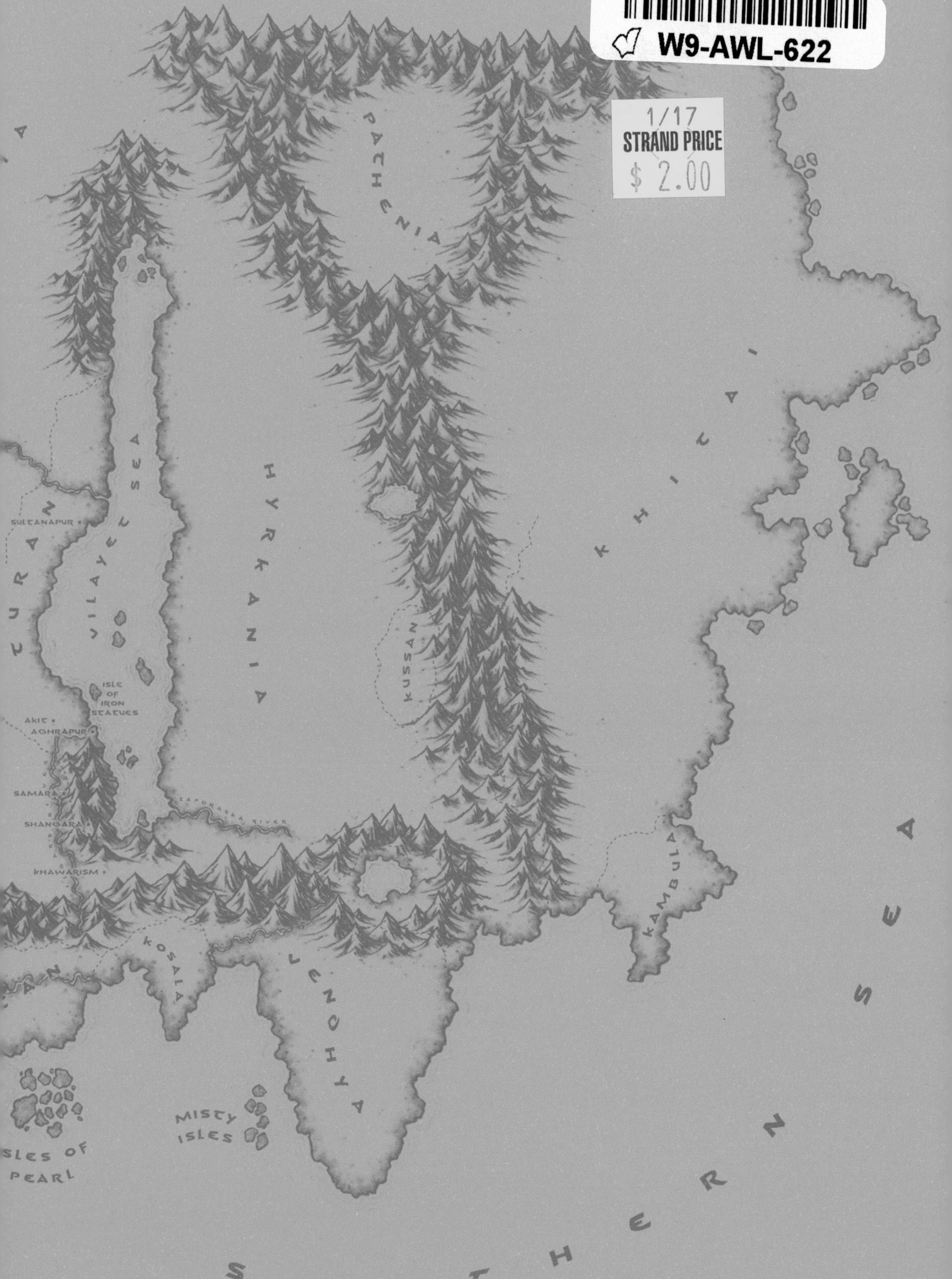
PATHENIA
HYRKANIA
KHITAI
VILAYET SEA
TURAN
SULTANAPUR
ISLE OF IRON STATUES
AKIT
AGHRAPUR
SAMARA
SHANGARA
KHAWARISM
ZAPOROSKA RIVER
KUSSAN
KAMBULA
KOSALA
VENDHYA
MISTY ISLES
SLES OF
PEARL
SOUTHERN SEA

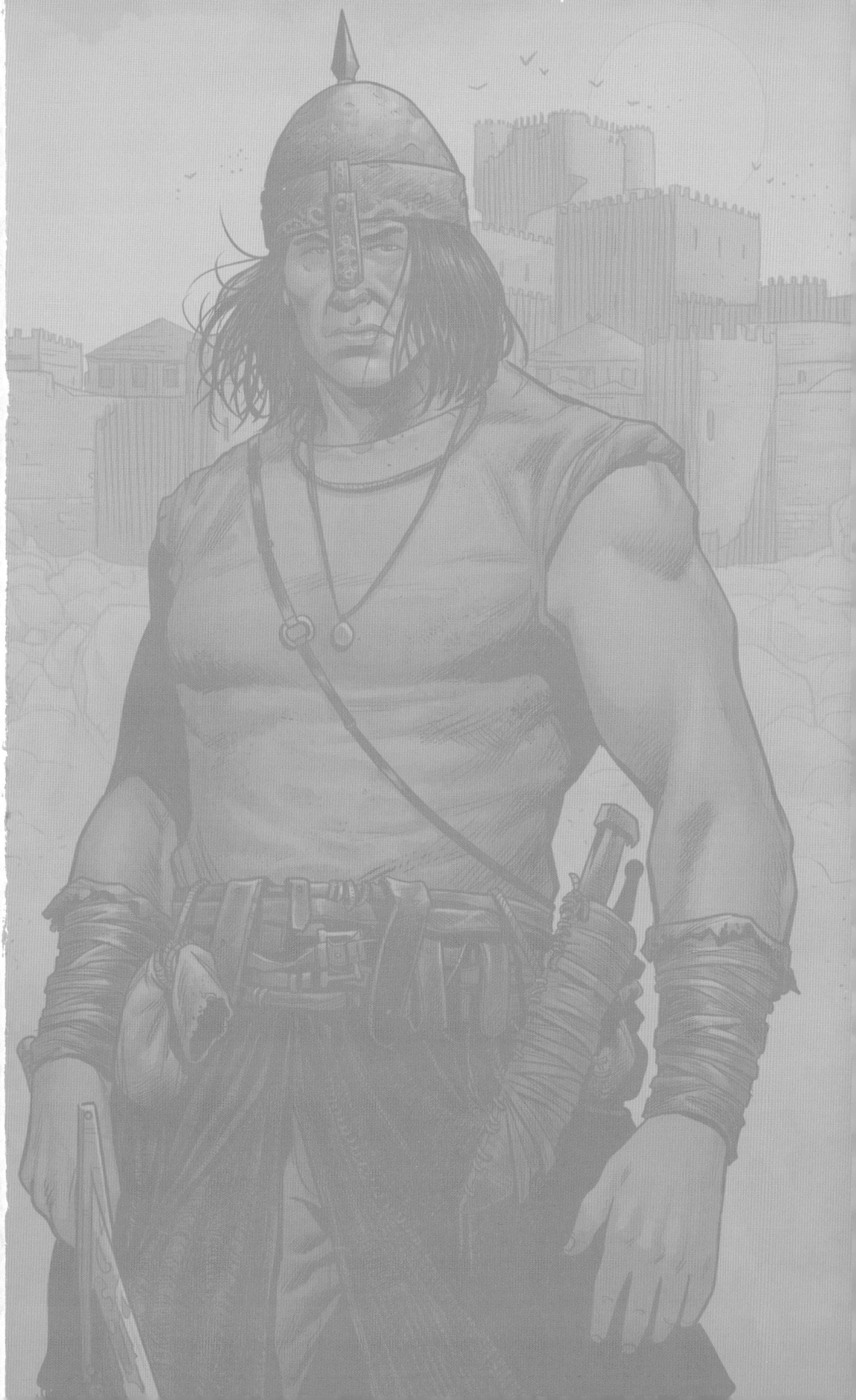

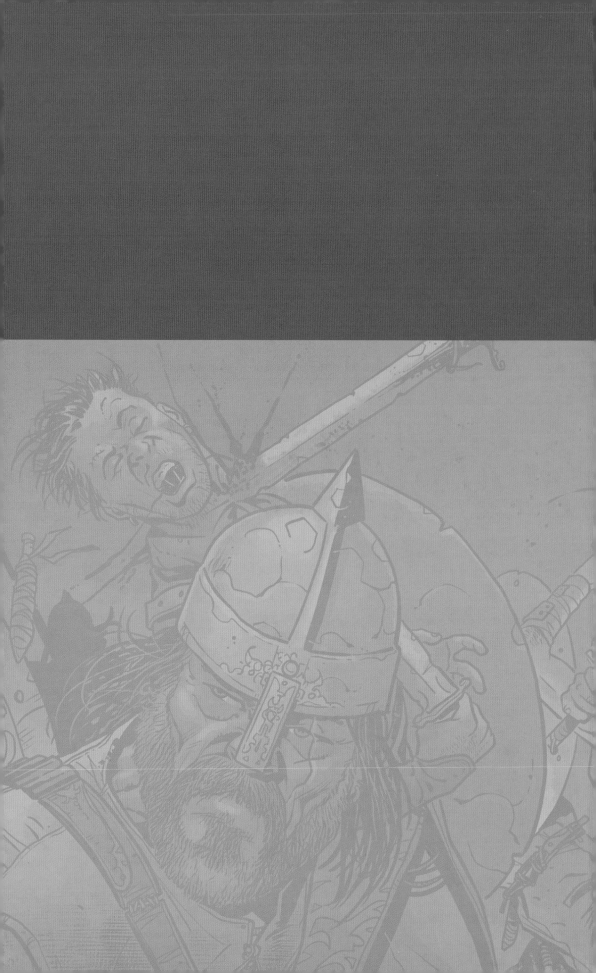

CONAN®

THE NIGHTMARE OF THE SHALLOWS

Writer BRIAN WOOD

Art by MIRKO COLAK (chapters 1–2)
ANDREA MUTTI
and PIERLUIGI BALDASSINI (chapter 3)
DAVIDE GIANFELICE (chapters 4–6)

Colors by DAVE STEWART

Letters by
RICHARD STARKINGS
and COMICRAFT'S JIMMY BETANCOURT

Cover and Chapter-Break Artist
MASSIMO CARNEVALE

Creator of Conan
ROBERT E. HOWARD

DARK HORSE BOOKS

Publisher MIKE RICHARDSON Designer KAT LARSON Digital Production CHRISTIANNE GOUDREAU Assistant Editor IAN TUCKER Editor DAVE MARSHALL

Special thanks to FREDRIK MALMBERG and JOAKIM ZETTERBERG at CONAN PROPERTIES.

This volume collects issues #13–#18 of the Dark Horse Comics monthly *Conan the Barbarian* series.

Published by Dark Horse Books
A division of Dark Horse Comics, Inc.
10956 SE Main Street
Milwaukie, OR 97222

DarkHorse.com

Library of Congress Cataloging-in-Publication Data

Wood, Brian, 1972- author.
Conan : the Nightmare of the Shallows / writer, Brian Wood ; art by Mirko Colak (chapters 1-2), Andrea Mutti and Pierluigi Baldassini (chapter 3), Davide Gianfelice (chapters 4-6) ; colors by Dave Stewart ; letters by Richard Starkings and Comicraft's Jimmy Betancourt ; cover and chapter-break artist, Massimo Carnevale ; creator of Conan, Robert E. Howard. -- First hardcover edition.
pages cm
ISBN 978-1-61655-233-6
1. Graphic novels. I. Colak, Mirko, 1975- illustrator. II. Mutti, Andrea, 1973- illustrator. III. Baldassini, Pierluigi, illustrator. IV. Gianfelice, Davide, illustrator. V. Stewart, Dave, illustrator. VI. Carnevale, Massimo, illustrator. VII. Howard, Robert E. (Robert Ervin), 1906-1936, creator. VIII. Title.
PN6728.C65W75 2014
741.5'973--dc23
2013034598

International Licensing: (503) 905-2377
To find a comics shop in your area, call the Comic Shop Locator Service toll-free at 1-888-266-4226

First hardcover edition: January 2014
ISBN 978-1-61655-233-6

10 9 8 7 6 5 4 3 2 1

Printed in China

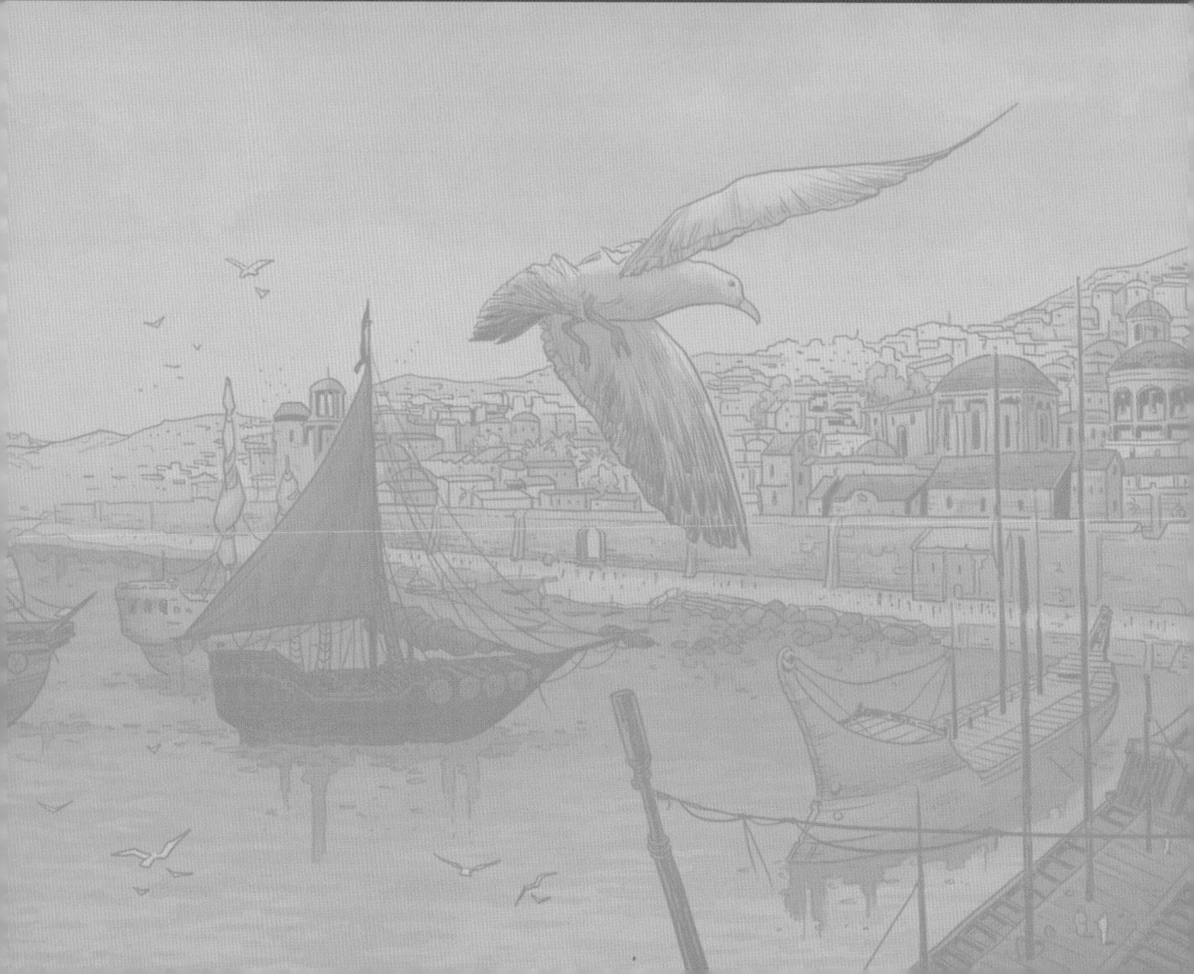

CHAPTER ONE

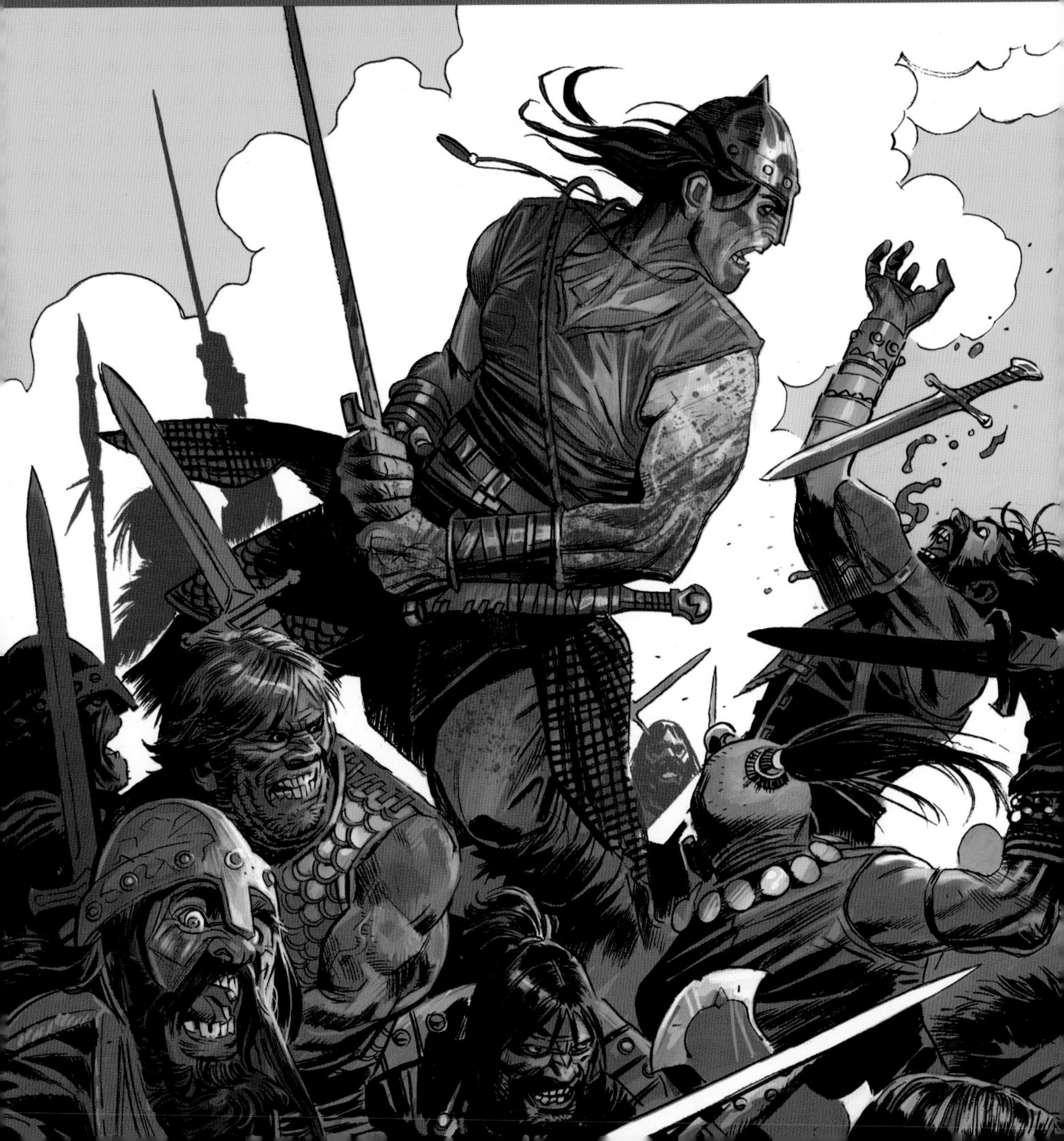

"Truly, it was a dark night when I first saw her, and she fairly shimmered. The ghost of the ramparts!"

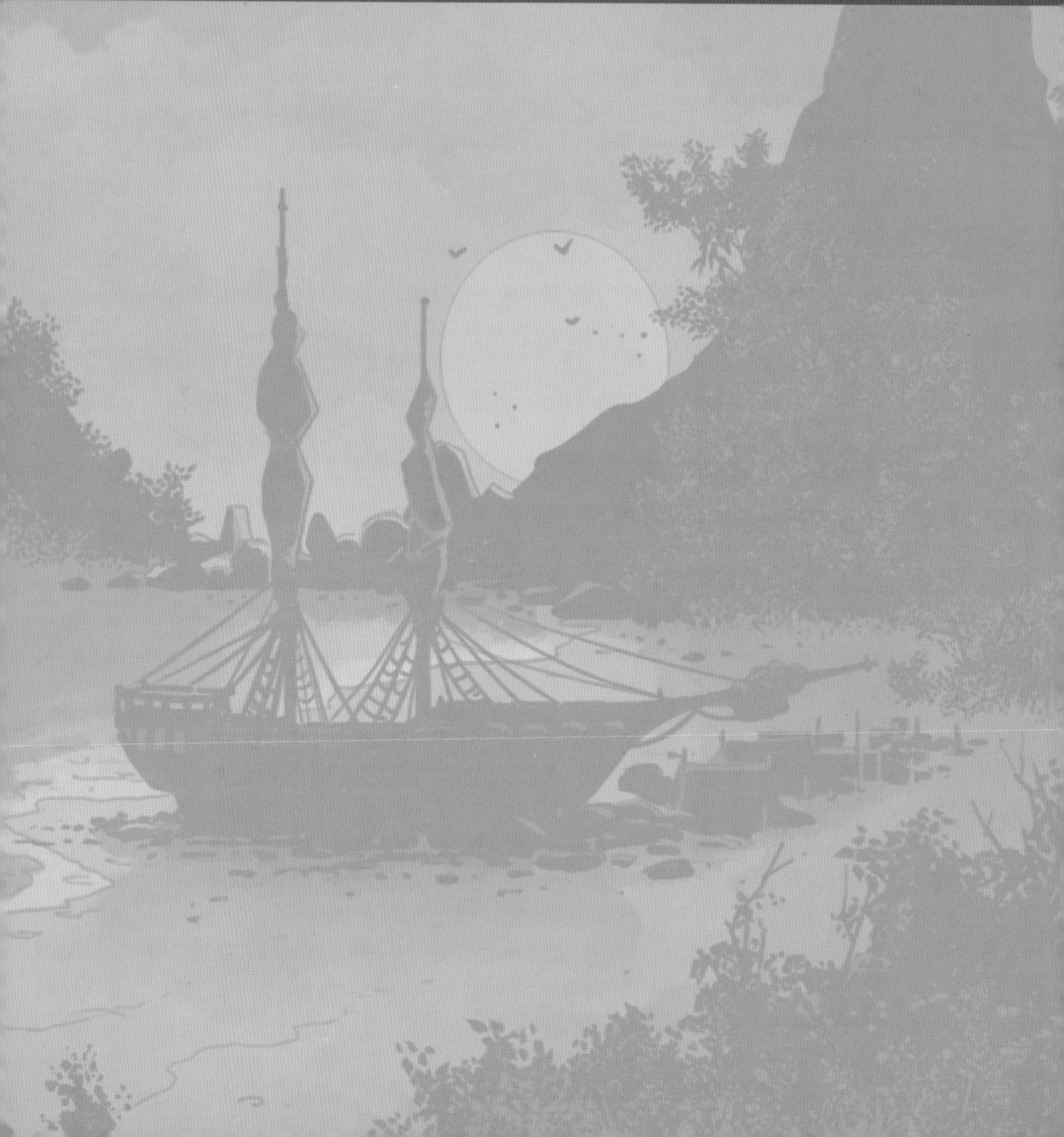

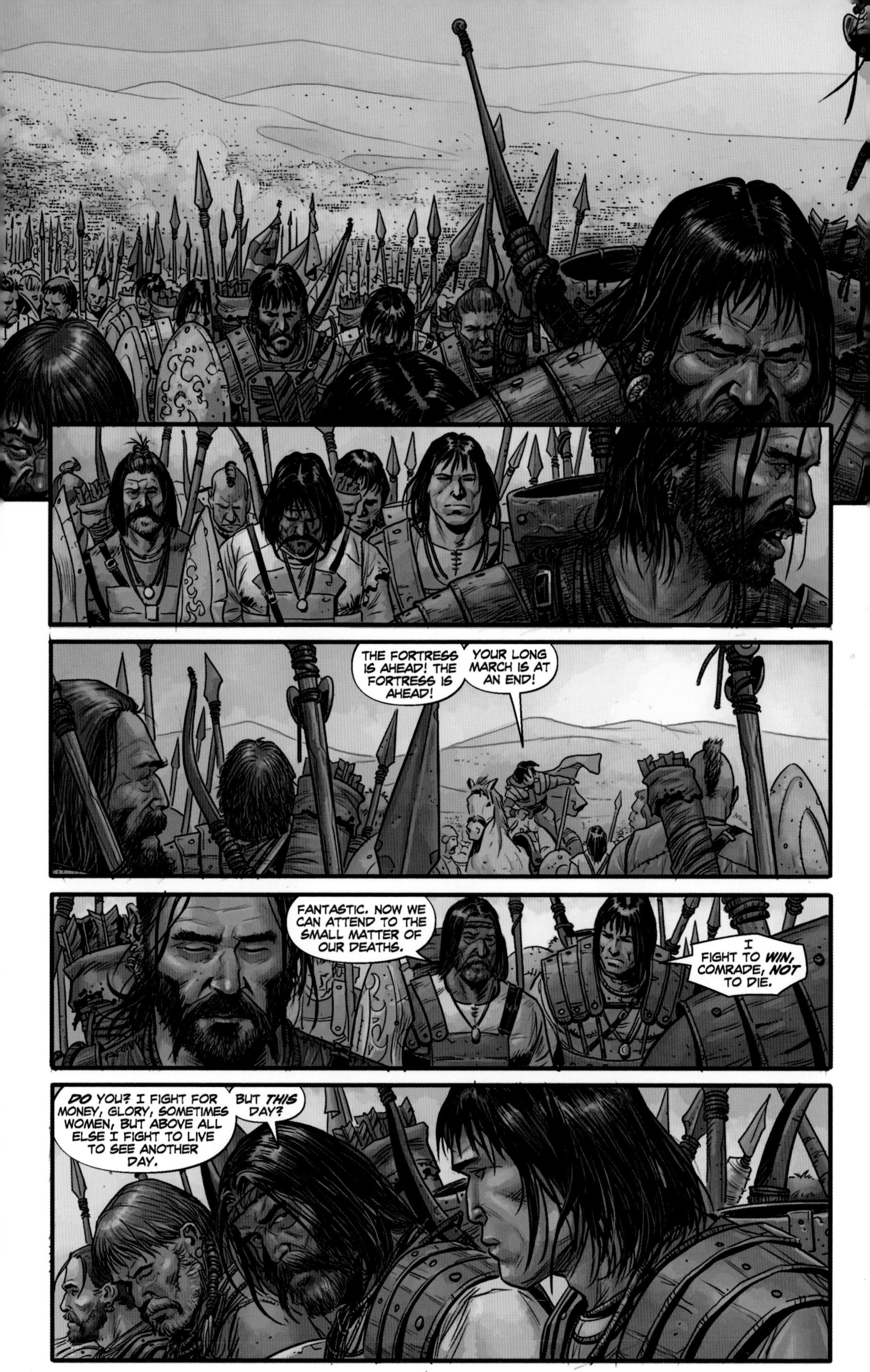
THE FORTRESS IS AHEAD! THE FORTRESS IS AHEAD!
YOUR LONG MARCH IS AT AN END!
FANTASTIC. NOW WE CAN ATTEND TO THE SMALL MATTER OF OUR DEATHS.
I FIGHT TO WIN, COMRADE, NOT TO DIE.
DO YOU? I FIGHT FOR MONEY, GLORY, SOMETIMES WOMEN, BUT ABOVE ALL ELSE I FIGHT TO LIVE TO SEE ANOTHER DAY.
BUT THIS DAY?

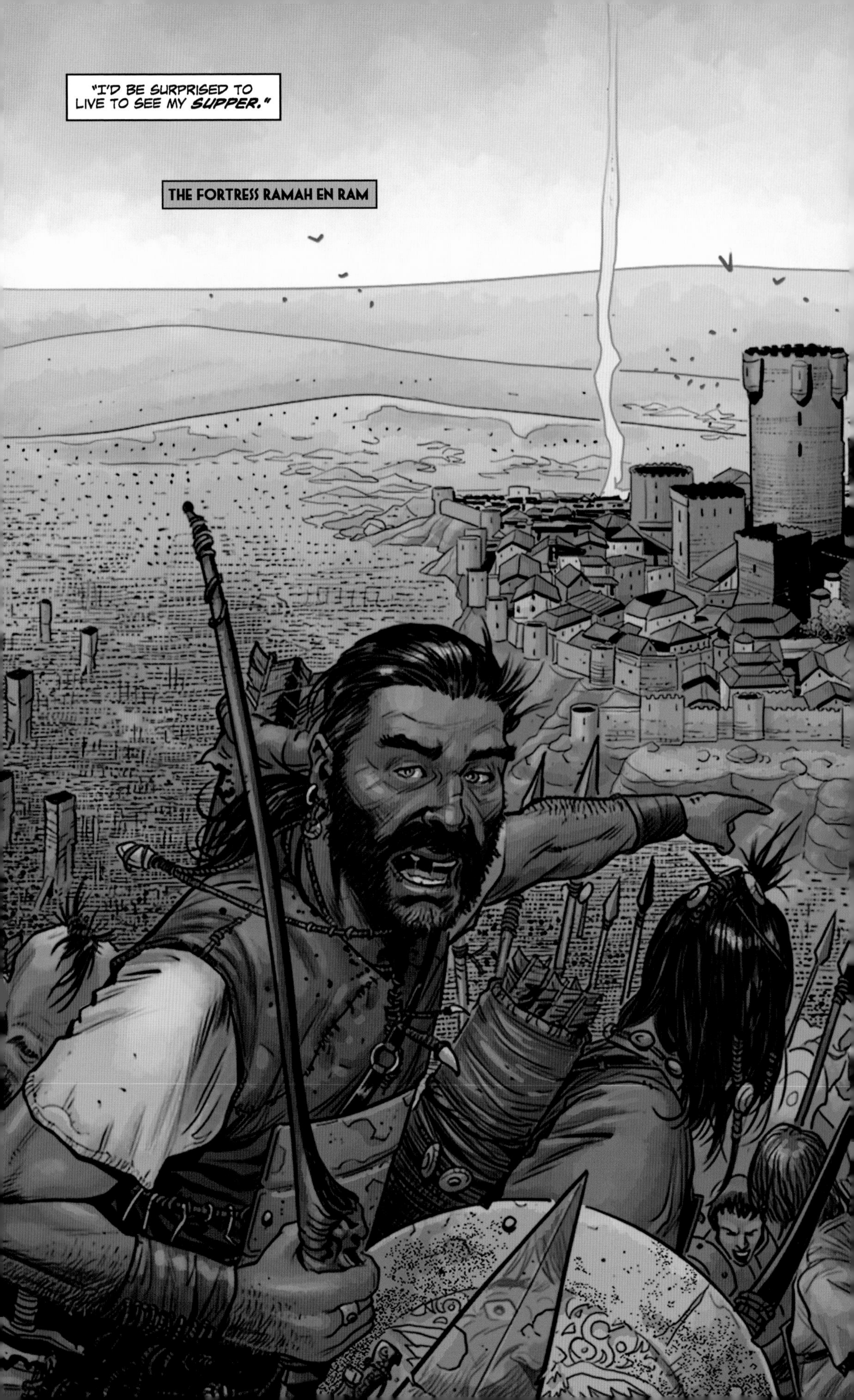
"I'D BE SURPRISED TO LIVE TO SEE MY SUPPER."
THE FORTRESS RAMAH EN RAM

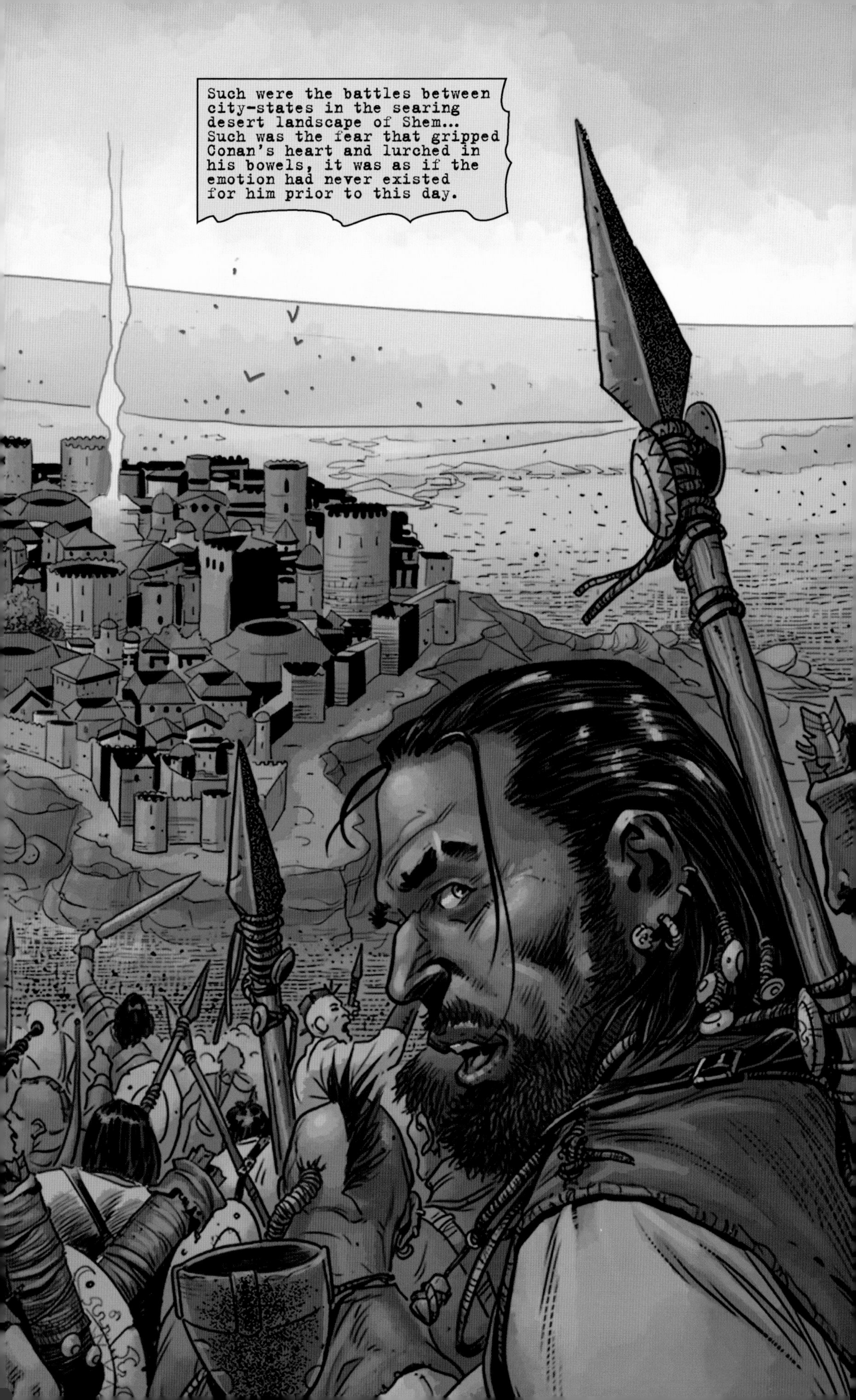
Such were the battles between city-states in the searing desert landscape of Shem... Such was the fear that gripped Conan's heart and lurched in his bowels, it was as if the emotion had never existed for him prior to this day.

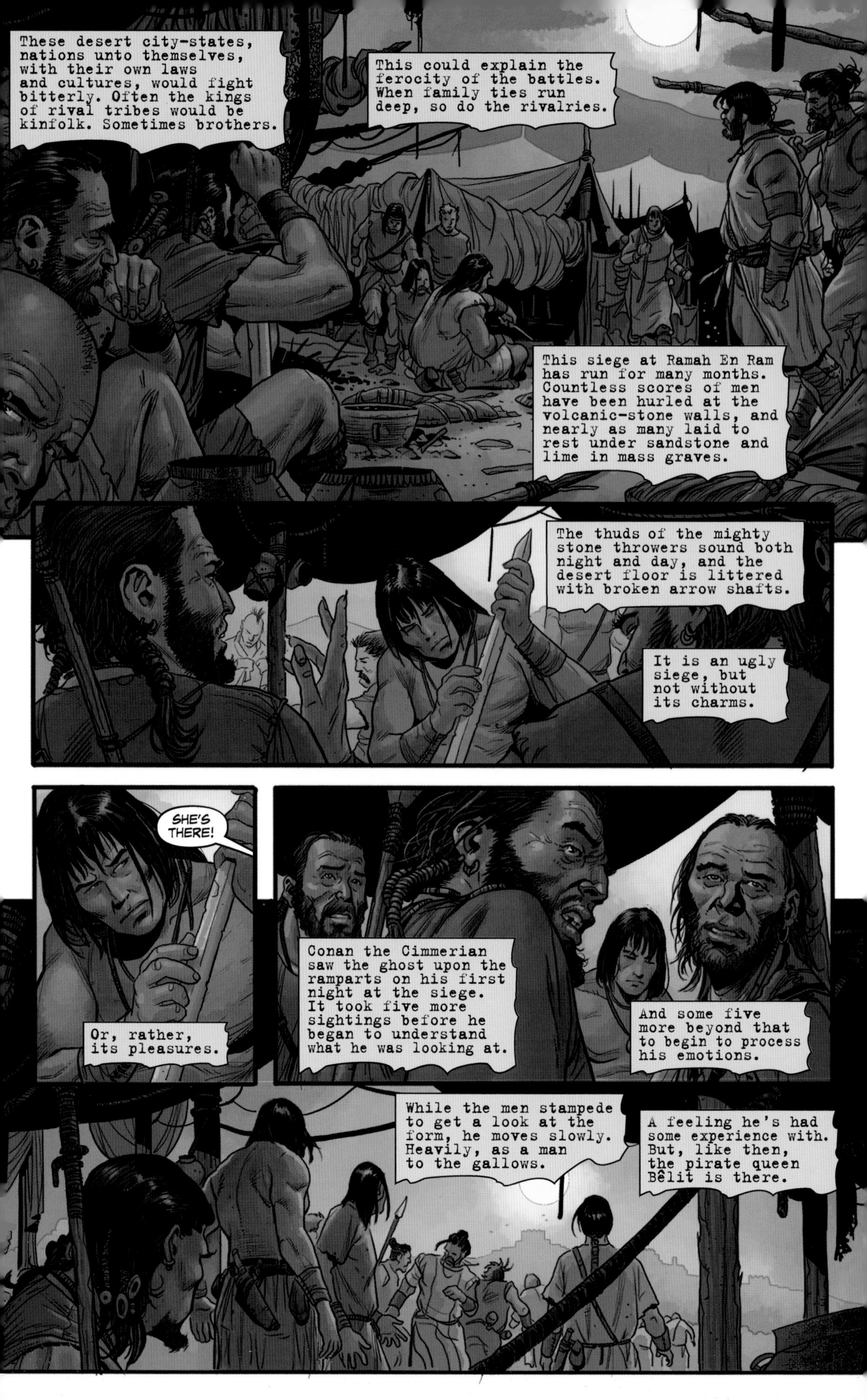
These desert city-states, nations unto themselves, with their own laws and cultures, would fight bitterly. Often the kings of rival tribes would be kinfolk. Sometimes brothers.
This could explain the ferocity of the battles. When family ties run deep, so do the rivalries.
This siege at Ramah En Ram has run for many months. Countless scores of men have been hurled at the volcanic-stone walls, and nearly as many laid to rest under sandstone and lime in mass graves.
The thuds of the mighty stone throwers sound both night and day, and the desert floor is littered with broken arrow shafts.
It is an ugly siege, but not without its charms.
SHE'S THERE!
Or, rather, its pleasures.
Conan the Cimmerian saw the ghost upon the ramparts on his first night at the siege. It took five more sightings before he began to understand what he was looking at.
And some five more beyond that to begin to process his emotions.
While the men stampede to get a look at the form, he moves slowly. Heavily, as a man to the gallows.
A feeling he's had some experience with. But, like then, the pirate queen Bêlit is there.

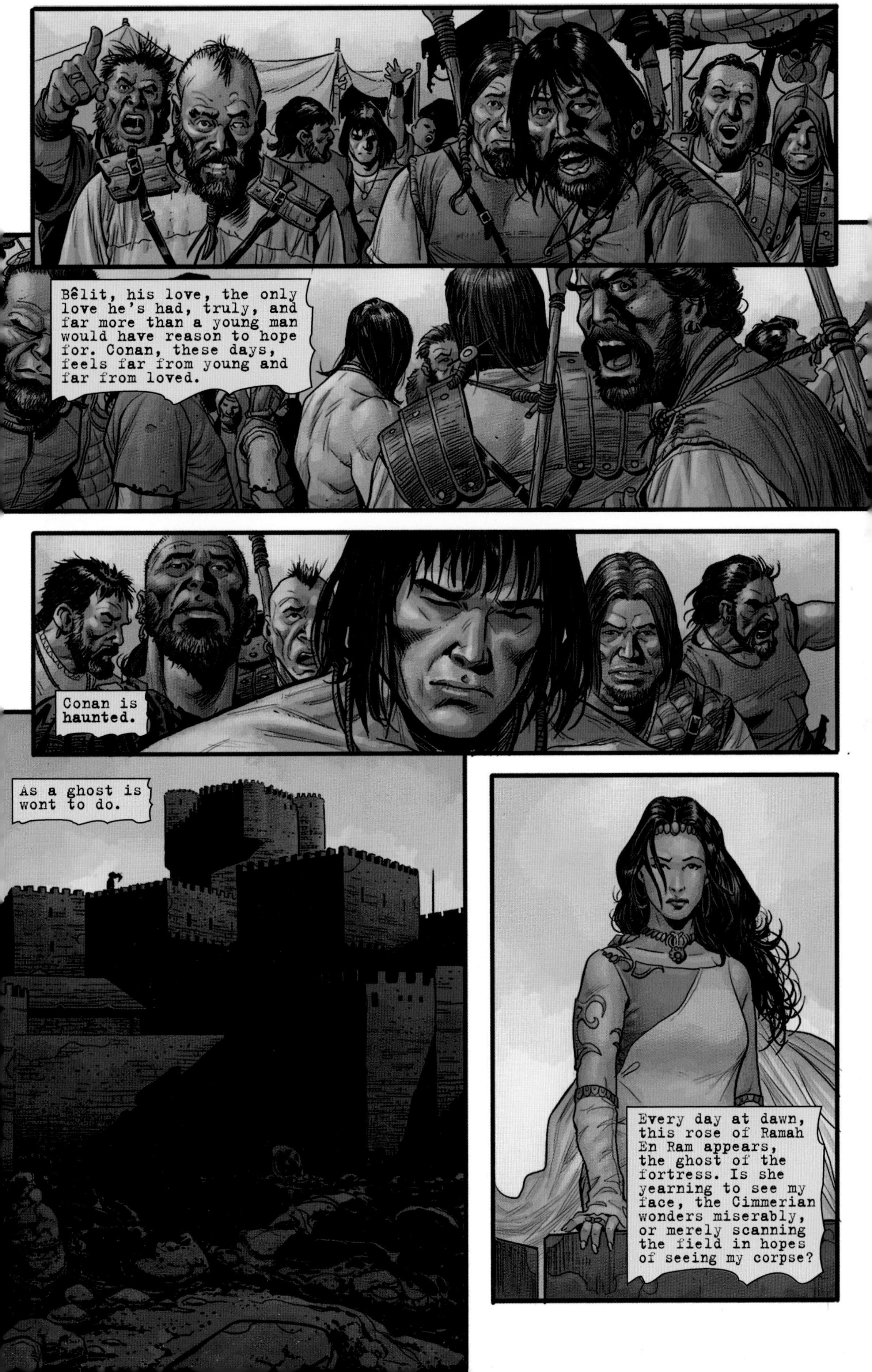
Bêlit, his love, the only love he's had, truly, and far more than a young man would have reason to hope for. Conan, these days, feels far from young and far from loved.
Conan is haunted.
As a ghost is wont to do.
Every day at dawn, this rose of Ramah En Ram appears, the ghost of the fortress. Is she yearning to see my face, the Cimmerian wonders miserably, or merely scanning the field in hopes of seeing my corpse?

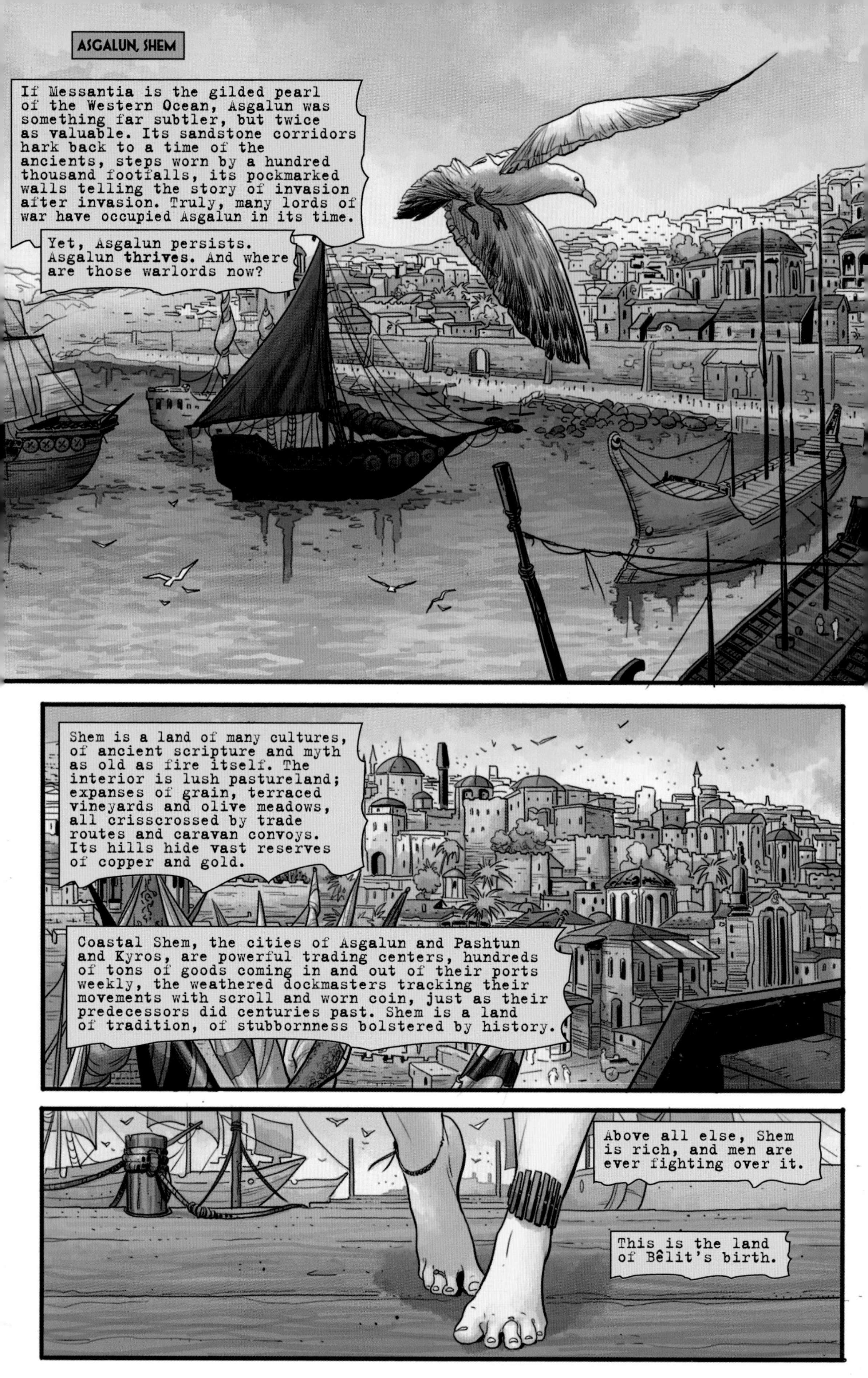
ASGALUN, SHEM
If Messantia is the gilded pearl of the Western Ocean, Asgalun was something far subtler, but twice as valuable. Its sandstone corridors hark back to a time of the ancients, steps worn by a hundred thousand footfalls, its pockmarked walls telling the story of invasion after invasion. Truly, many lords of war have occupied Asgalun in its time.
Yet, Asgalun persists. Asgalun thrives. And where are those warlords now?
Shem is a land of many cultures, of ancient scripture and myth as old as fire itself. The interior is lush pastureland; expanses of grain, terraced vineyards and olive meadows, all crisscrossed by trade routes and caravan convoys. Its hills hide vast reserves of copper and gold.
Coastal Shem, the cities of Asgalun and Pashtun and Kyros, are powerful trading centers, hundreds of tons of goods coming in and out of their ports weekly, the weathered dockmasters tracking their movements with scroll and worn coin, just as their predecessors did centuries past. Shem is a land of tradition, of stubbornness bolstered by history.
Above all else, Shem is rich, and men are ever fighting over it.
This is the land of Bêlit's birth.

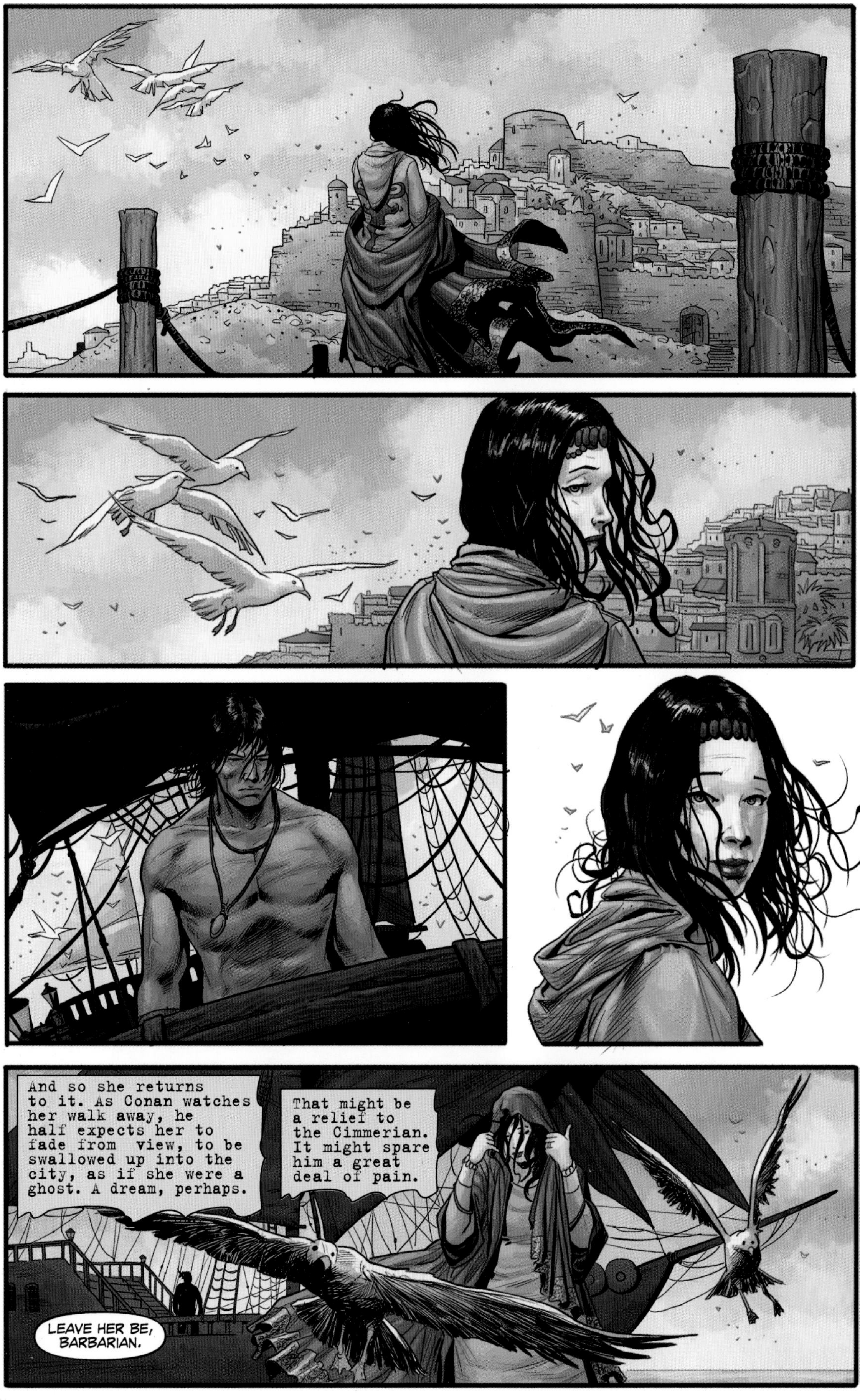
And so she returns to it. As Conan watches her walk away, he half expects her to fade from view, to be swallowed up into the city, as if she were a ghost. A dream, perhaps.
That might be a relief to the Cimmerian. It might spare him a great deal of pain.
LEAVE HER BE, BARBARIAN.

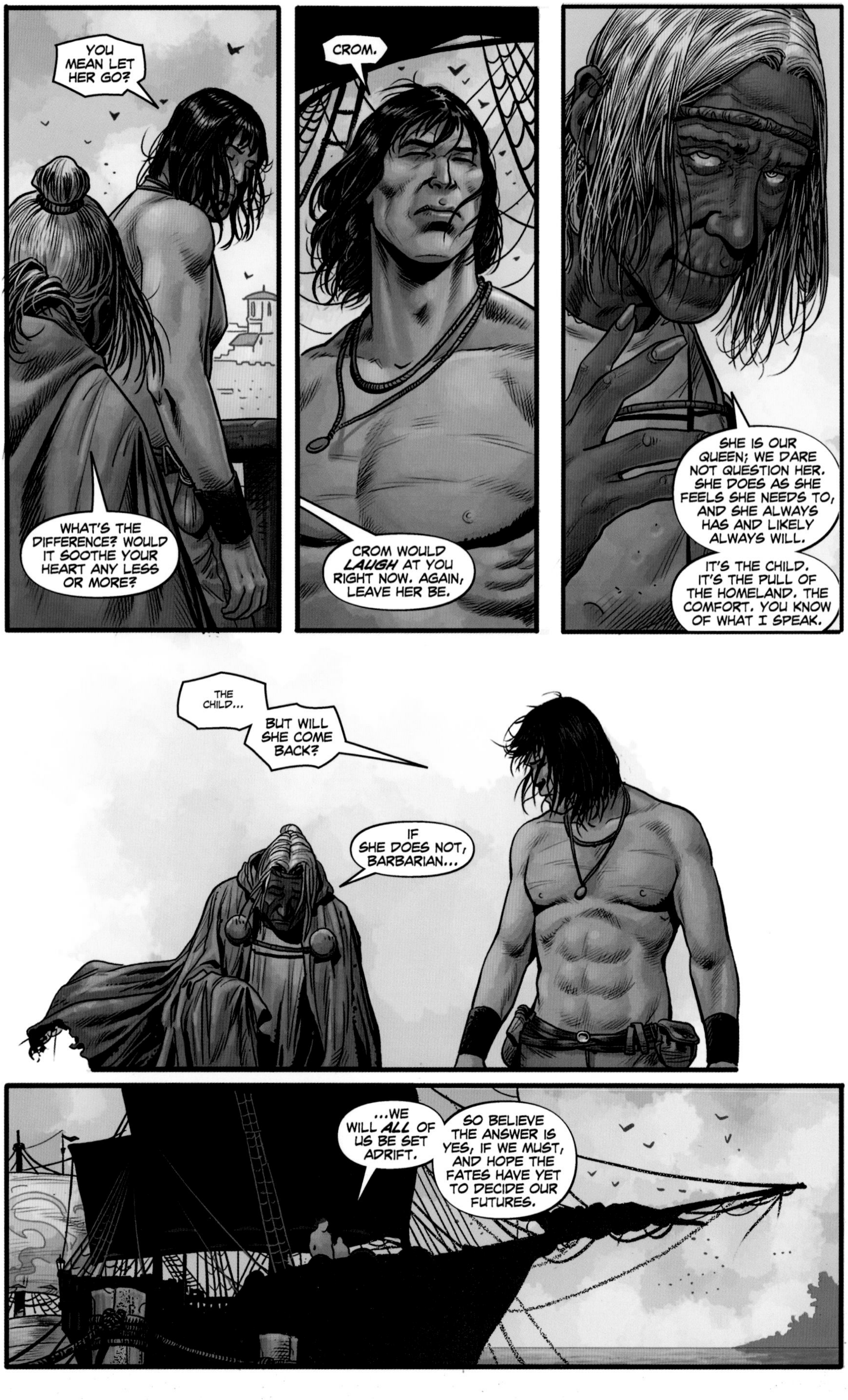
YOU MEAN LET HER GO?
WHAT'S THE DIFFERENCE? WOULD IT SOOTHE YOUR HEART ANY LESS OR MORE?
CROM.
CROM WOULD LAUGH AT YOU RIGHT NOW. AGAIN, LEAVE HER BE.
SHE IS OUR QUEEN; WE DARE NOT QUESTION HER. SHE DOES AS SHE FEELS SHE NEEDS TO, AND SHE ALWAYS HAS AND LIKELY ALWAYS WILL.
IT'S THE CHILD. IT'S THE PULL OF THE HOMELAND. THE COMFORT. YOU KNOW OF WHAT I SPEAK.
THE CHILD...
BUT WILL SHE COME BACK?
IF SHE DOES NOT, BARBARIAN...
...WE WILL ALL OF US BE SET ADRIFT.
SO BELIEVE THE ANSWER IS YES, IF WE MUST, AND HOPE THE FATES HAVE YET TO DECIDE OUR FUTURES.

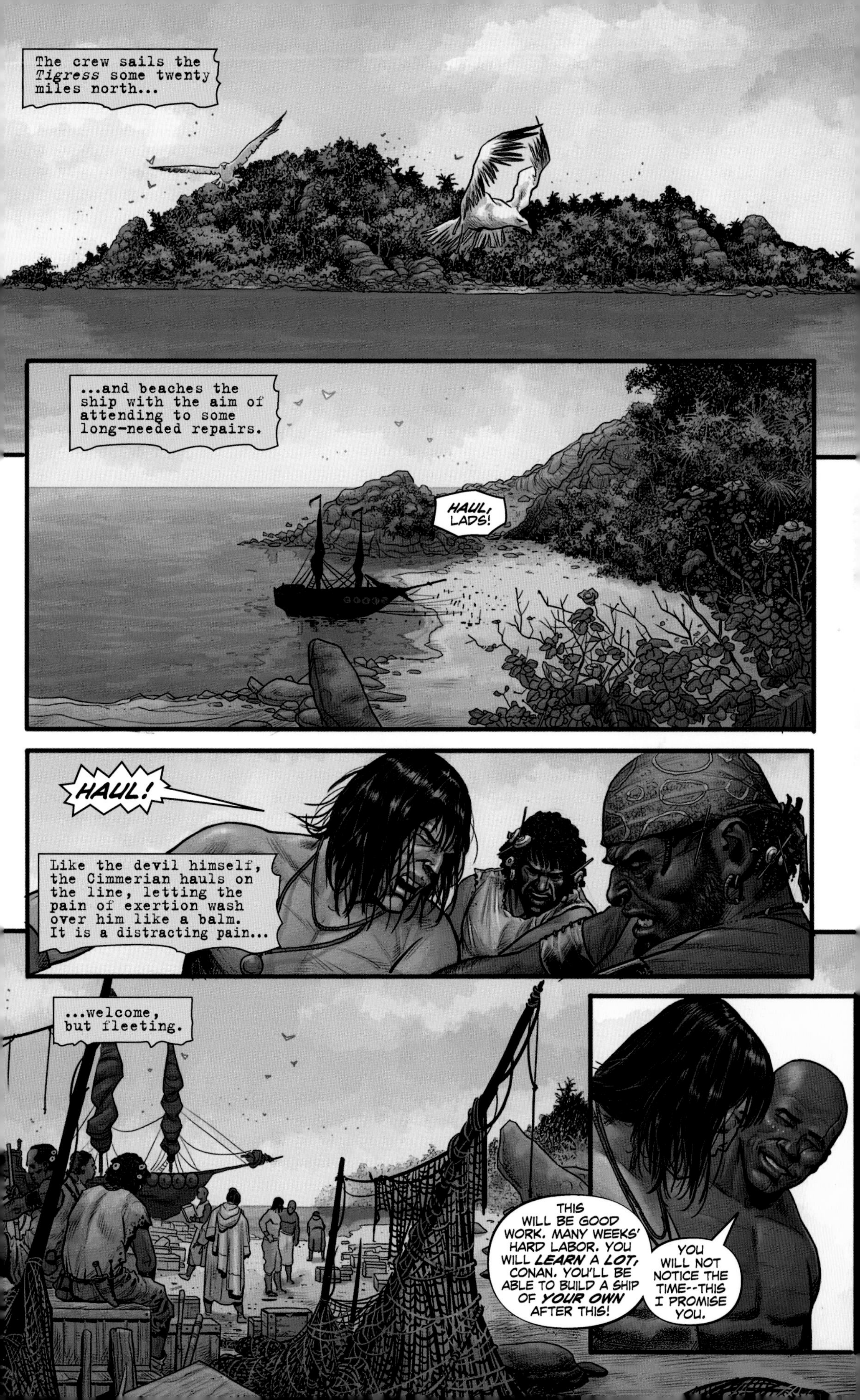

The crew sails the *Tigress* some twenty miles north...
...and beaches the ship with the aim of attending to some long-needed repairs.
HAUL, LADS!
HAUL!
Like the devil himself, the Cimmerian hauls on the line, letting the pain of exertion wash over him like a balm. It is a distracting pain...
...welcome, but fleeting.
THIS WILL BE GOOD WORK. MANY WEEKS' HARD LABOR. YOU WILL LEARN A LOT, CONAN. YOU'LL BE ABLE TO BUILD A SHIP OF YOUR OWN AFTER THIS!
YOU WILL NOT NOTICE THE TIME--THIS I PROMISE YOU.

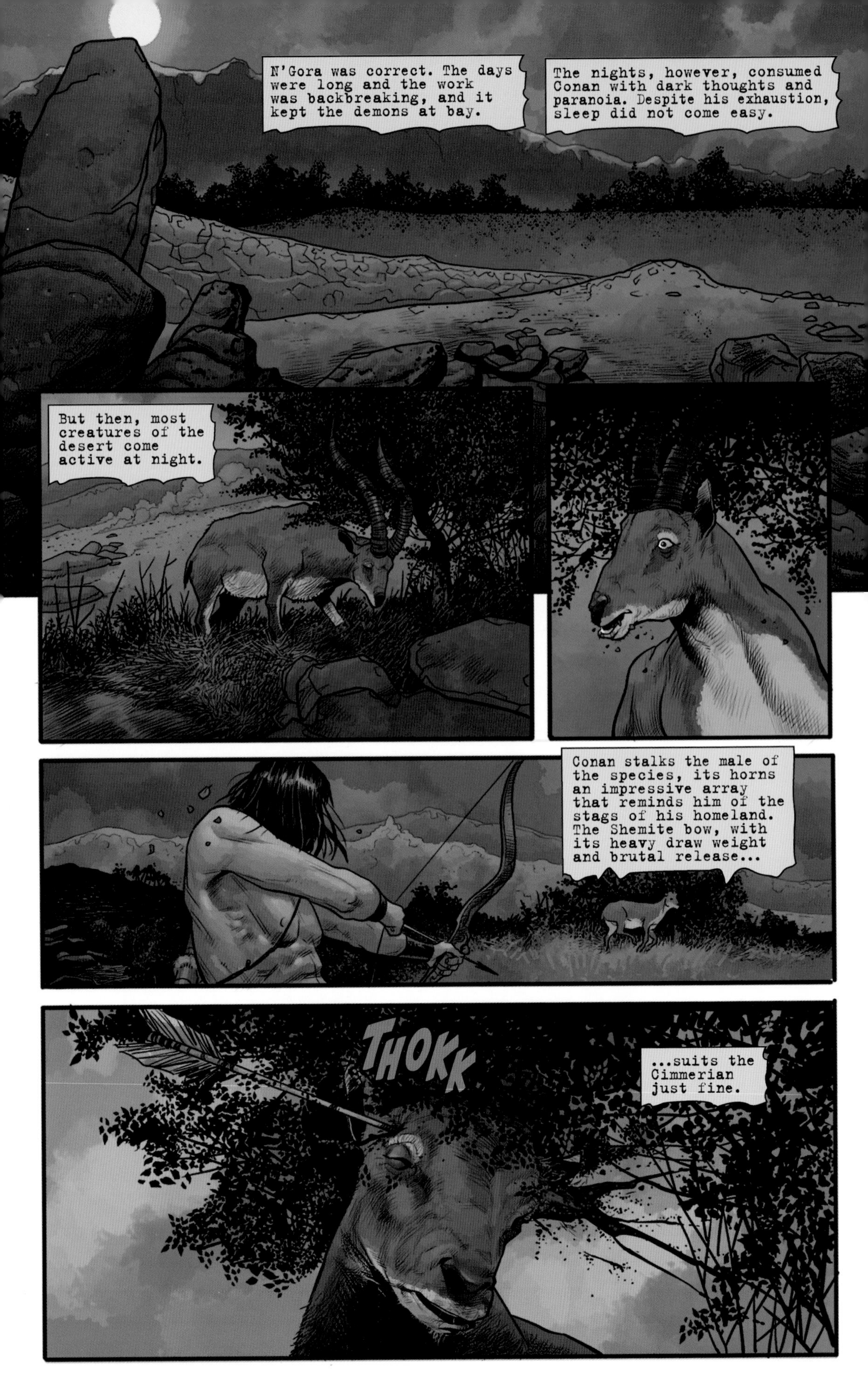
N'Gora was correct. The days were long and the work was backbreaking, and it kept the demons at bay.
The nights, however, consumed Conan with dark thoughts and paranoia. Despite his exhaustion, sleep did not come easy.
But then, most creatures of the desert come active at night.
Conan stalks the male of the species, its horns an impressive array that reminds him of the stags of his homeland. The Shemite bow, with its heavy draw weight and brutal release...
THOKK
...suits the Cimmerian just fine.

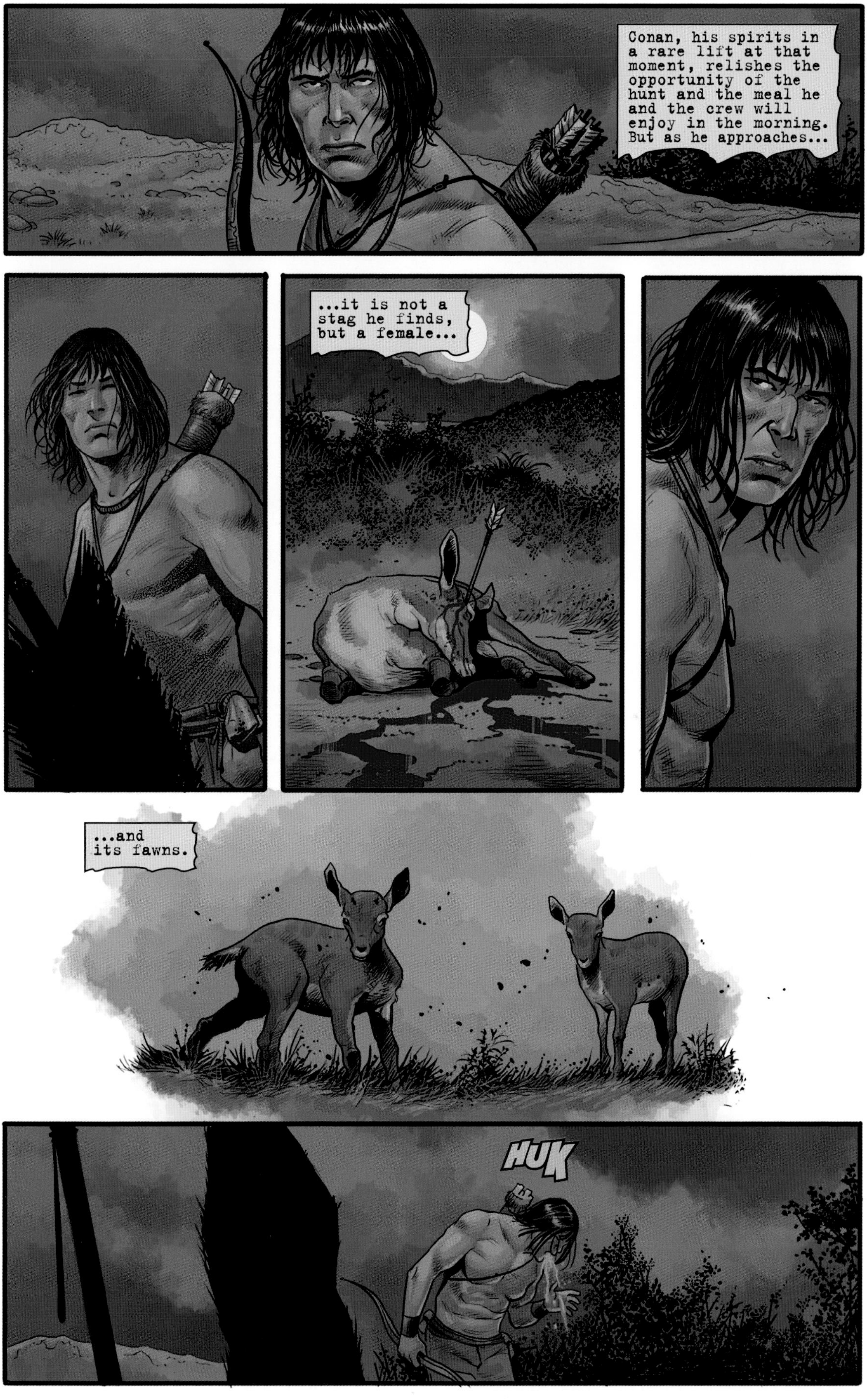

Conan, his spirits in a rare lift at that moment, relishes the opportunity of the hunt and the meal he and the crew will enjoy in the morning. But as he approaches...
...it is not a stag he finds, but a female...
...and its fawns.
HUK

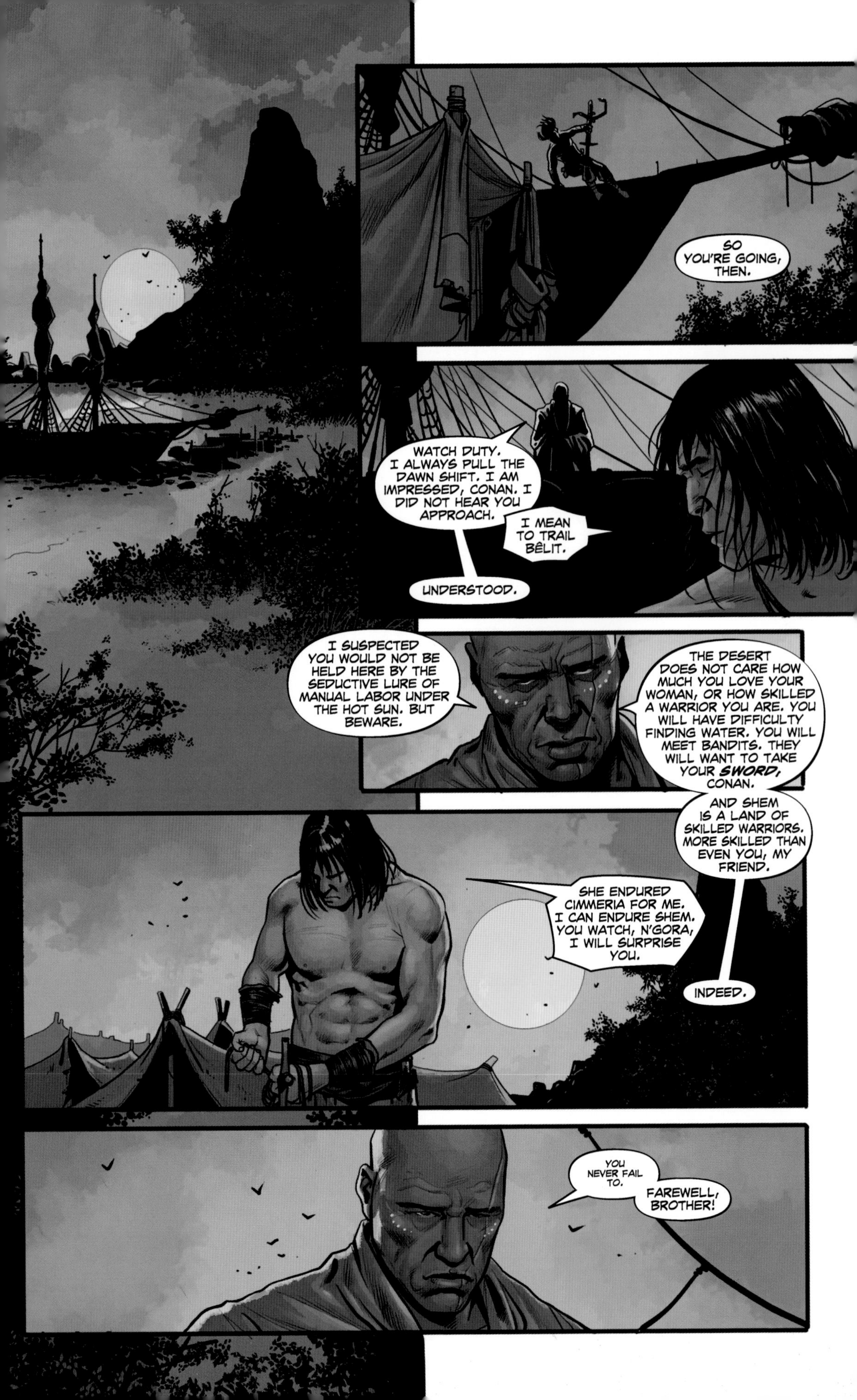
SO YOU'RE GOING, THEN.
WATCH DUTY. I ALWAYS PULL THE DAWN SHIFT. I AM IMPRESSED, CONAN. I DID NOT HEAR YOU APPROACH.
I MEAN TO TRAIL BÊLIT.
UNDERSTOOD.
I SUSPECTED YOU WOULD NOT BE HELD HERE BY THE SEDUCTIVE LURE OF MANUAL LABOR UNDER THE HOT SUN. BUT BEWARE.
THE DESERT DOES NOT CARE HOW MUCH YOU LOVE YOUR WOMAN, OR HOW SKILLED A WARRIOR YOU ARE. YOU WILL HAVE DIFFICULTY FINDING WATER. YOU WILL MEET BANDITS. THEY WILL WANT TO TAKE YOUR ***SWORD,*** CONAN.
AND SHEM IS A LAND OF SKILLED WARRIORS. MORE SKILLED THAN EVEN YOU, MY FRIEND.
SHE ENDURED CIMMERIA FOR ME. I CAN ENDURE SHEM. YOU WATCH, N'GORA, I WILL SURPRISE YOU.
INDEED.
YOU NEVER FAIL TO.
FAREWELL, BROTHER!

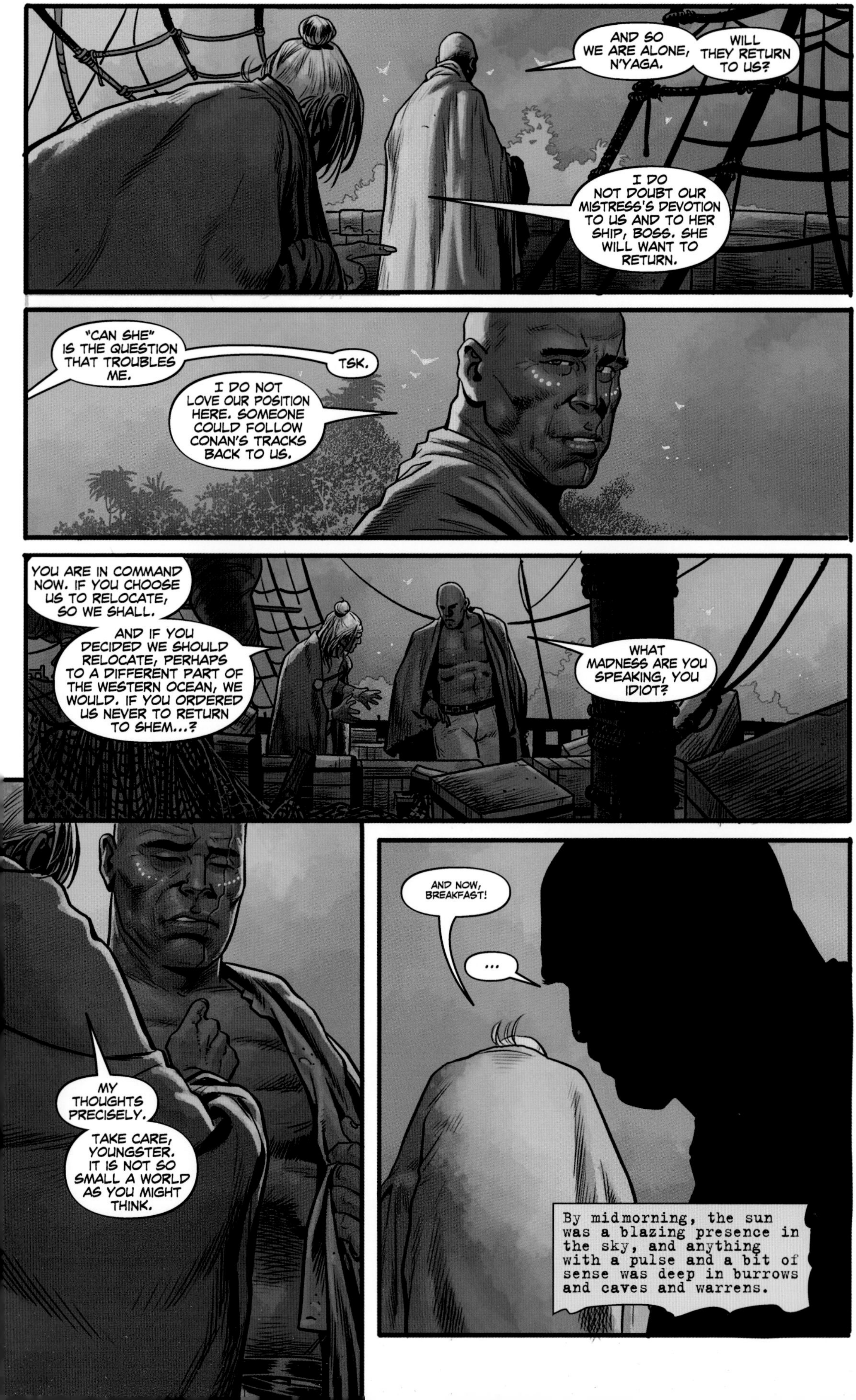
AND SO WE ARE ALONE, N'YAGA.
WILL THEY RETURN TO US?
I DO NOT DOUBT OUR MISTRESS'S DEVOTION TO US AND TO HER SHIP, BOSS. SHE WILL WANT TO RETURN.
"CAN SHE" IS THE QUESTION THAT TROUBLES ME.
TSK.
I DO NOT LOVE OUR POSITION HERE. SOMEONE COULD FOLLOW CONAN'S TRACKS BACK TO US.
YOU ARE IN COMMAND NOW. IF YOU CHOOSE US TO RELOCATE, SO WE SHALL.
AND IF YOU DECIDED WE SHOULD RELOCATE, PERHAPS TO A DIFFERENT PART OF THE WESTERN OCEAN, WE WOULD. IF YOU ORDERED US NEVER TO RETURN TO SHEM...?
WHAT MADNESS ARE YOU SPEAKING, YOU IDIOT?
MY THOUGHTS PRECISELY.
TAKE CARE, YOUNGSTER. IT IS NOT SO SMALL A WORLD AS YOU MIGHT THINK.
AND NOW, BREAKFAST!
...
By midmorning, the sun was a blazing presence in the sky, and anything with a pulse and a bit of sense was deep in burrows and caves and warrens.

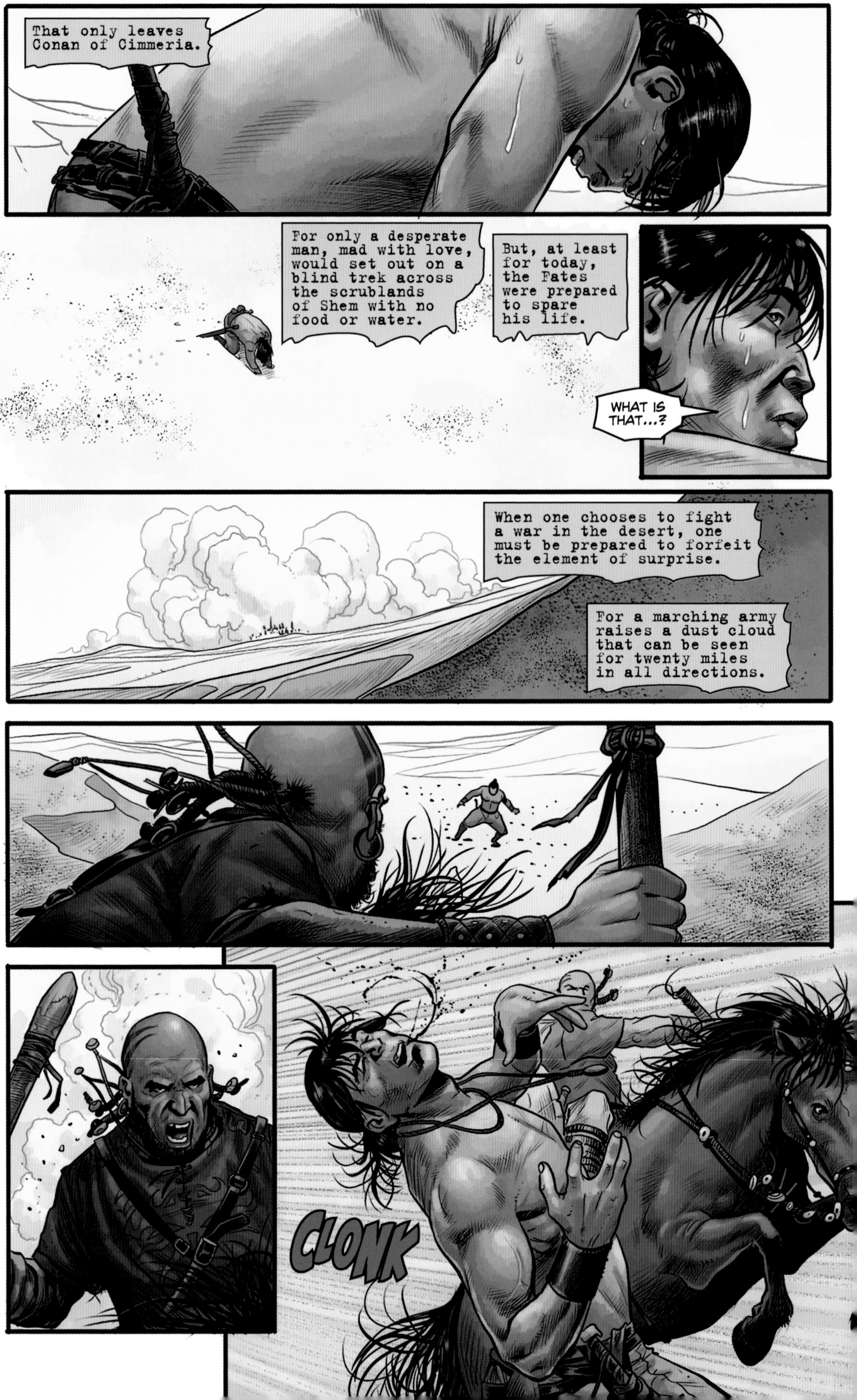
That only leaves Conan of Cimmeria.
For only a desperate man, mad with love, would set out on a blind trek across the scrublands of Shem with no food or water.
But, at least for today, the Fates were prepared to spare his life.
WHAT IS THAT...?
When one chooses to fight a war in the desert, one must be prepared to forfeit the element of surprise.
For a marching army raises a dust cloud that can be seen for twenty miles in all directions.
CLONK

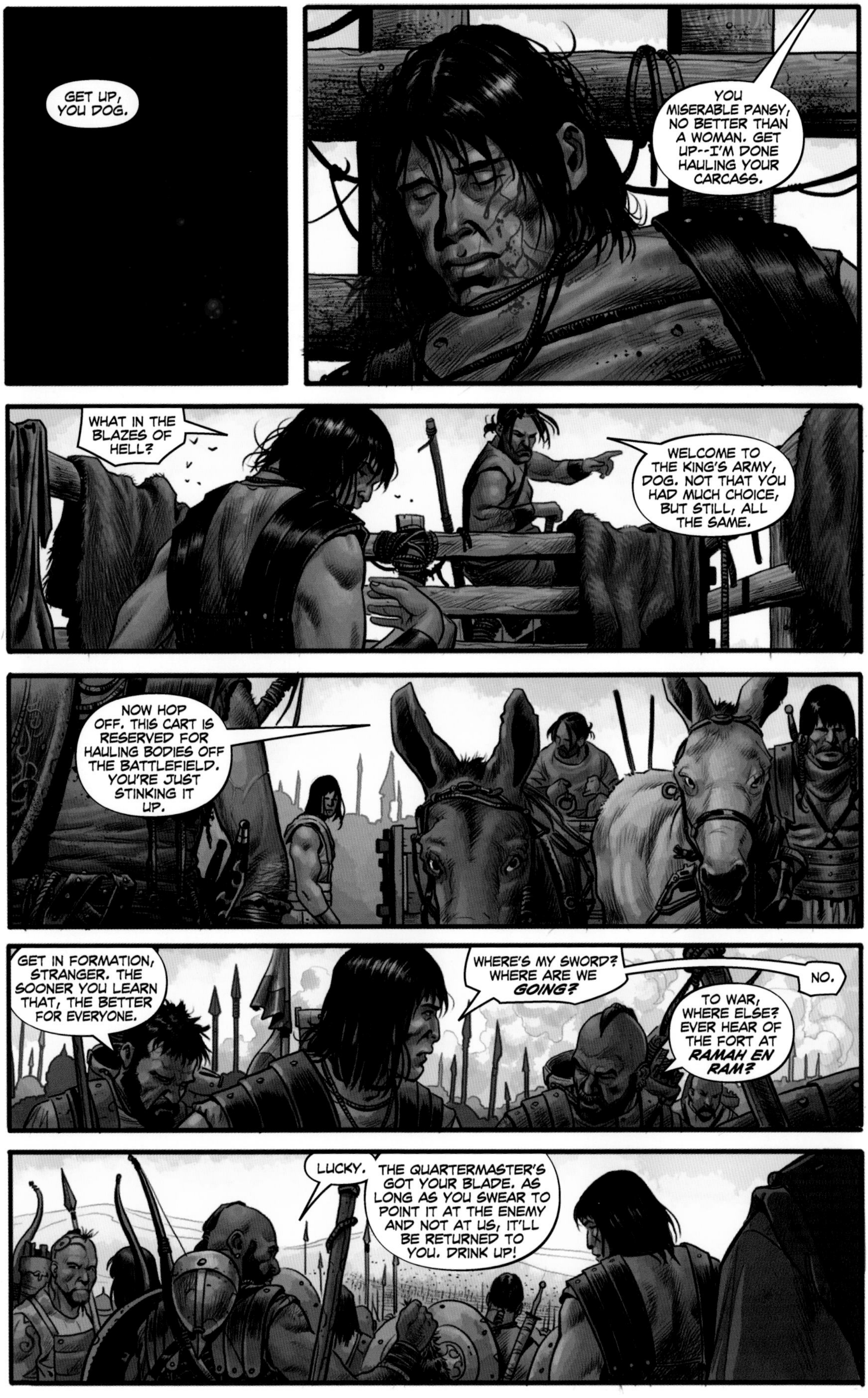
GET UP, YOU DOG.
YOU MISERABLE PANSY, NO BETTER THAN A WOMAN. GET UP--I'M DONE HAULING YOUR CARCASS.
WHAT IN THE BLAZES OF HELL?
WELCOME TO THE KING'S ARMY, DOG. NOT THAT YOU HAD MUCH CHOICE, BUT STILL, ALL THE SAME.
NOW HOP OFF. THIS CART IS RESERVED FOR HAULING BODIES OFF THE BATTLEFIELD. YOU'RE JUST STINKING IT UP.
GET IN FORMATION, STRANGER. THE SOONER YOU LEARN THAT, THE BETTER FOR EVERYONE.
WHERE'S MY SWORD? WHERE ARE WE *GOING?*
TO WAR, WHERE ELSE? EVER HEAR OF THE FORT AT *RAMAH EN RAM?*
NO.
LUCKY.
THE QUARTERMASTER'S GOT YOUR BLADE. AS LONG AS YOU SWEAR TO POINT IT AT THE ENEMY AND NOT AT US, IT'LL BE RETURNED TO YOU. DRINK UP!

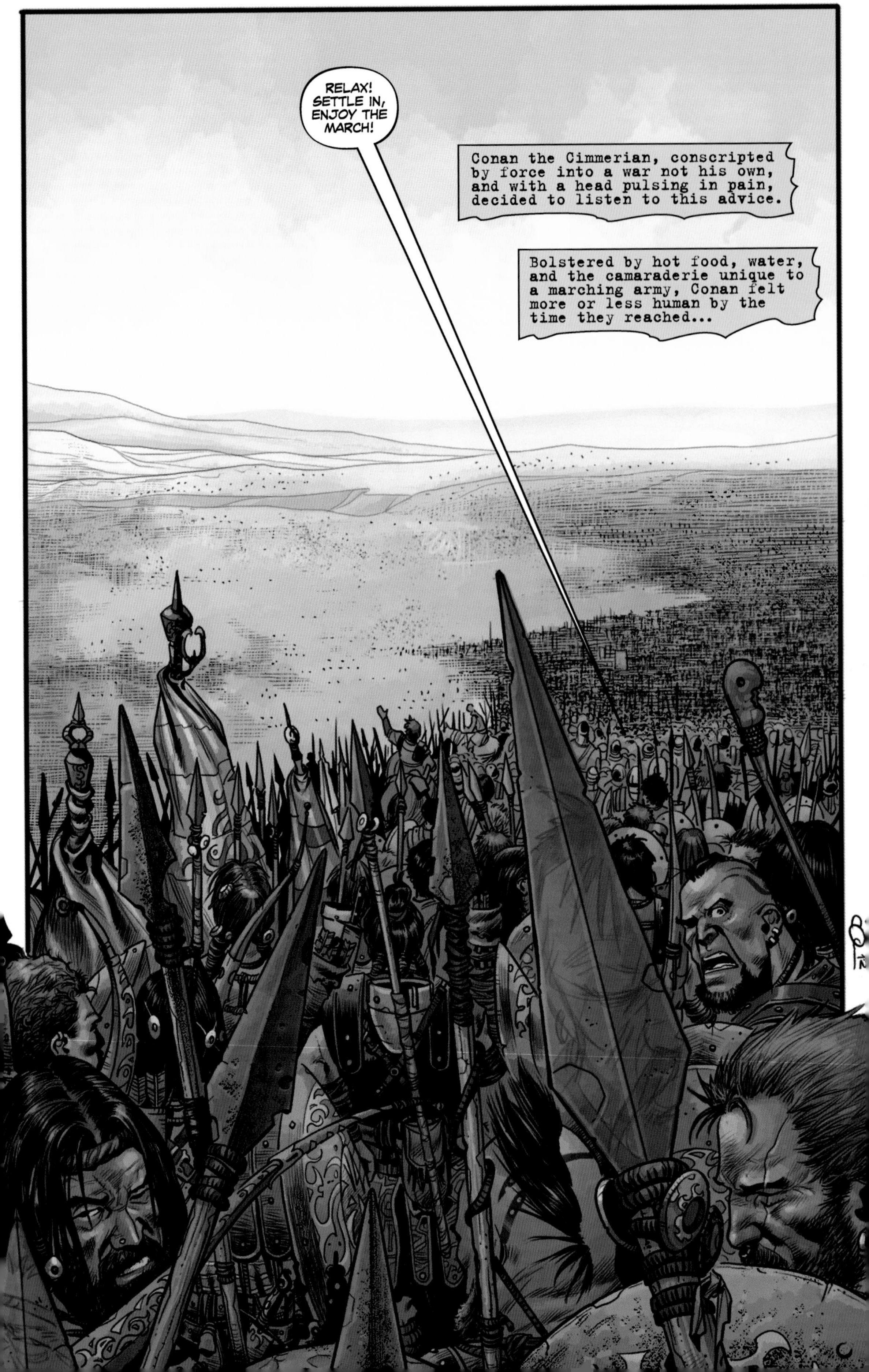
RELAX! SETTLE IN, ENJOY THE MARCH!
Conan the Cimmerian, conscripted by force into a war not his own, and with a head pulsing in pain, decided to listen to this advice.
Bolstered by hot food, water, and the camaraderie unique to a marching army, Conan felt more or less human by the time they reached...

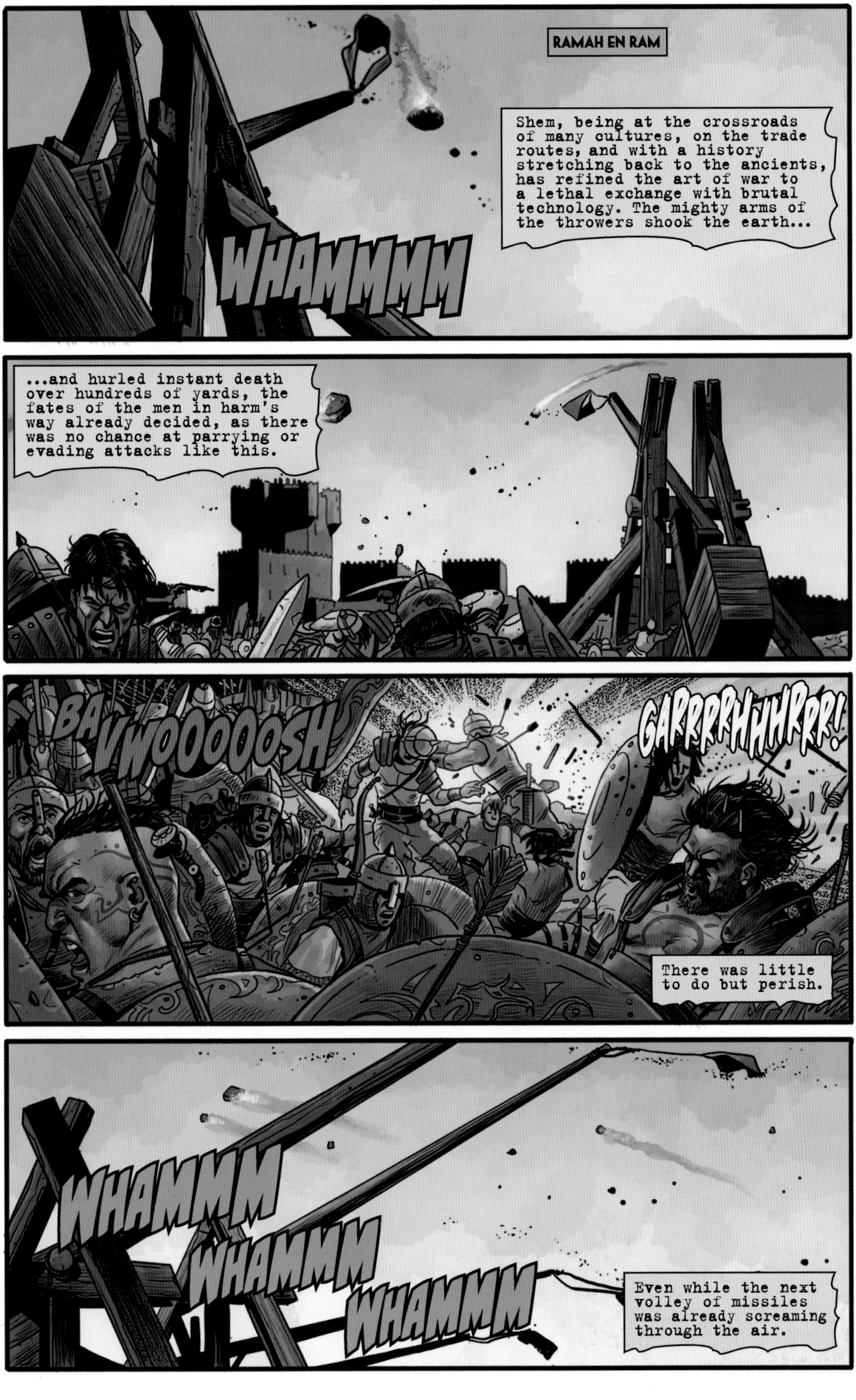

RAMAH EN RAM
Shem, being at the crossroads of many cultures, on the trade routes, and with a history stretching back to the ancients, has refined the art of war to a lethal exchange with brutal technology. The mighty arms of the throwers shook the earth...
WHAMMMMM
...and hurled instant death over hundreds of yards, the fates of the men in harm's way already decided, as there was no chance at parrying or evading attacks like this.
BAVWOOOOOSH
GARRRHHHRRR!
There was little to do but perish.
WHAMMM
WHAMMM
WHAMMM
Even while the next volley of missiles was already screaming through the air.

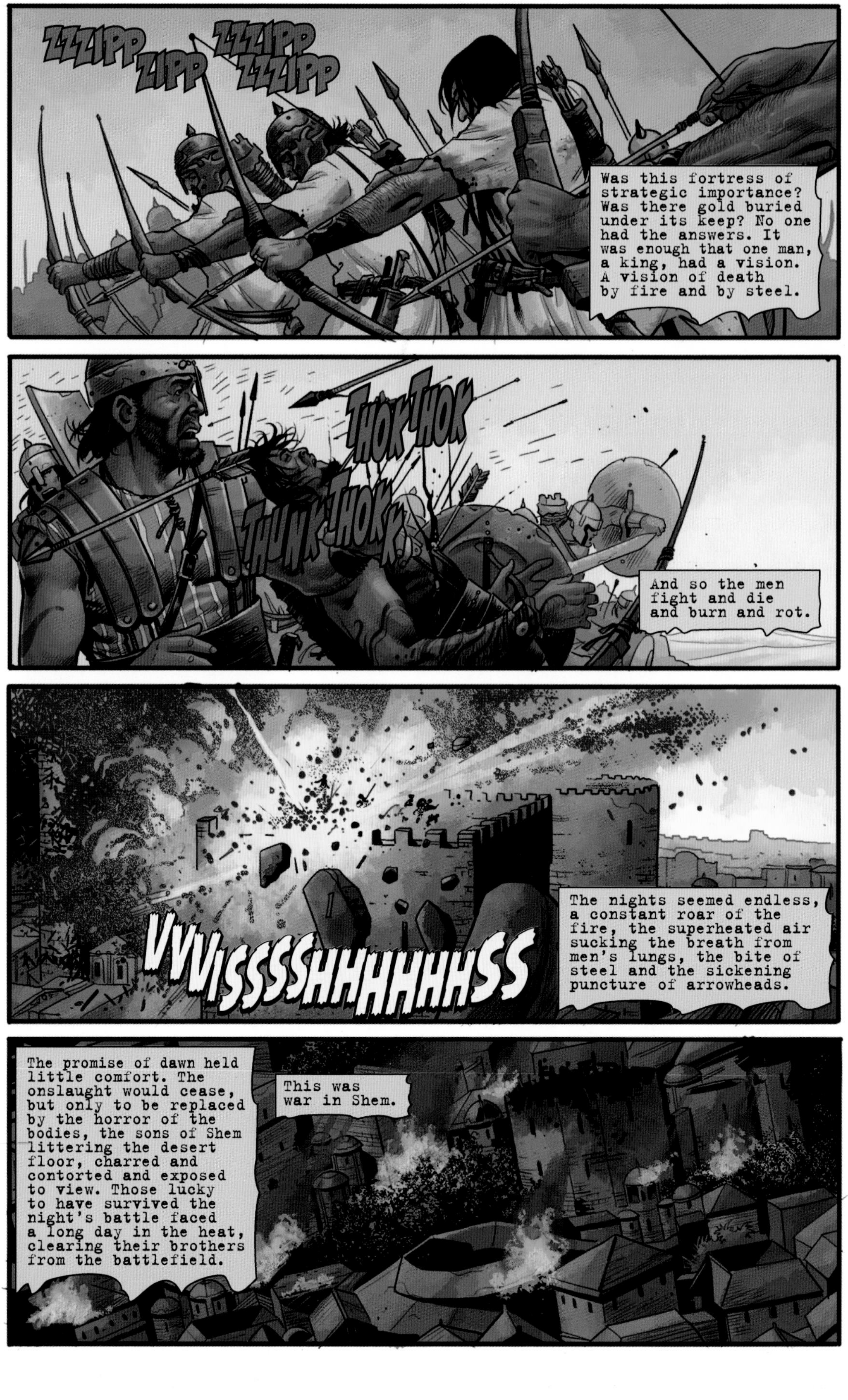
ZZZIPP
ZIPP
ZZZIPP
ZZZIPP
Was this fortress of strategic importance? Was there gold buried under its keep? No one had the answers. It was enough that one man, a king, had a vision. A vision of death by fire and by steel.
THOK THOK
THUNK
THOKK
And so the men fight and die and burn and rot.
The nights seemed endless, a constant roar of the fire, the superheated air sucking the breath from men's lungs, the bite of steel and the sickening puncture of arrowheads.
VVVISSSSHHHHHHSS
The promise of dawn held little comfort. The onslaught would cease, but only to be replaced by the horror of the bodies, the sons of Shem littering the desert floor, charred and contorted and exposed to view. Those lucky to have survived the night's battle faced a long day in the heat, clearing their brothers from the battlefield.
This was war in Shem.

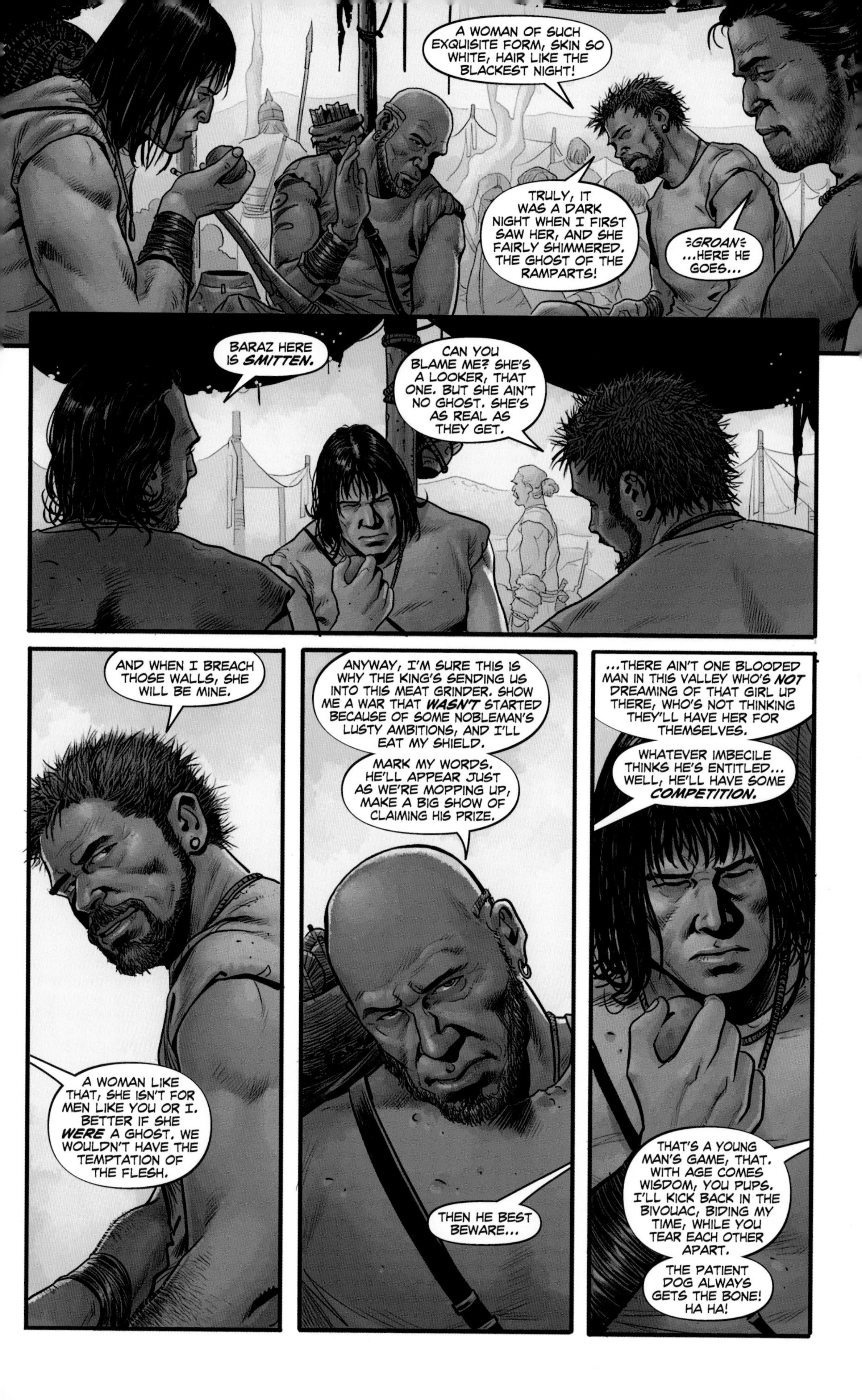
A WOMAN OF SUCH EXQUISITE FORM, SKIN SO WHITE, HAIR LIKE THE BLACKEST NIGHT!
TRULY, IT WAS A DARK NIGHT WHEN I FIRST SAW HER, AND SHE FAIRLY SHIMMERED. THE GHOST OF THE RAMPARTS!
GROAN ...HERE HE GOES...
BARAZ HERE IS *SMITTEN.*
CAN YOU BLAME ME? SHE'S A LOOKER, THAT ONE. BUT SHE AIN'T NO GHOST. SHE'S AS REAL AS THEY GET.
AND WHEN I BREACH THOSE WALLS, SHE WILL BE MINE.
A WOMAN LIKE THAT, SHE ISN'T FOR MEN LIKE YOU OR I. BETTER IF SHE *WERE* A GHOST. WE WOULDN'T HAVE THE TEMPTATION OF THE FLESH.
ANYWAY, I'M SURE THIS IS WHY THE KING'S SENDING US INTO THIS MEAT GRINDER. SHOW ME A WAR THAT *WASN'T* STARTED BECAUSE OF SOME NOBLEMAN'S LUSTY AMBITIONS, AND I'LL EAT MY SHIELD.
MARK MY WORDS. HE'LL APPEAR JUST AS WE'RE MOPPING UP, MAKE A BIG SHOW OF CLAIMING HIS PRIZE.
THEN HE BEST BEWARE...
...THERE AIN'T ONE BLOODED MAN IN THIS VALLEY WHO'S *NOT* DREAMING OF THAT GIRL UP THERE, WHO'S NOT THINKING THEY'LL HAVE HER FOR THEMSELVES.
WHATEVER IMBECILE THINKS HE'S ENTITLED... WELL, HE'LL HAVE SOME *COMPETITION.*
THAT'S A YOUNG MAN'S GAME, THAT. WITH AGE COMES WISDOM, YOU PUPS. I'LL KICK BACK IN THE BIVOUAC, BIDING MY TIME, WHILE YOU TEAR EACH OTHER APART.
THE PATIENT DOG ALWAYS GETS THE BONE! HA HA!

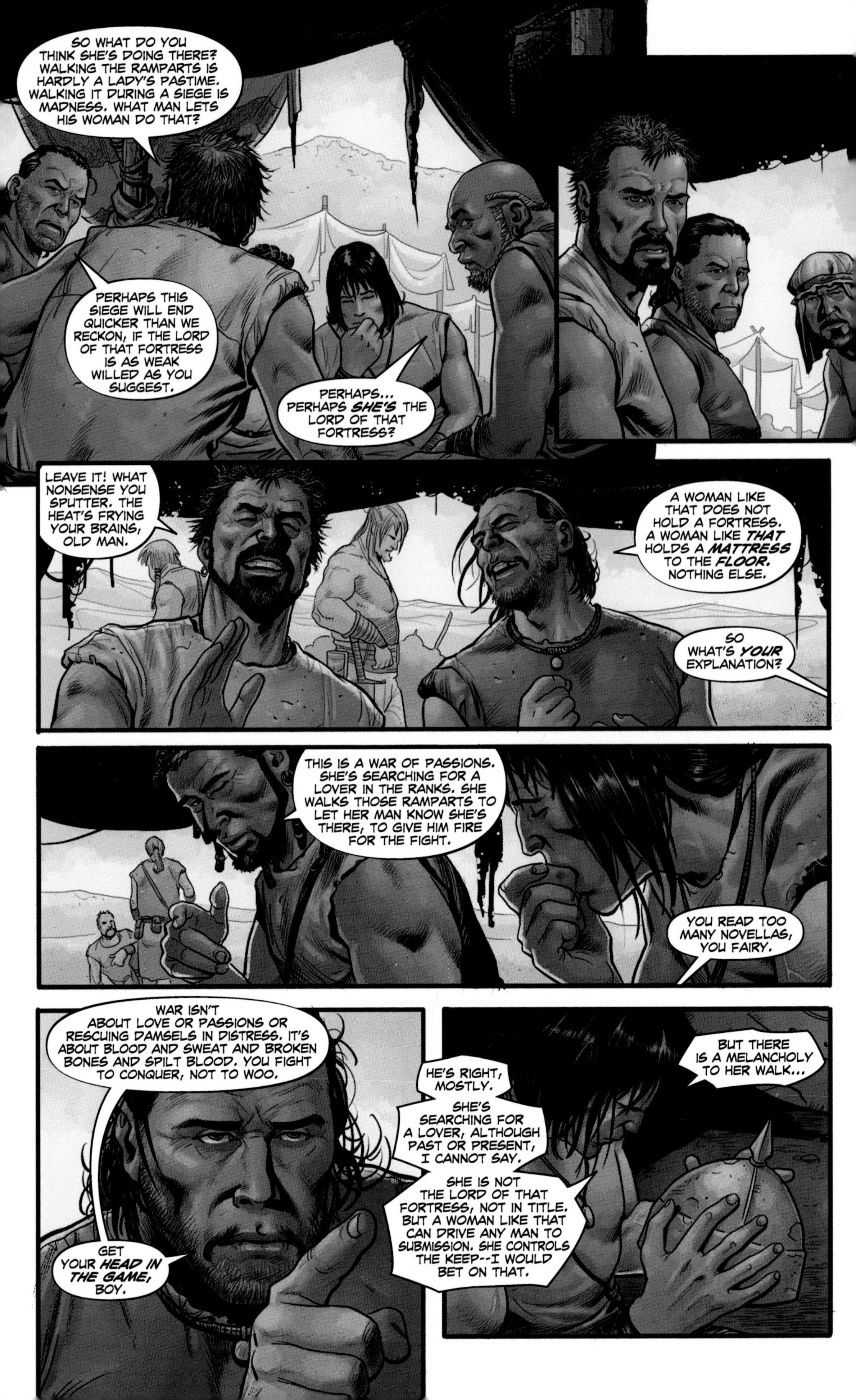
SO WHAT DO YOU THINK SHE'S DOING THERE? WALKING THE RAMPARTS IS HARDLY A LADY'S PASTIME. WALKING IT DURING A SIEGE IS MADNESS. WHAT MAN LETS HIS WOMAN DO THAT?
PERHAPS THIS SIEGE WILL END QUICKER THAN WE RECKON, IF THE LORD OF THAT FORTRESS IS AS WEAK WILLED AS YOU SUGGEST.
PERHAPS... PERHAPS SHE'S THE LORD OF THAT FORTRESS?
LEAVE IT! WHAT NONSENSE YOU SPUTTER. THE HEAT'S FRYING YOUR BRAINS, OLD MAN.
A WOMAN LIKE THAT DOES NOT HOLD A FORTRESS. A WOMAN LIKE THAT HOLDS A MATTRESS TO THE FLOOR. NOTHING ELSE.
SO WHAT'S YOUR EXPLANATION?
THIS IS A WAR OF PASSIONS. SHE'S SEARCHING FOR A LOVER IN THE RANKS. SHE WALKS THOSE RAMPARTS TO LET HER MAN KNOW SHE'S THERE, TO GIVE HIM FIRE FOR THE FIGHT.
YOU READ TOO MANY NOVELLAS, YOU FAIRY.
WAR ISN'T ABOUT LOVE OR PASSIONS OR RESCUING DAMSELS IN DISTRESS. IT'S ABOUT BLOOD AND SWEAT AND BROKEN BONES AND SPILT BLOOD. YOU FIGHT TO CONQUER, NOT TO WOO.
GET YOUR HEAD IN THE GAME, BOY.
HE'S RIGHT, MOSTLY.
SHE'S SEARCHING FOR A LOVER, ALTHOUGH PAST OR PRESENT, I CANNOT SAY.
SHE IS NOT THE LORD OF THAT FORTRESS, NOT IN TITLE. BUT A WOMAN LIKE THAT CAN DRIVE ANY MAN TO SUBMISSION. SHE CONTROLS THE KEEP--I WOULD BET ON THAT.
BUT THERE IS A MELANCHOLY TO HER WALK...

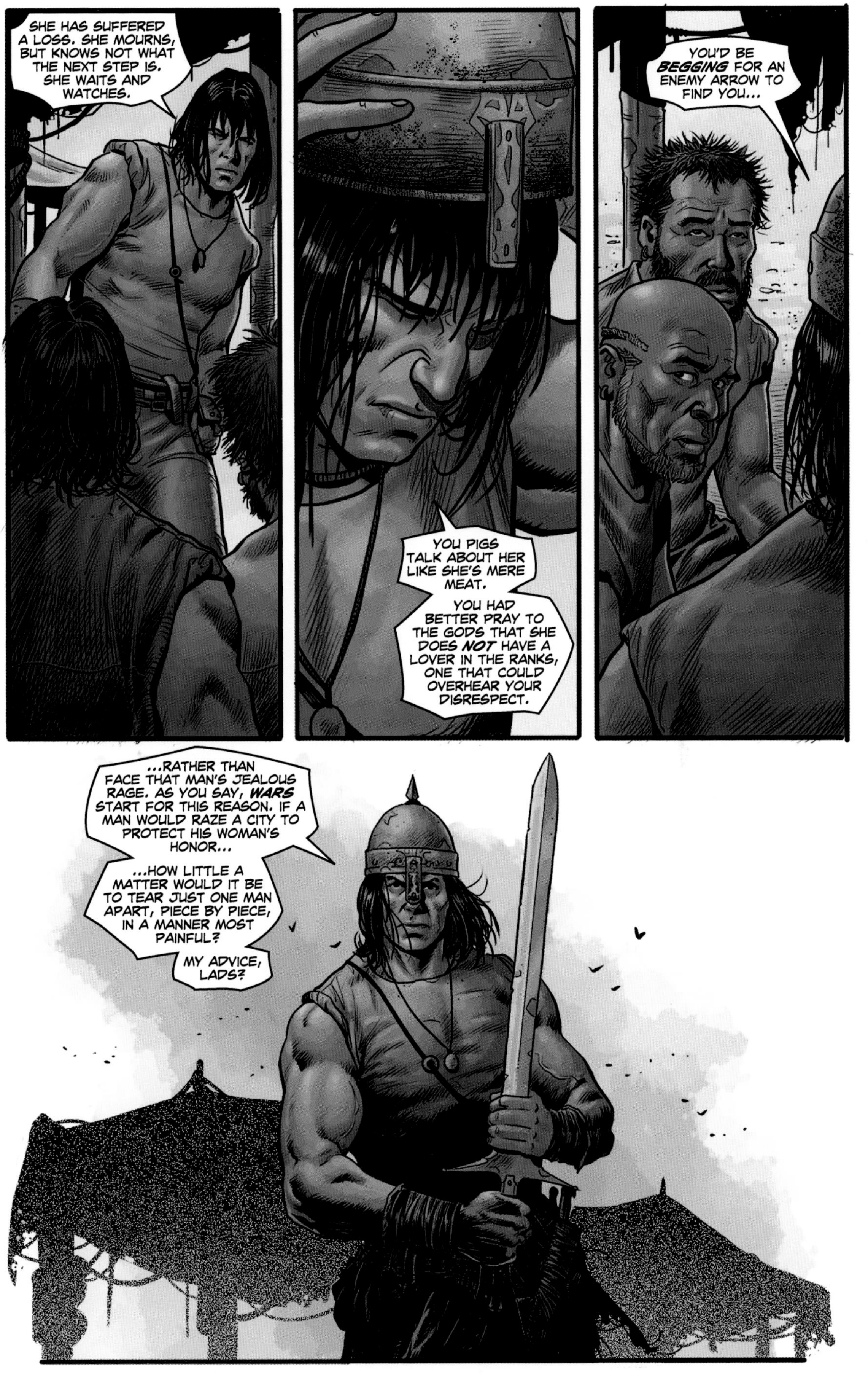
SHE HAS SUFFERED A LOSS. SHE MOURNS, BUT KNOWS NOT WHAT THE NEXT STEP IS. SHE WAITS AND WATCHES.
YOU PIGS TALK ABOUT HER LIKE SHE'S MERE MEAT.
YOU HAD BETTER PRAY TO THE GODS THAT SHE DOES *NOT* HAVE A LOVER IN THE RANKS, ONE THAT COULD OVERHEAR YOUR DISRESPECT.
YOU'D BE *BEGGING* FOR AN ENEMY ARROW TO FIND YOU...
...RATHER THAN FACE THAT MAN'S JEALOUS RAGE. AS YOU SAY, *WARS* START FOR THIS REASON. IF A MAN WOULD RAZE A CITY TO PROTECT HIS WOMAN'S HONOR...
...HOW LITTLE A MATTER WOULD IT BE TO TEAR JUST ONE MAN APART, PIECE BY PIECE, IN A MANNER MOST PAINFUL?
MY ADVICE, LADS?

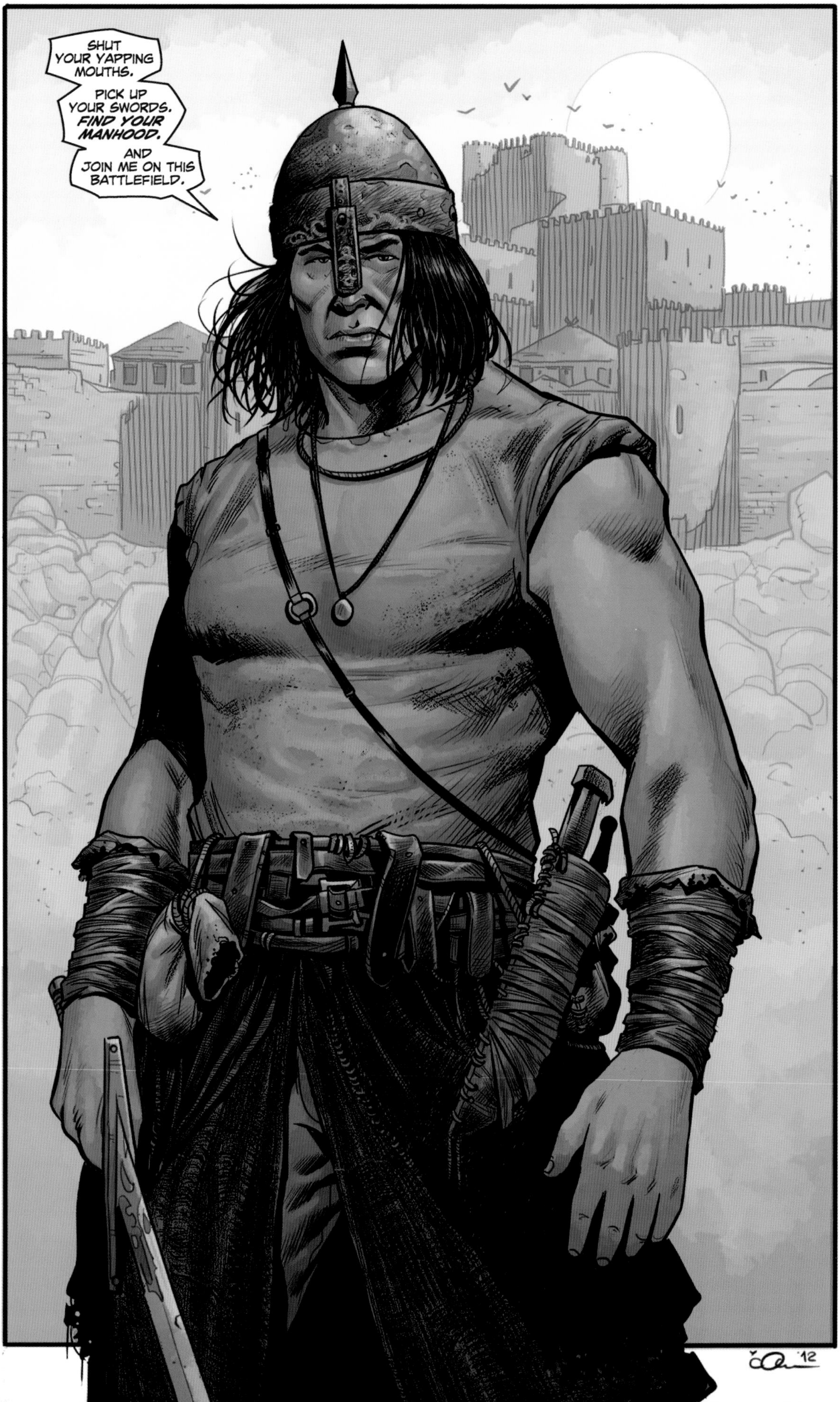
SHUT YOUR YAPPING MOUTHS.
PICK UP YOUR SWORDS. FIND YOUR MANHOOD.
AND JOIN ME ON THIS BATTLEFIELD.

CHAPTER TWO

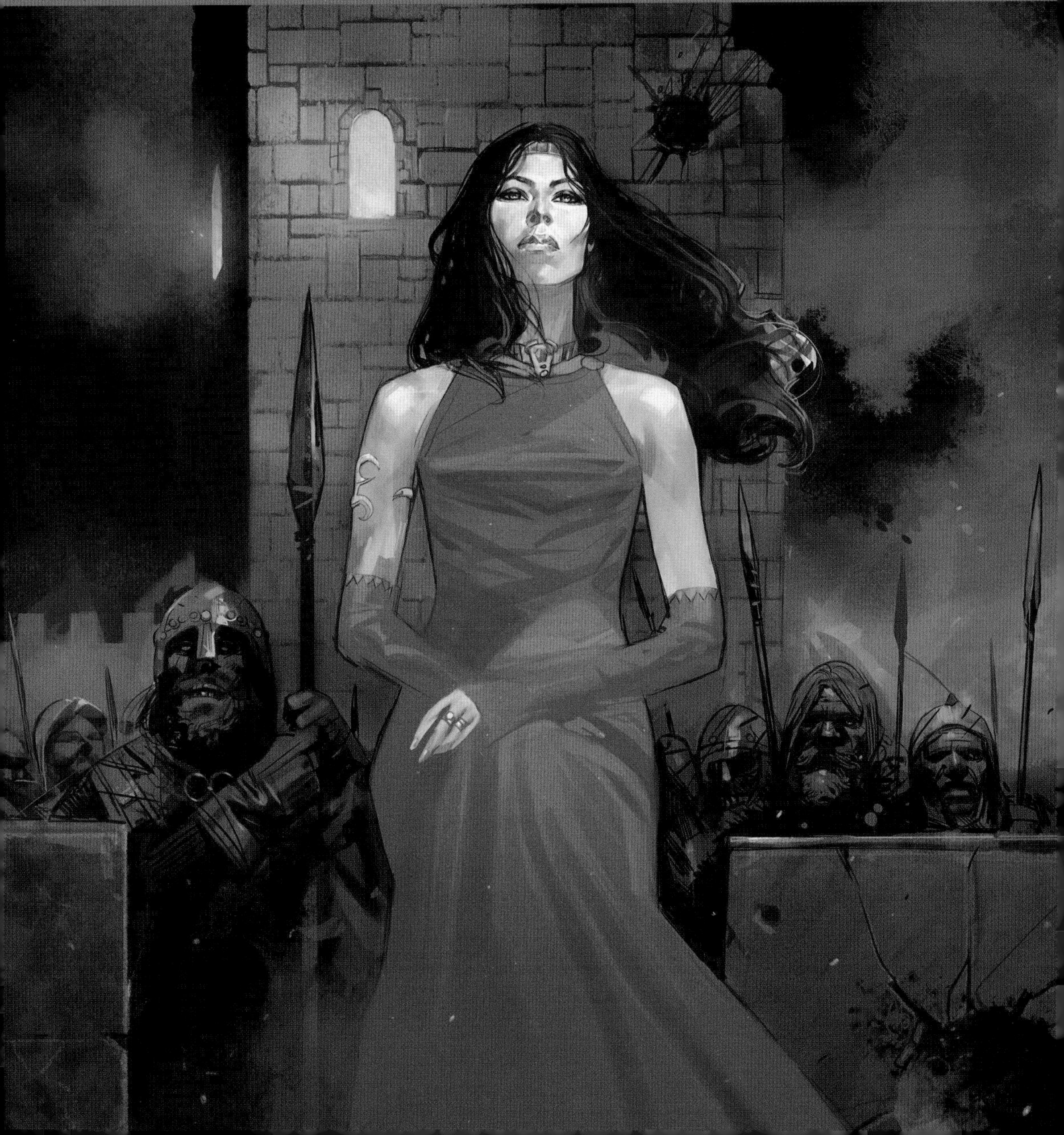

"You may command my men,
but you do not command me, Conan!"

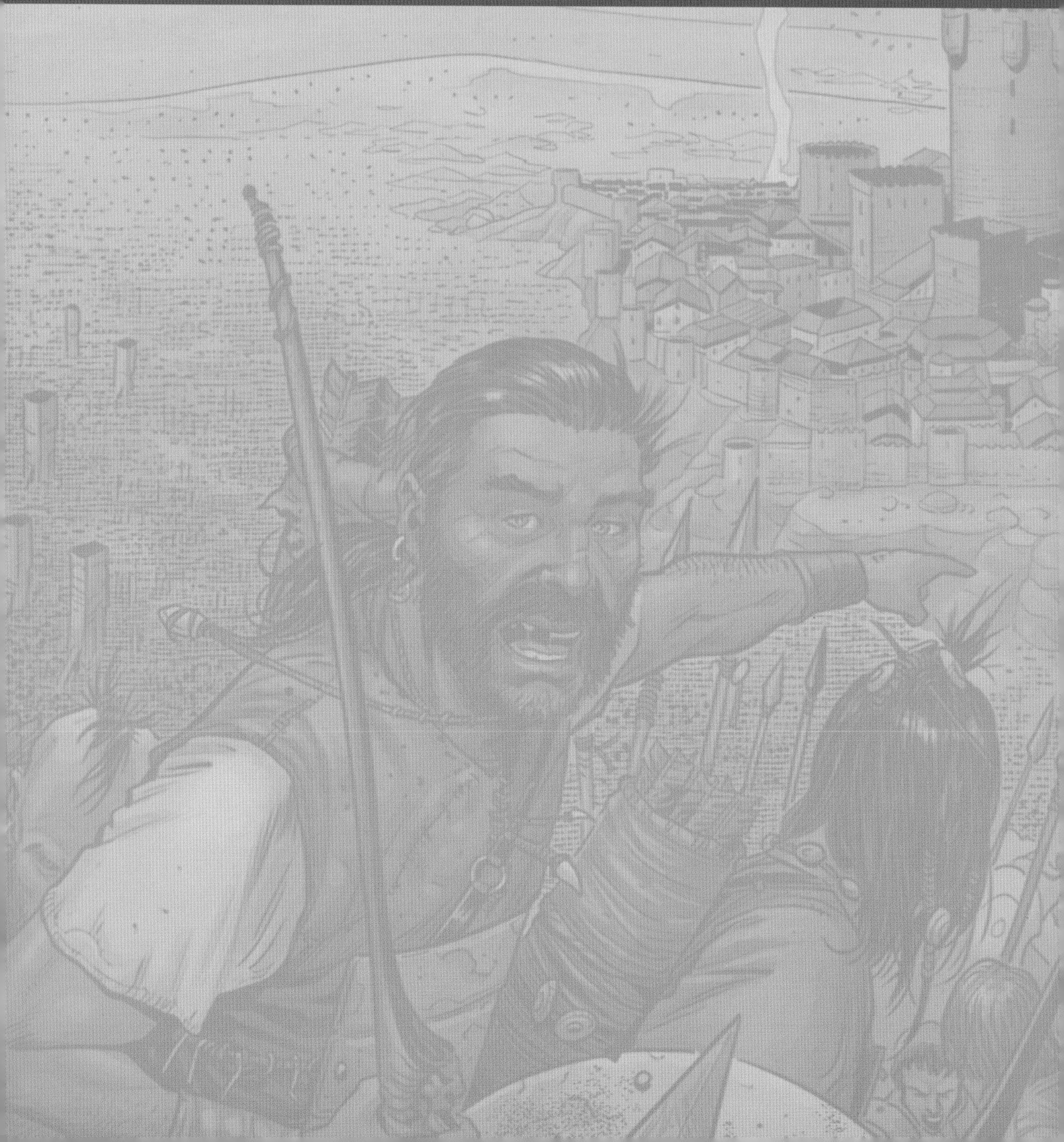

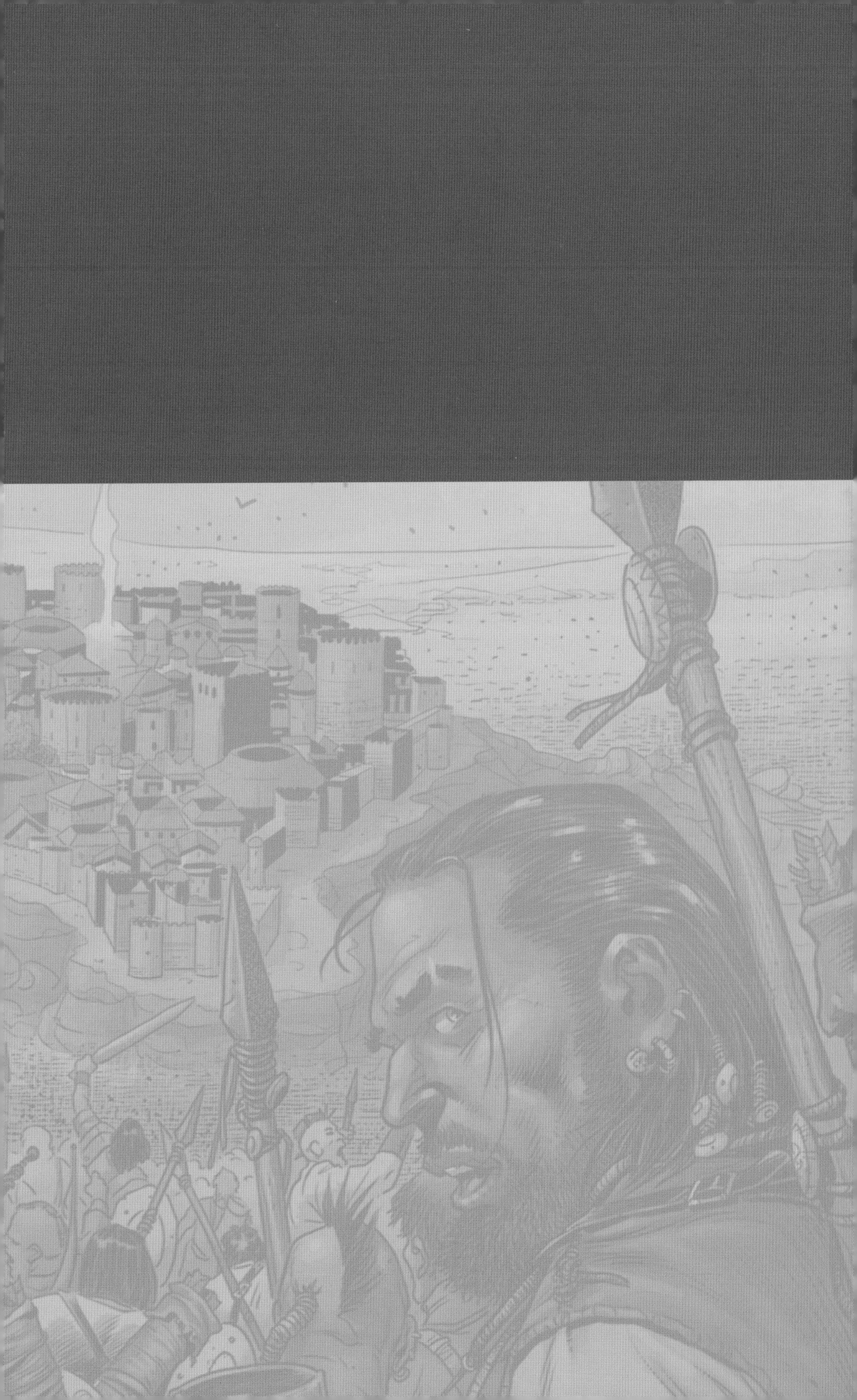

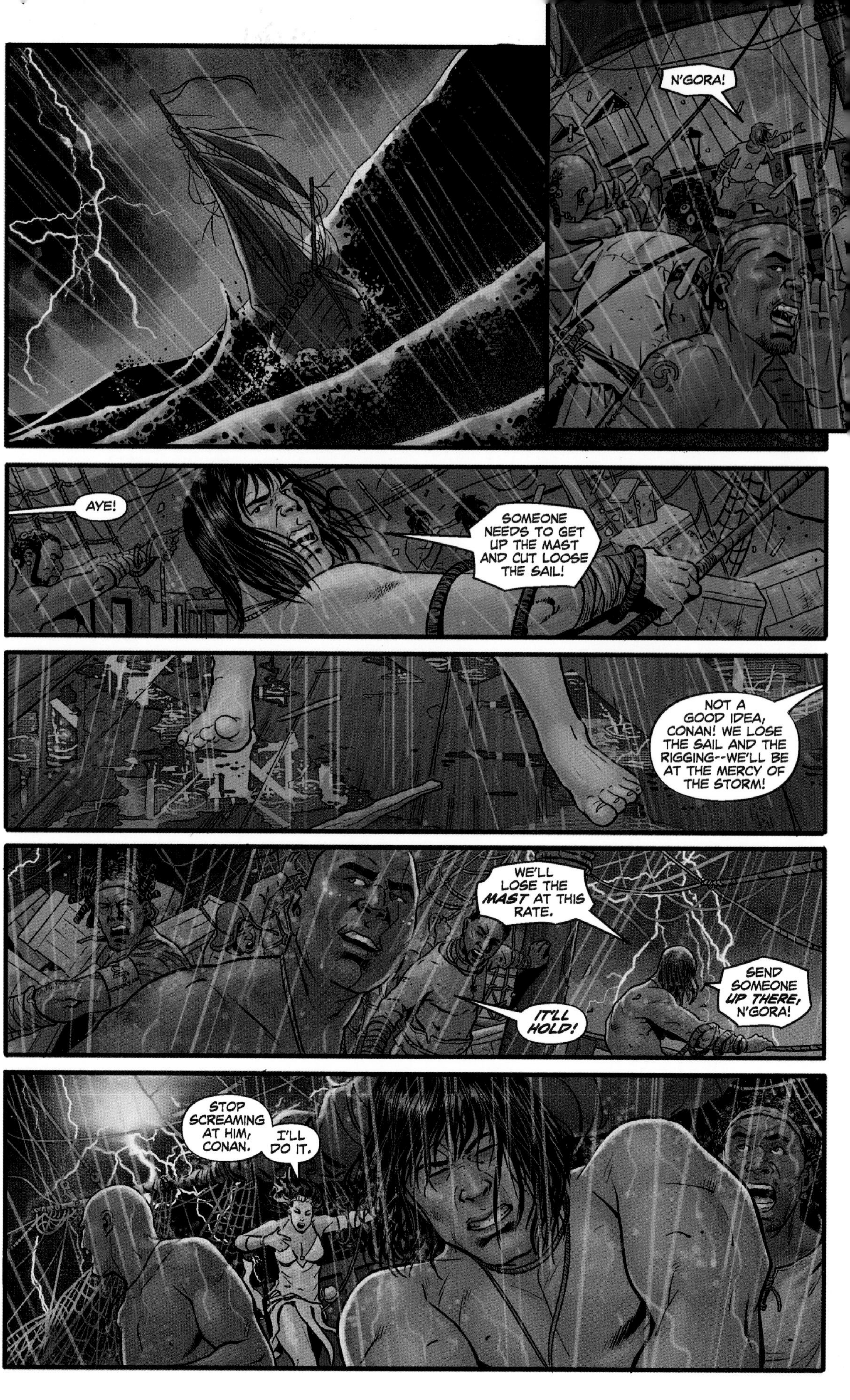
N'GORA!
AYE!
SOMEONE NEEDS TO GET UP THE MAST AND CUT LOOSE THE SAIL!
NOT A GOOD IDEA, CONAN! WE LOSE THE SAIL AND THE RIGGING--WE'LL BE AT THE MERCY OF THE STORM!
WE'LL LOSE THE MAST AT THIS RATE.
SEND SOMEONE UP THERE, N'GORA!
IT'LL HOLD!
STOP SCREAMING AT HIM, CONAN.
I'LL DO IT.

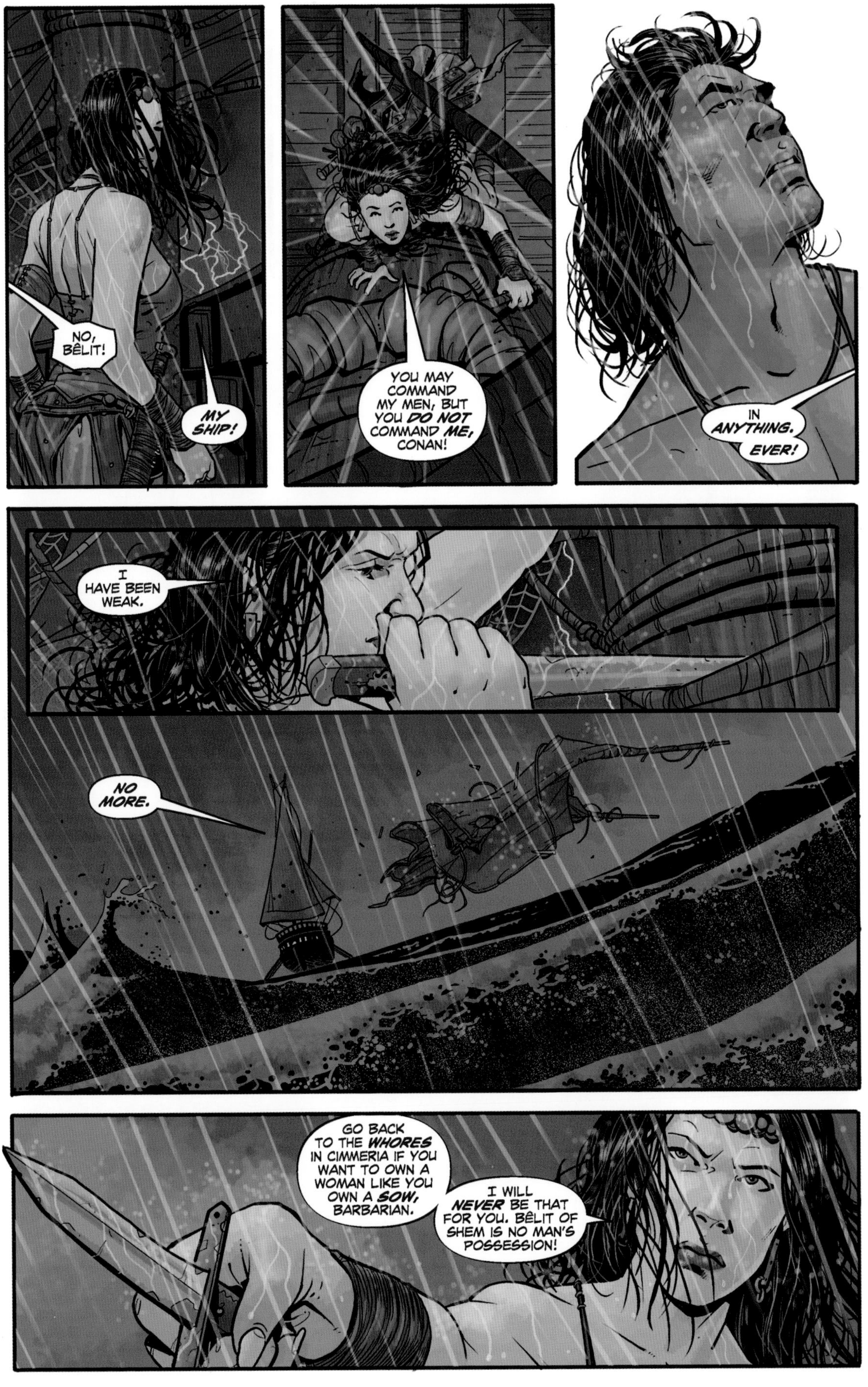
NO, BÊLIT!
MY SHIP!
YOU MAY COMMAND MY MEN, BUT YOU DO NOT COMMAND ME, CONAN!
IN ANYTHING.
EVER!
I HAVE BEEN WEAK.
NO MORE.
GO BACK TO THE WHORES IN CIMMERIA IF YOU WANT TO OWN A WOMAN LIKE YOU OWN A SOW, BARBARIAN.
I WILL NEVER BE THAT FOR YOU. BÊLIT OF SHEM IS NO MAN'S POSSESSION!

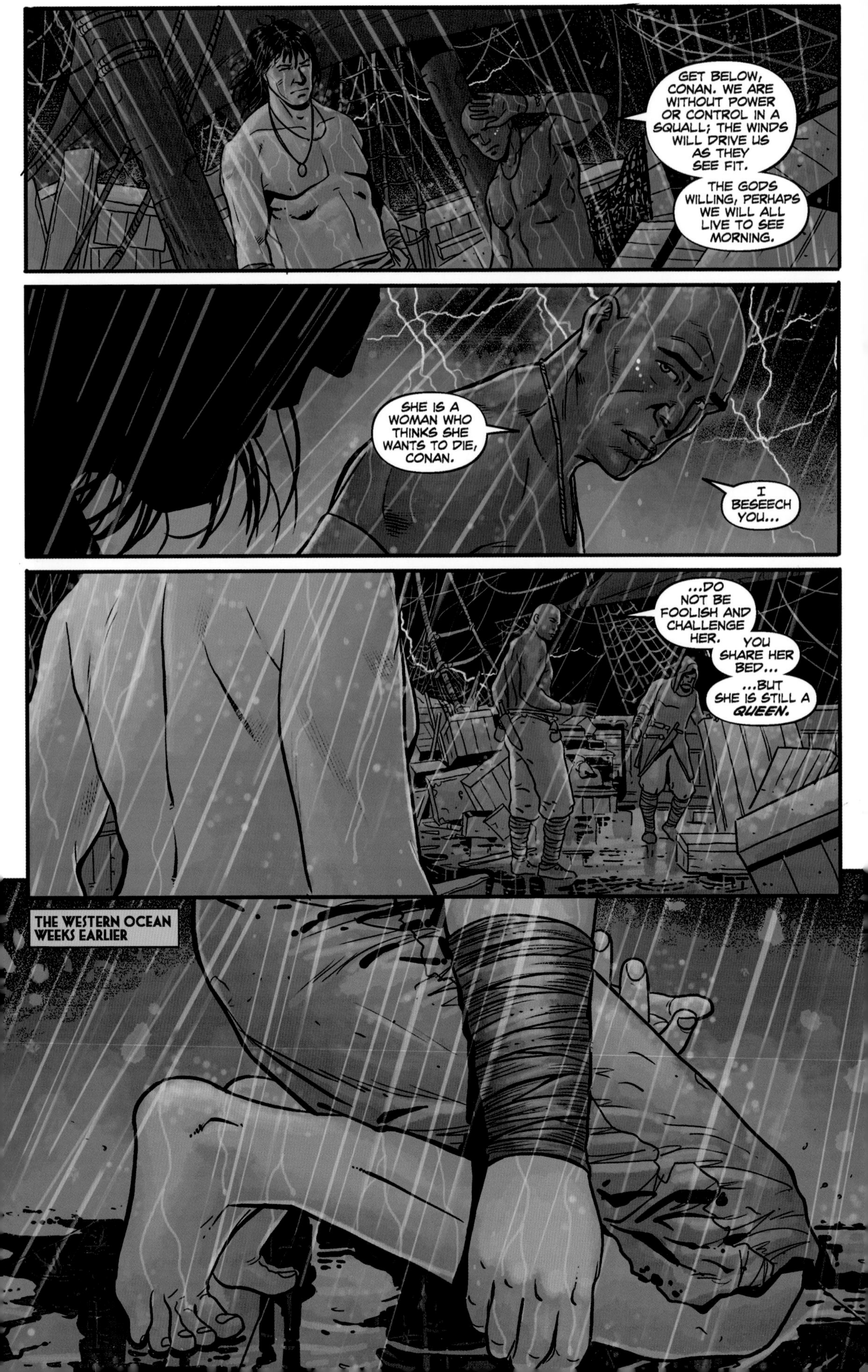

GET BELOW, CONAN. WE ARE WITHOUT POWER OR CONTROL IN A SQUALL; THE WINDS WILL DRIVE US AS THEY SEE FIT.
THE GODS WILLING, PERHAPS WE WILL ALL LIVE TO SEE MORNING.
SHE IS A WOMAN WHO THINKS SHE WANTS TO DIE, CONAN.
I BESEECH YOU...
...DO NOT BE FOOLISH AND CHALLENGE HER.
YOU SHARE HER BED...
...BUT SHE IS STILL A *QUEEN*.
THE WESTERN OCEAN WEEKS EARLIER

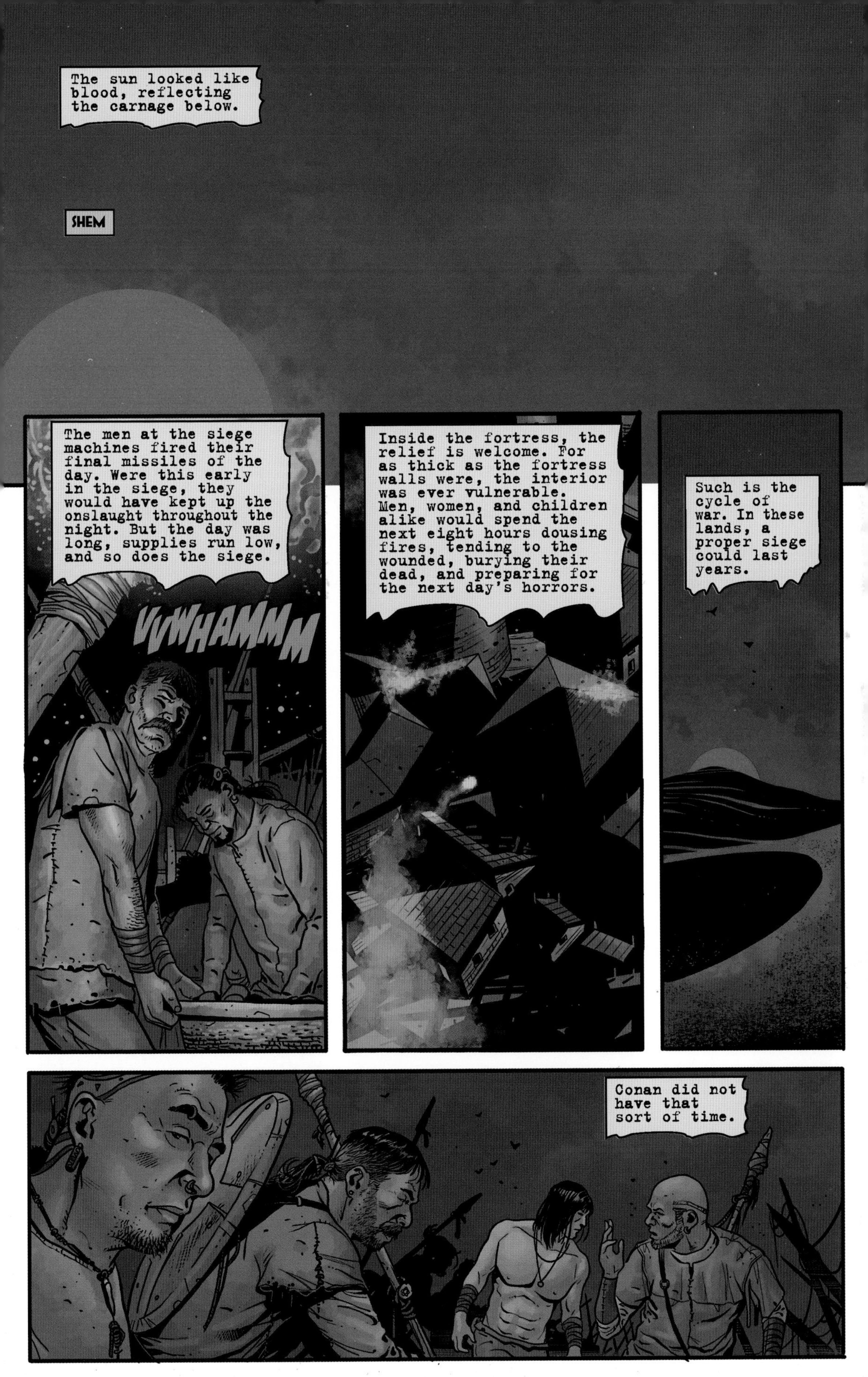
The sun looked like blood, reflecting the carnage below.
SHEM
The men at the siege machines fired their final missiles of the day. Were this early in the siege, they would have kept up the onslaught throughout the night. But the day was long, supplies run low, and so does the siege.
VVWHAMMM
Inside the fortress, the relief is welcome. For as thick as the fortress walls were, the interior was ever vulnerable. Men, women, and children alike would spend the next eight hours dousing fires, tending to the wounded, burying their dead, and preparing for the next day's horrors.
Such is the cycle of war. In these lands, a proper siege could last years.
Conan did not have that sort of time.

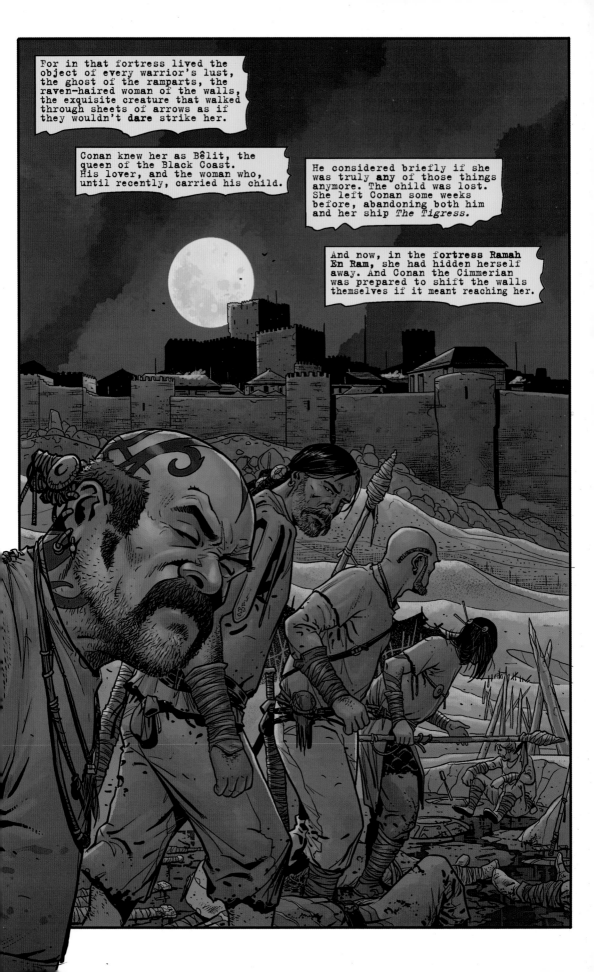

For in that fortress lived the object of every warrior's lust, the ghost of the ramparts, the raven-haired woman of the walls, the exquisite creature that walked through sheets of arrows as if they wouldn't **dare** strike her.

Conan knew her as Bêlit, the queen of the Black Coast. His lover, and the woman who, until recently, carried his child.

He considered briefly if she was truly **any of those things** anymore. The child was lost. She left Conan some weeks before, abandoning both him and her ship *The Tigress*.

And now, in the fortress **Ramah En Ram**, she had hidden herself away. And Conan the Cimmerian was prepared to shift the walls themselves if it meant reaching her.

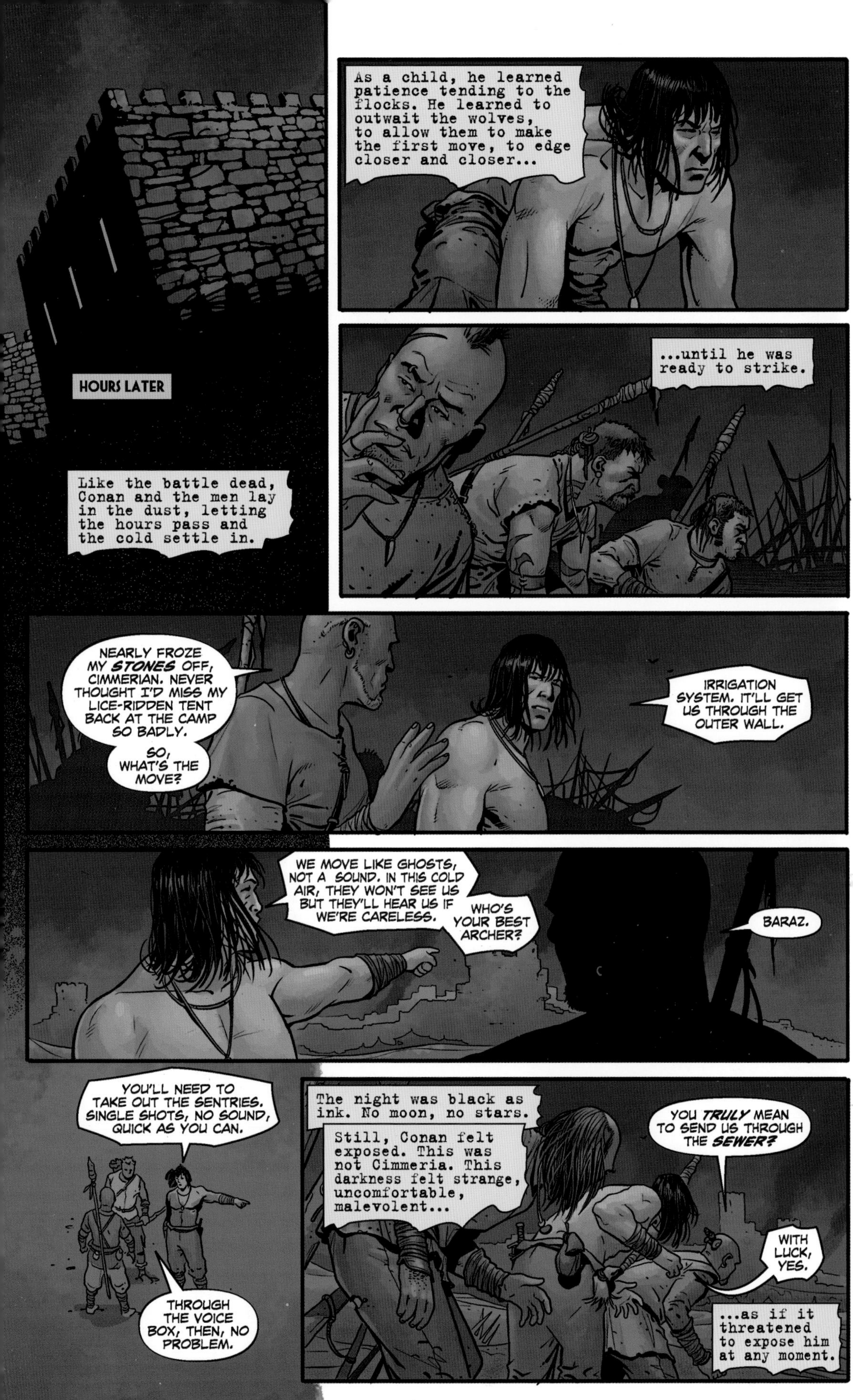
HOURS LATER
As a child, he learned patience tending to the flocks. He learned to outwait the wolves, to allow them to make the first move, to edge closer and closer...
Like the battle dead, Conan and the men lay in the dust, letting the hours pass and the cold settle in.
...until he was ready to strike.
NEARLY FROZE MY STONES OFF, CIMMERIAN. NEVER THOUGHT I'D MISS MY LICE-RIDDEN TENT BACK AT THE CAMP SO BADLY.
SO, WHAT'S THE MOVE?
IRRIGATION SYSTEM. IT'LL GET US THROUGH THE OUTER WALL.
WE MOVE LIKE GHOSTS, NOT A SOUND. IN THIS COLD AIR, THEY WON'T SEE US BUT THEY'LL HEAR US IF WE'RE CARELESS.
WHO'S YOUR BEST ARCHER?
BARAZ.
YOU'LL NEED TO TAKE OUT THE SENTRIES. SINGLE SHOTS, NO SOUND, QUICK AS YOU CAN.
THROUGH THE VOICE BOX, THEN, NO PROBLEM.
The night was black as ink. No moon, no stars.
Still, Conan felt exposed. This was not Cimmeria. This darkness felt strange, uncomfortable, malevolent...
YOU TRULY MEAN TO SEND US THROUGH THE SEWER?
WITH LUCK, YES.
...as if it threatened to expose him at any moment.

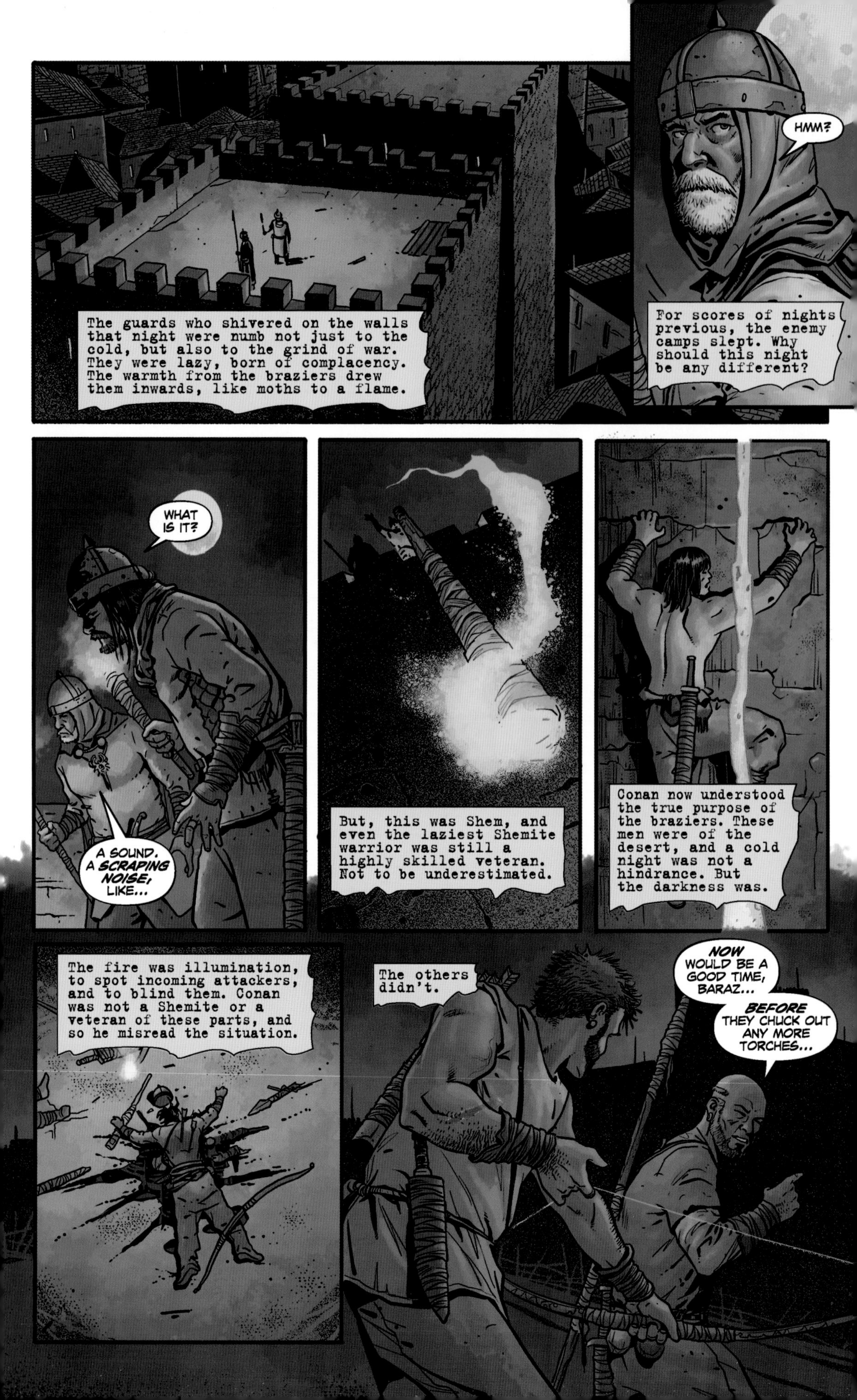

The guards who shivered on the walls that night were numb not just to the cold, but also to the grind of war. They were lazy, born of complacency. The warmth from the braziers drew them inwards, like moths to a flame.
HMM?
For scores of nights previous, the enemy camps slept. Why should this night be any different?
WHAT IS IT?
A SOUND. A SCRAPING NOISE; LIKE...
But, this was Shem, and even the laziest Shemite warrior was still a highly skilled veteran. Not to be underestimated.
Conan now understood the true purpose of the braziers. These men were of the desert, and a cold night was not a hindrance. But the darkness was.
The fire was illumination, to spot incoming attackers, and to blind them. Conan was not a Shemite or a veteran of these parts, and so he misread the situation.
The others didn't.
NOW WOULD BE A GOOD TIME, BARAZ...
BEFORE THEY CHUCK OUT ANY MORE TORCHES...

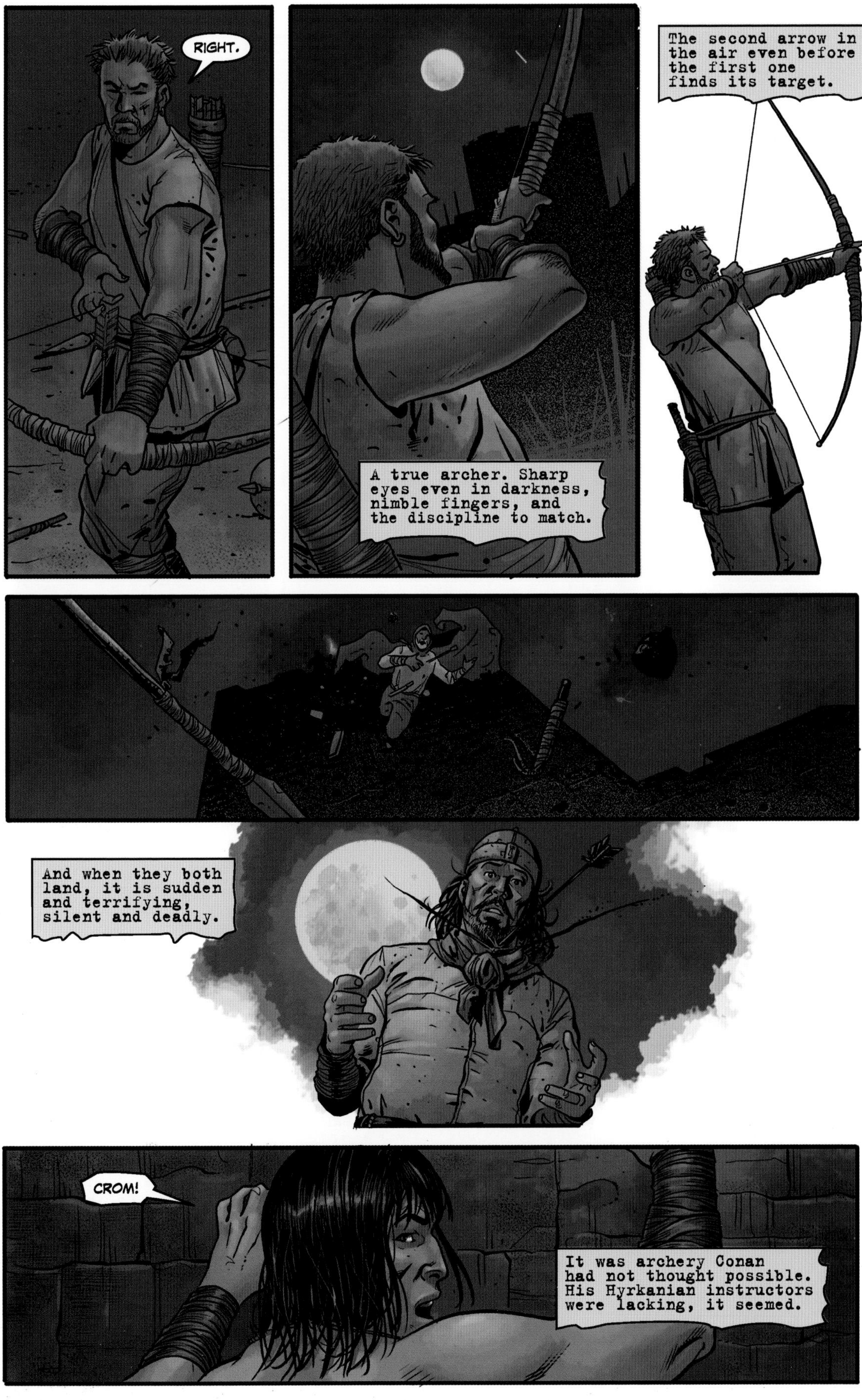
RIGHT.
A true archer. Sharp eyes even in darkness, nimble fingers, and the discipline to match.
The second arrow in the air even before the first one finds its target.
And when they both land, it is sudden and terrifying, silent and deadly.
CROM!
It was archery Conan had not thought possible. His Hyrkanian instructors were lacking, it seemed.

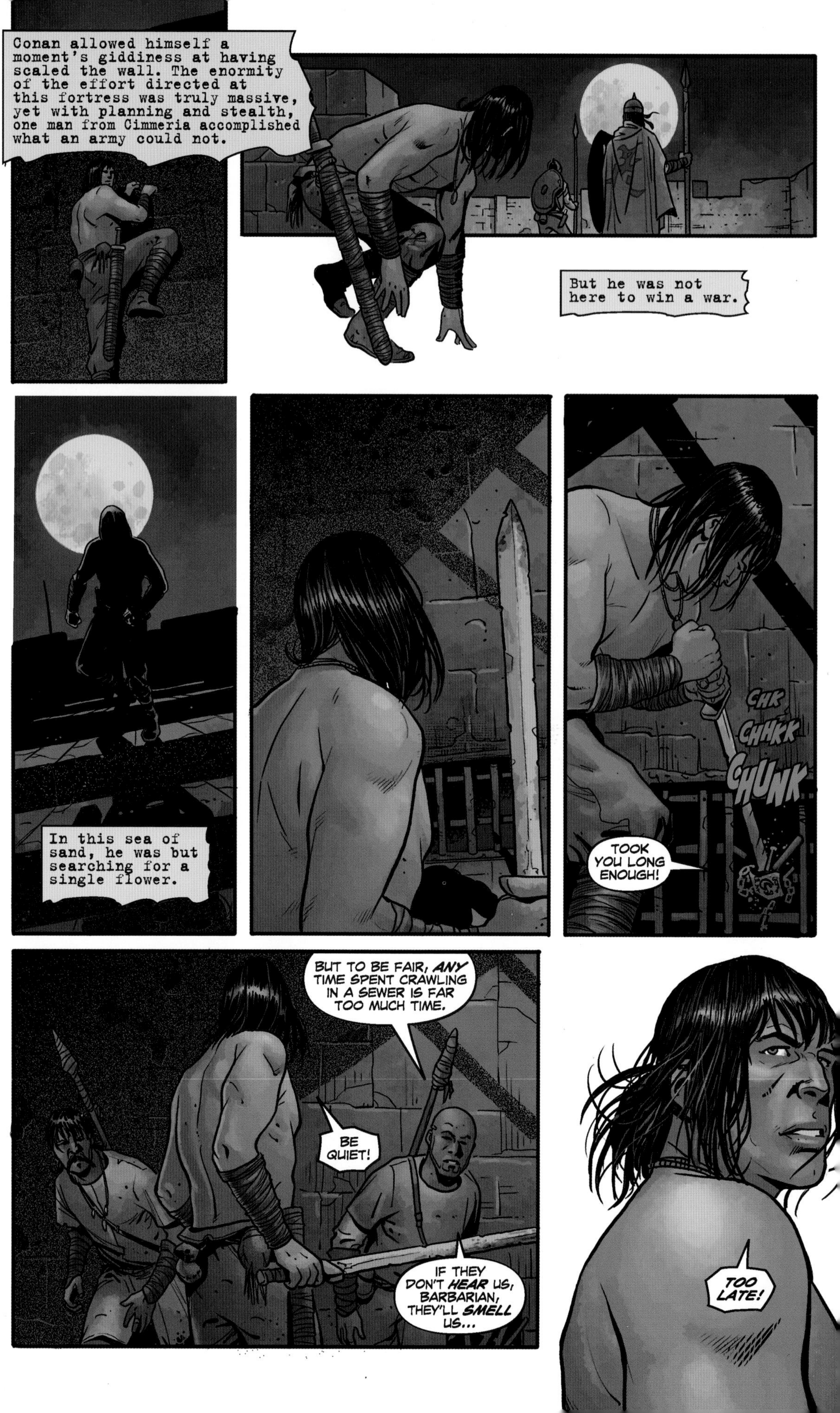
Conan allowed himself a moment's giddiness at having scaled the wall. The enormity of the effort directed at this fortress was truly massive, yet with planning and stealth, one man from Cimmeria accomplished what an army could not.
But he was not here to win a war.
In this sea of sand, he was but searching for a single flower.
CHK
CHHKK
CHUNK
TOOK YOU LONG ENOUGH!
BUT TO BE FAIR, ANY TIME SPENT CRAWLING IN A SEWER IS FAR TOO MUCH TIME.
BE QUIET!
IF THEY DON'T HEAR US, BARBARIAN, THEY'LL SMELL US...
TOO LATE!

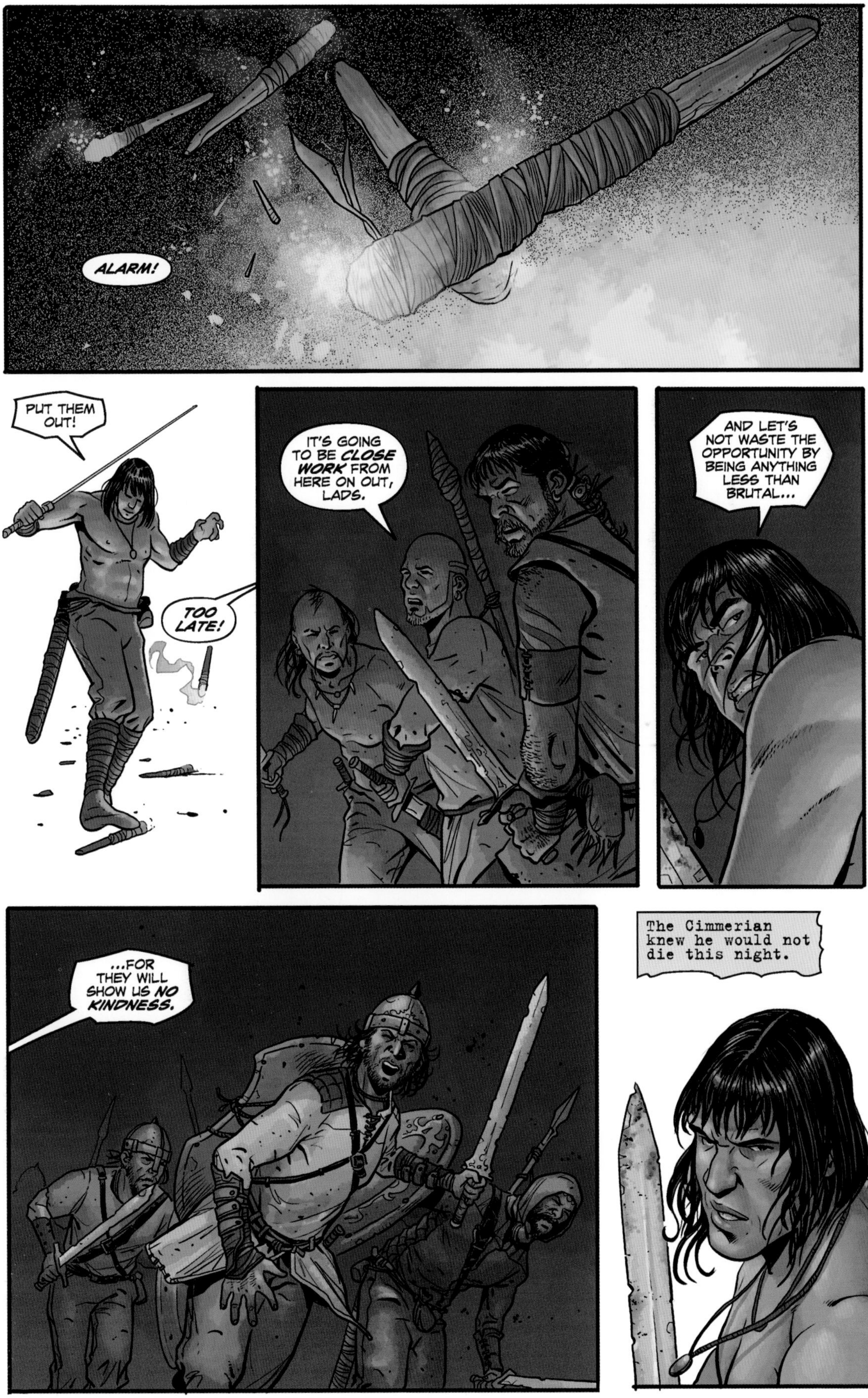
ALARM!
PUT THEM OUT!
TOO LATE!
IT'S GOING TO BE CLOSE WORK FROM HERE ON OUT, LADS.
AND LET'S NOT WASTE THE OPPORTUNITY BY BEING ANYTHING LESS THAN BRUTAL...
...FOR THEY WILL SHOW US NO KINDNESS.
The Cimmerian knew he would not die this night.

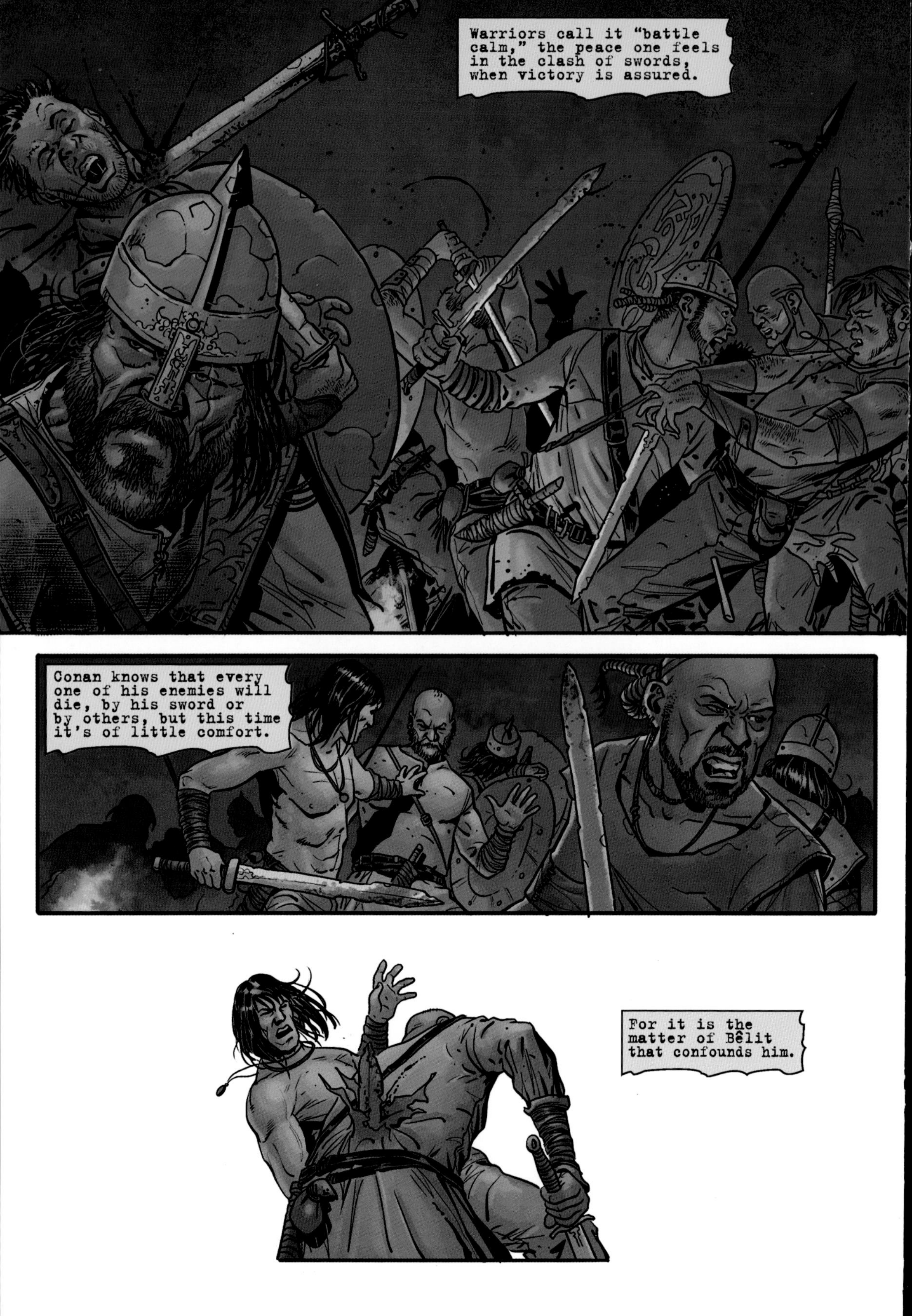
Warriors call it "battle calm," the peace one feels in the clash of swords, when victory is assured.
Conan knows that every one of his enemies will die, by his sword or by others, but this time it's of little comfort.
For it is the matter of Bêlit that confounds him.

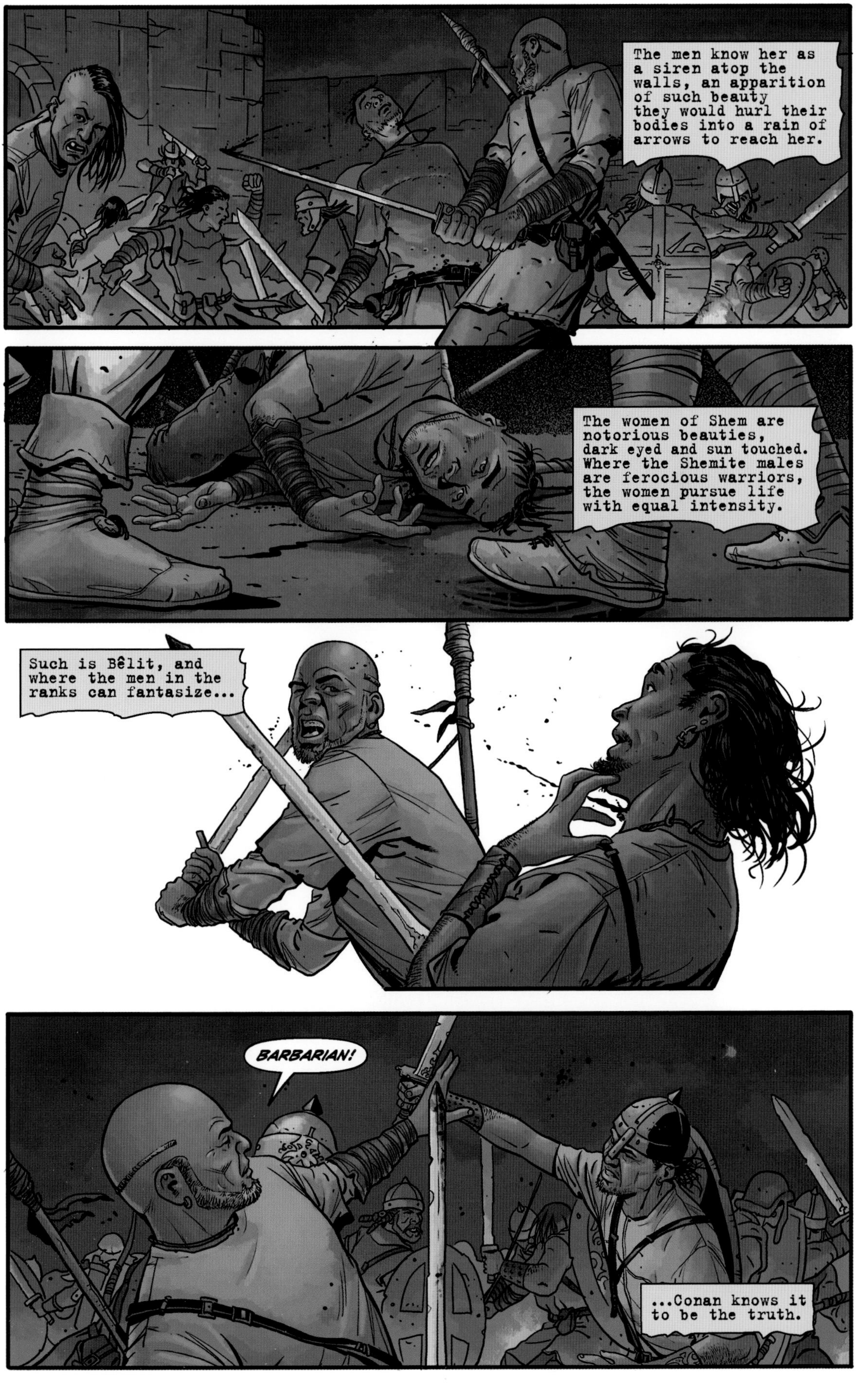
The men know her as a siren atop the walls, an apparition of such beauty they would hurl their bodies into a rain of arrows to reach her.
The women of Shem are notorious beauties, dark eyed and sun touched. Where the Shemite males are ferocious warriors, the women pursue life with equal intensity.
Such is Bêlit, and where the men in the ranks can fantasize...
BARBARIAN!
...Conan knows it to be the truth.

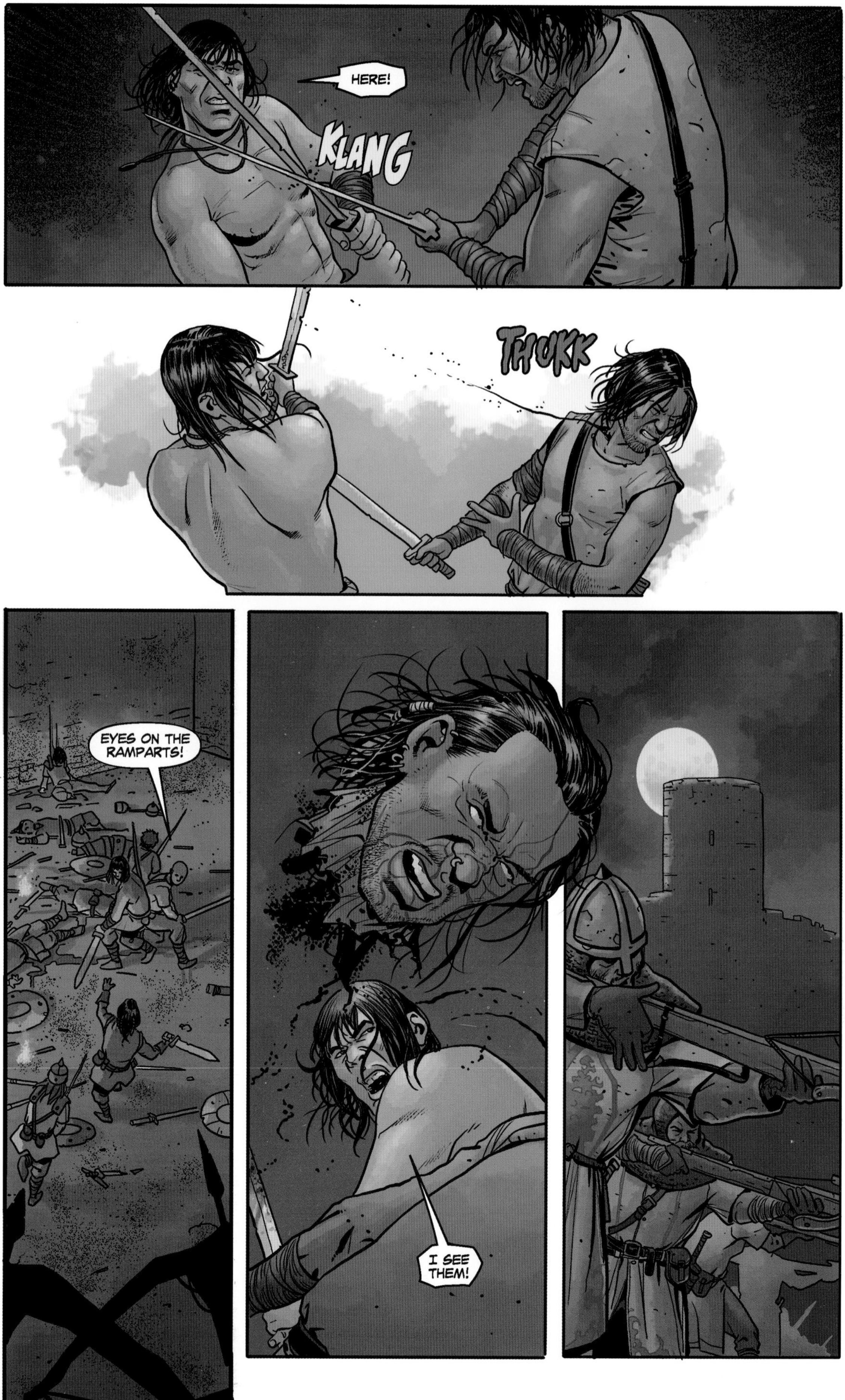
HERE!
KLANG
THUKK
EYES ON THE RAMPARTS!
I SEE THEM!

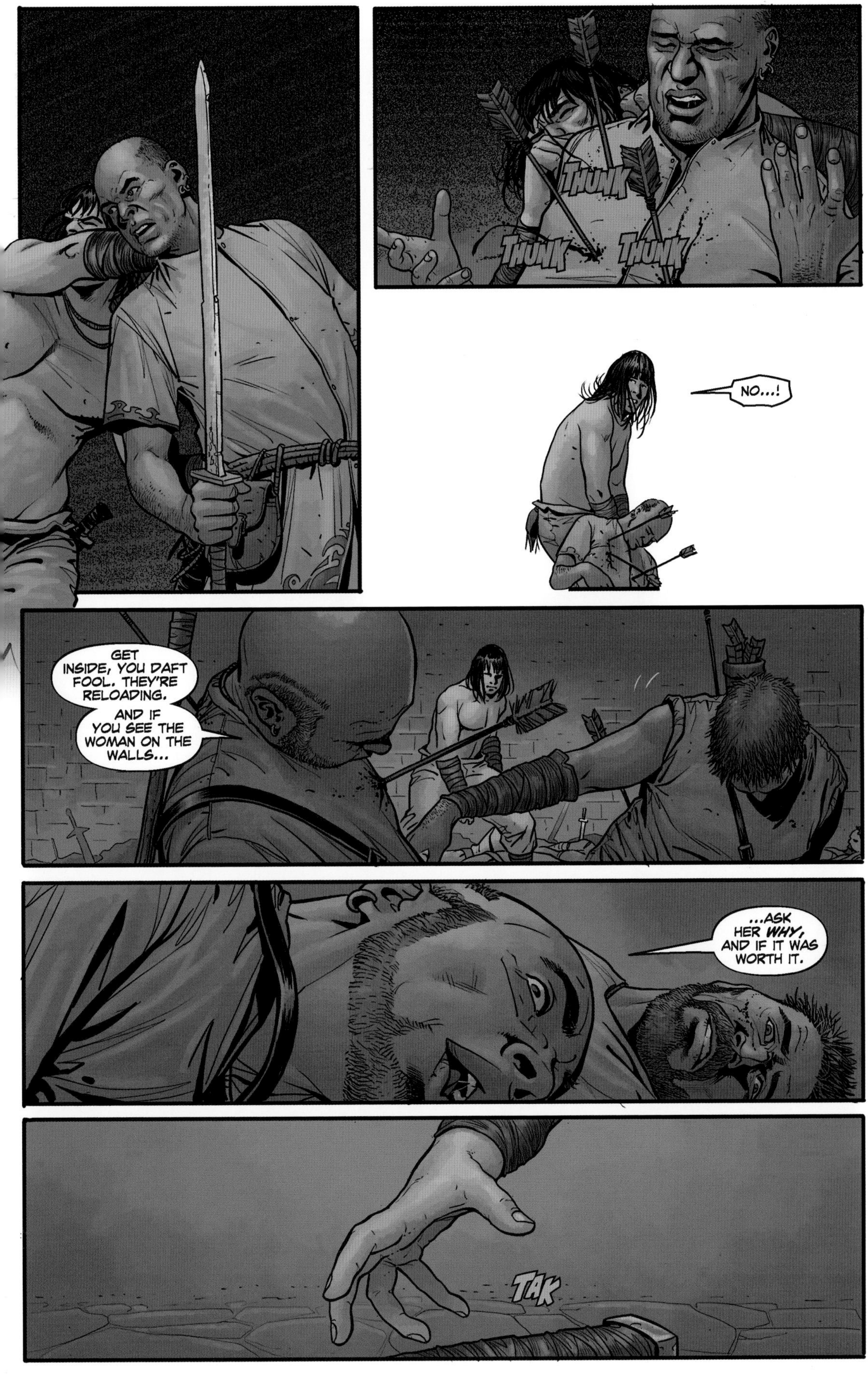
THUNK
THUNK
THUNK
NO...!
GET INSIDE, YOU DAFT FOOL. THEY'RE RELOADING.
AND IF YOU SEE THE WOMAN ON THE WALLS...
...ASK HER WHY, AND IF IT WAS WORTH IT.
TAK

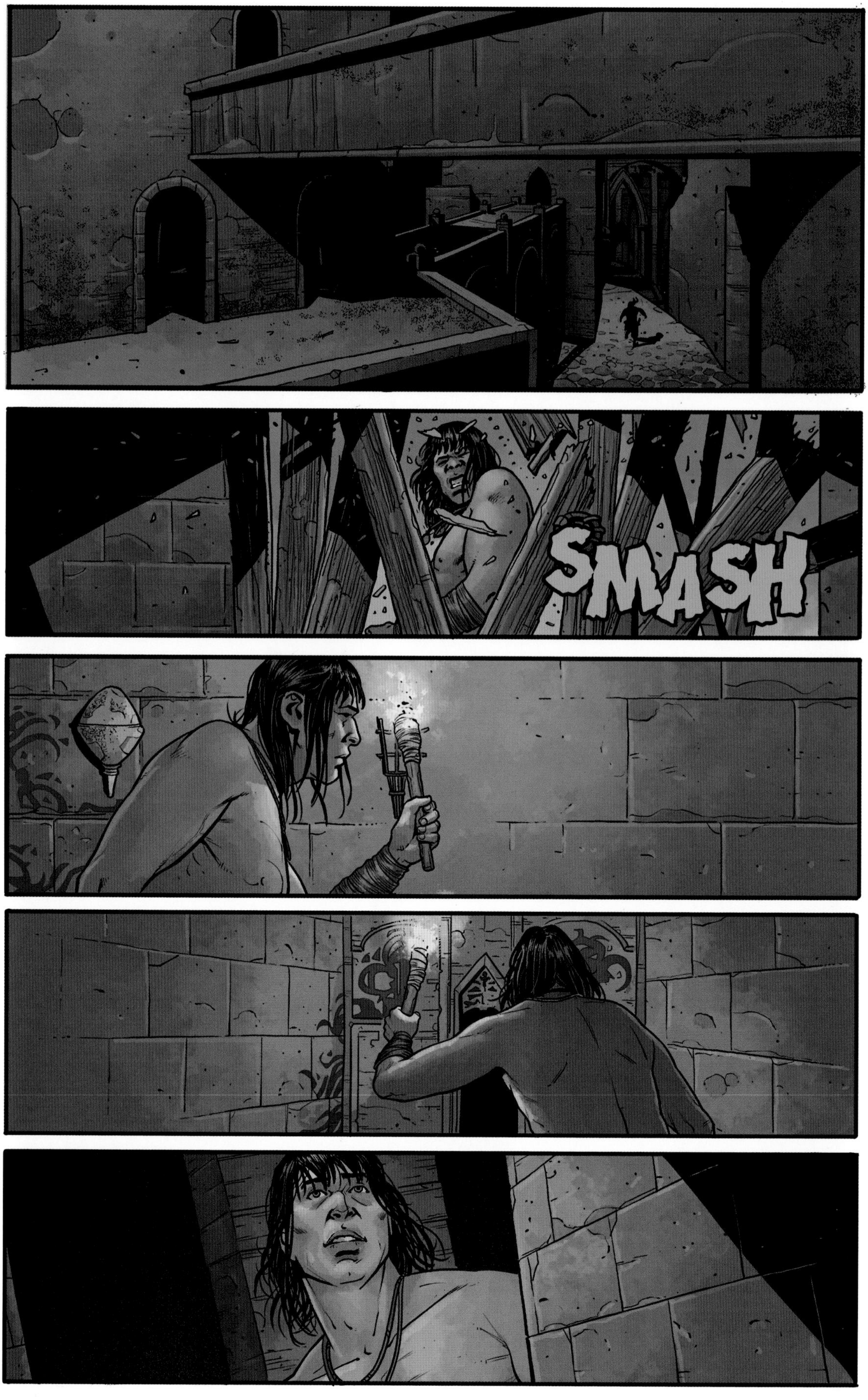
SMASH

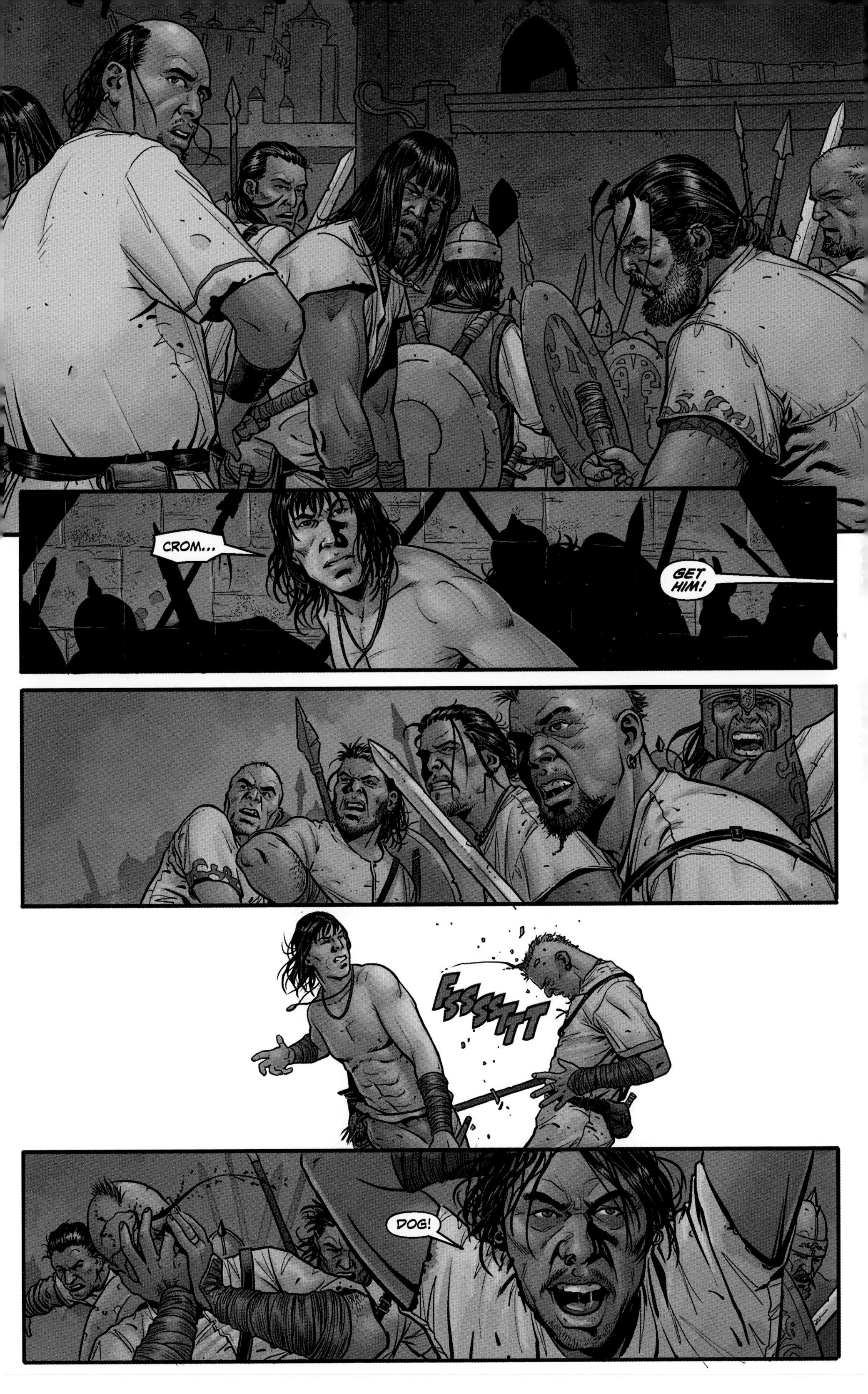
CROM...
GET HIM!
FSSSTTT
DOG!

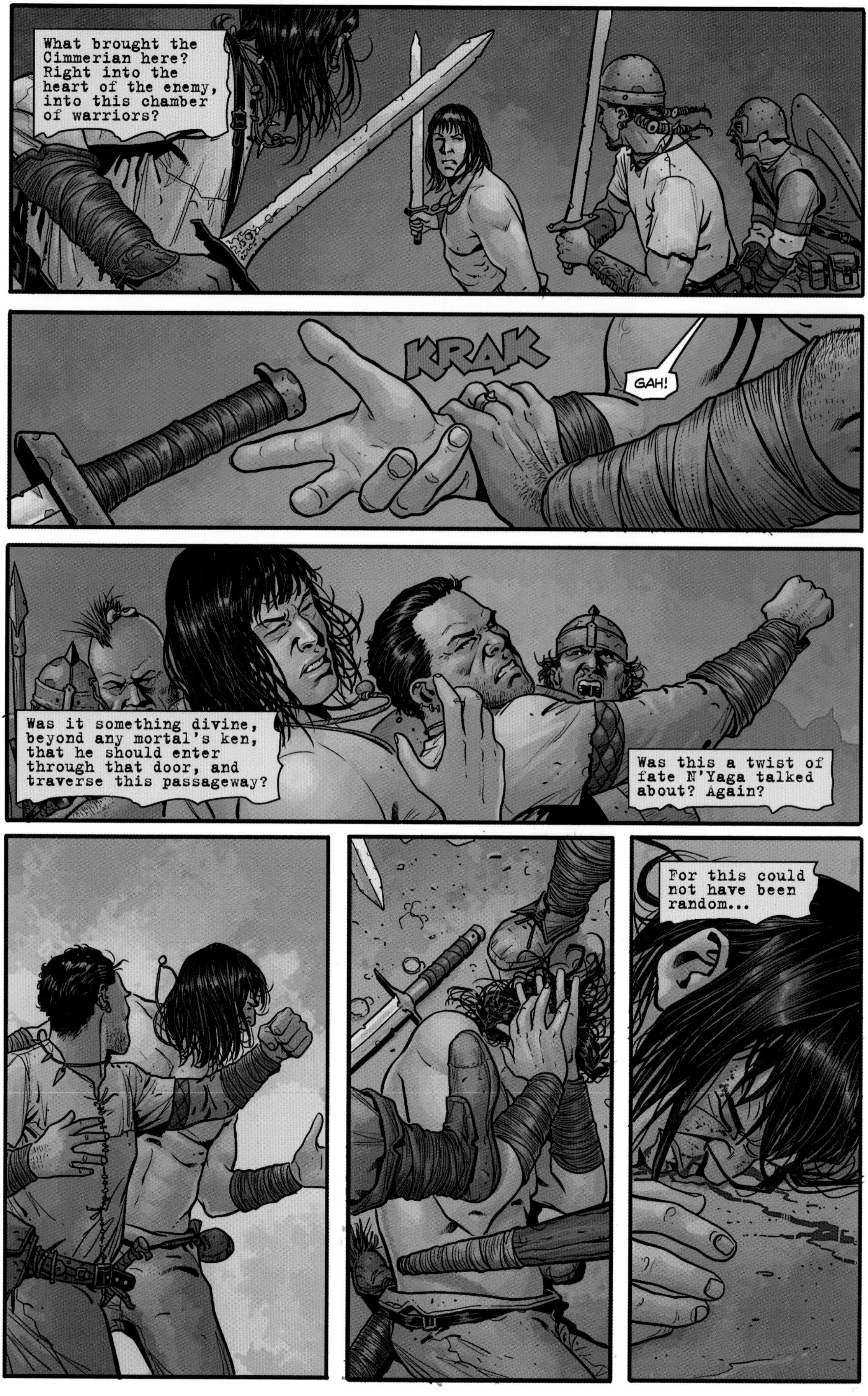
What brought the Cimmerian here? Right into the heart of the enemy, into this chamber of warriors?
KRAK
GAH!
Was it something divine, beyond any mortal's ken, that he should enter through that door, and traverse this passageway?
Was this a twist of fate N'Yaga talked about? Again?
For this could not have been random...

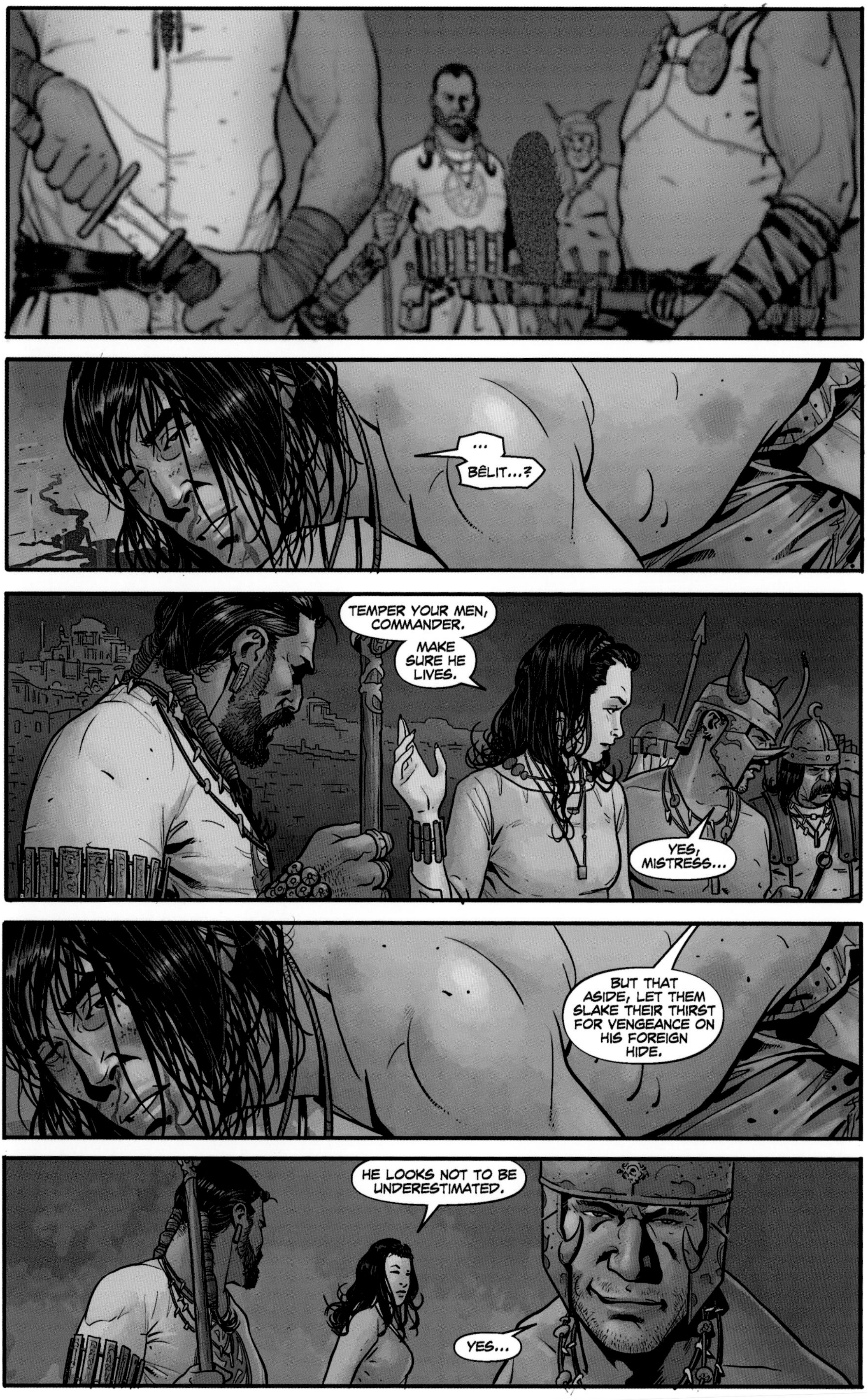
...
BÊLIT...?
TEMPER YOUR MEN, COMMANDER.
MAKE SURE HE LIVES.
YES, MISTRESS...
BUT THAT ASIDE, LET THEM SLAKE THEIR THIRST FOR VENGEANCE ON HIS FOREIGN HIDE.
HE LOOKS NOT TO BE UNDERESTIMATED.
YES...

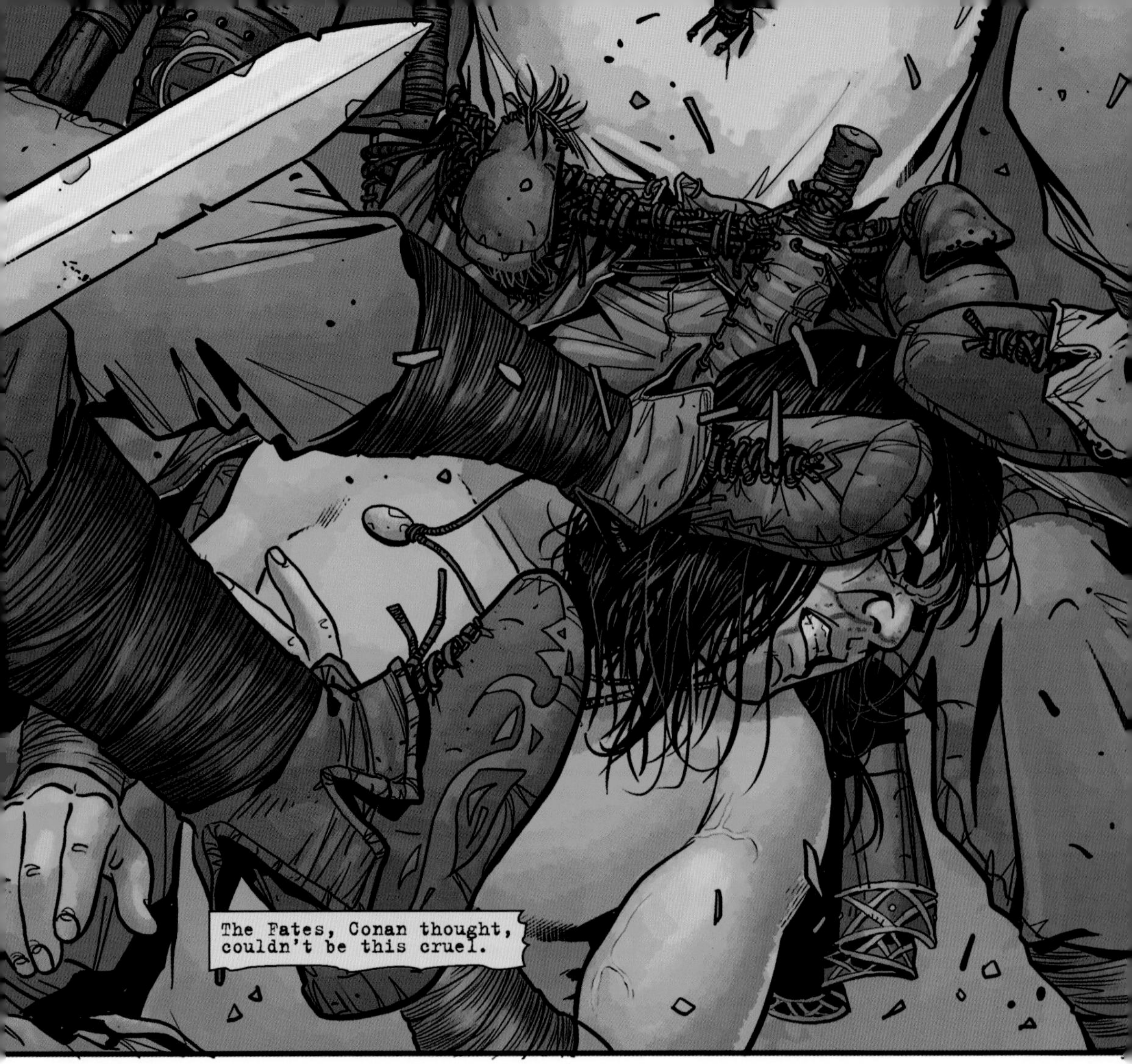
The Fates, Conan thought, couldn't be this cruel.

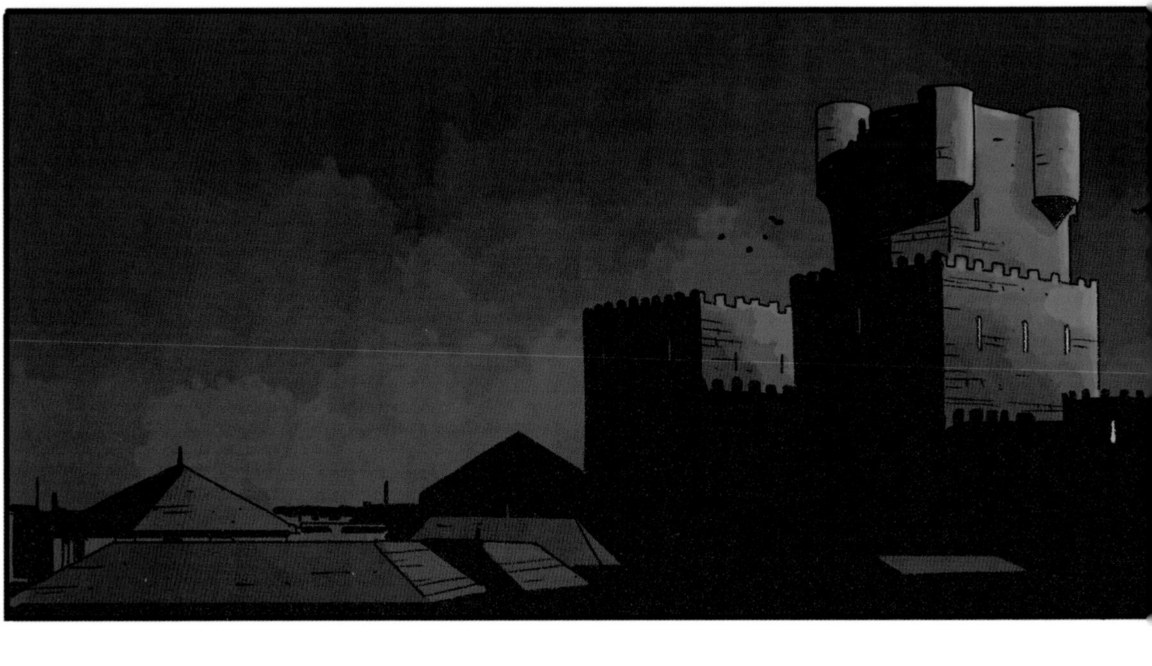

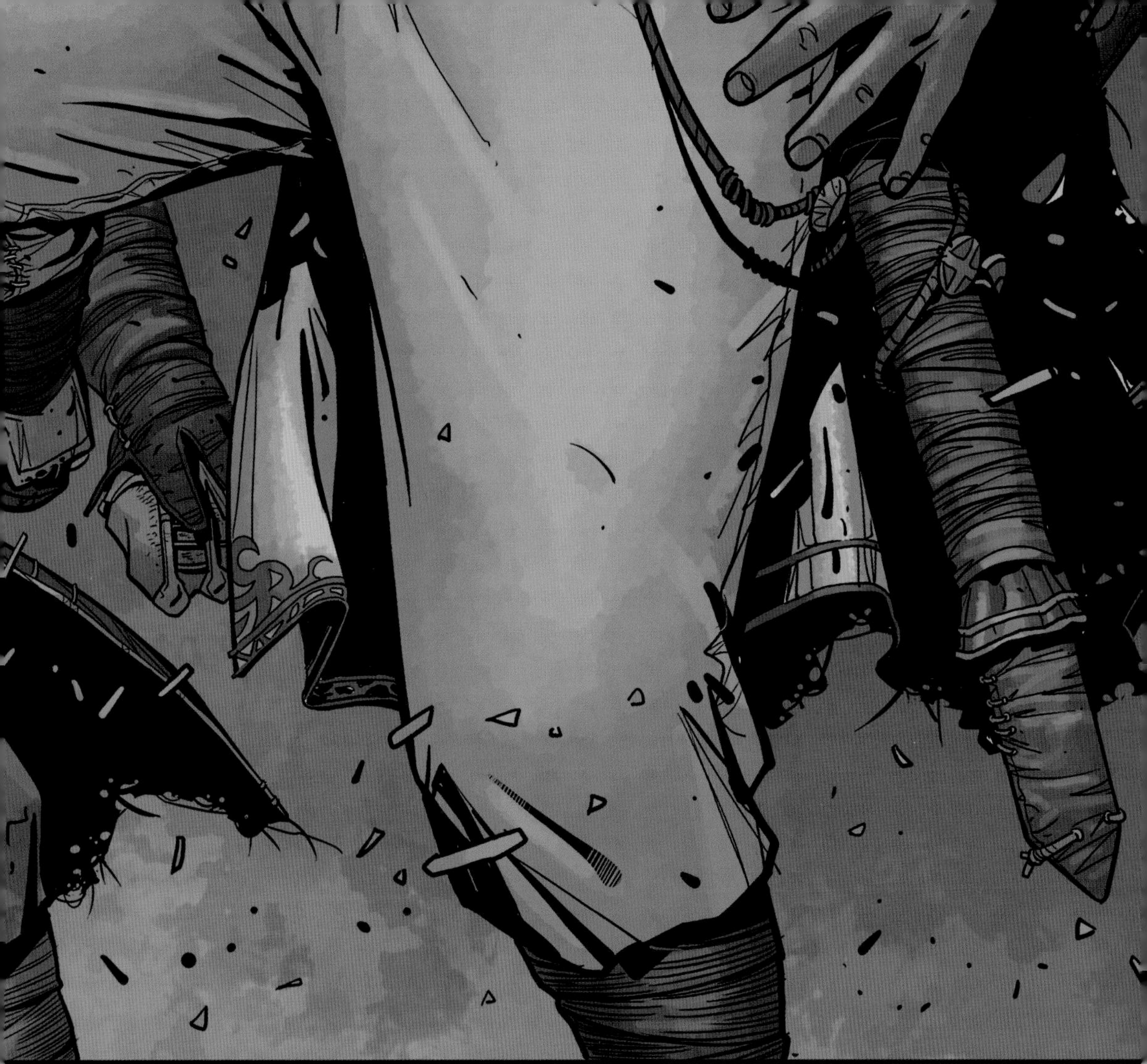

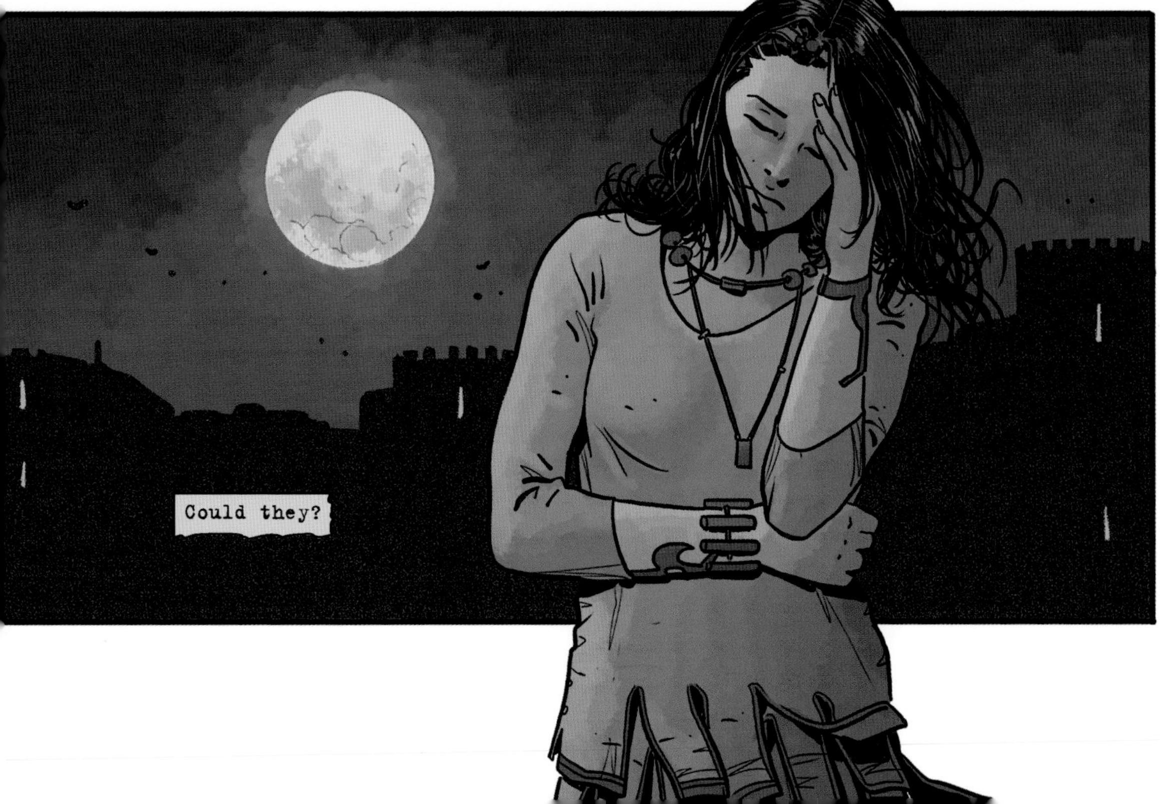
Could they?

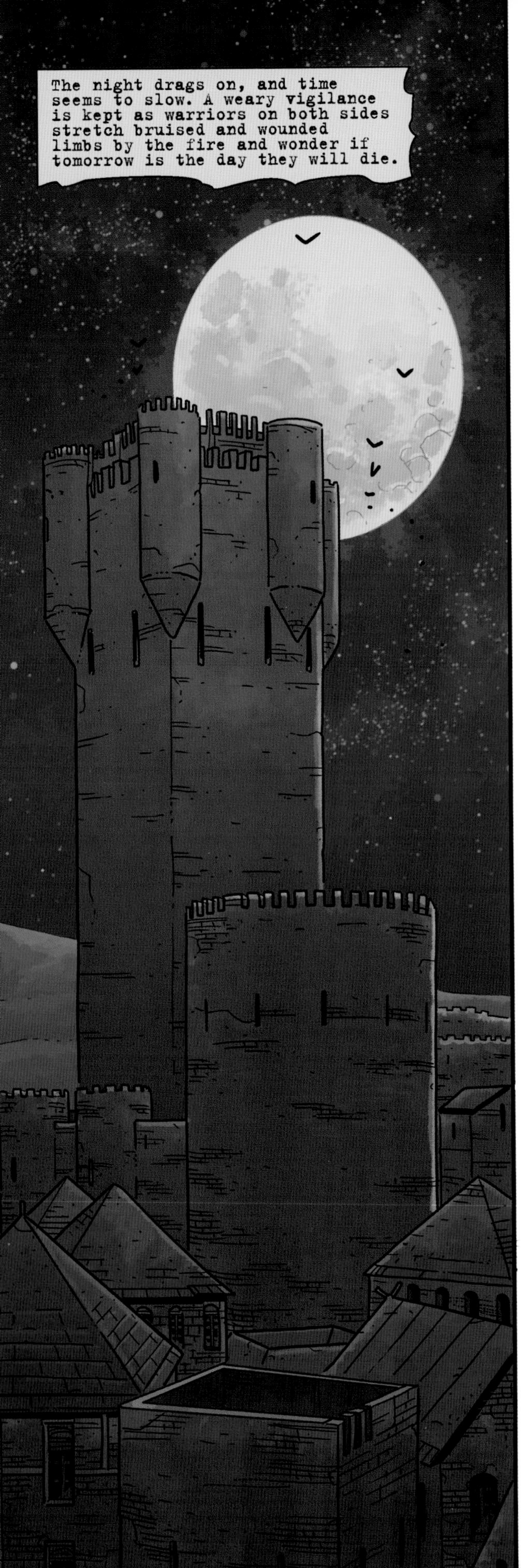
The night drags on, and time seems to slow. A weary vigilance is kept as warriors on both sides stretch bruised and wounded limbs by the fire and wonder if tomorrow is the day they will die.

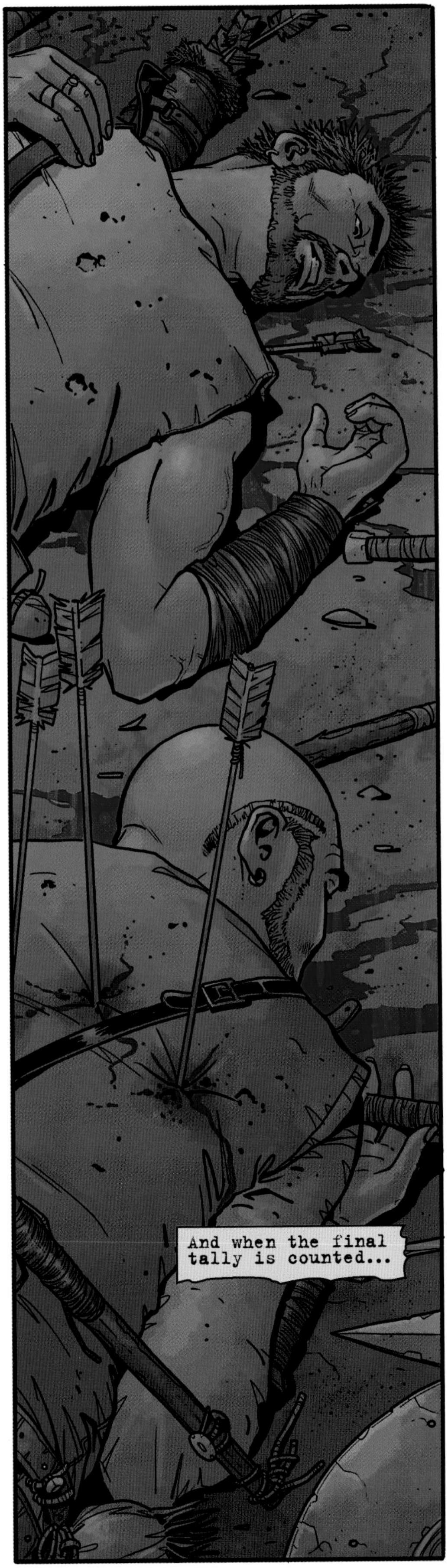
And when the final tally is counted...

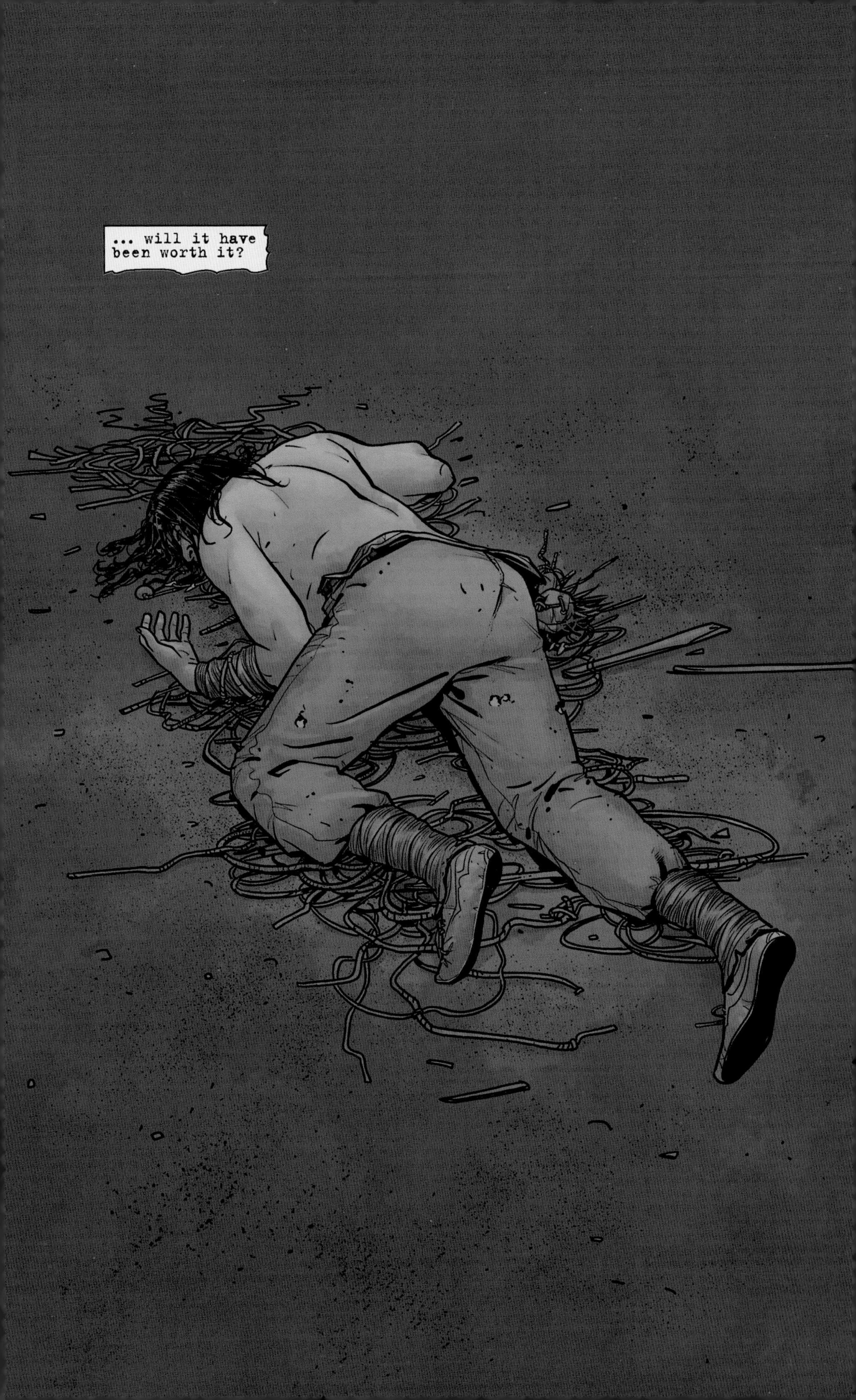
... will it have
been worth it?

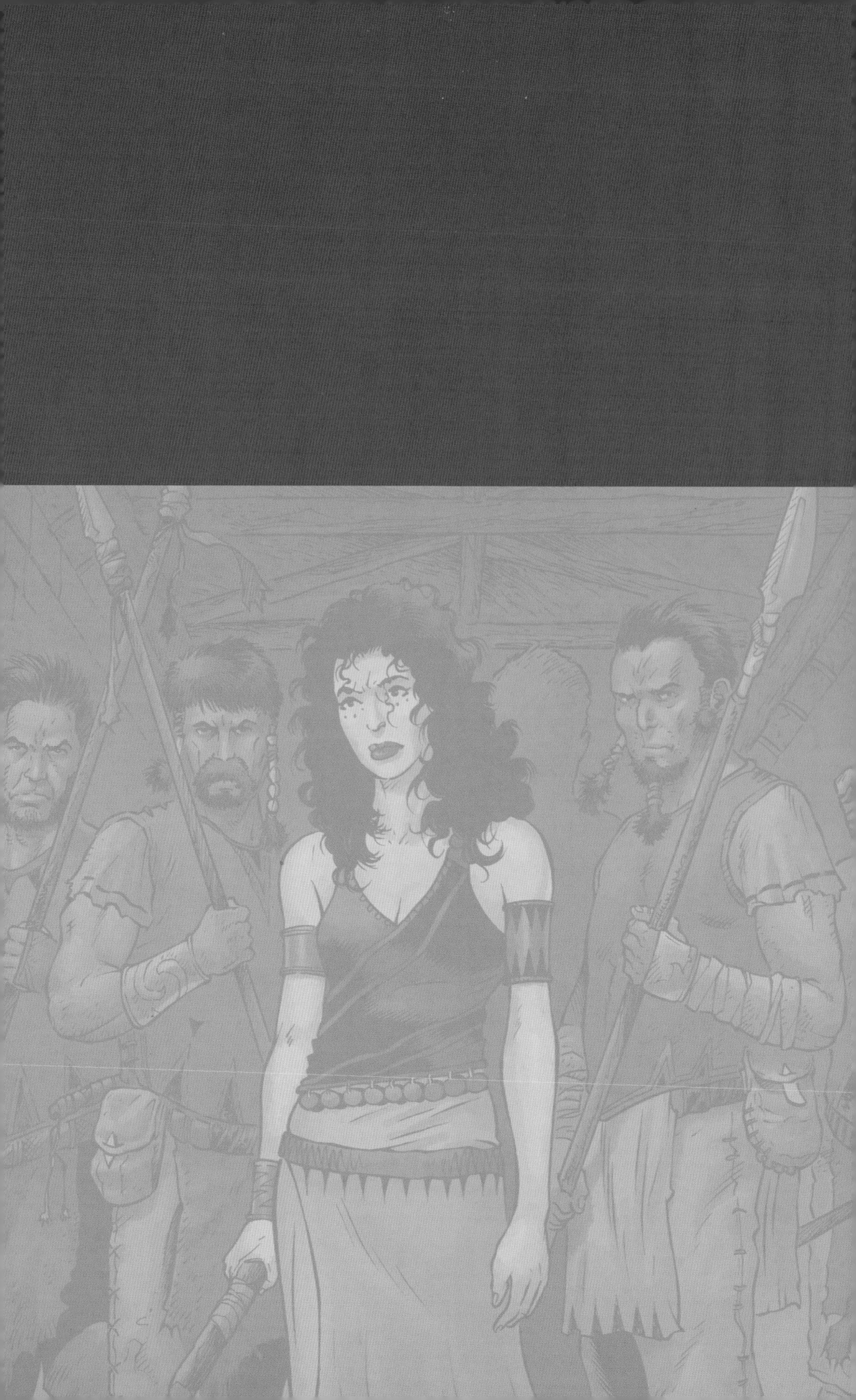

CHAPTER THREE

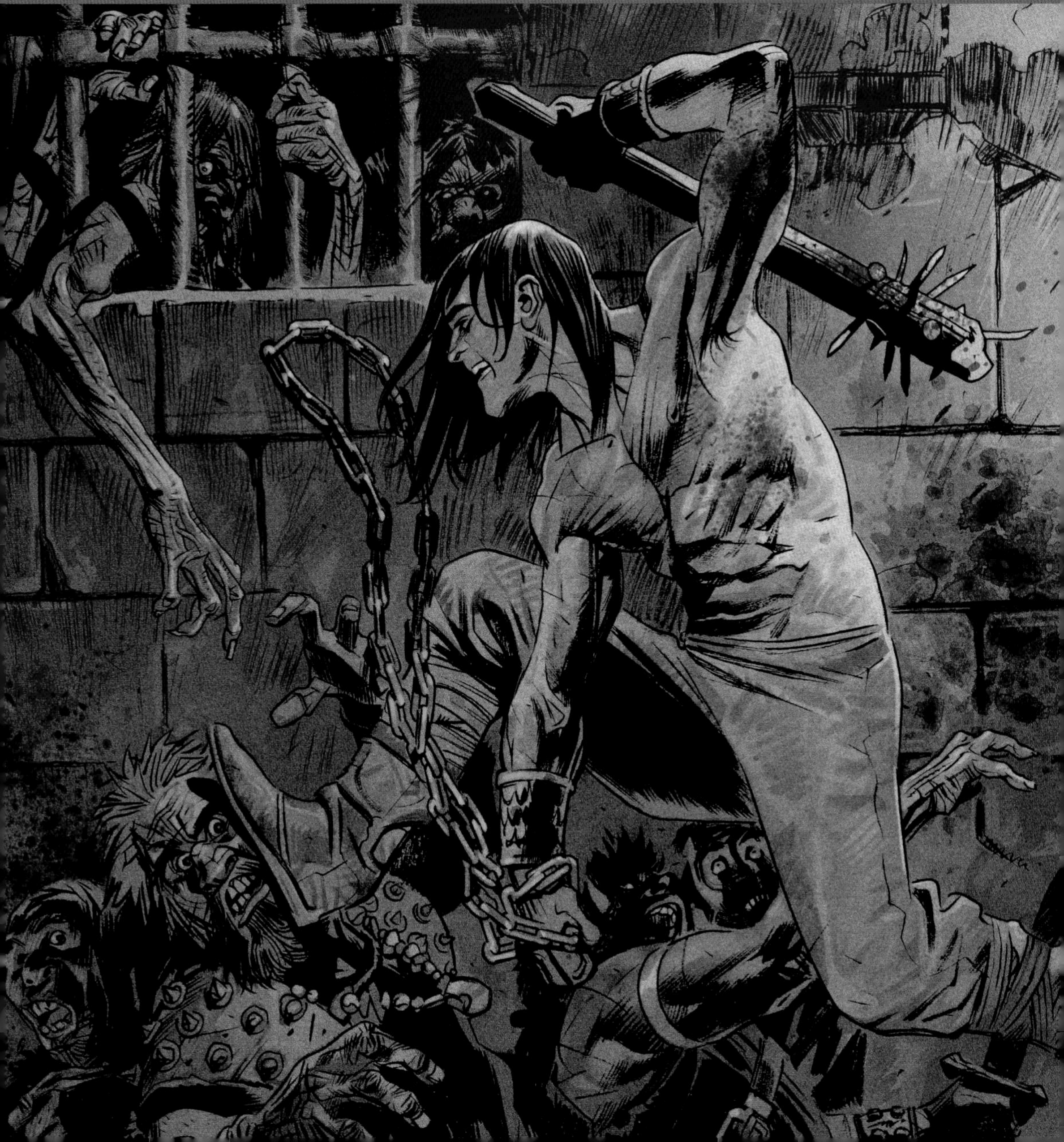

"This is Shem, you dolt.
Conflict is never over, only deferred."

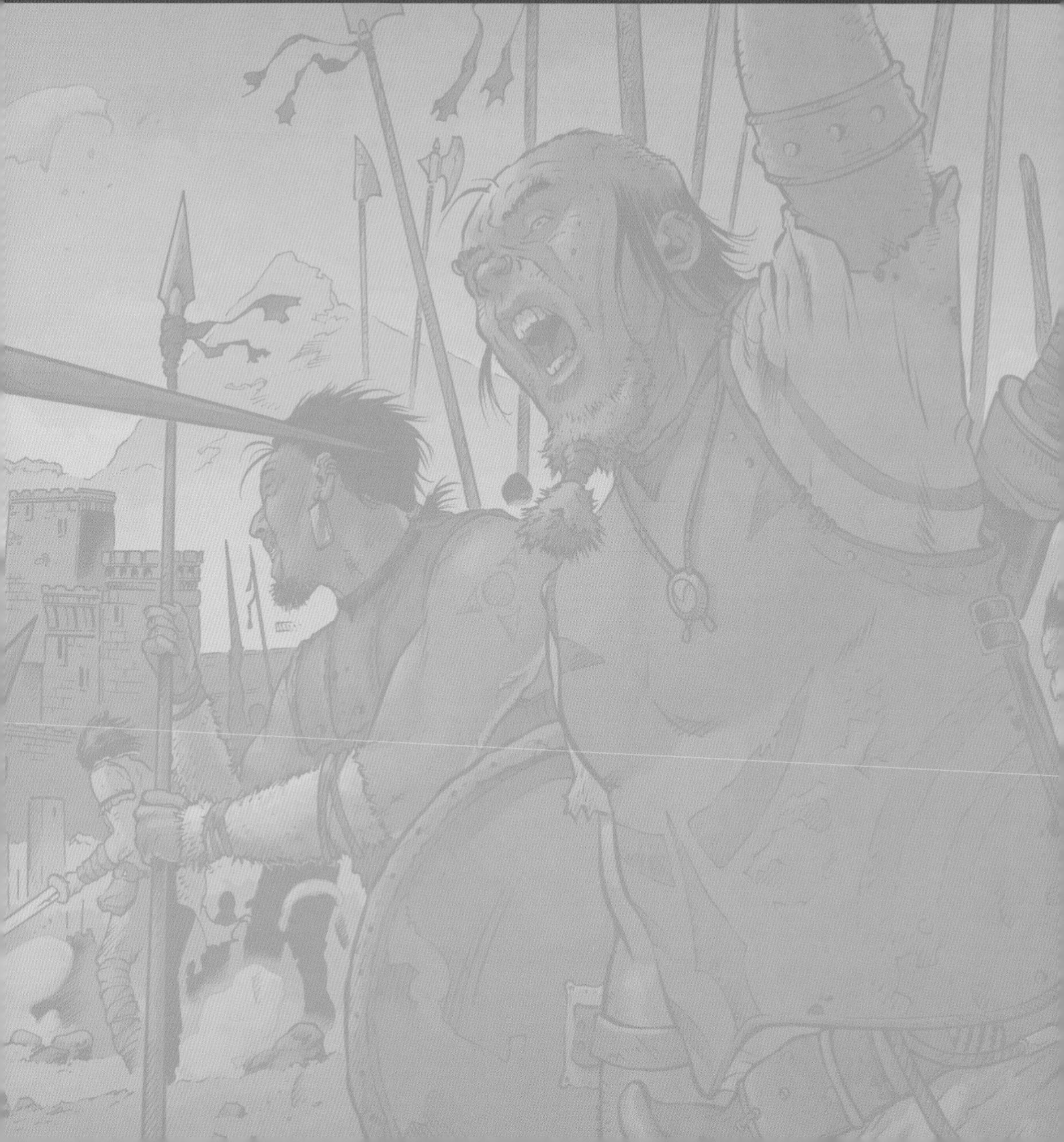

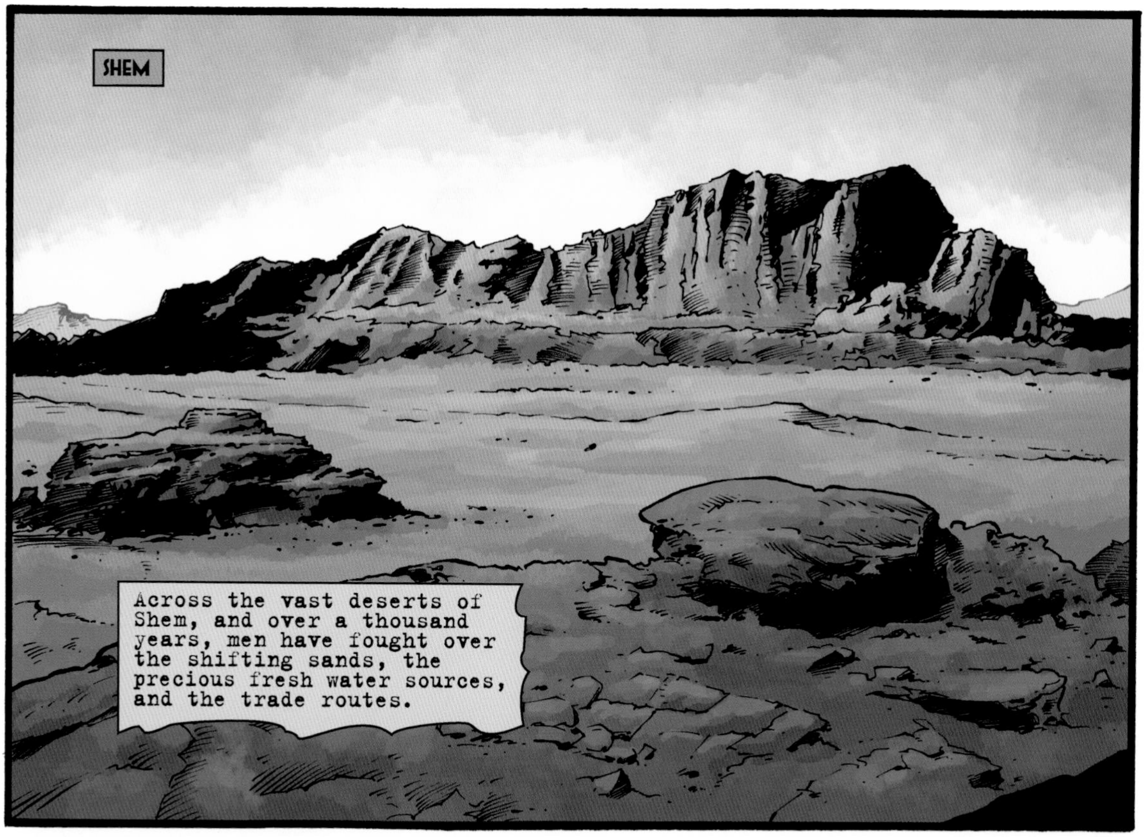
SHEM
Across the vast deserts of Shem, and over a thousand years, men have fought over the shifting sands, the precious fresh water sources, and the trade routes.

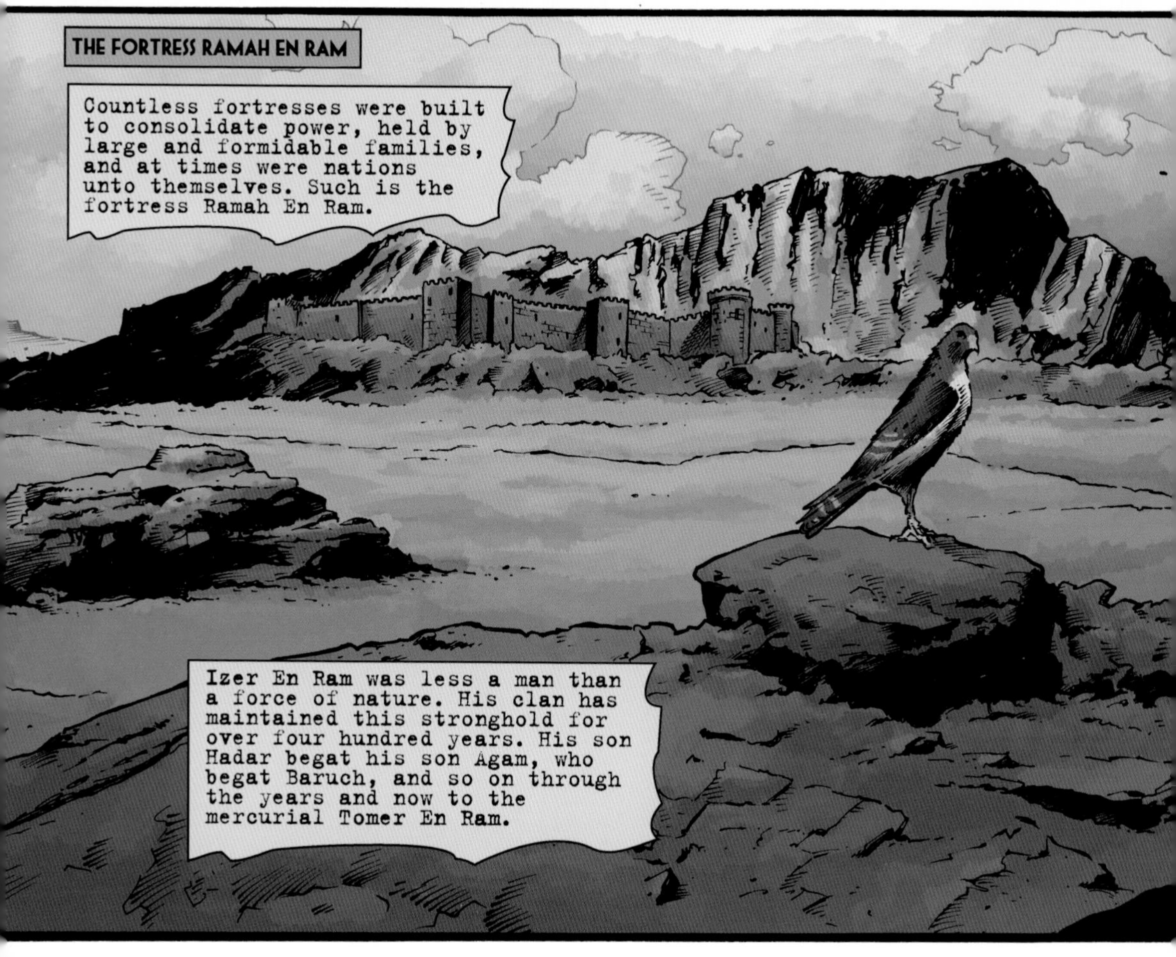
THE FORTRESS RAMAH EN RAM
Countless fortresses were built to consolidate power, held by large and formidable families, and at times were nations unto themselves. Such is the fortress Ramah En Ram.
Izer En Ram was less a man than a force of nature. His clan has maintained this stronghold for over four hundred years. His son Hadar begat his son Agam, who begat Baruch, and so on through the years and now to the mercurial Tomer En Ram.

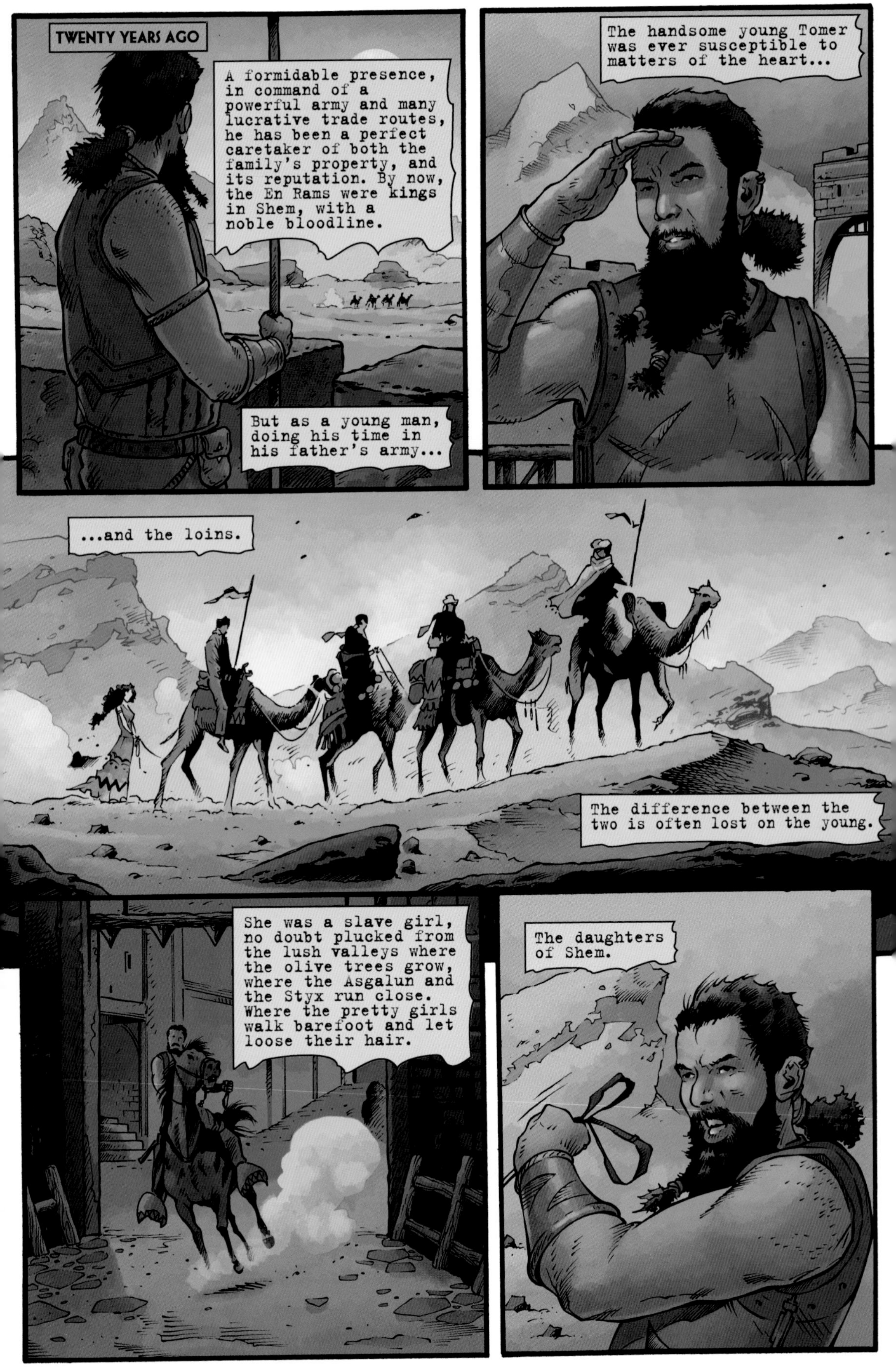
TWENTY YEARS AGO
A formidable presence, in command of a powerful army and many lucrative trade routes, he has been a perfect caretaker of both the family's property, and its reputation. By now, the En Rams were kings in Shem, with a noble bloodline.
But as a young man, doing his time in his father's army...
The handsome young Tomer was ever susceptible to matters of the heart...
...and the loins.
The difference between the two is often lost on the young.
She was a slave girl, no doubt plucked from the lush valleys where the olive trees grow, where the Asgalun and the Styx run close. Where the pretty girls walk barefoot and let loose their hair.
The daughters of Shem.

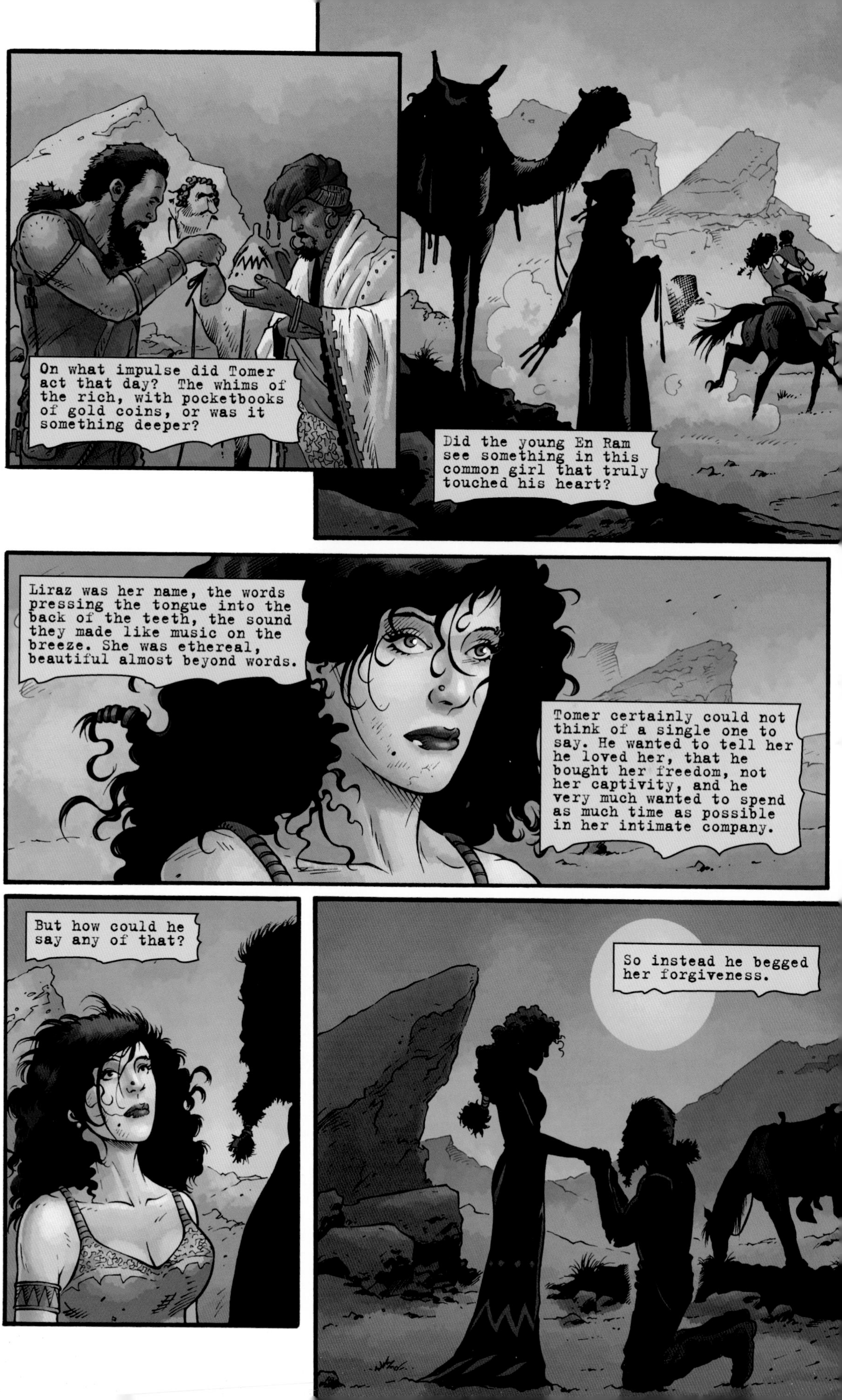
On what impulse did Tomer act that day? The whims of the rich, with pocketbooks of gold coins, or was it something deeper?
Did the young En Ram see something in this common girl that truly touched his heart?
Liraz was her name, the words pressing the tongue into the back of the teeth, the sound they made like music on the breeze. She was ethereal, beautiful almost beyond words.
Tomer certainly could not think of a single one to say. He wanted to tell her he loved her, that he bought her freedom, not her captivity, and he very much wanted to spend as much time as possible in her intimate company.
But how could he say any of that?
So instead he begged her forgiveness.

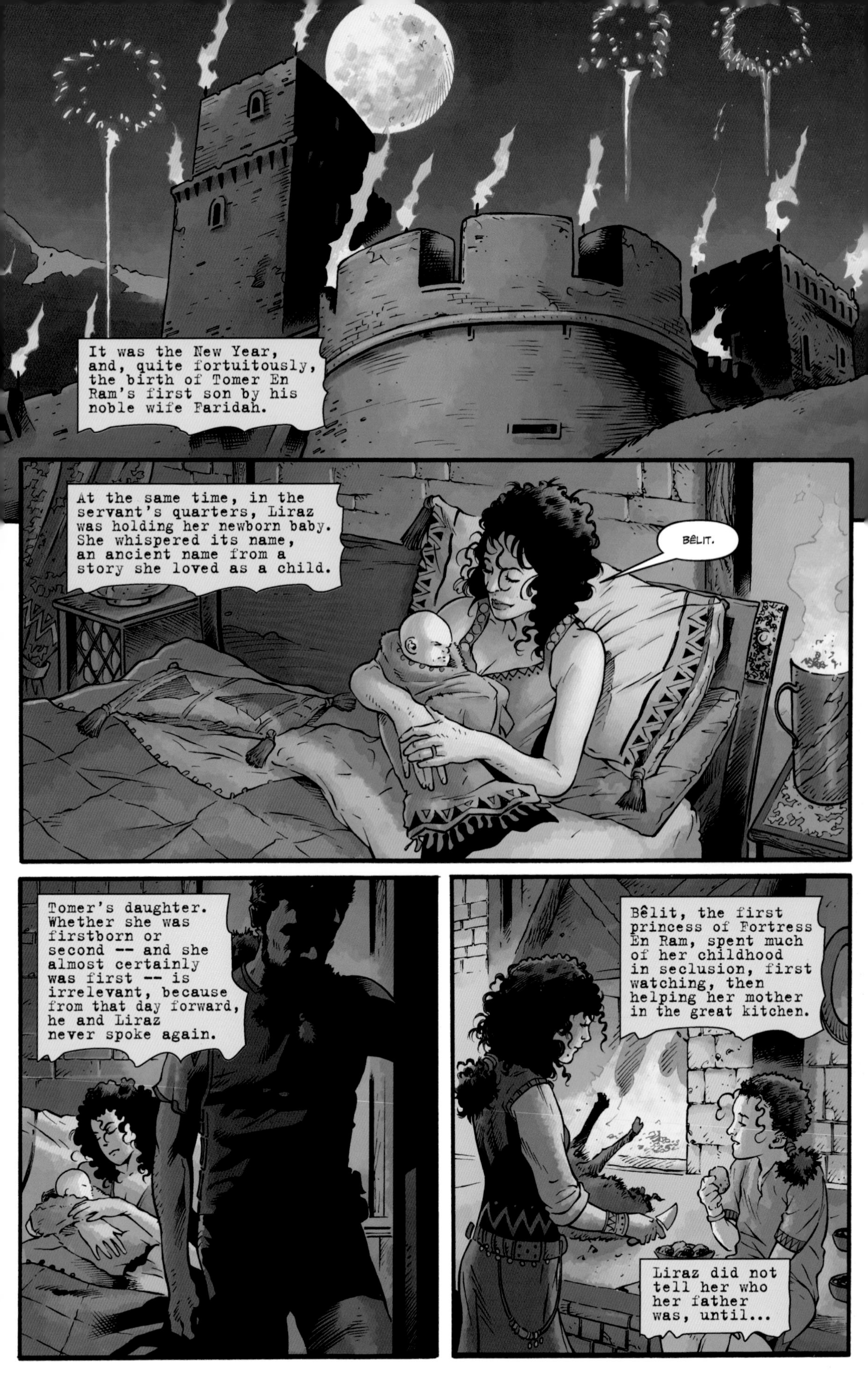
It was the New Year, and, quite fortuitously, the birth of Tomer En Ram's first son by his noble wife Faridah.
At the same time, in the servant's quarters, Liraz was holding her newborn baby. She whispered its name, an ancient name from a story she loved as a child.
BÊLIT.
Tomer's daughter. Whether she was firstborn or second -- and she almost certainly was first -- is irrelevant, because from that day forward, he and Liraz never spoke again.
Bêlit, the first princess of Fortress En Ram, spent much of her childhood in seclusion, first watching, then helping her mother in the great kitchen.
Liraz did not tell her who her father was, until...

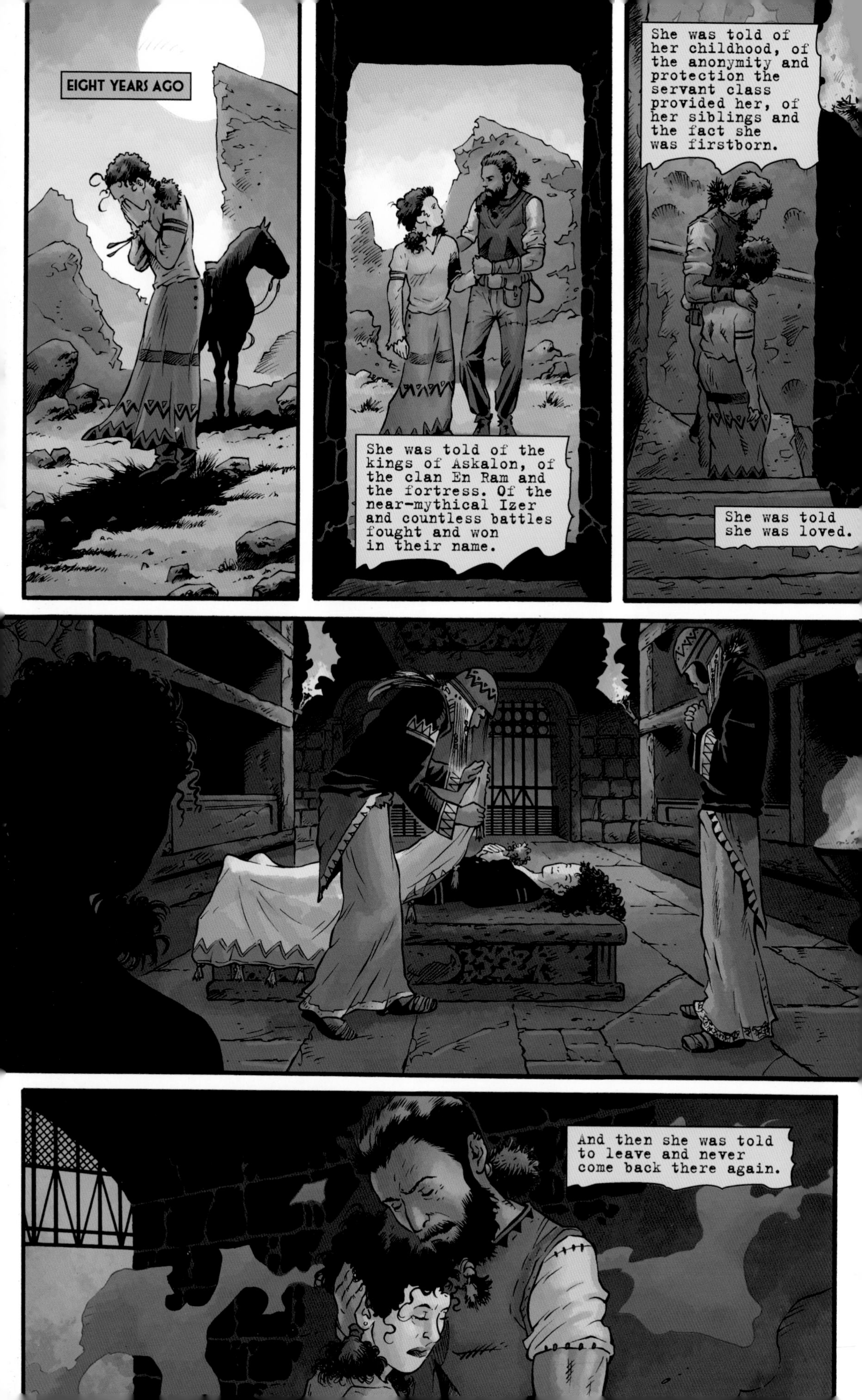
EIGHT YEARS AGO
She was told of the kings of Askalon, of the clan En Ram and the fortress. Of the near-mythical Izer and countless battles fought and won in their name.
She was told of her childhood, of the anonymity and protection the servant class provided her, of her siblings and the fact she was firstborn.
She was told she was loved.
And then she was told to leave and never come back there again.

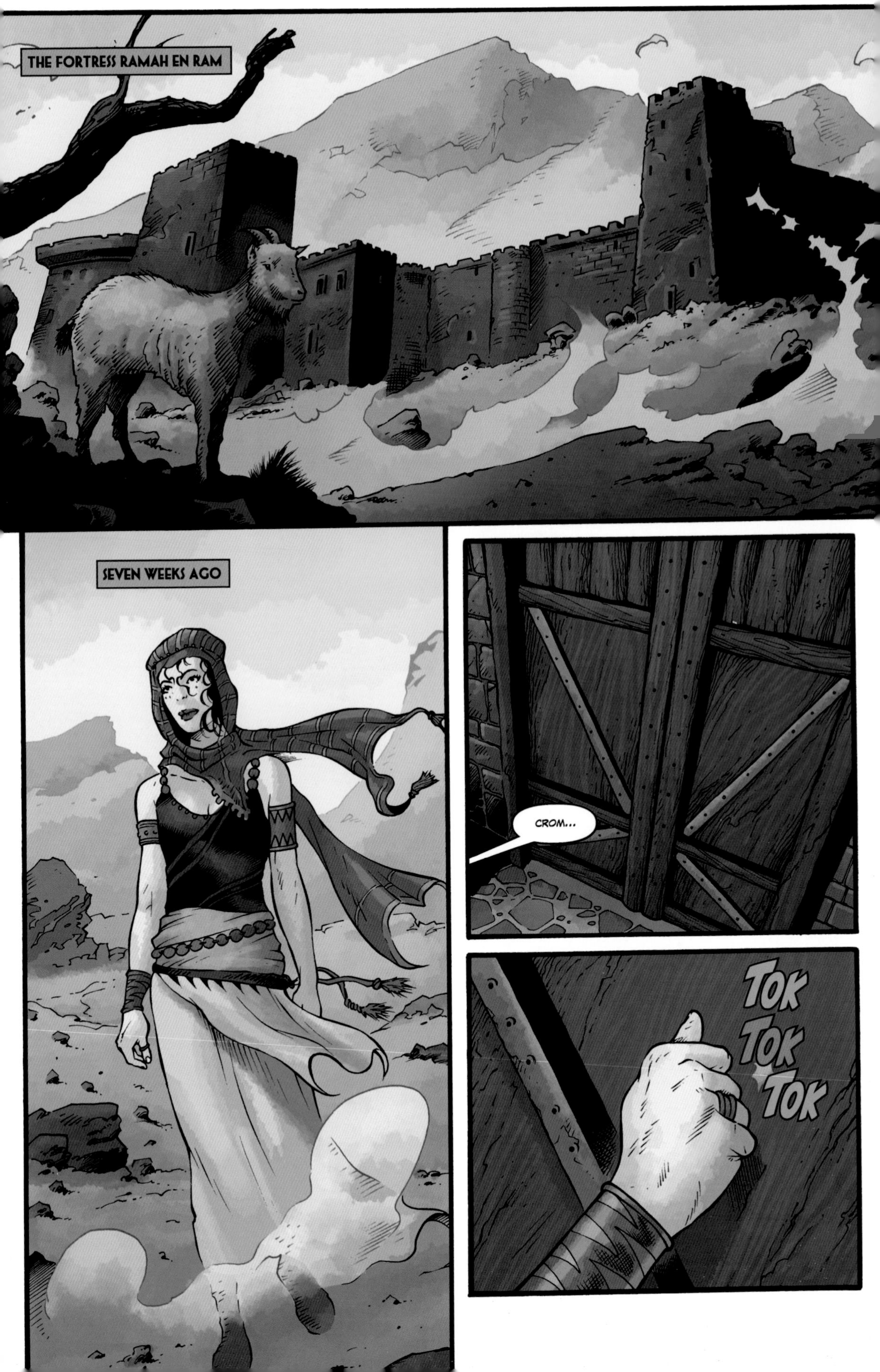
THE FORTRESS RAMAH EN RAM
SEVEN WEEKS AGO
CROM...
TOK
TOK
TOK

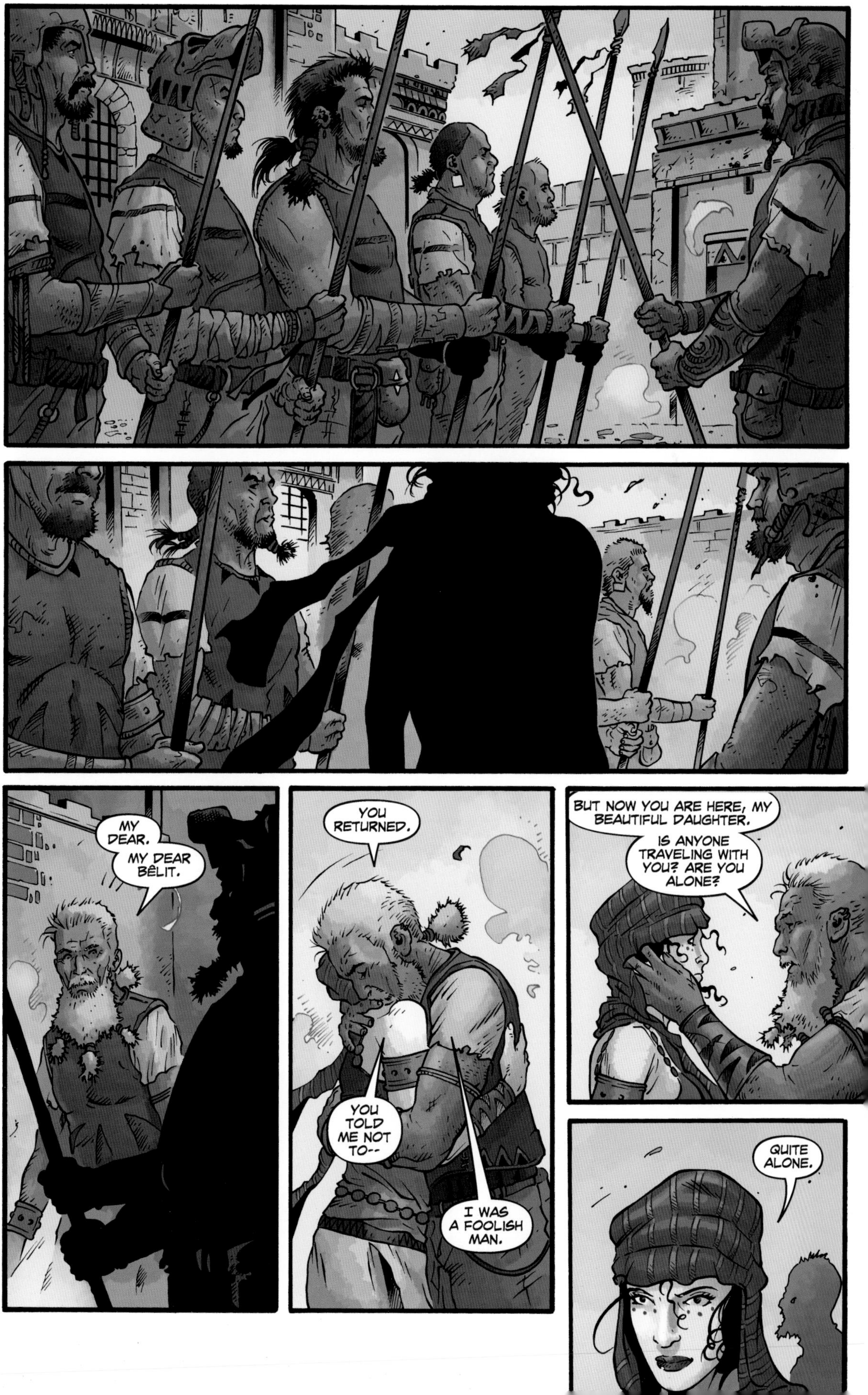
MY DEAR.
MY DEAR BÊLIT.
YOU RETURNED.
YOU TOLD ME NOT TO--
I WAS A FOOLISH MAN.
BUT NOW YOU ARE HERE, MY BEAUTIFUL DAUGHTER.
IS ANYONE TRAVELING WITH YOU? ARE YOU ALONE?
QUITE ALONE.

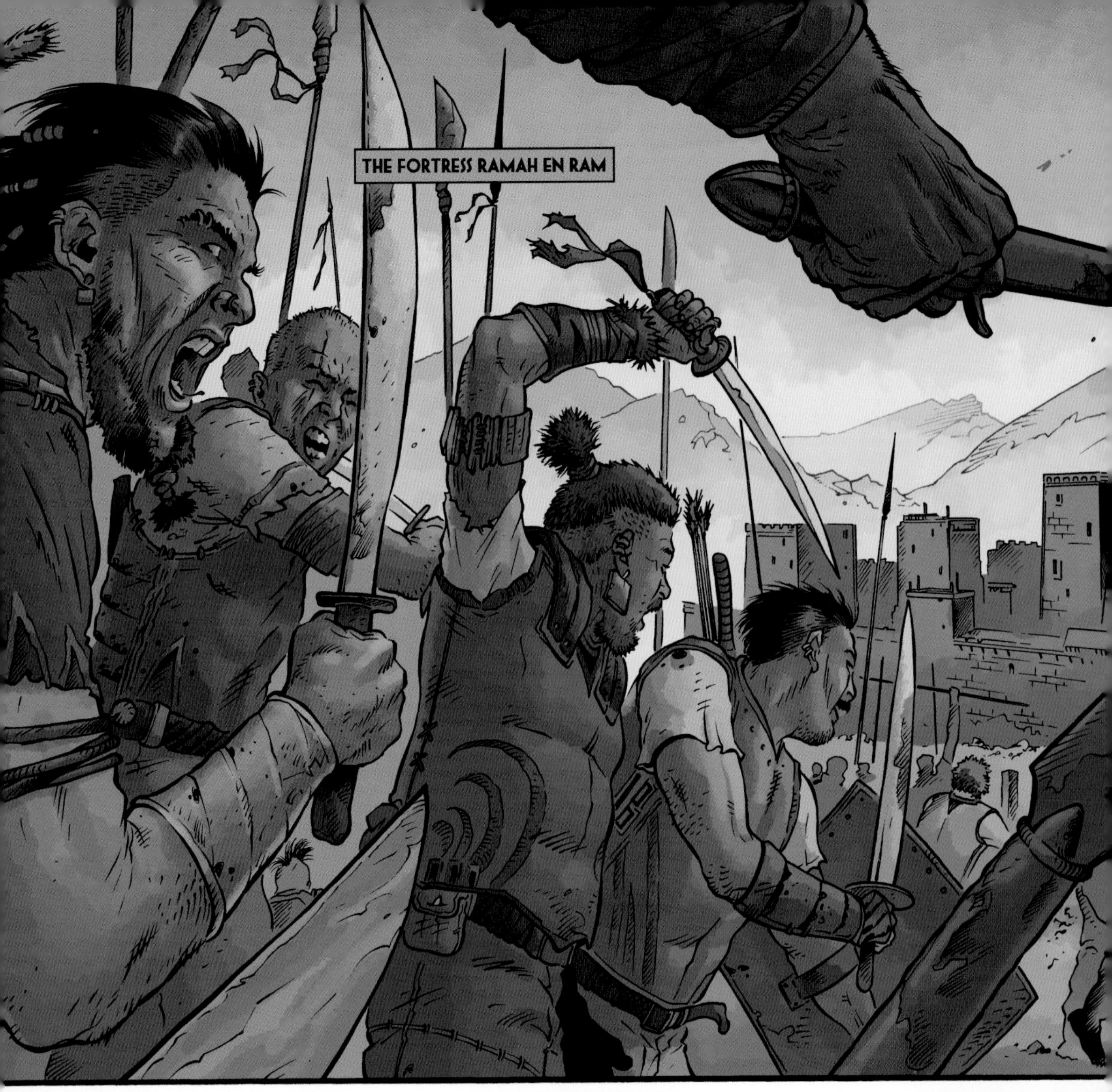
THE FORTRESS RAMAH EN RAM

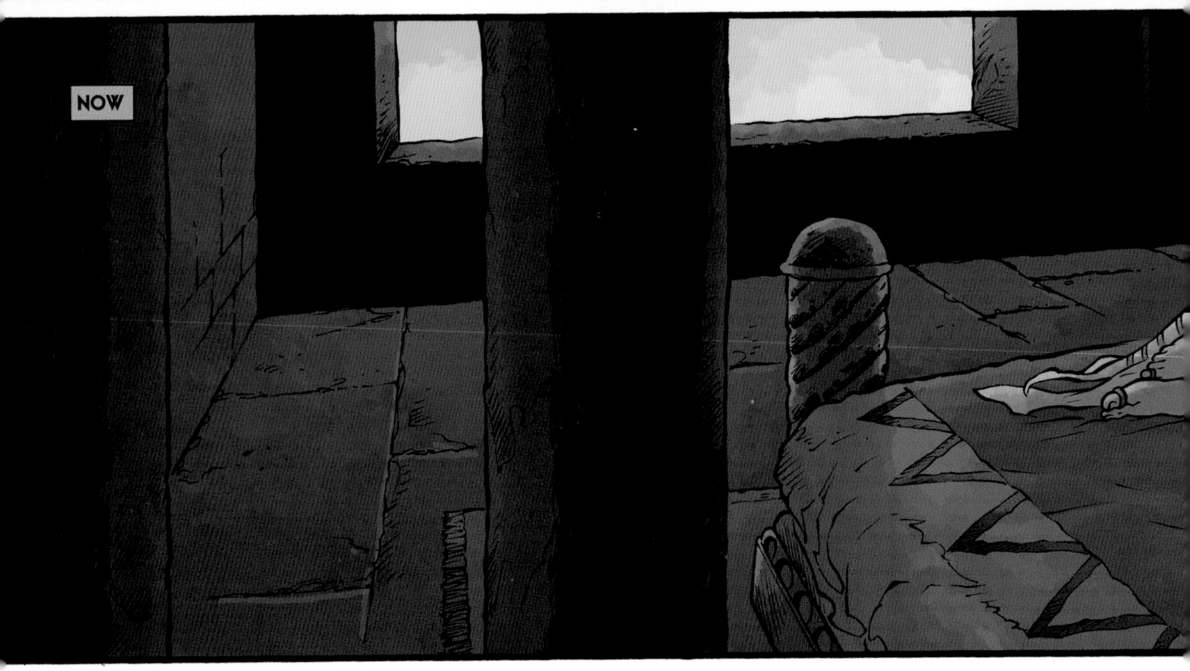
NOW

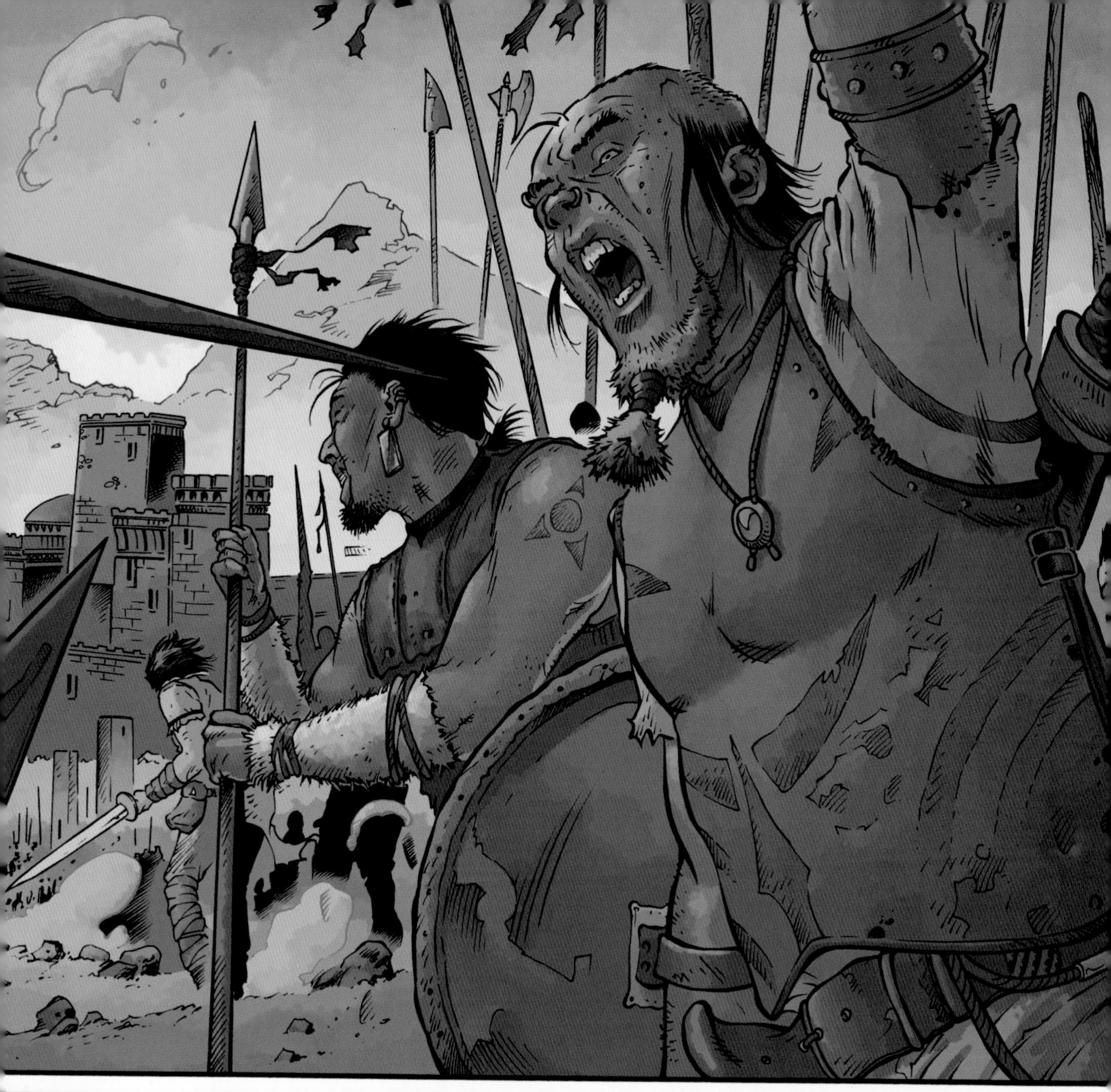
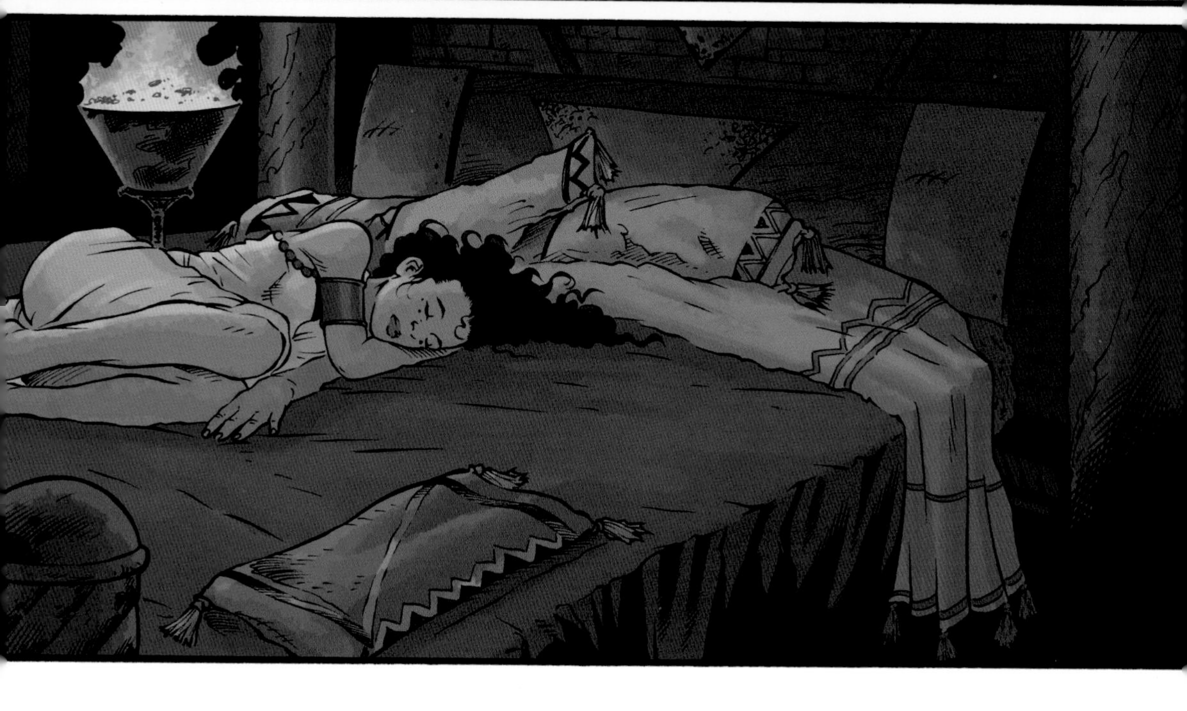

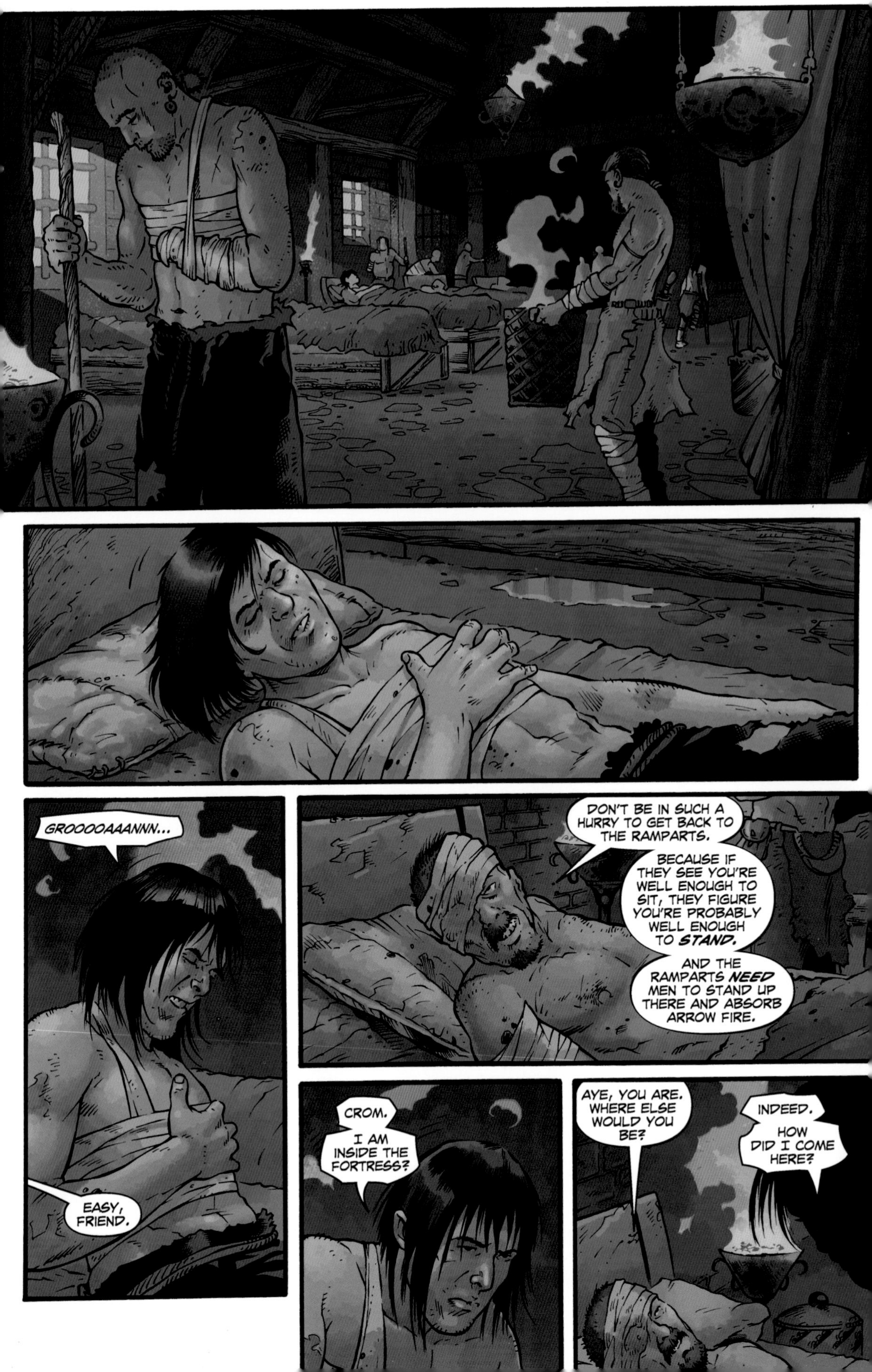
GROOOOAAANNN...
EASY, FRIEND.
DON'T BE IN SUCH A HURRY TO GET BACK TO THE RAMPARTS.
BECAUSE IF THEY SEE YOU'RE WELL ENOUGH TO SIT, THEY FIGURE YOU'RE PROBABLY WELL ENOUGH TO *STAND.*
AND THE RAMPARTS *NEED* MEN TO STAND UP THERE AND ABSORB ARROW FIRE.
CROM.
I AM INSIDE THE FORTRESS?
AYE, YOU ARE. WHERE ELSE WOULD YOU BE?
INDEED.
HOW DID I COME HERE?

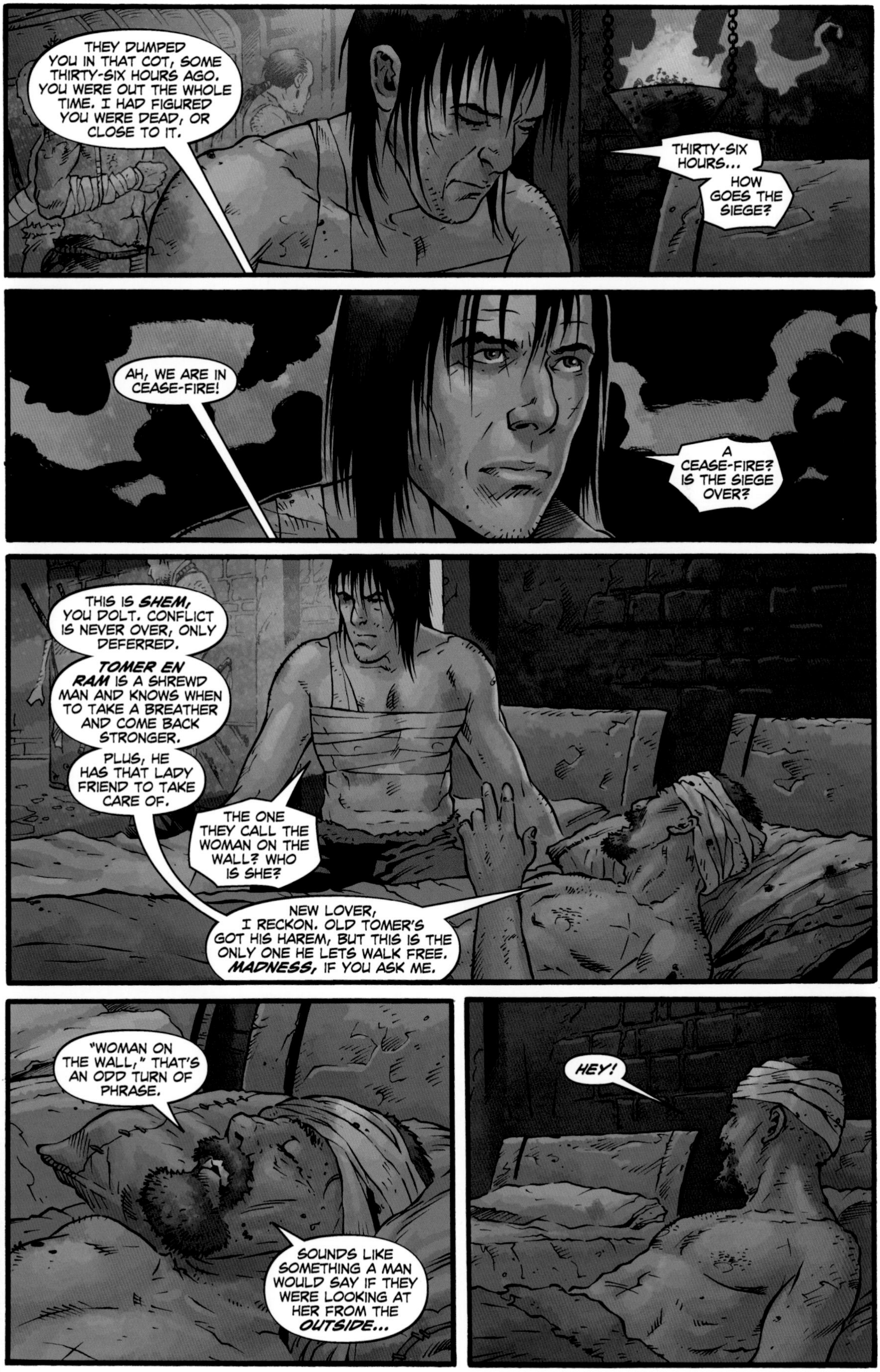
THEY DUMPED YOU IN THAT COT, SOME THIRTY-SIX HOURS AGO. YOU WERE OUT THE WHOLE TIME. I HAD FIGURED YOU WERE DEAD, OR CLOSE TO IT.
THIRTY-SIX HOURS... HOW GOES THE SIEGE?
AH, WE ARE IN CEASE-FIRE!
A CEASE-FIRE? IS THE SIEGE OVER?
THIS IS *SHEM,* YOU DOLT. CONFLICT IS NEVER OVER, ONLY DEFERRED.
TOMER EN RAM IS A SHREWD MAN AND KNOWS WHEN TO TAKE A BREATHER AND COME BACK STRONGER.
PLUS, HE HAS THAT LADY FRIEND TO TAKE CARE OF.
THE ONE THEY CALL THE WOMAN ON THE WALL? WHO IS SHE?
NEW LOVER, I RECKON. OLD TOMER'S GOT HIS HAREM, BUT THIS IS THE ONLY ONE HE LETS WALK FREE. *MADNESS,* IF YOU ASK ME.
"WOMAN ON THE WALL," THAT'S AN ODD TURN OF PHRASE.
SOUNDS LIKE SOMETHING A MAN WOULD SAY IF THEY WERE LOOKING AT HER FROM THE *OUTSIDE...*
HEY!

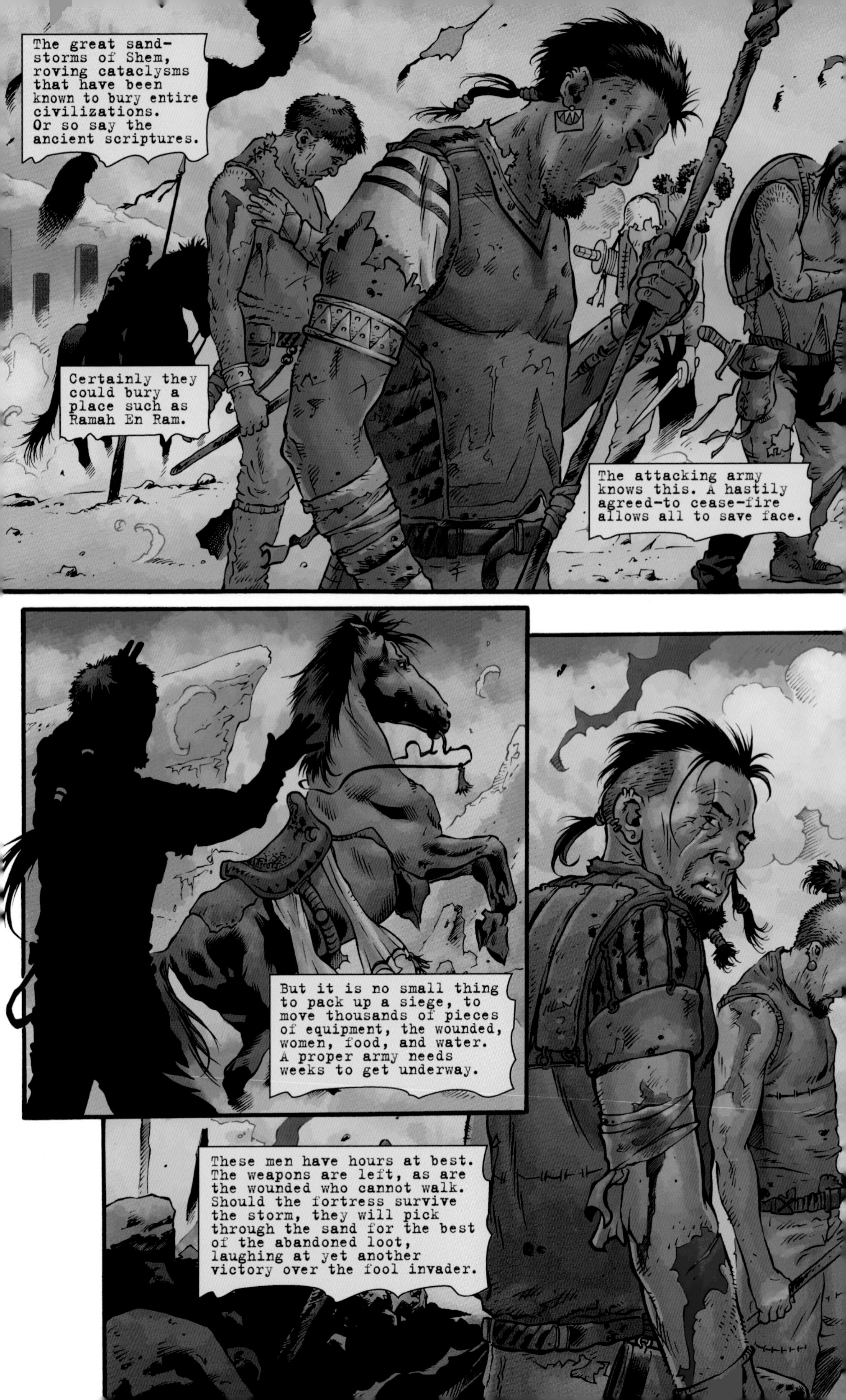
The great sand-storms of Shem, roving cataclysms that have been known to bury entire civilizations. Or so say the ancient scriptures.
Certainly they could bury a place such as Ramah En Ram.
The attacking army knows this. A hastily agreed-to cease-fire allows all to save face.
But it is no small thing to pack up a siege, to move thousands of pieces of equipment, the wounded, women, food, and water. A proper army needs weeks to get underway.
These men have hours at best. The weapons are left, as are the wounded who cannot walk. Should the fortress survive the storm, they will pick through the sand for the best of the abandoned loot, laughing at yet another victory over the fool invader.

The Cimmerian thinks he's seen storms before, and to be sure the North has its share of punishing weather. But that is cold, and cold kills by inches. It creeps, it drains life slowly, relentlessly.

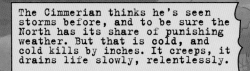

A sandstorm such as this arrives like a wall and hits like rock, wind that feels as if a man's flesh could be pulled from bone. A storm like this doesn't damage or kill so much as erases from existence.

For the thousandth time this day, Conan thinks of Bêlit, of this land of her birth, this terrible, violent, brutal place, so like and so profoundly unlike his own home. He understands her that much more with each thought.

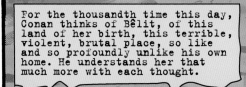

And understands her that much less at the same time.

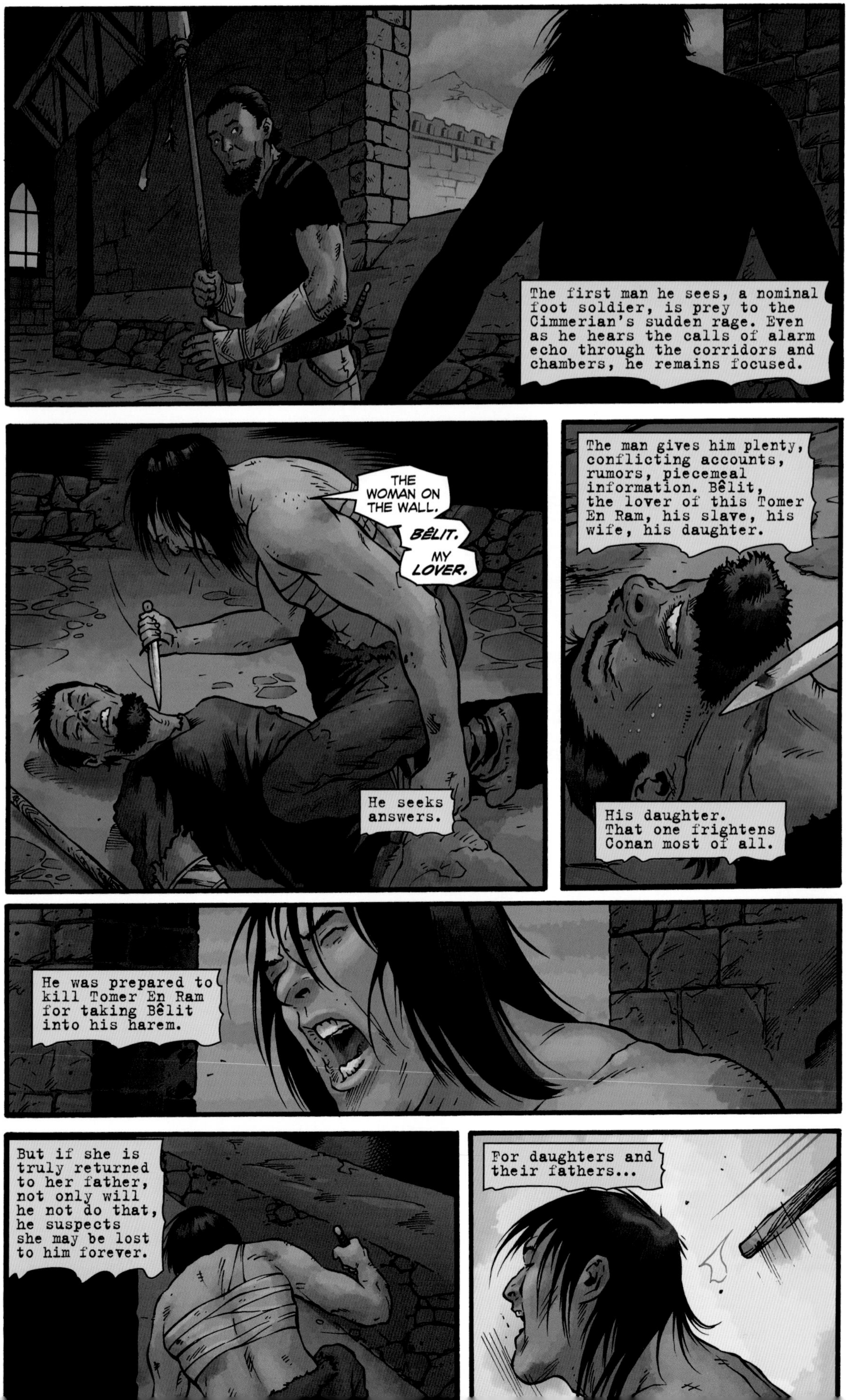
The first man he sees, a nominal foot soldier, is prey to the Cimmerian's sudden rage. Even as he hears the calls of alarm echo through the corridors and chambers, he remains focused.
THE WOMAN ON THE WALL.
BÊLIT.
MY LOVER.
He seeks answers.
The man gives him plenty, conflicting accounts, rumors, piecemeal information. Bêlit, the lover of this Tomer En Ram, his slave, his wife, his daughter.
His daughter. That one frightens Conan most of all.
He was prepared to kill Tomer En Ram for taking Bêlit into his harem.
But if she is truly returned to her father, not only will he not do that, he suspects she may be lost to him forever.
For daughters and their fathers...

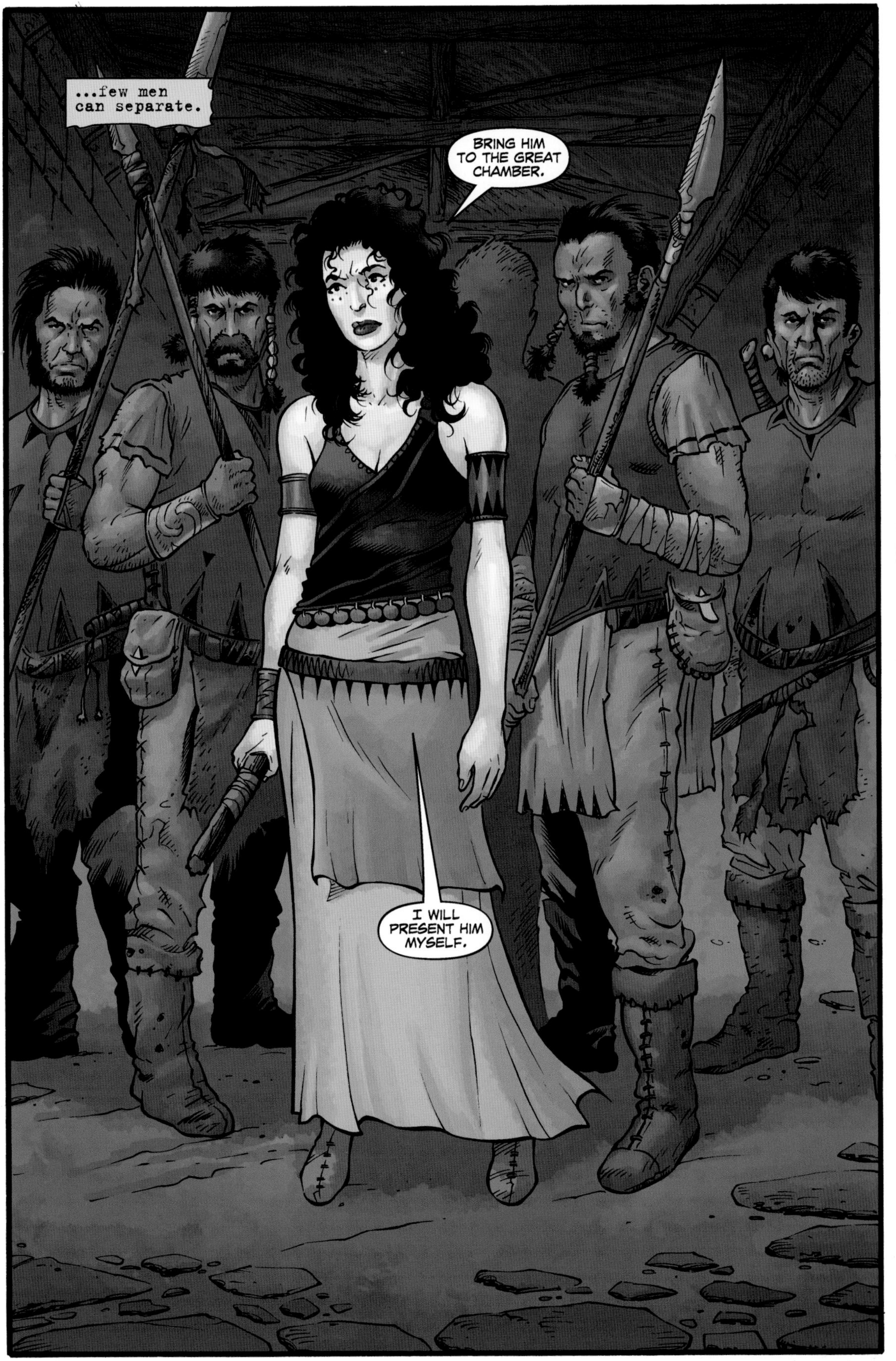
...few men
can separate.
BRING HIM
TO THE GREAT
CHAMBER.
I WILL
PRESENT HIM
MYSELF.

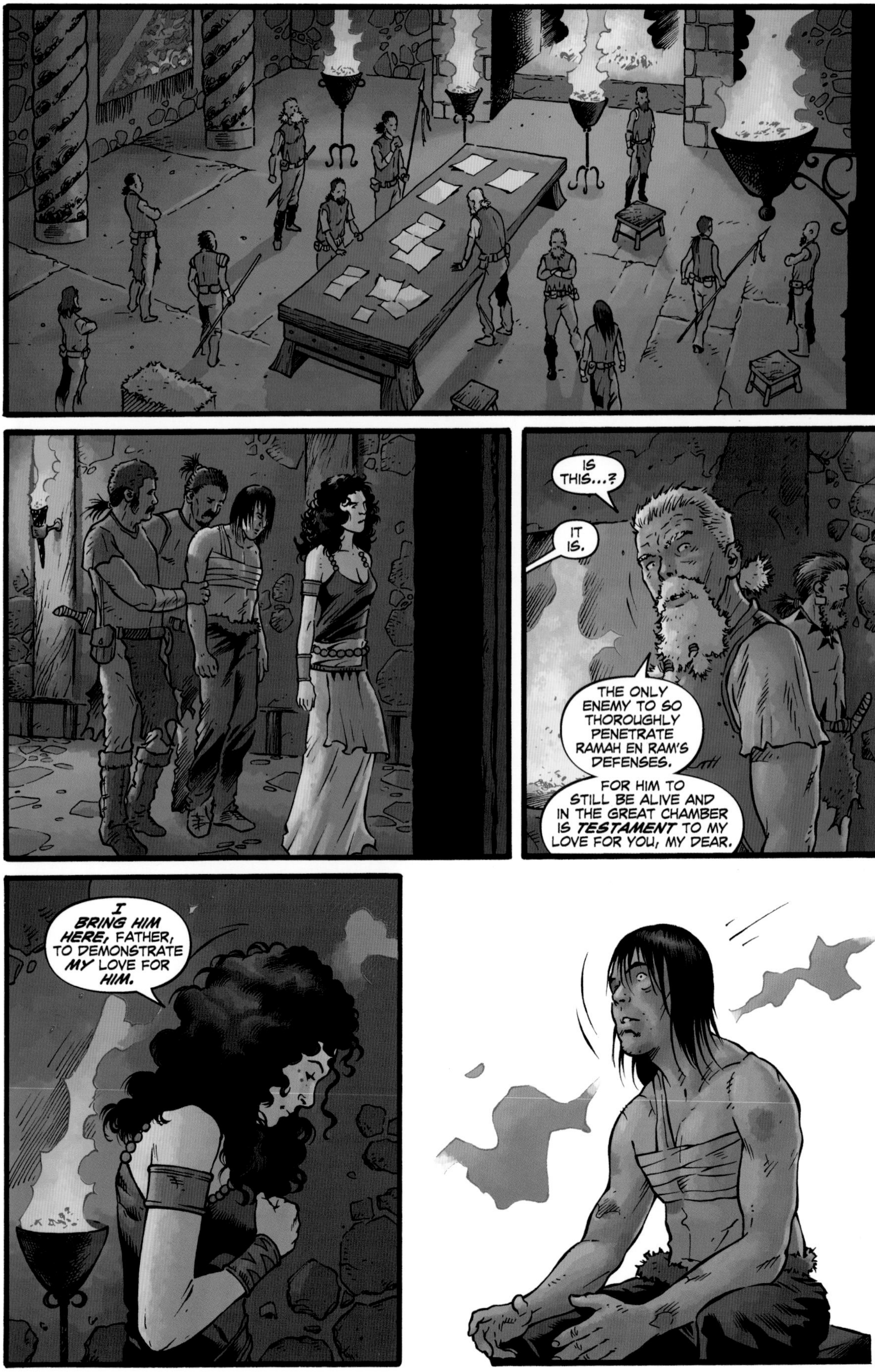
IS THIS...?
IT IS.
THE ONLY ENEMY TO SO THOROUGHLY PENETRATE RAMAH EN RAM'S DEFENSES.
FOR HIM TO STILL BE ALIVE AND IN THE GREAT CHAMBER IS TESTAMENT TO MY LOVE FOR YOU, MY DEAR.
I BRING HIM HERE, FATHER, TO DEMONSTRATE MY LOVE FOR HIM.

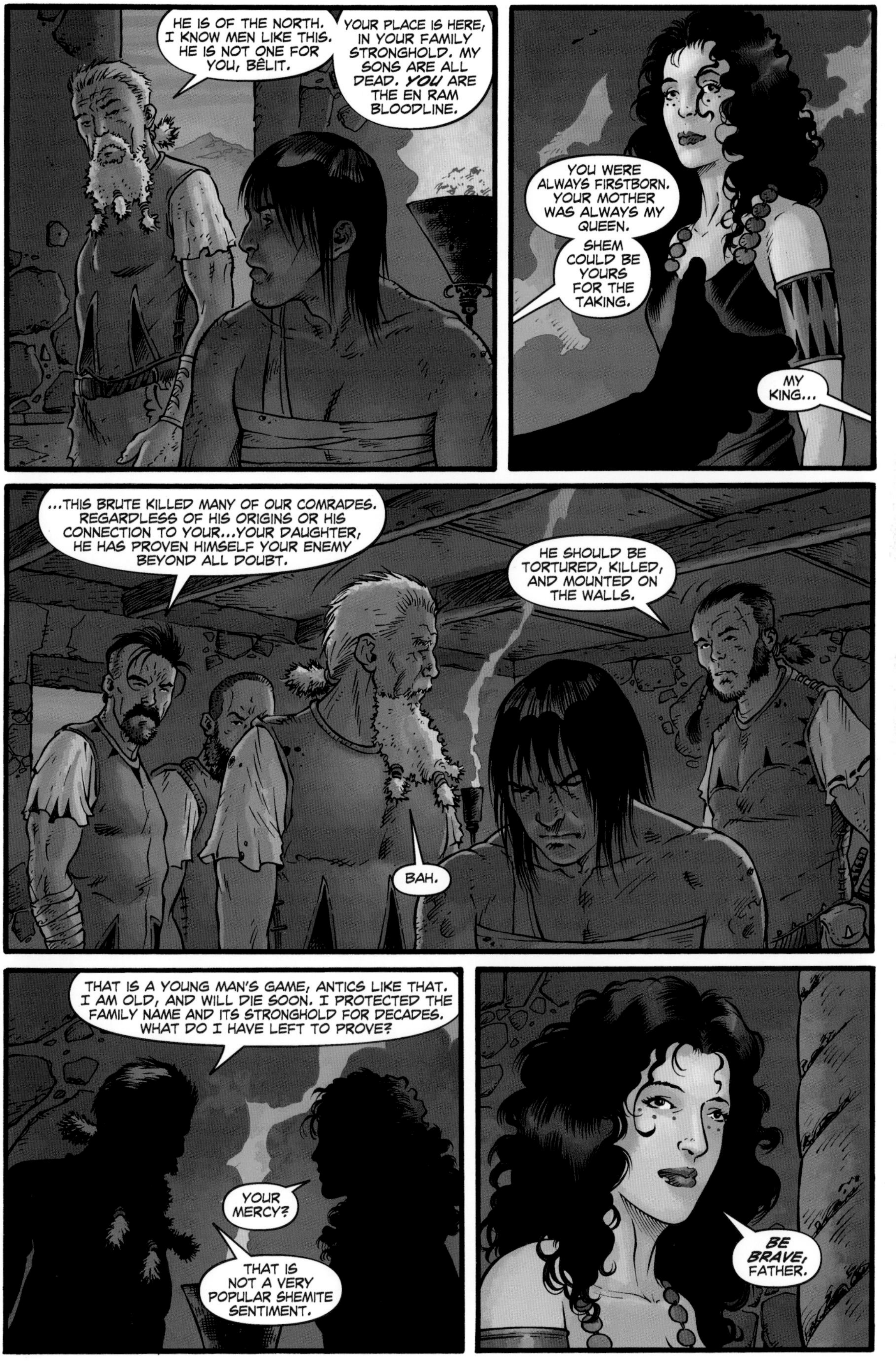
HE IS OF THE NORTH. I KNOW MEN LIKE THIS. HE IS NOT ONE FOR YOU, BÊLIT.
YOUR PLACE IS HERE, IN YOUR FAMILY STRONGHOLD. MY SONS ARE ALL DEAD. YOU ARE THE EN RAM BLOODLINE.
YOU WERE ALWAYS FIRSTBORN. YOUR MOTHER WAS ALWAYS MY QUEEN.
SHEM COULD BE YOURS FOR THE TAKING.
MY KING...
...THIS BRUTE KILLED MANY OF OUR COMRADES. REGARDLESS OF HIS ORIGINS OR HIS CONNECTION TO YOUR...YOUR DAUGHTER, HE HAS PROVEN HIMSELF YOUR ENEMY BEYOND ALL DOUBT.
HE SHOULD BE TORTURED, KILLED, AND MOUNTED ON THE WALLS.
BAH.
THAT IS A YOUNG MAN'S GAME, ANTICS LIKE THAT. I AM OLD, AND WILL DIE SOON. I PROTECTED THE FAMILY NAME AND ITS STRONGHOLD FOR DECADES. WHAT DO I HAVE LEFT TO PROVE?
YOUR MERCY?
THAT IS NOT A VERY POPULAR SHEMITE SENTIMENT.
BE BRAVE, FATHER.

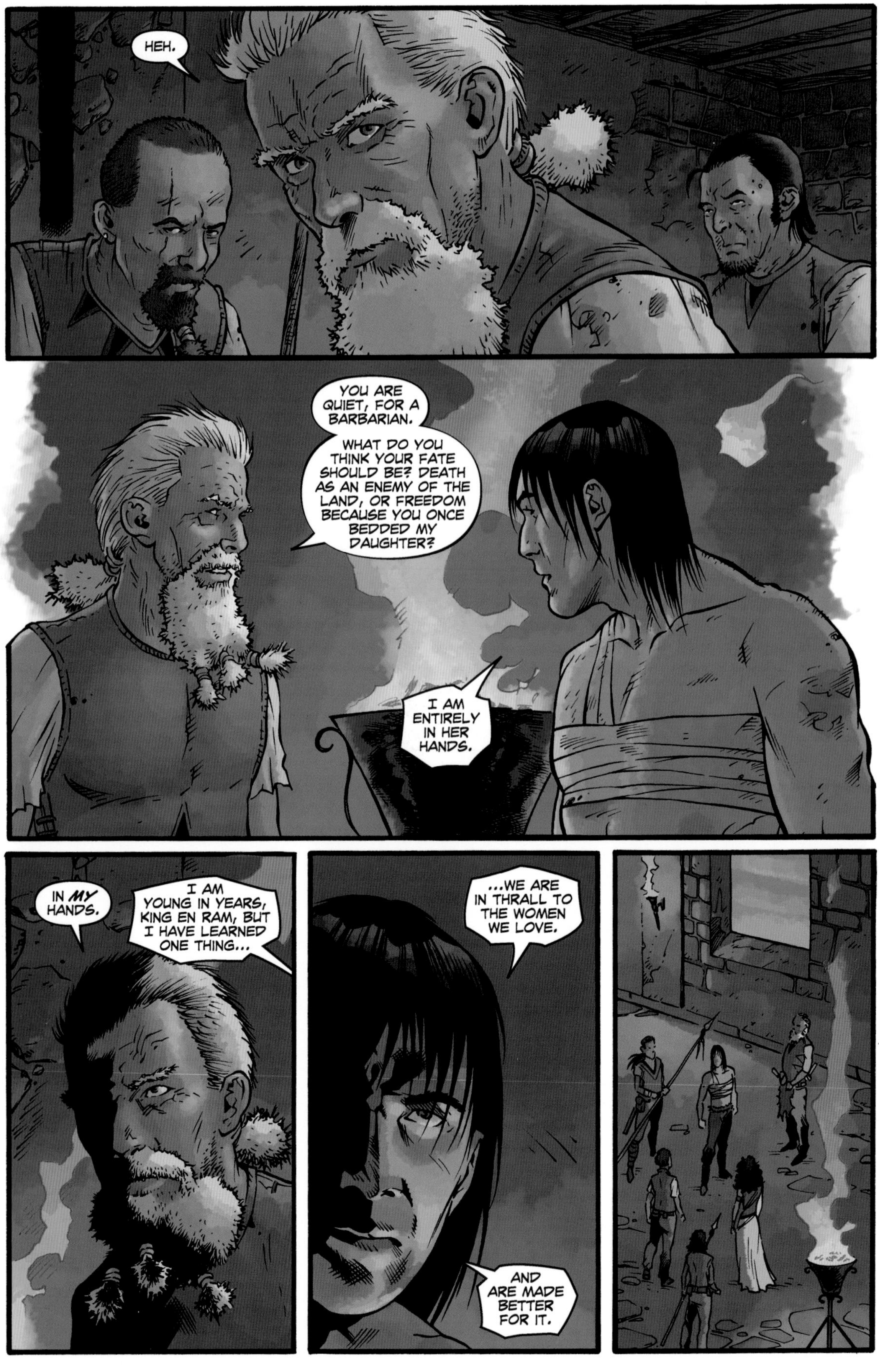
HEH.
YOU ARE QUIET, FOR A BARBARIAN.
WHAT DO YOU THINK YOUR FATE SHOULD BE? DEATH AS AN ENEMY OF THE LAND, OR FREEDOM BECAUSE YOU ONCE BEDDED MY DAUGHTER?
I AM ENTIRELY IN HER HANDS.
IN MY HANDS.
I AM YOUNG IN YEARS, KING EN RAM, BUT I HAVE LEARNED ONE THING...
...WE ARE IN THRALL TO THE WOMEN WE LOVE.
AND ARE MADE BETTER FOR IT.

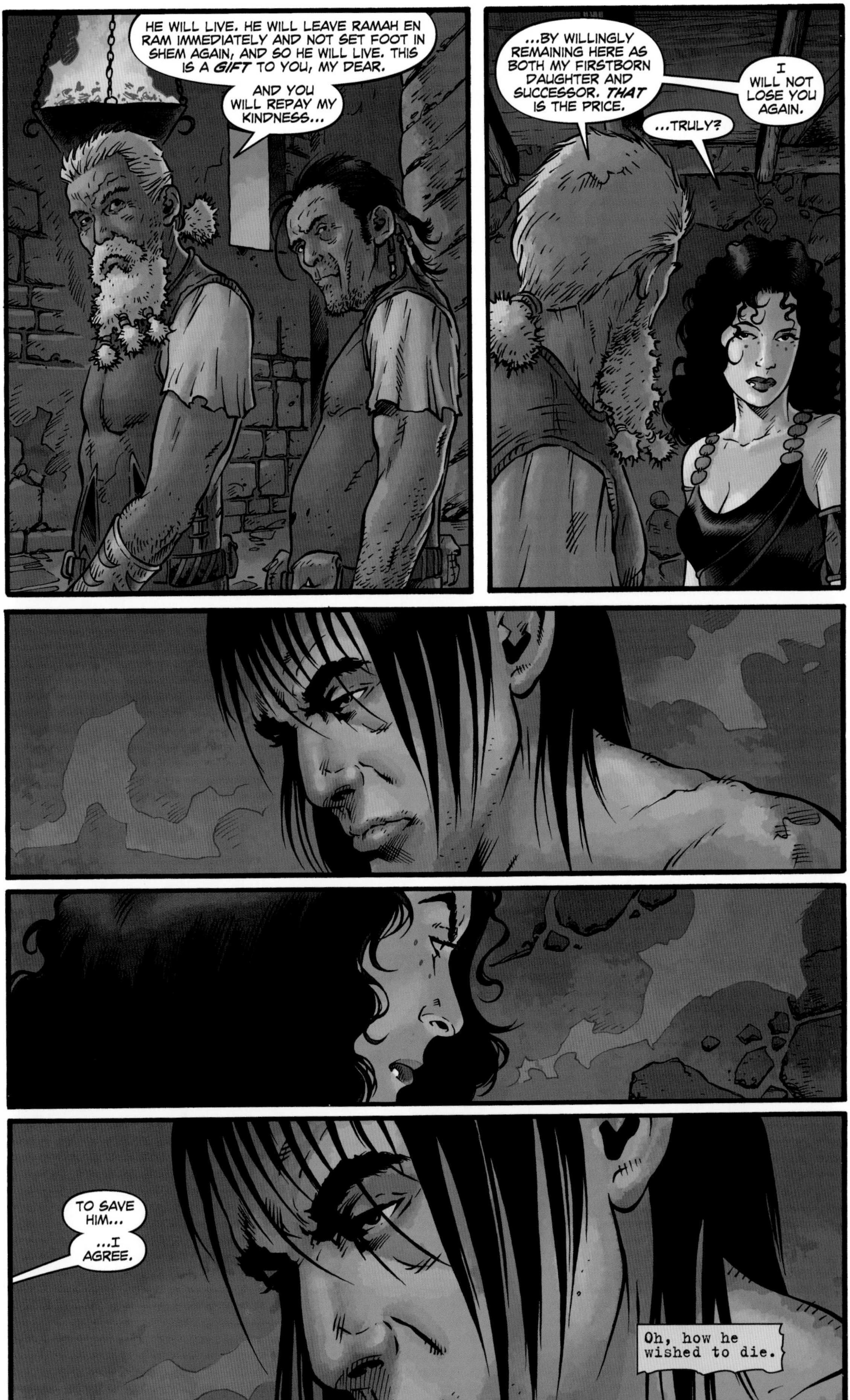
HE WILL LIVE. HE WILL LEAVE RAMAH EN RAM IMMEDIATELY AND NOT SET FOOT IN SHEM AGAIN, AND SO HE WILL LIVE. THIS IS A *GIFT* TO YOU, MY DEAR.
AND YOU WILL REPAY MY KINDNESS...
...BY WILLINGLY REMAINING HERE AS BOTH MY FIRSTBORN DAUGHTER AND SUCCESSOR. *THAT* IS THE PRICE.
I WILL NOT LOSE YOU AGAIN.
...TRULY?
TO SAVE HIM...
...I AGREE.
Oh, how he wished to die.

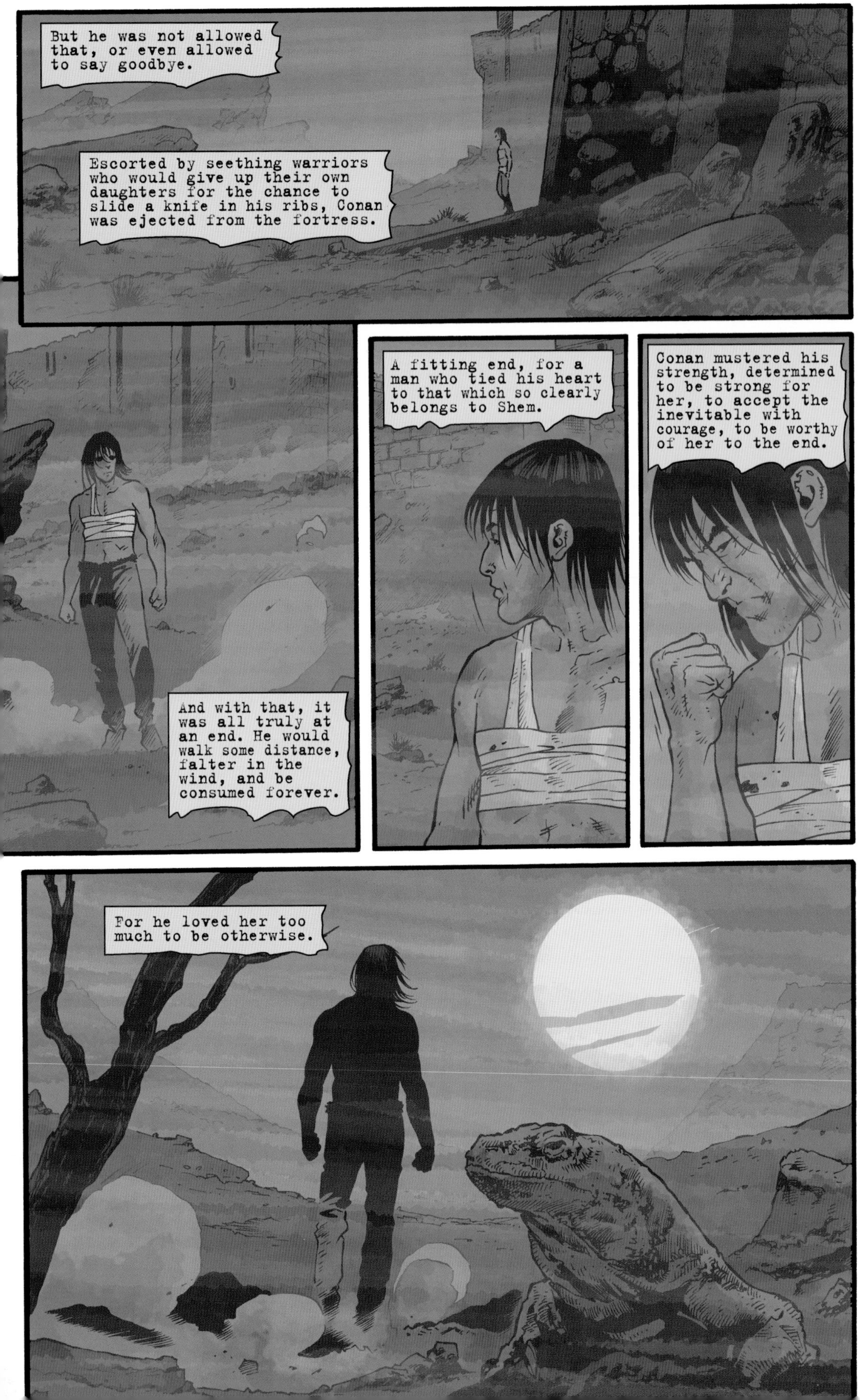
But he was not allowed that, or even allowed to say goodbye.
Escorted by seething warriors who would give up their own daughters for the chance to slide a knife in his ribs, Conan was ejected from the fortress.
And with that, it was all truly at an end. He would walk some distance, falter in the wind, and be consumed forever.
A fitting end, for a man who tied his heart to that which so clearly belongs to Shem.
Conan mustered his strength, determined to be strong for her, to accept the inevitable with courage, to be worthy of her to the end.
For he loved her too much to be otherwise.

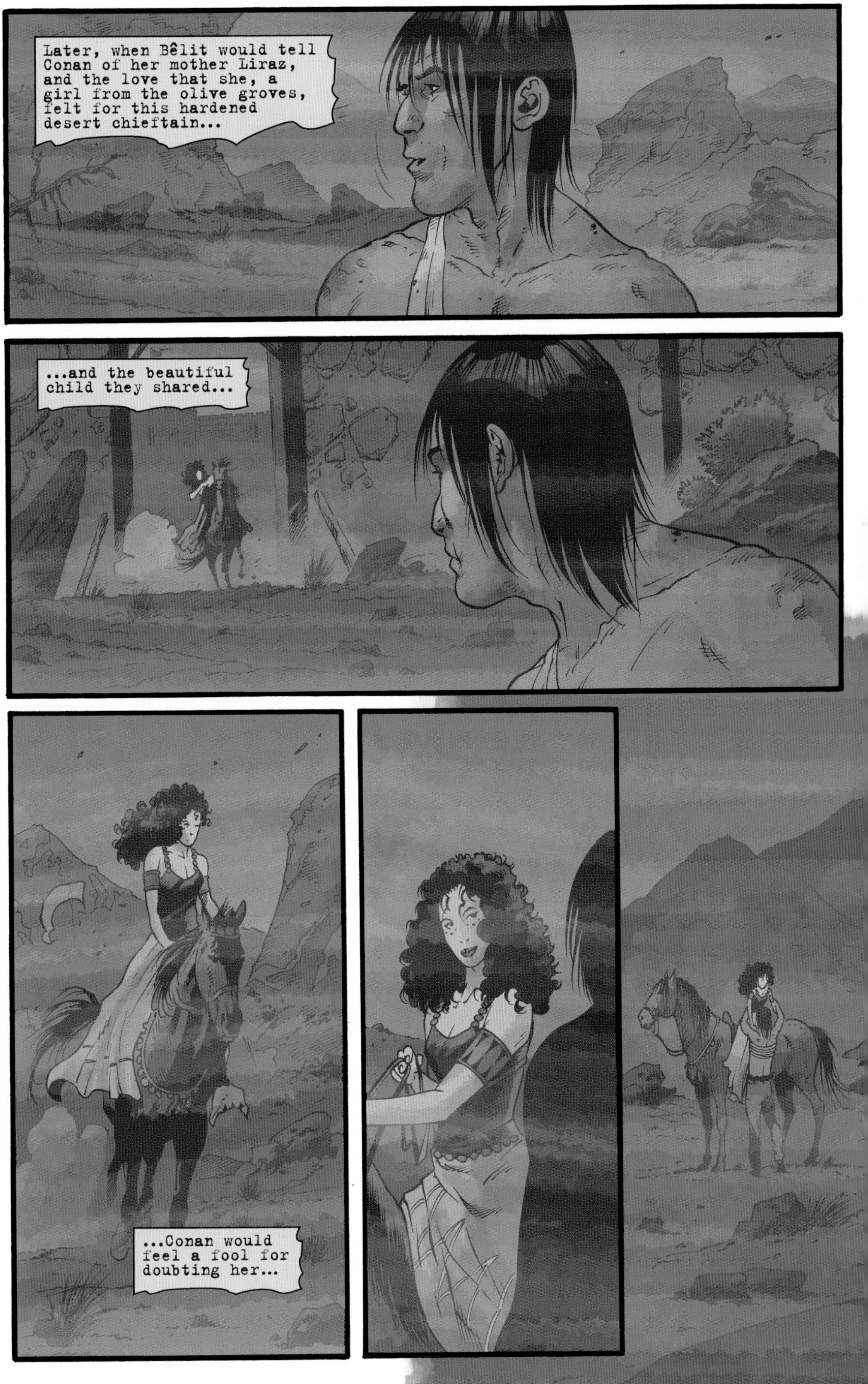
Later, when Bêlit would tell Conan of her mother Liraz, and the love that she, a girl from the olive groves, felt for this hardened desert chieftain...
...and the beautiful child they shared...
...Conan would feel a fool for doubting her...

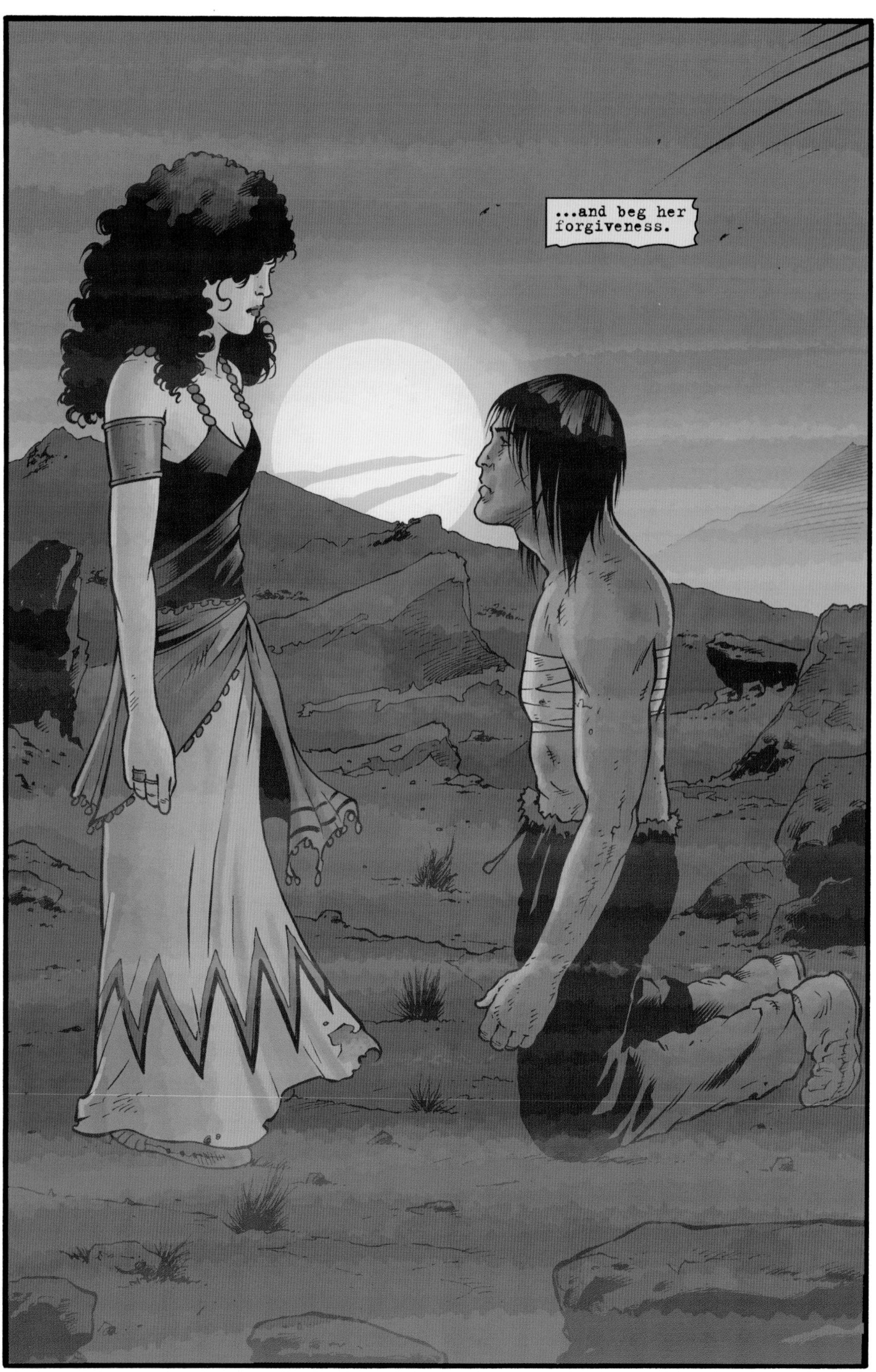
...and beg her forgiveness.

CHAPTER FOUR

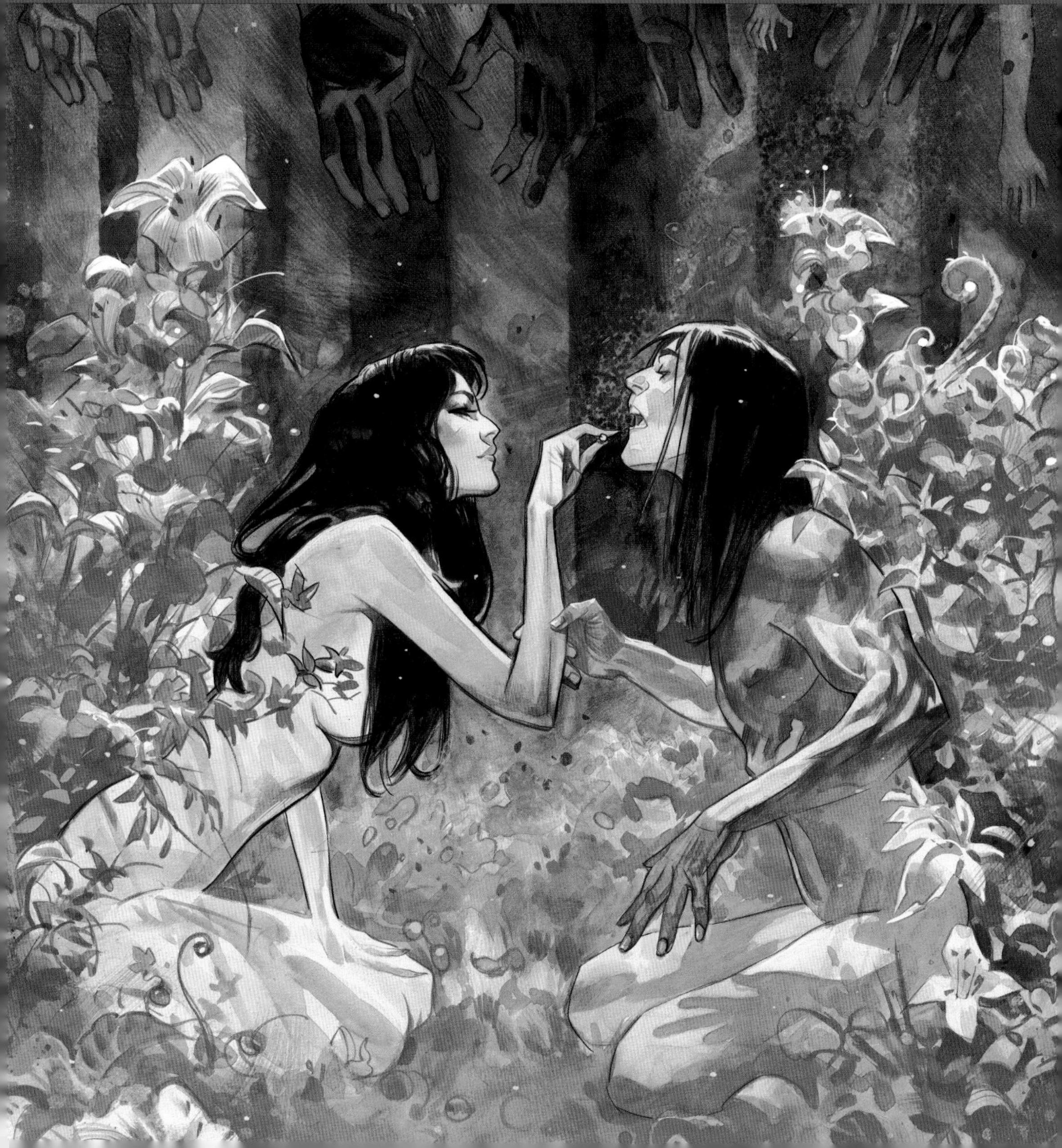

"You lash out in anger and pain,
looking for answers in sword strokes.
But there are none."

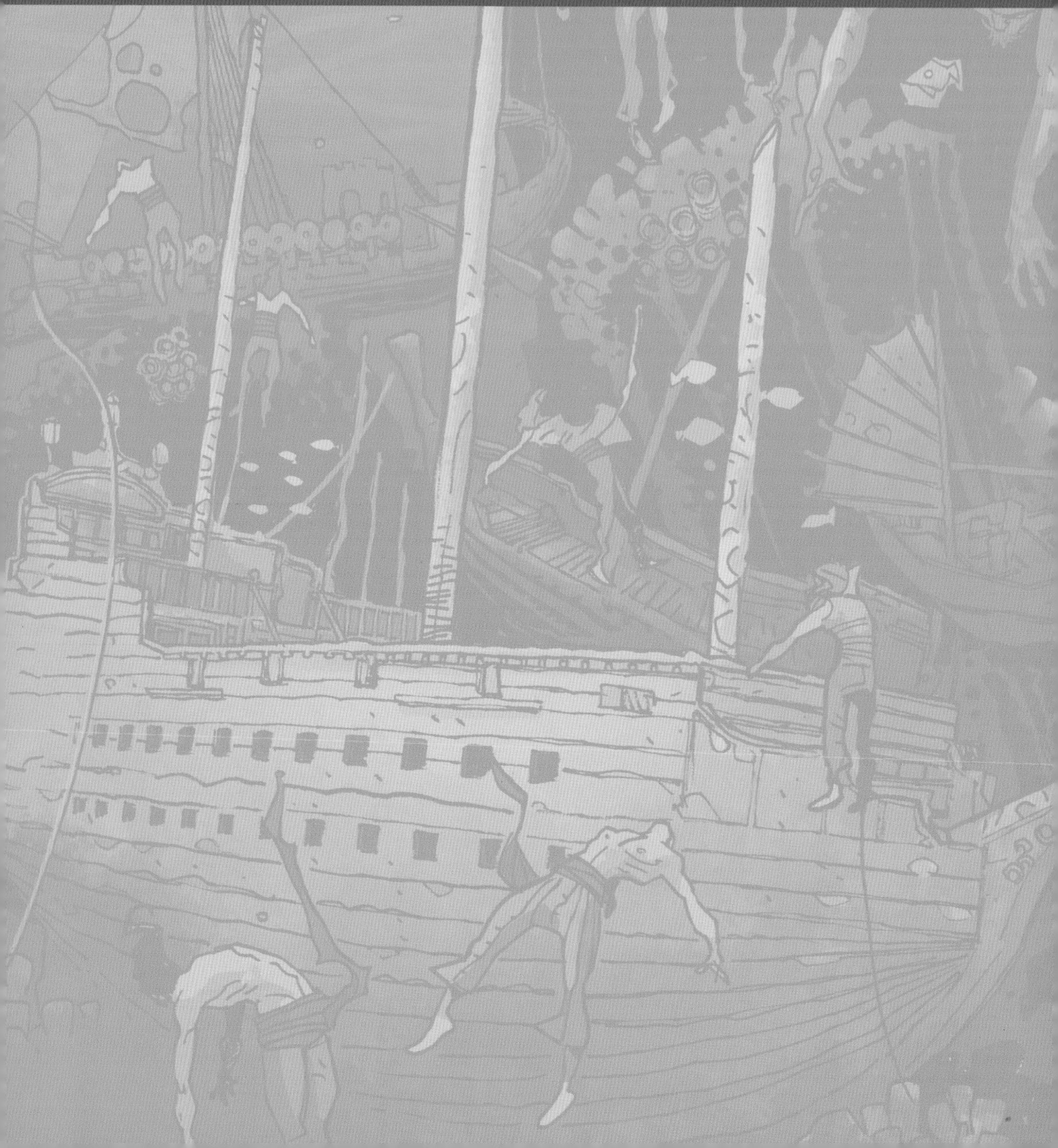

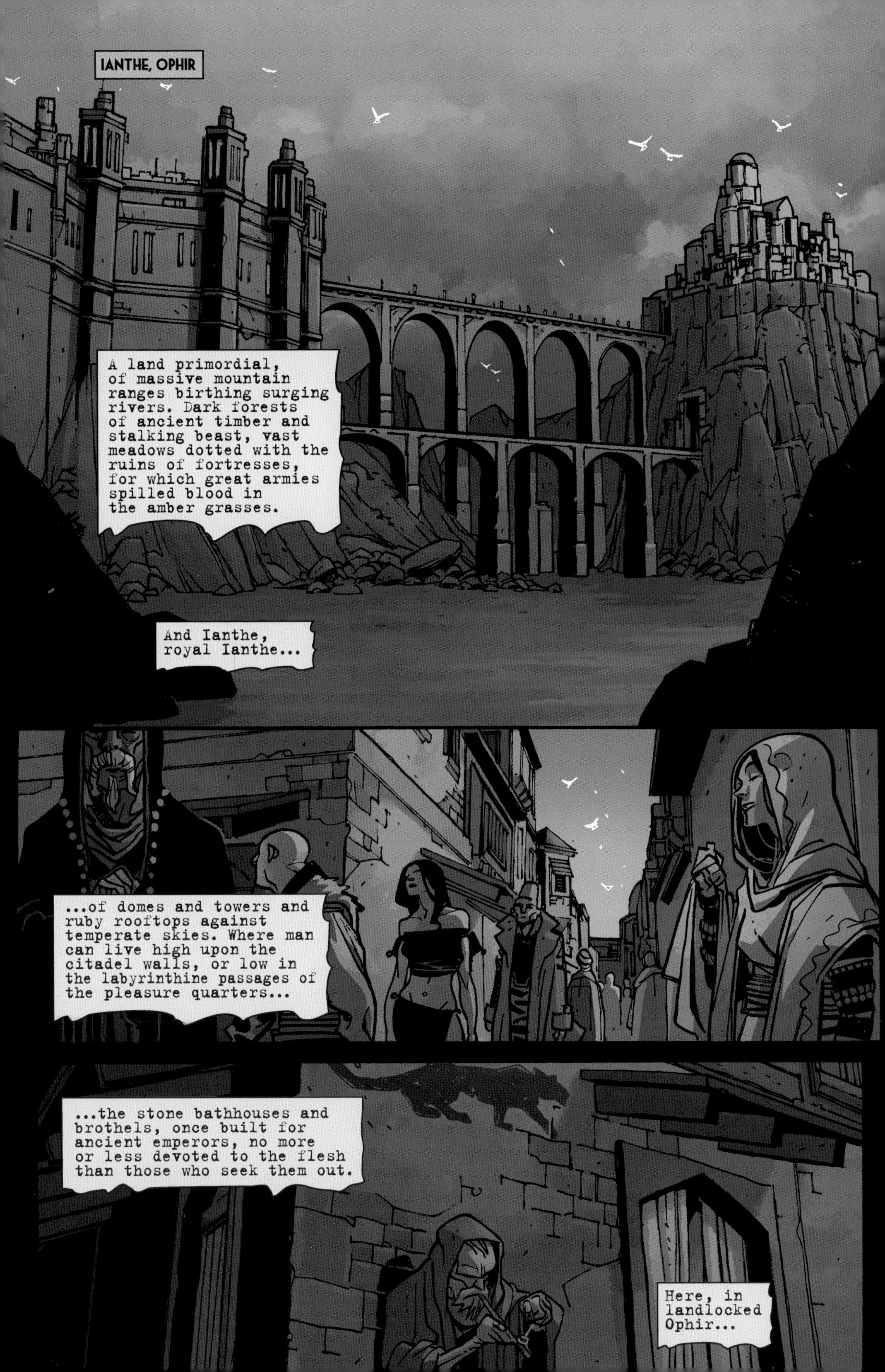
IANTHE, OPHIR
A land primordial, of massive mountain ranges birthing surging rivers. Dark forests of ancient timber and stalking beast, vast meadows dotted with the ruins of fortresses, for which great armies spilled blood in the amber grasses.
And Ianthe, royal Ianthe...
...of domes and towers and ruby rooftops against temperate skies. Where man can live high upon the citadel walls, or low in the labyrinthine passages of the pleasure quarters...
...the stone bathhouses and brothels, once built for ancient emperors, no more or less devoted to the flesh than those who seek them out.
Here, in landlocked Ophir...

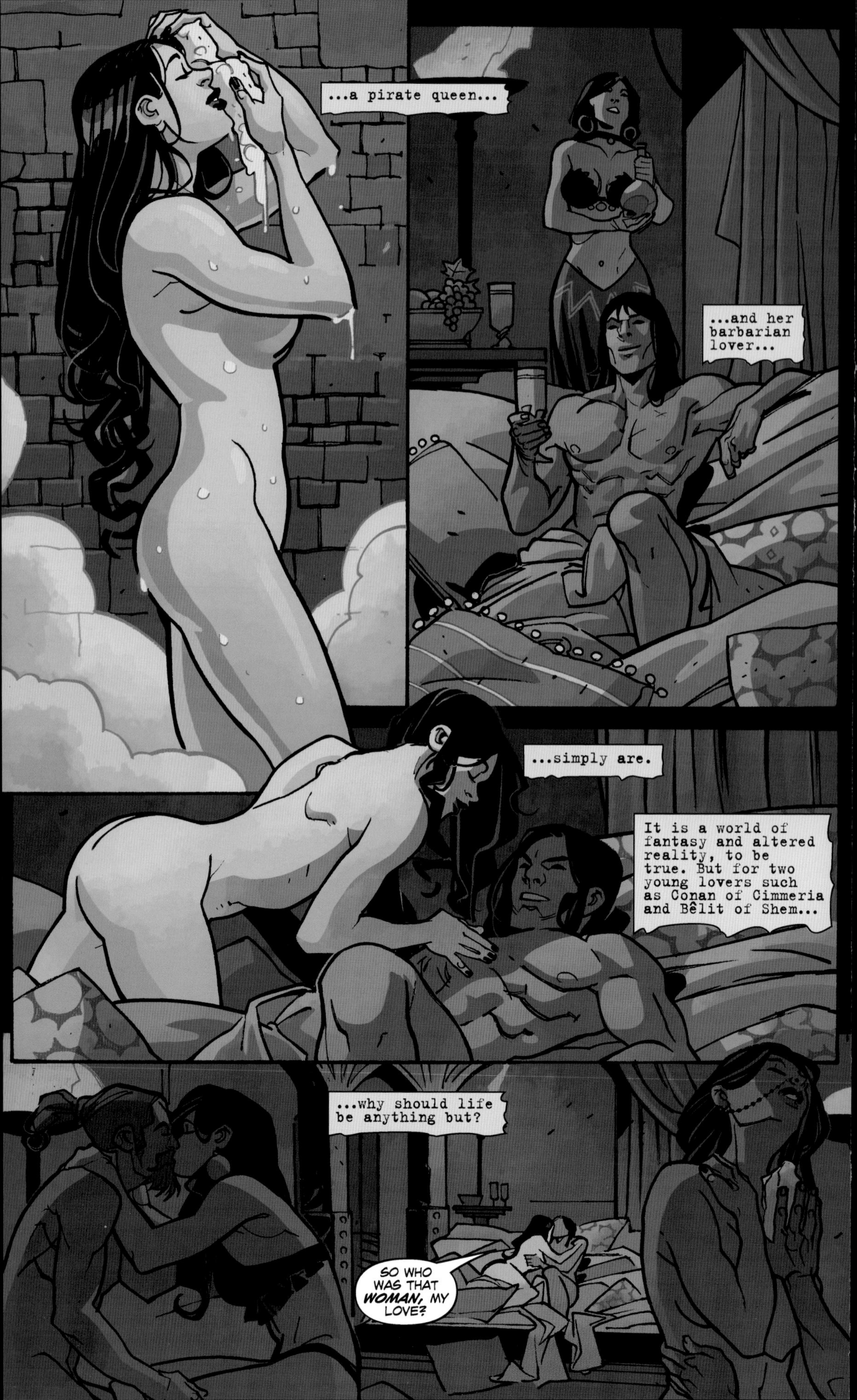
...a pirate queen...
...and her barbarian lover...
...simply are.
It is a world of fantasy and altered reality, to be true. But for two young lovers such as Conan of Cimmeria and Bêlit of Shem...
...why should life be anything but?
SO WHO WAS THAT *WOMAN,* MY LOVE?

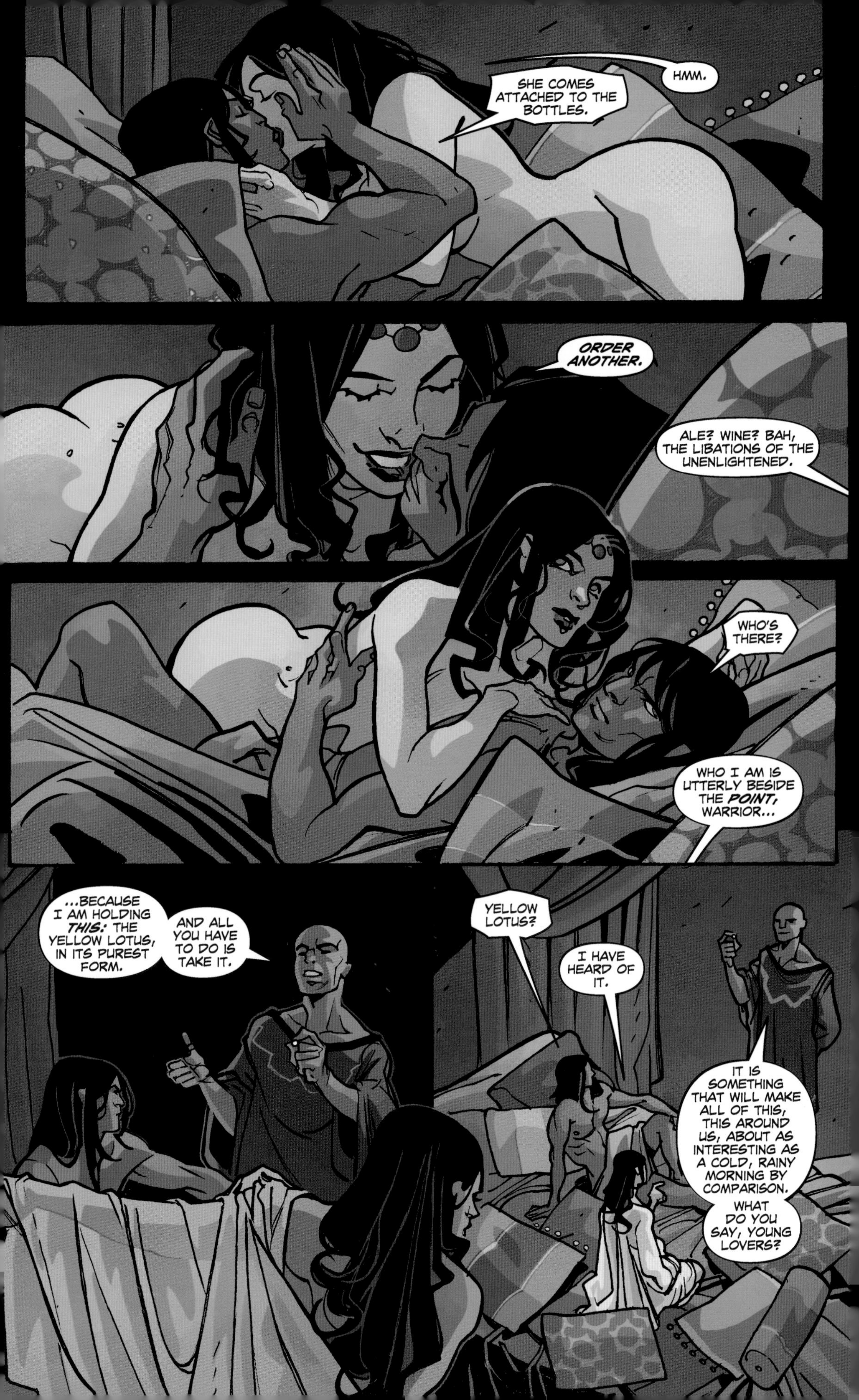
SHE COMES ATTACHED TO THE BOTTLES.
HMM.
ORDER ANOTHER.
ALE? WINE? BAH, THE LIBATIONS OF THE UNENLIGHTENED.
WHO'S THERE?
WHO I AM IS UTTERLY BESIDE THE POINT, WARRIOR...
...BECAUSE I AM HOLDING THIS: THE YELLOW LOTUS, IN ITS PUREST FORM.
AND ALL YOU HAVE TO DO IS TAKE IT.
YELLOW LOTUS?
I HAVE HEARD OF IT.
IT IS SOMETHING THAT WILL MAKE ALL OF THIS, THIS AROUND US, ABOUT AS INTERESTING AS A COLD, RAINY MORNING BY COMPARISON.
WHAT DO YOU SAY, YOUNG LOVERS?

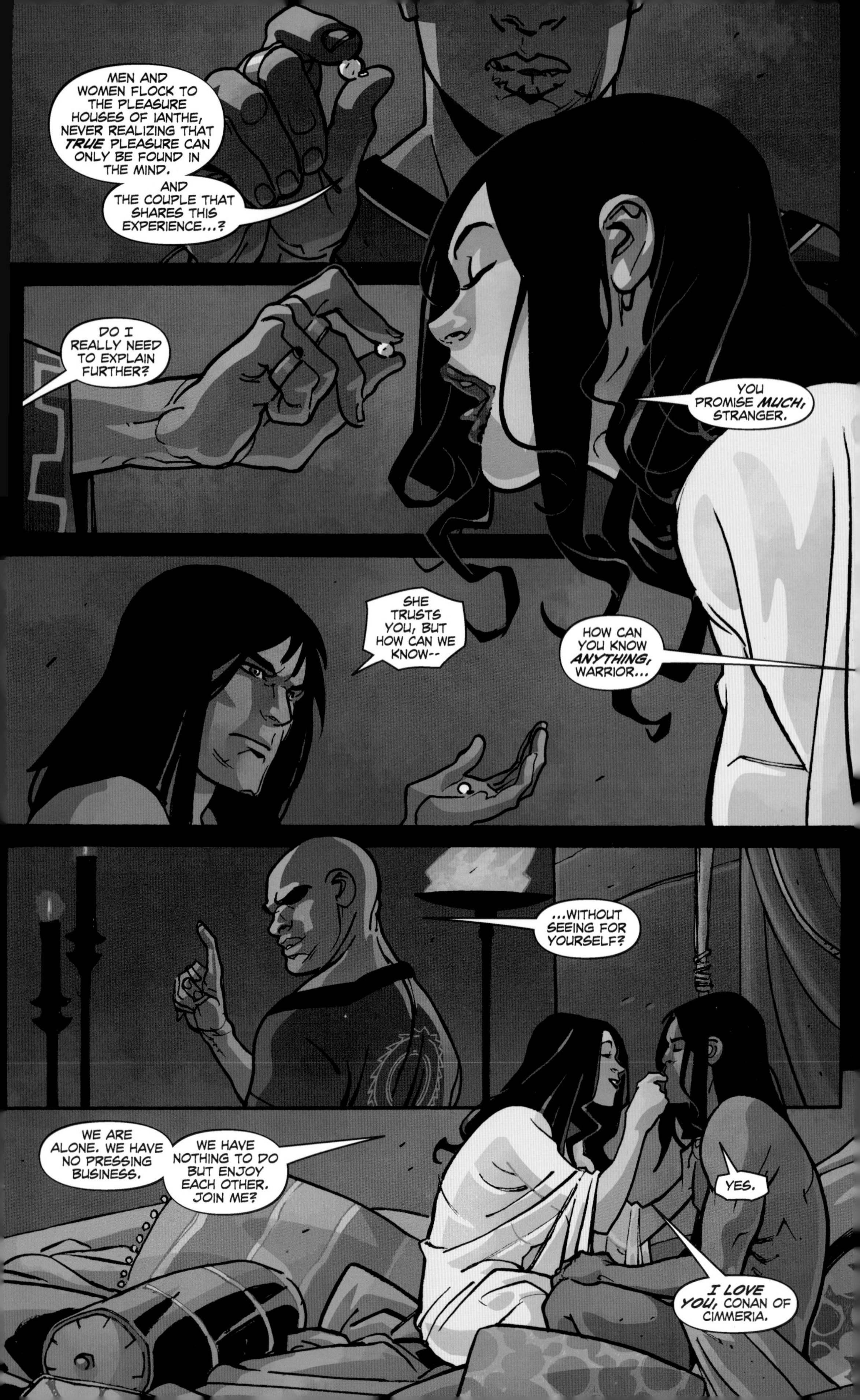
MEN AND WOMEN FLOCK TO THE PLEASURE HOUSES OF IANTHE, NEVER REALIZING THAT *TRUE* PLEASURE CAN ONLY BE FOUND IN THE MIND.
AND THE COUPLE THAT SHARES THIS EXPERIENCE...?
DO I REALLY NEED TO EXPLAIN FURTHER?
YOU PROMISE *MUCH,* STRANGER.
SHE TRUSTS YOU, BUT HOW CAN WE KNOW--
HOW CAN YOU KNOW *ANYTHING,* WARRIOR...
...WITHOUT SEEING FOR YOURSELF?
WE ARE ALONE. WE HAVE NO PRESSING BUSINESS.
WE HAVE NOTHING TO DO BUT ENJOY EACH OTHER. JOIN ME?
YES.
I LOVE YOU, CONAN OF CIMMERIA.

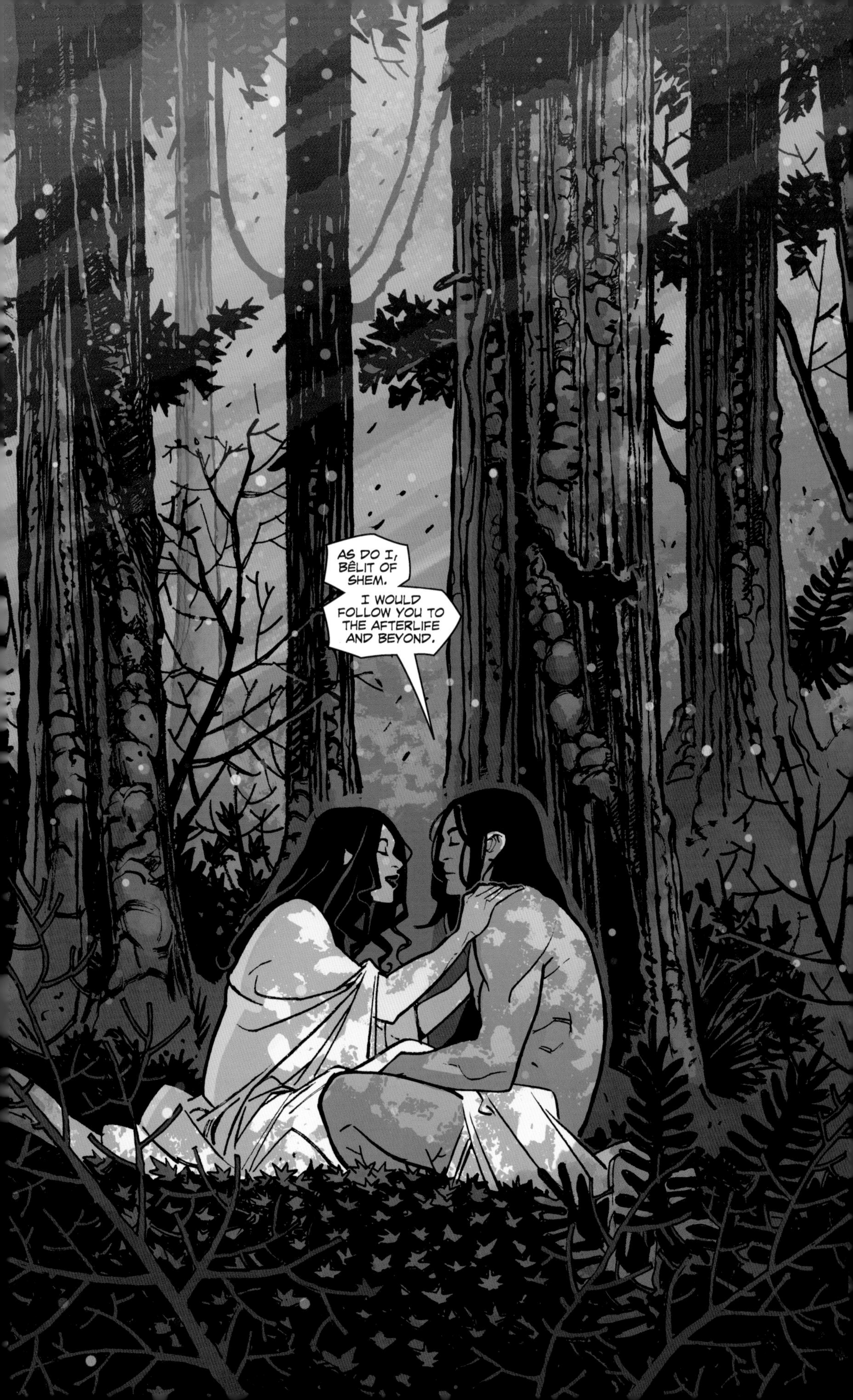
AS DO I, BÊLIT OF SHEM.
I WOULD FOLLOW YOU TO THE AFTERLIFE AND BEYOND.

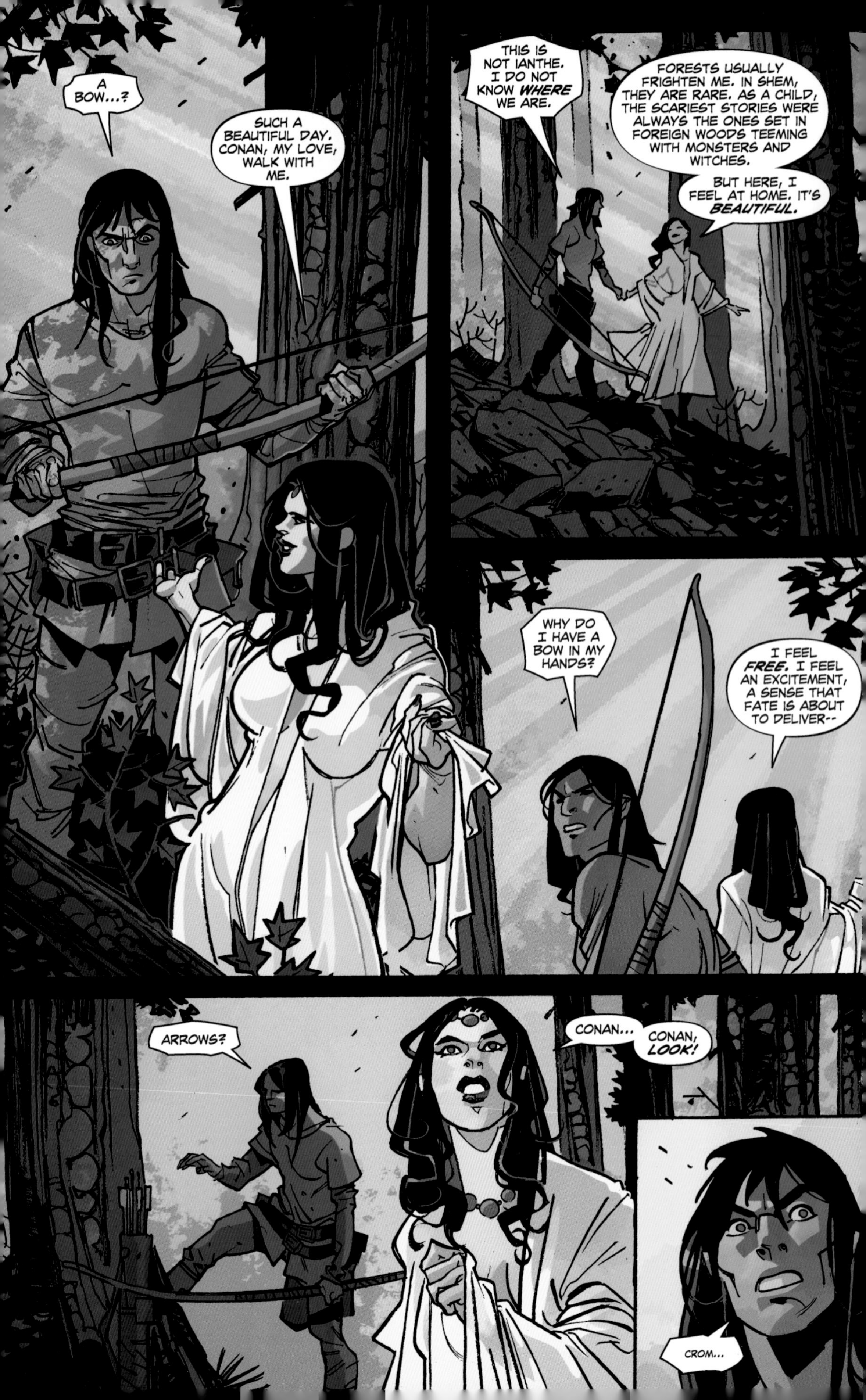
A BOW...?
SUCH A BEAUTIFUL DAY. CONAN, MY LOVE, WALK WITH ME.
THIS IS NOT IANTHE. I DO NOT KNOW *WHERE* WE ARE.
FORESTS USUALLY FRIGHTEN ME. IN SHEM, THEY ARE RARE. AS A CHILD, THE SCARIEST STORIES WERE ALWAYS THE ONES SET IN FOREIGN WOODS TEEMING WITH MONSTERS AND WITCHES.
BUT HERE, I FEEL AT HOME. IT'S ***BEAUTIFUL.***
WHY DO I HAVE A BOW IN MY HANDS?
I FEEL ***FREE.*** I FEEL AN EXCITEMENT, A SENSE THAT FATE IS ABOUT TO DELIVER--
ARROWS?
CONAN...
CONAN, ***LOOK!***
CROM...

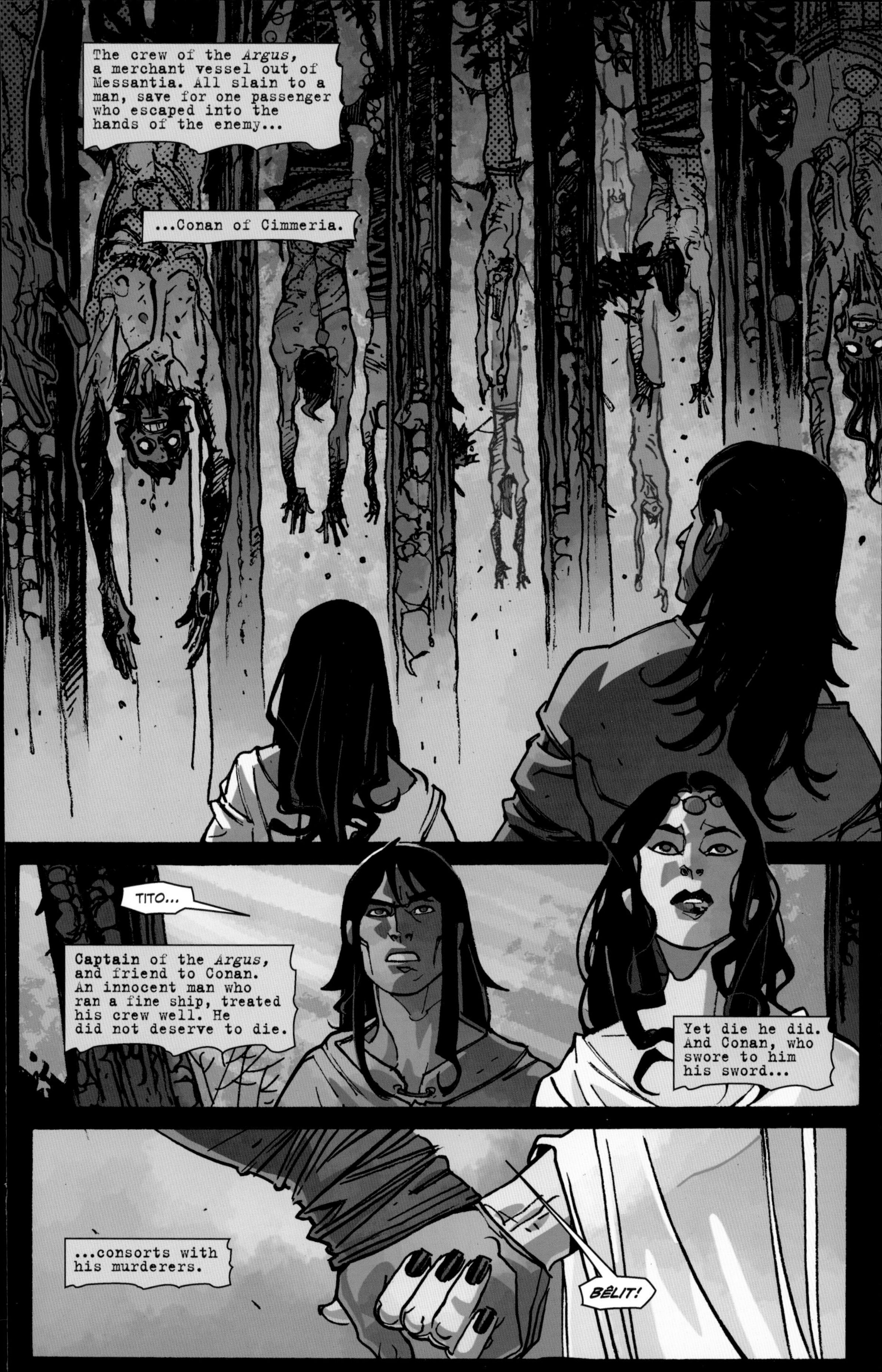

The crew of the *Argus*, a merchant vessel out of Messantia. All slain to a man, save for one passenger who escaped into the hands of the enemy...
...Conan of Cimmeria.
TITO...
Captain of the *Argus*, and friend to Conan. An innocent man who ran a fine ship, treated his crew well. He did not deserve to die.
Yet die he did. And Conan, who swore to him his sword...
...consorts with his murderers.
BÊLIT!

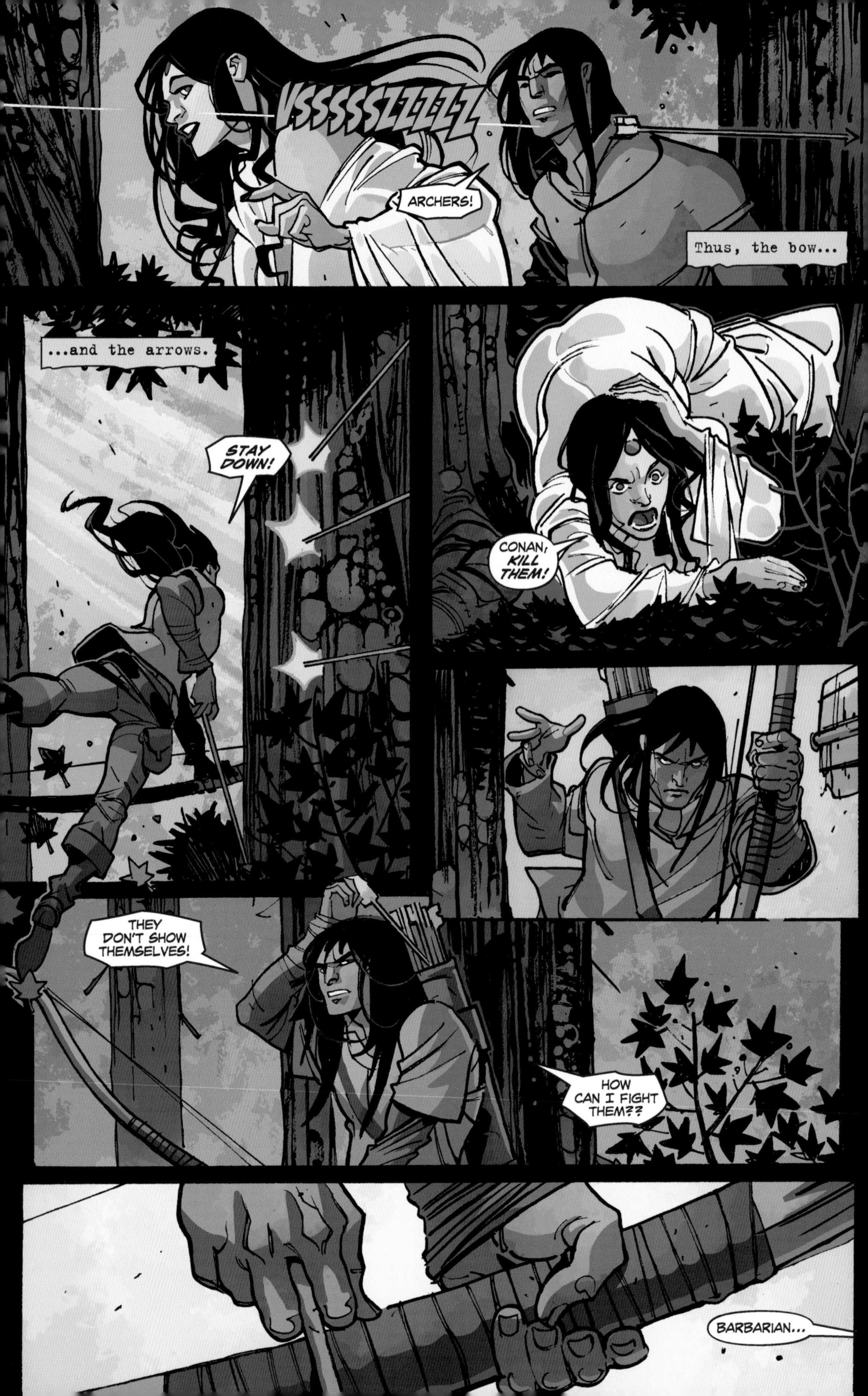
VSSSSSZZZZZ
ARCHERS!
Thus, the bow...
...and the arrows.
STAY DOWN!
CONAN, KILL THEM!
THEY DON'T SHOW THEMSELVES!
HOW CAN I FIGHT THEM??
BARBARIAN...

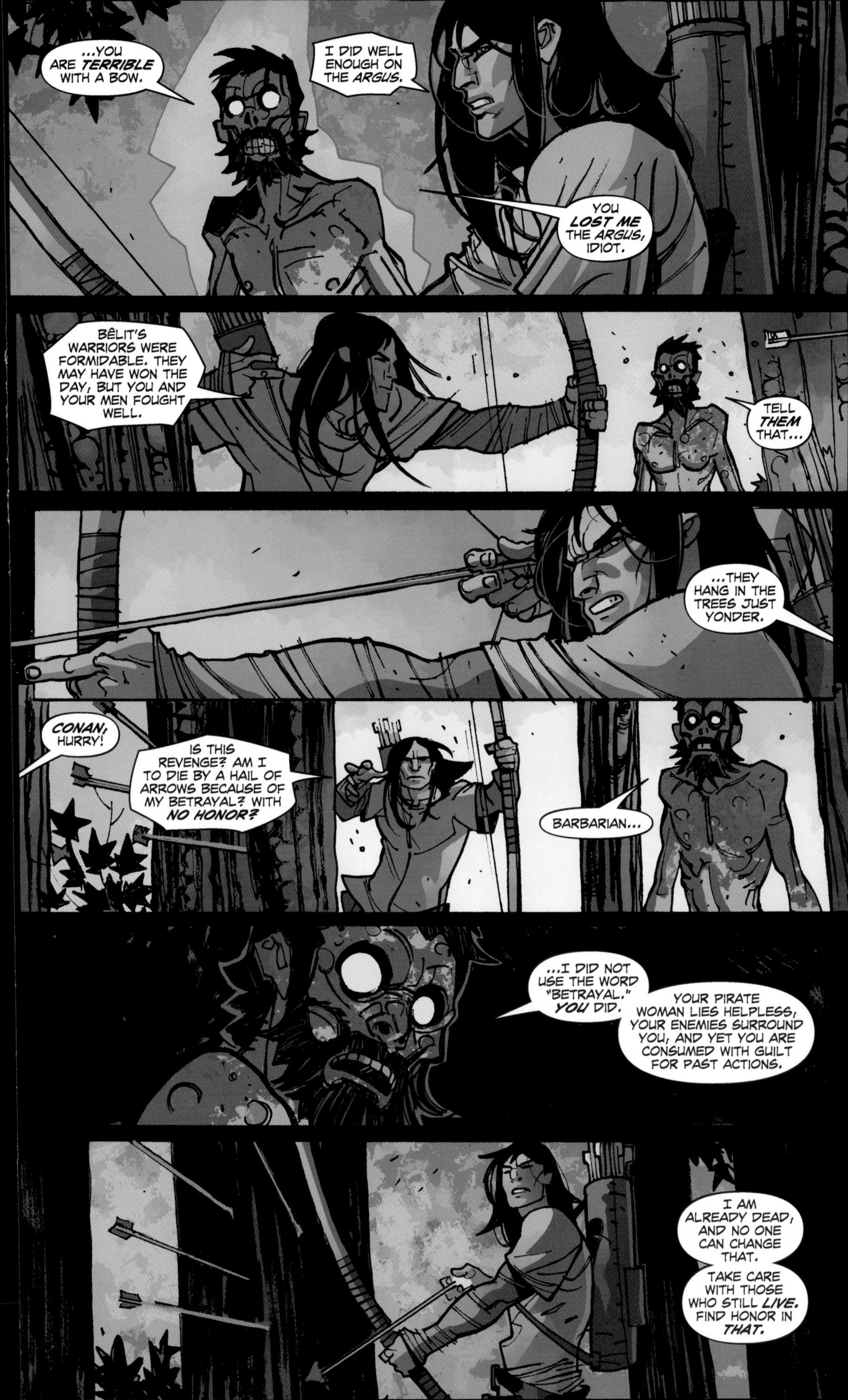

...YOU ARE TERRIBLE WITH A BOW.
I DID WELL ENOUGH ON THE ARGUS.
YOU LOST ME THE ARGUS, IDIOT.
BÊLIT'S WARRIORS WERE FORMIDABLE. THEY MAY HAVE WON THE DAY, BUT YOU AND YOUR MEN FOUGHT WELL.
TELL THEM THAT...
...THEY HANG IN THE TREES JUST YONDER.
CONAN, HURRY!
IS THIS REVENGE? AM I TO DIE BY A HAIL OF ARROWS BECAUSE OF MY BETRAYAL? WITH NO HONOR?
BARBARIAN...
...I DID NOT USE THE WORD "BETRAYAL." YOU DID.
YOUR PIRATE WOMAN LIES HELPLESS, YOUR ENEMIES SURROUND YOU, AND YET YOU ARE CONSUMED WITH GUILT FOR PAST ACTIONS.
I AM ALREADY DEAD, AND NO ONE CAN CHANGE THAT.
TAKE CARE WITH THOSE WHO STILL LIVE. FIND HONOR IN THAT.

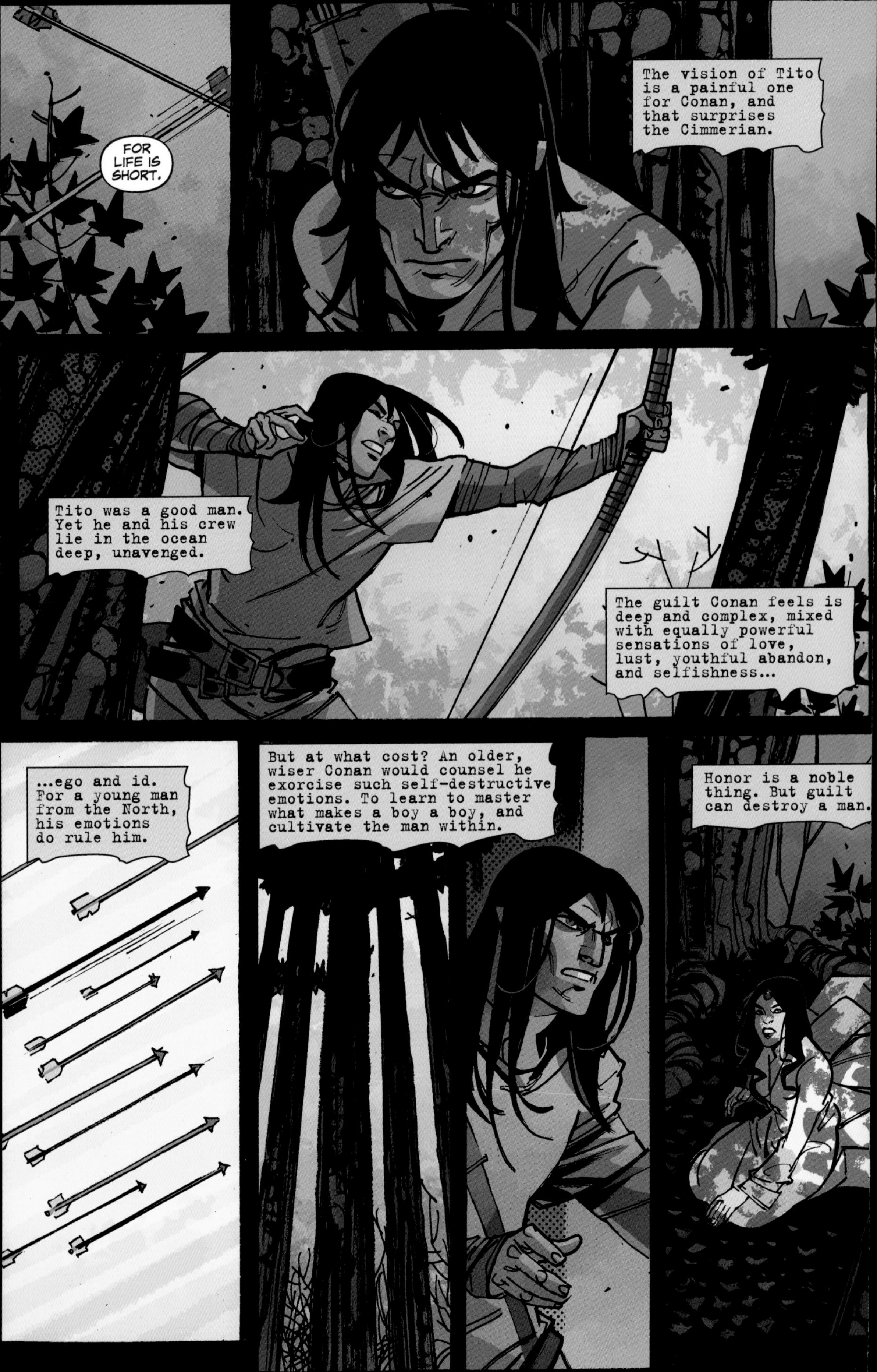
FOR LIFE IS SHORT.
The vision of Tito is a painful one for Conan, and that surprises the Cimmerian.
Tito was a good man. Yet he and his crew lie in the ocean deep, unavenged.
The guilt Conan feels is deep and complex, mixed with equally powerful sensations of love, lust, youthful abandon, and selfishness...
...ego and id. For a young man from the North, his emotions do rule him.
But at what cost? An older, wiser Conan would counsel he exorcise such self-destructive emotions. To learn to master what makes a boy a boy, and cultivate the man within.
Honor is a noble thing. But guilt can destroy a man.

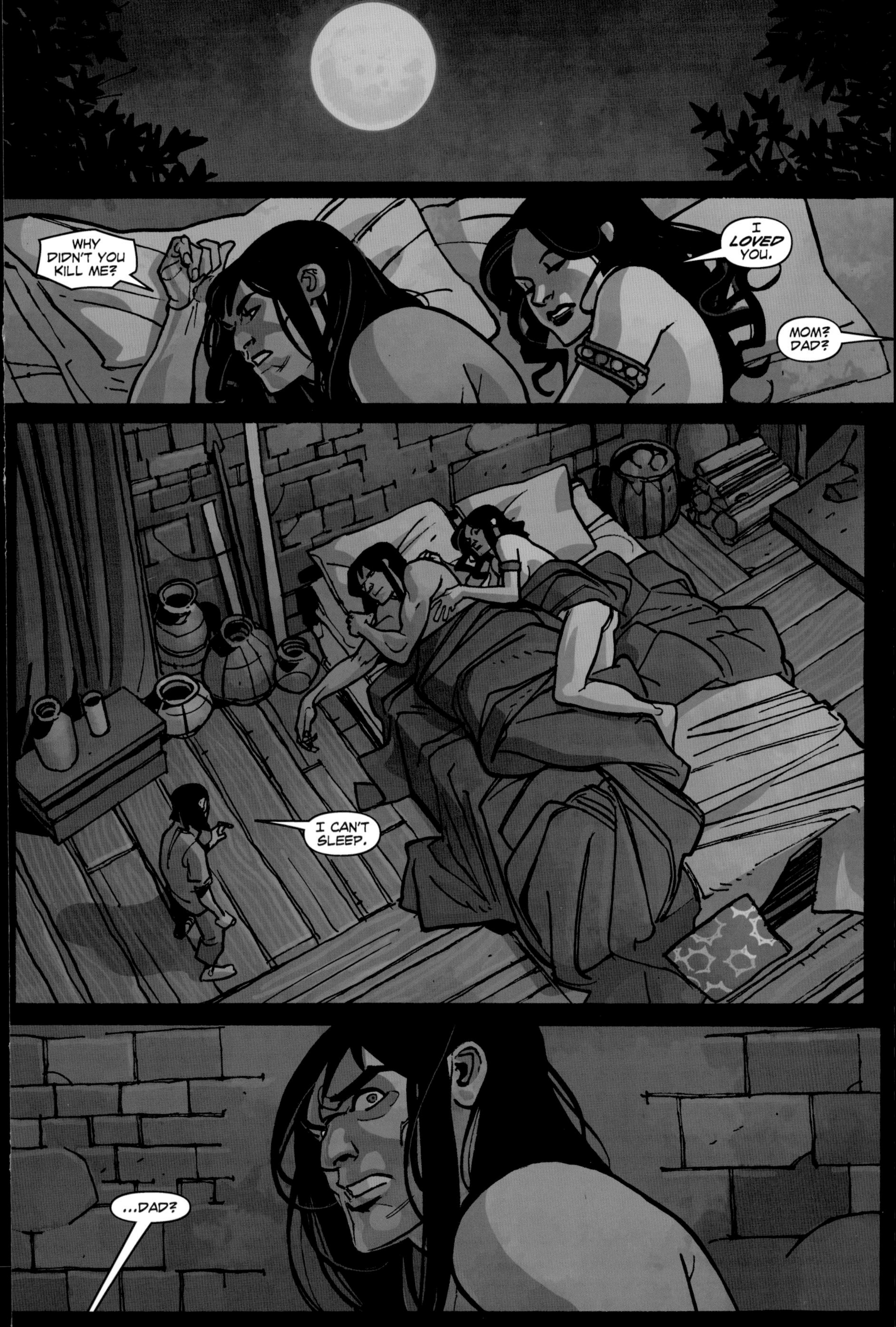
WHY DIDN'T YOU KILL ME?
I *LOVED* YOU.
MOM? DAD?
I CAN'T SLEEP.
...DAD?

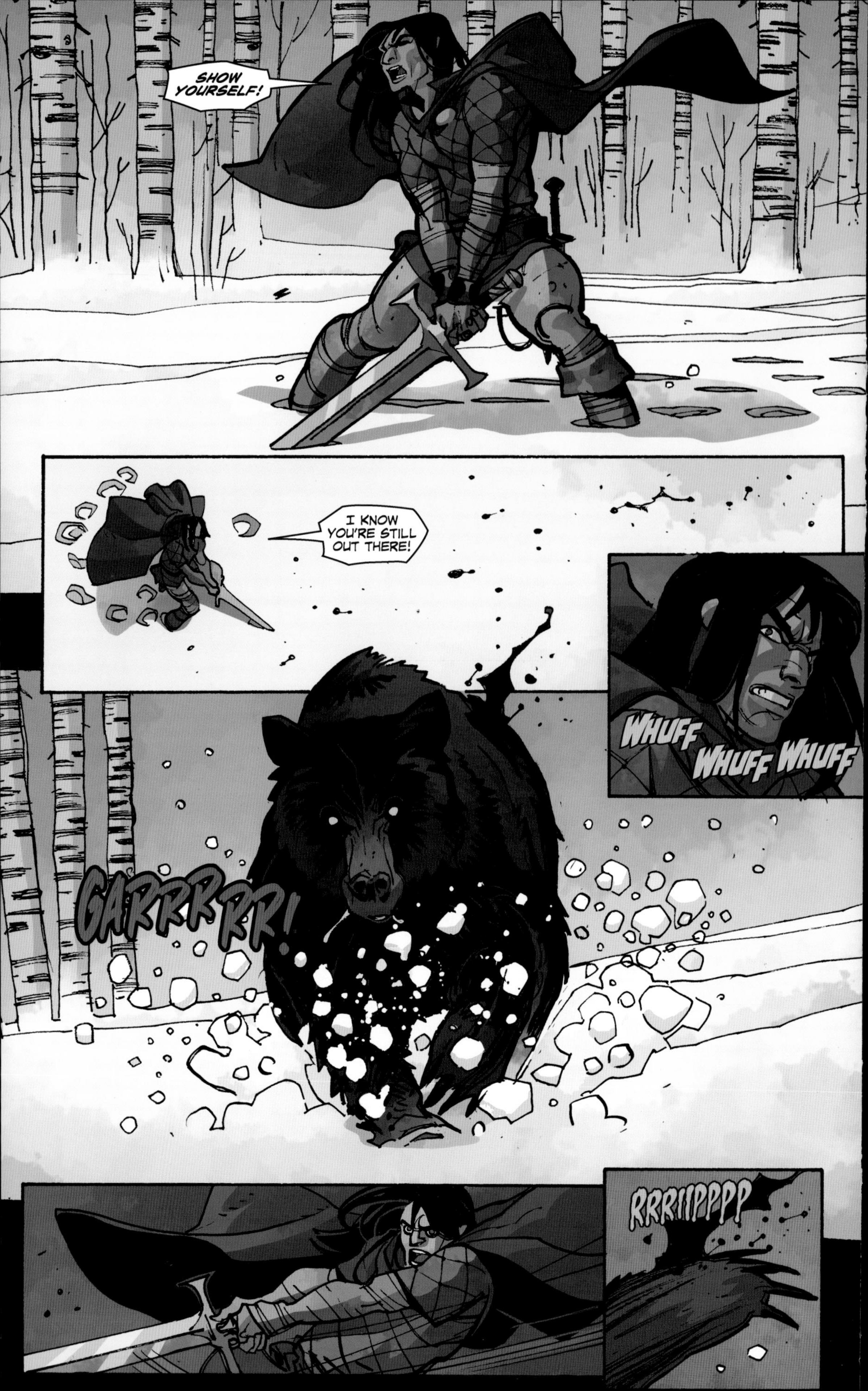
SHOW YOURSELF!
I KNOW YOU'RE STILL OUT THERE!
WHUFF WHUFF WHUFF
GARRRRRR!
RRRIIPPPP

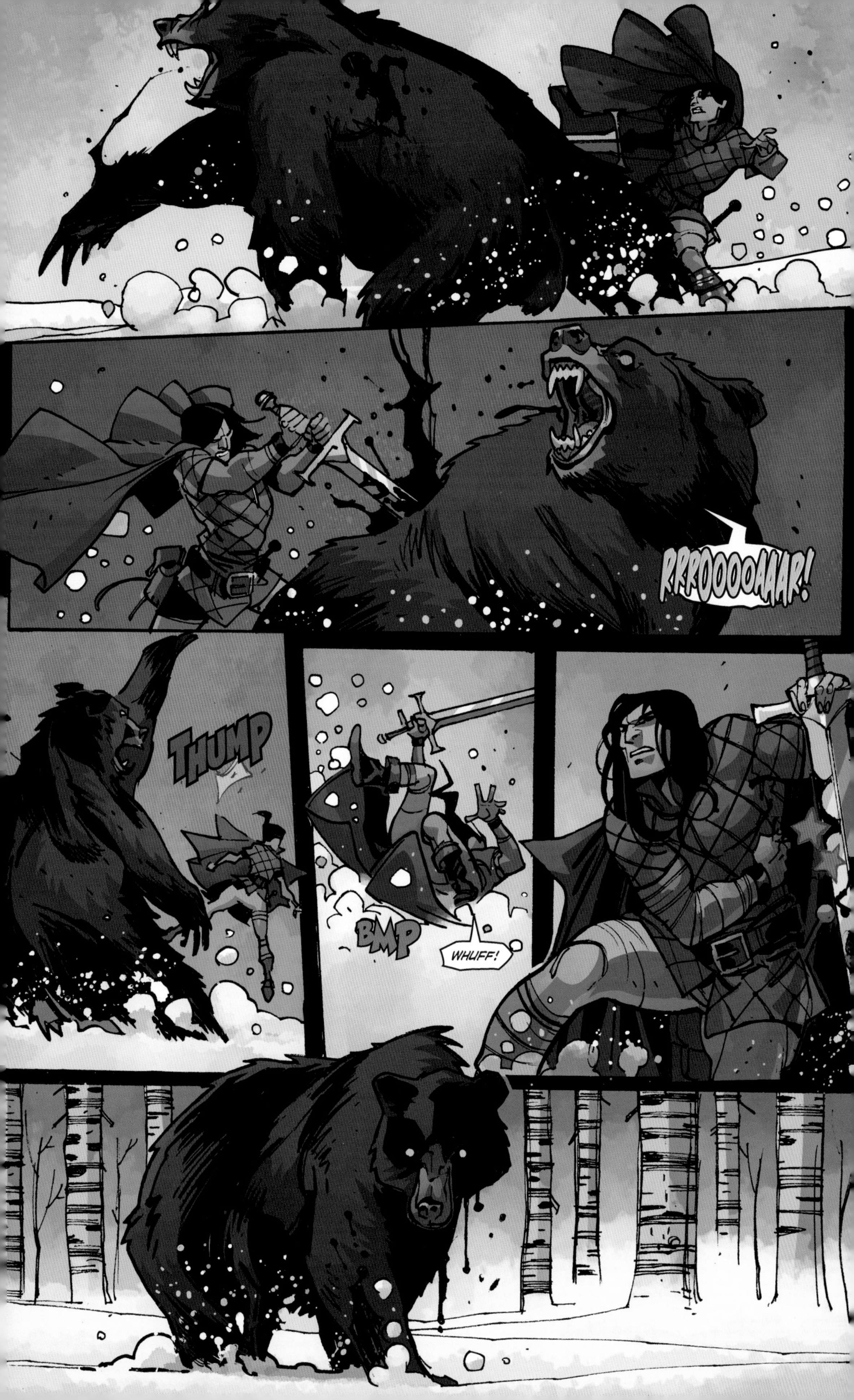
RRROOOOAAAR!
THUMP
BMP
WHUFF!

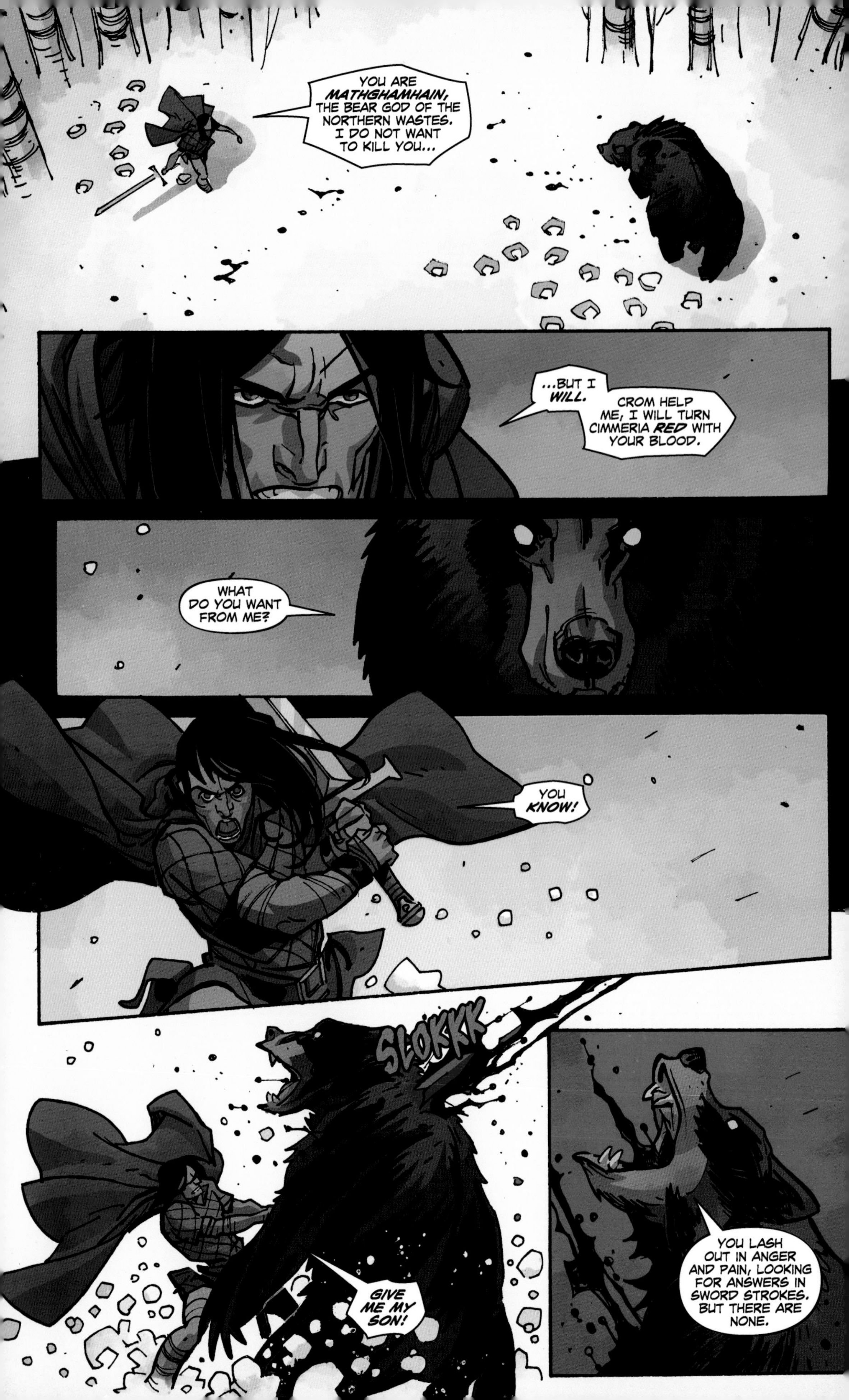
YOU ARE MATHGHAMHAIN, THE BEAR GOD OF THE NORTHERN WASTES. I DO NOT WANT TO KILL YOU...
...BUT I WILL.
CROM HELP ME, I WILL TURN CIMMERIA RED WITH YOUR BLOOD.
WHAT DO YOU WANT FROM ME?
YOU KNOW!
SLOKKK
GIVE ME MY SON!
YOU LASH OUT IN ANGER AND PAIN, LOOKING FOR ANSWERS IN SWORD STROKES. BUT THERE ARE NONE.

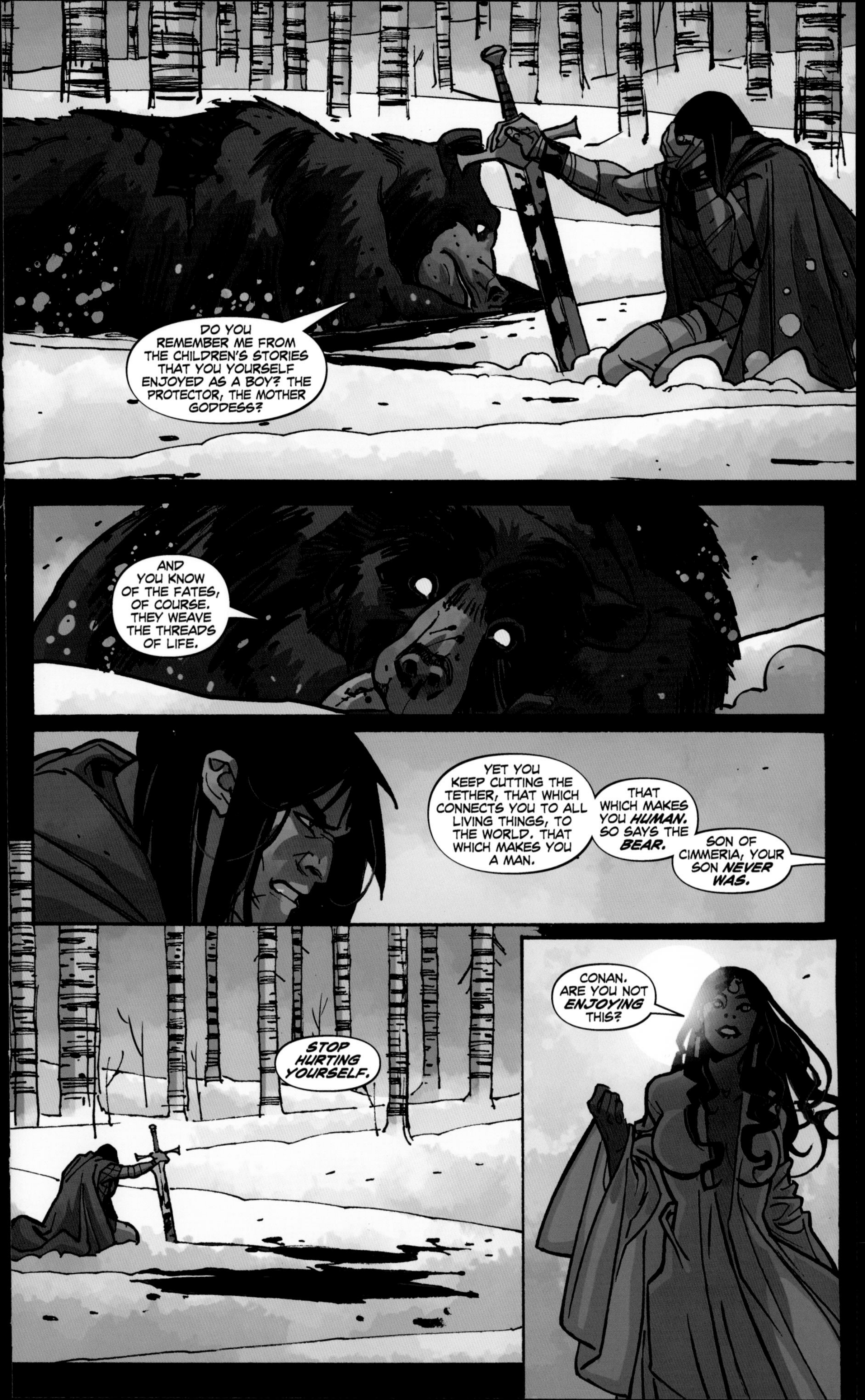
DO YOU REMEMBER ME FROM THE CHILDREN'S STORIES THAT YOU YOURSELF ENJOYED AS A BOY? THE PROTECTOR, THE MOTHER GODDESS?
AND YOU KNOW OF THE FATES, OF COURSE. THEY WEAVE THE THREADS OF LIFE.
YET YOU KEEP CUTTING THE TETHER, THAT WHICH CONNECTS YOU TO ALL LIVING THINGS, TO THE WORLD. THAT WHICH MAKES YOU A MAN.
THAT WHICH MAKES YOU *HUMAN.* SO SAYS THE *BEAR.*
SON OF CIMMERIA, YOUR SON *NEVER WAS.*
STOP HURTING YOURSELF.
CONAN. ARE YOU NOT *ENJOYING* THIS?

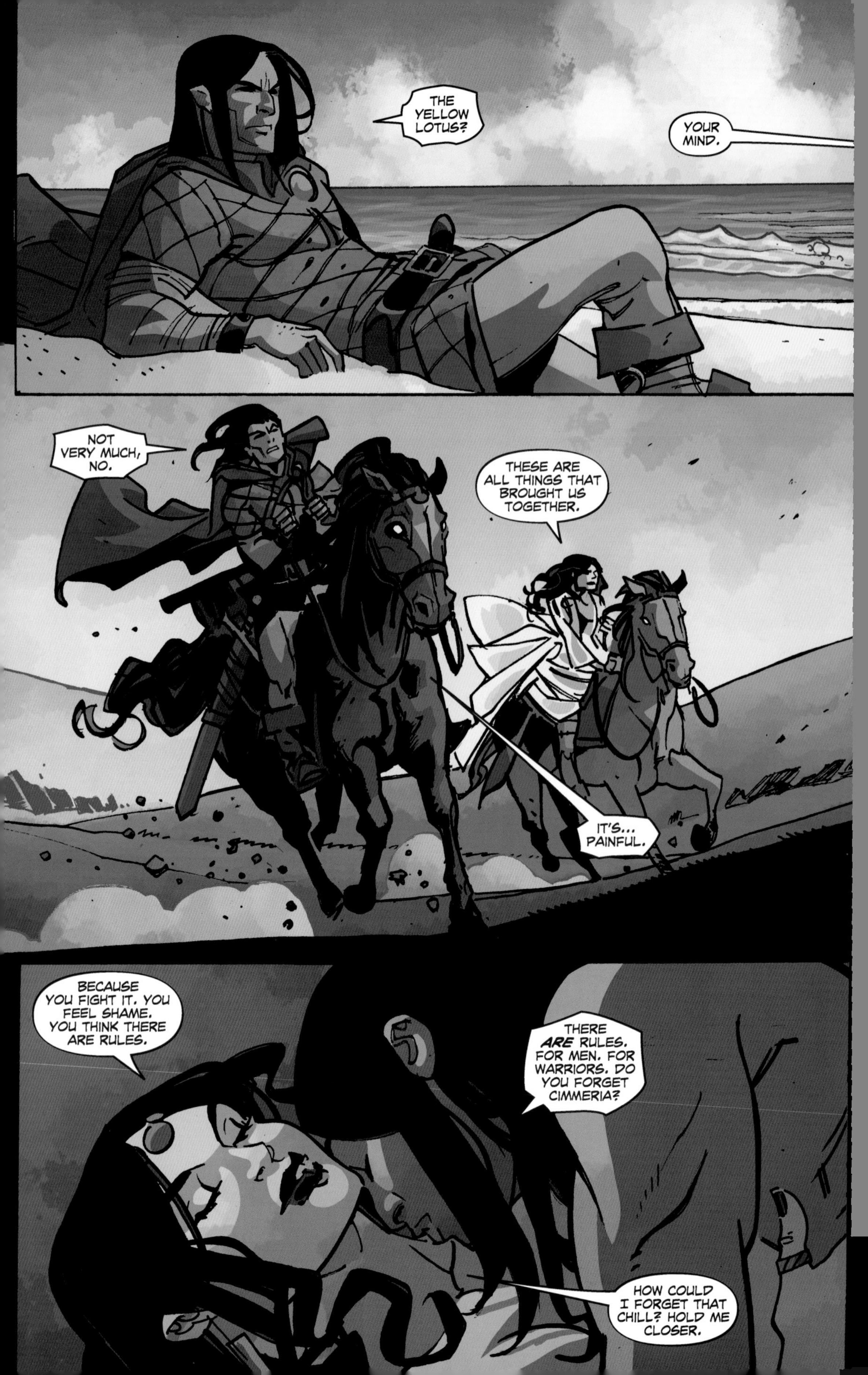
THE YELLOW LOTUS?
YOUR MIND.
NOT VERY MUCH, NO.
THESE ARE ALL THINGS THAT BROUGHT US TOGETHER.
IT'S... PAINFUL.
BECAUSE YOU FIGHT IT. YOU FEEL SHAME. YOU THINK THERE ARE RULES.
THERE *ARE* RULES. FOR MEN. FOR WARRIORS. DO YOU FORGET CIMMERIA?
HOW COULD I FORGET THAT CHILL? HOLD ME CLOSER.

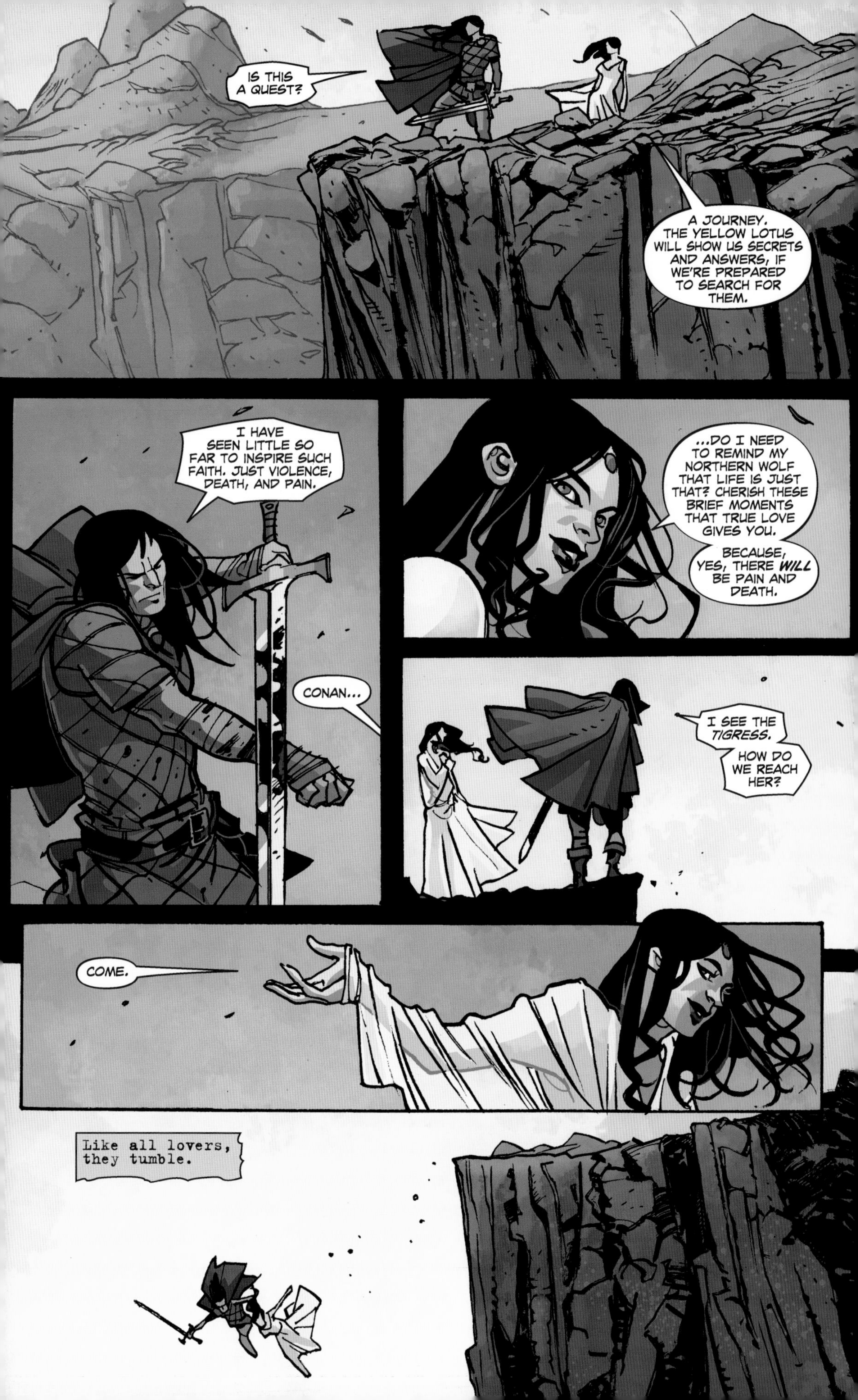
IS THIS A QUEST?
A JOURNEY. THE YELLOW LOTUS WILL SHOW US SECRETS AND ANSWERS, IF WE'RE PREPARED TO SEARCH FOR THEM.
I HAVE SEEN LITTLE SO FAR TO INSPIRE SUCH FAITH. JUST VIOLENCE, DEATH, AND PAIN.
CONAN...
...DO I NEED TO REMIND MY NORTHERN WOLF THAT LIFE IS JUST THAT? CHERISH THESE BRIEF MOMENTS THAT TRUE LOVE GIVES YOU.
BECAUSE, YES, THERE *WILL* BE PAIN AND DEATH.
I SEE THE *TIGRESS.*
HOW DO WE REACH HER?
COME.
Like all lovers, they tumble.

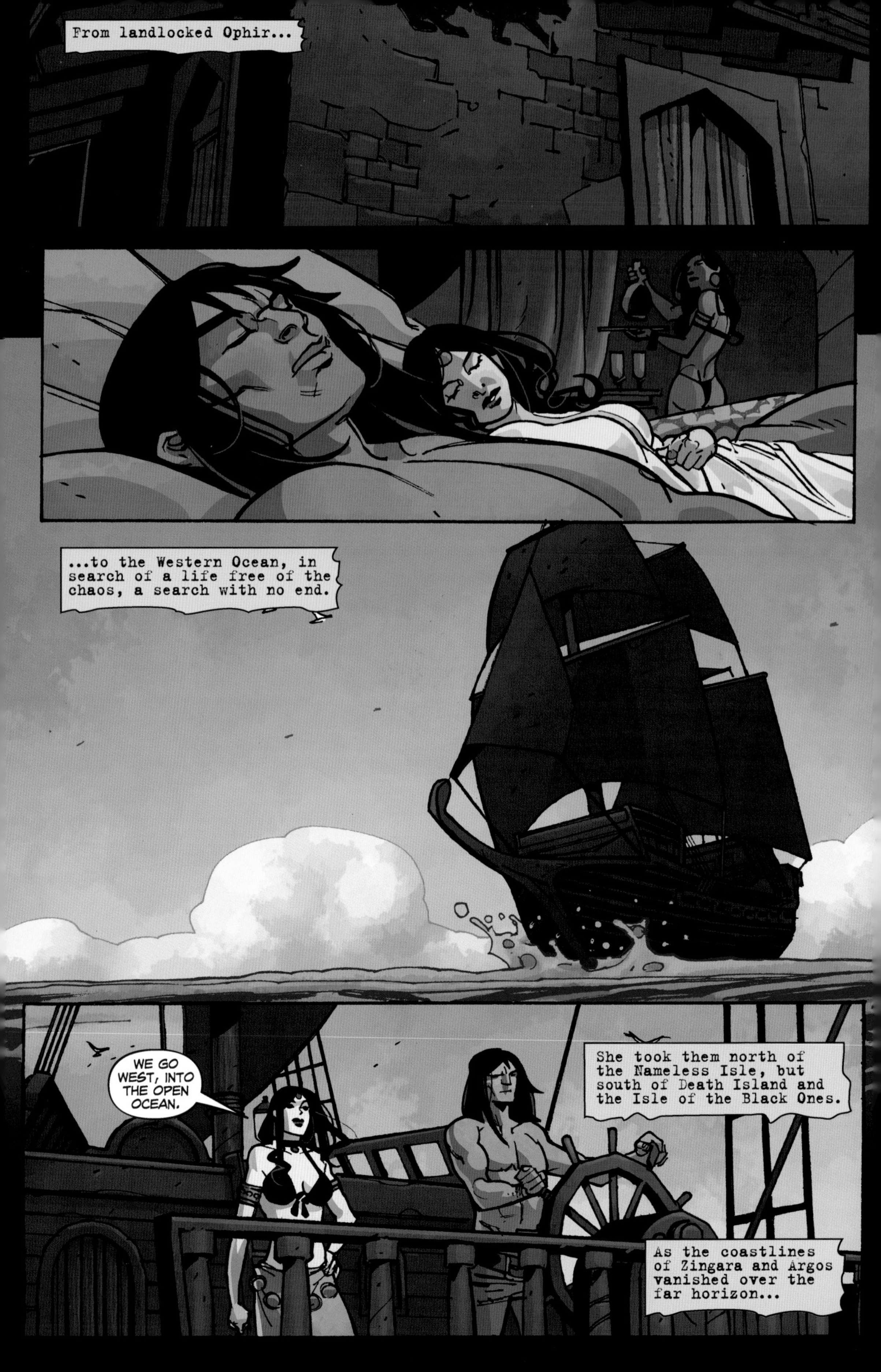

From landlocked Ophir...
...to the Western Ocean, in search of a life free of the chaos, a search with no end.
WE GO WEST, INTO THE OPEN OCEAN.
She took them north of the Nameless Isle, but south of Death Island and the Isle of the Black Ones.
As the coastlines of Zingara and Argos vanished over the far horizon...

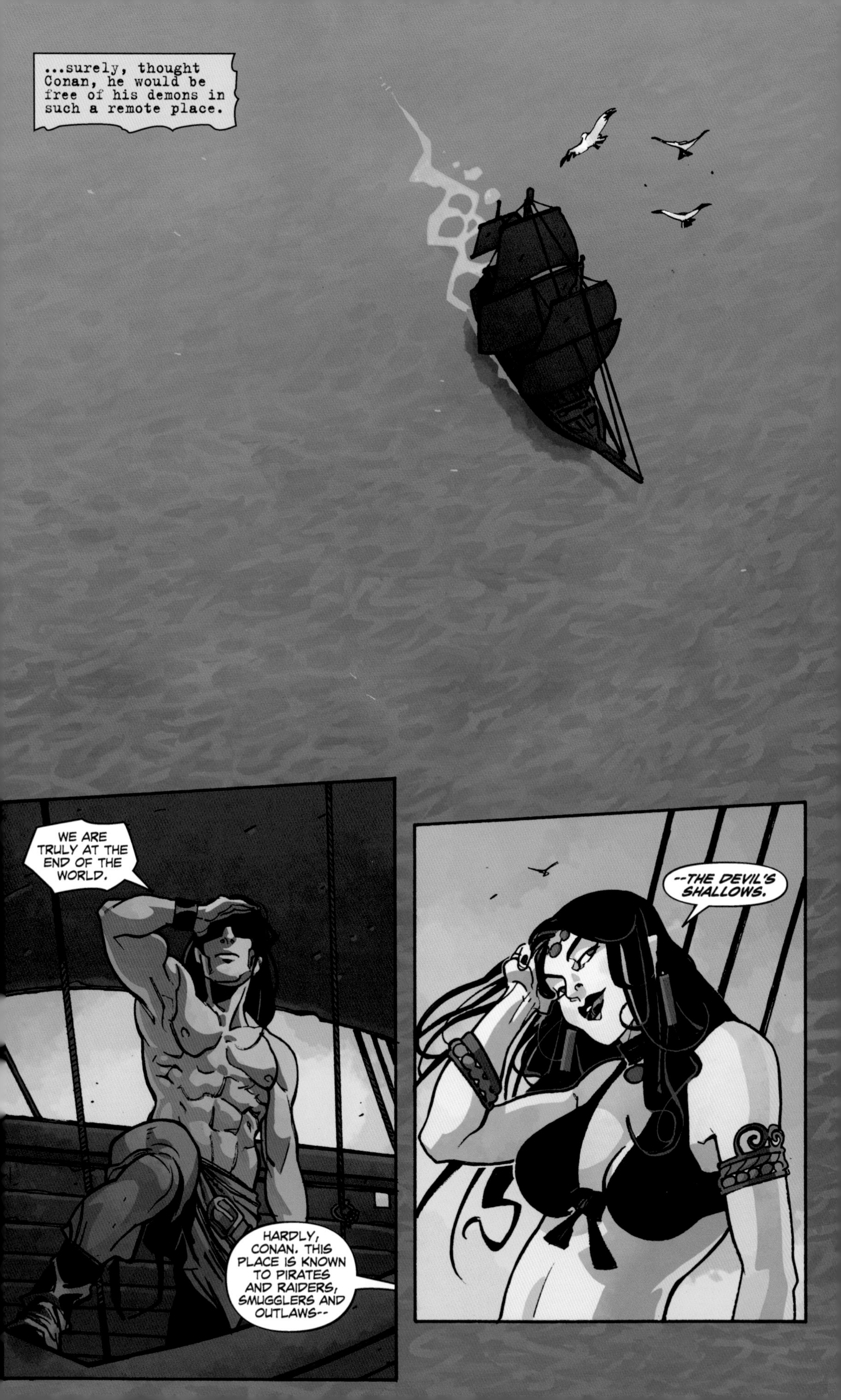
...surely, thought Conan, he would be free of his demons in such a remote place.
WE ARE TRULY AT THE END OF THE WORLD.
HARDLY, CONAN. THIS PLACE IS KNOWN TO PIRATES AND RAIDERS, SMUGGLERS AND OUTLAWS--
--THE DEVIL'S SHALLOWS.

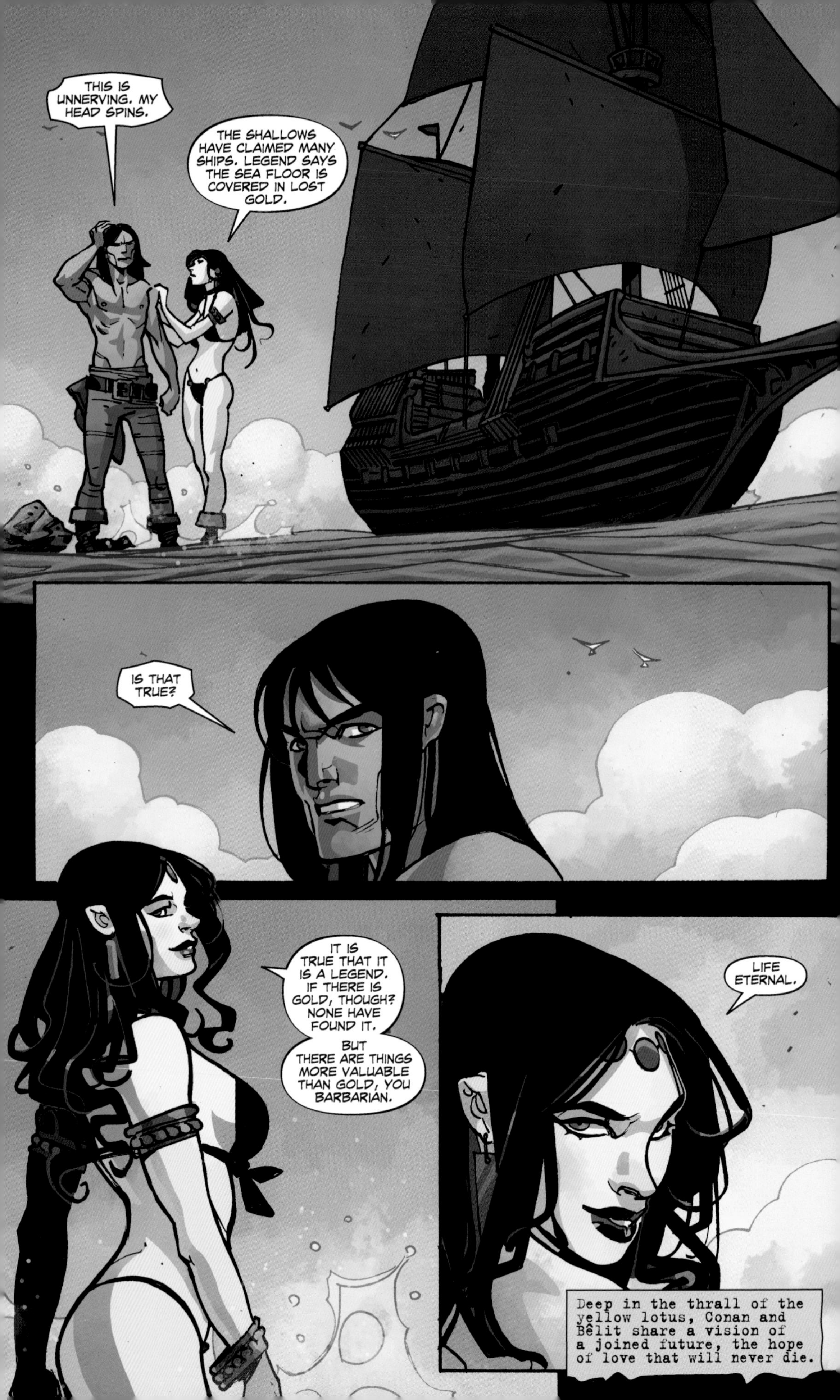
THIS IS UNNERVING. MY HEAD SPINS.
THE SHALLOWS HAVE CLAIMED MANY SHIPS. LEGEND SAYS THE SEA FLOOR IS COVERED IN LOST GOLD.
IS THAT TRUE?
IT IS TRUE THAT IT IS A LEGEND. IF THERE IS GOLD, THOUGH? NONE HAVE FOUND IT.
BUT THERE ARE THINGS MORE VALUABLE THAN GOLD, YOU BARBARIAN.
LIFE ETERNAL.
Deep in the thrall of the yellow lotus, Conan and Bêlit share a vision of a joined future, the hope of love that will never die.

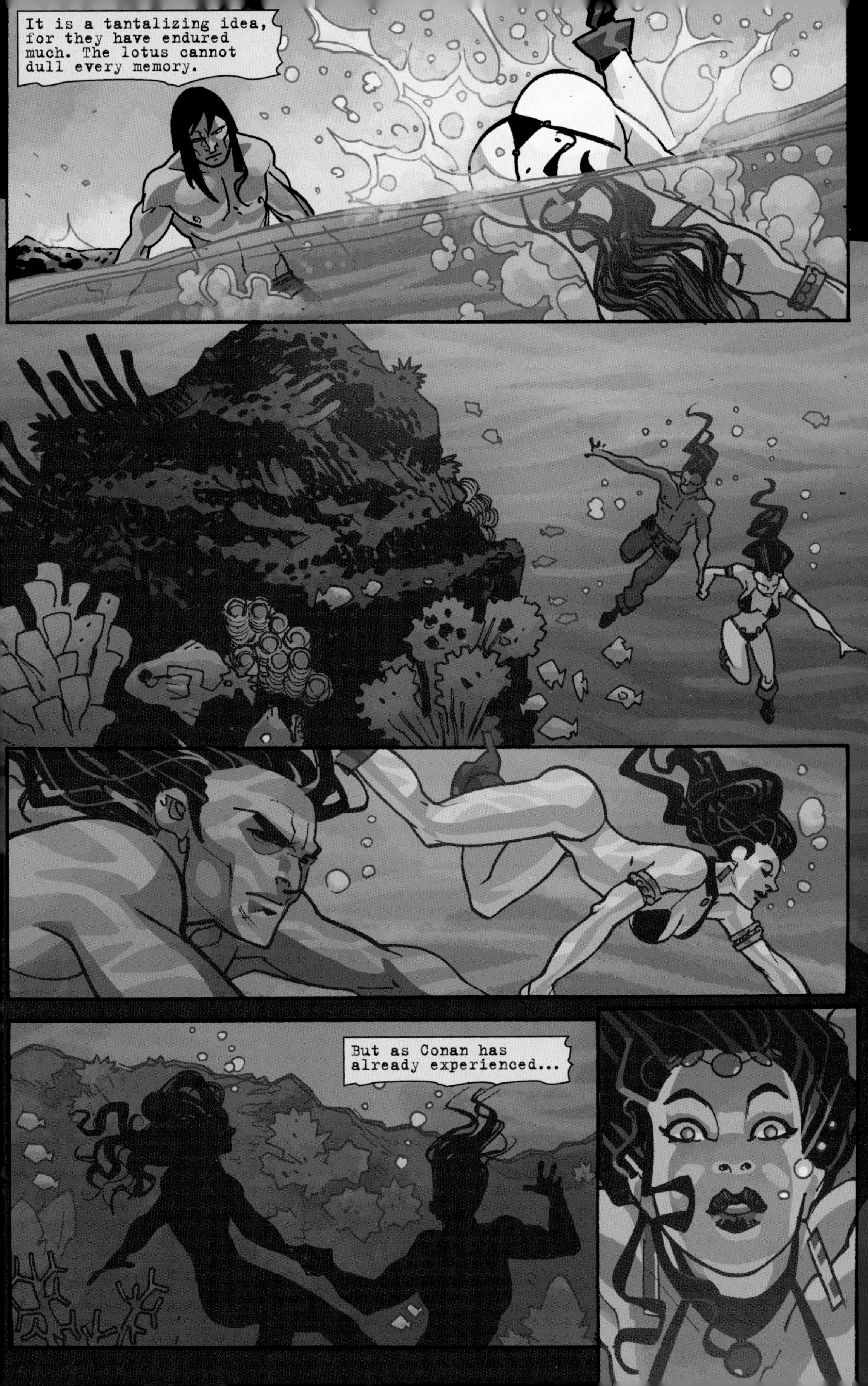
It is a tantalizing idea, for they have endured much. The lotus cannot dull every memory.
But as Conan has already experienced...

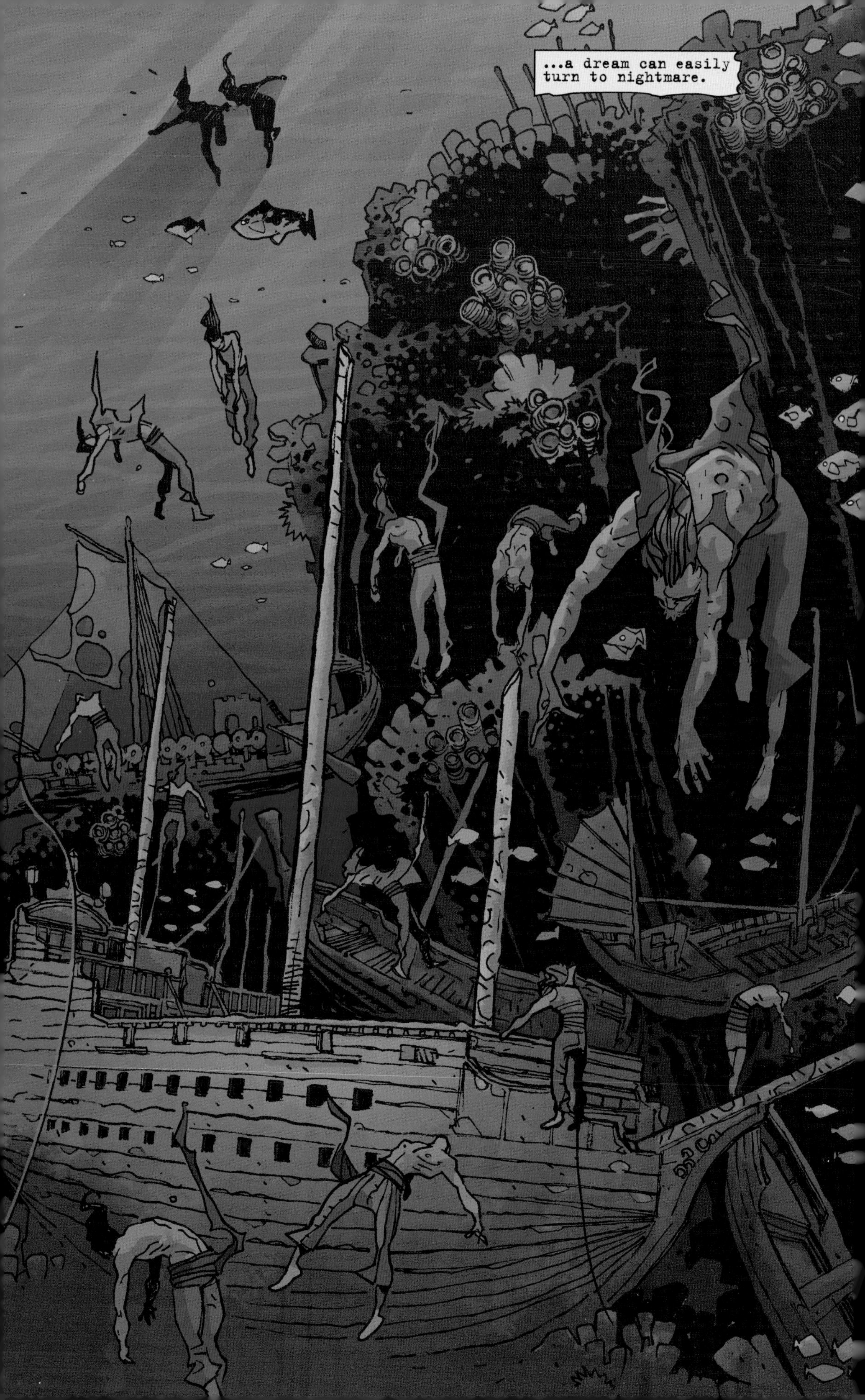
...a dream can easily turn to nightmare.

CHAPTER FIVE

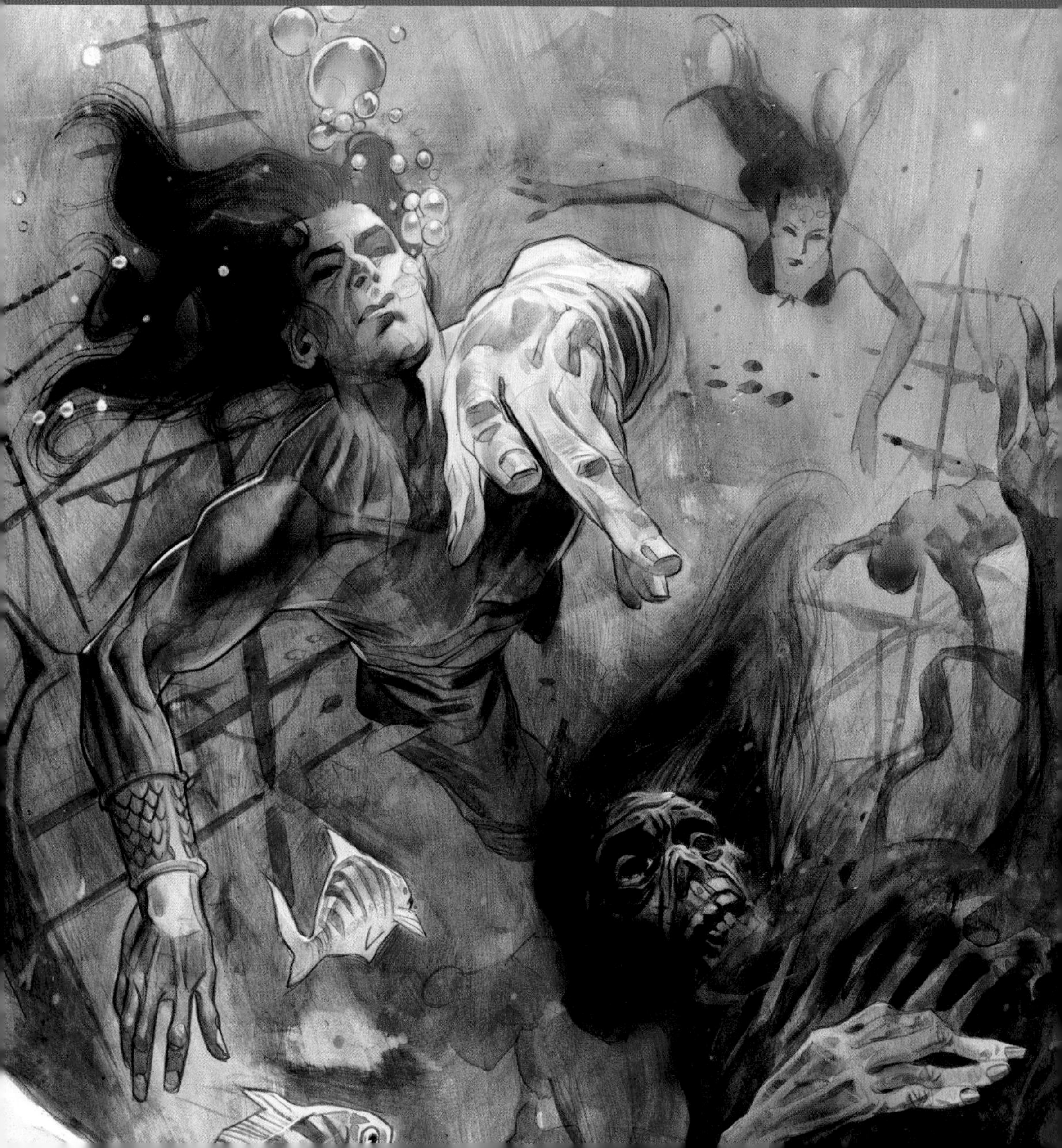

"I am your killer from the North, your wolf.
But up until now, I did only your bidding."

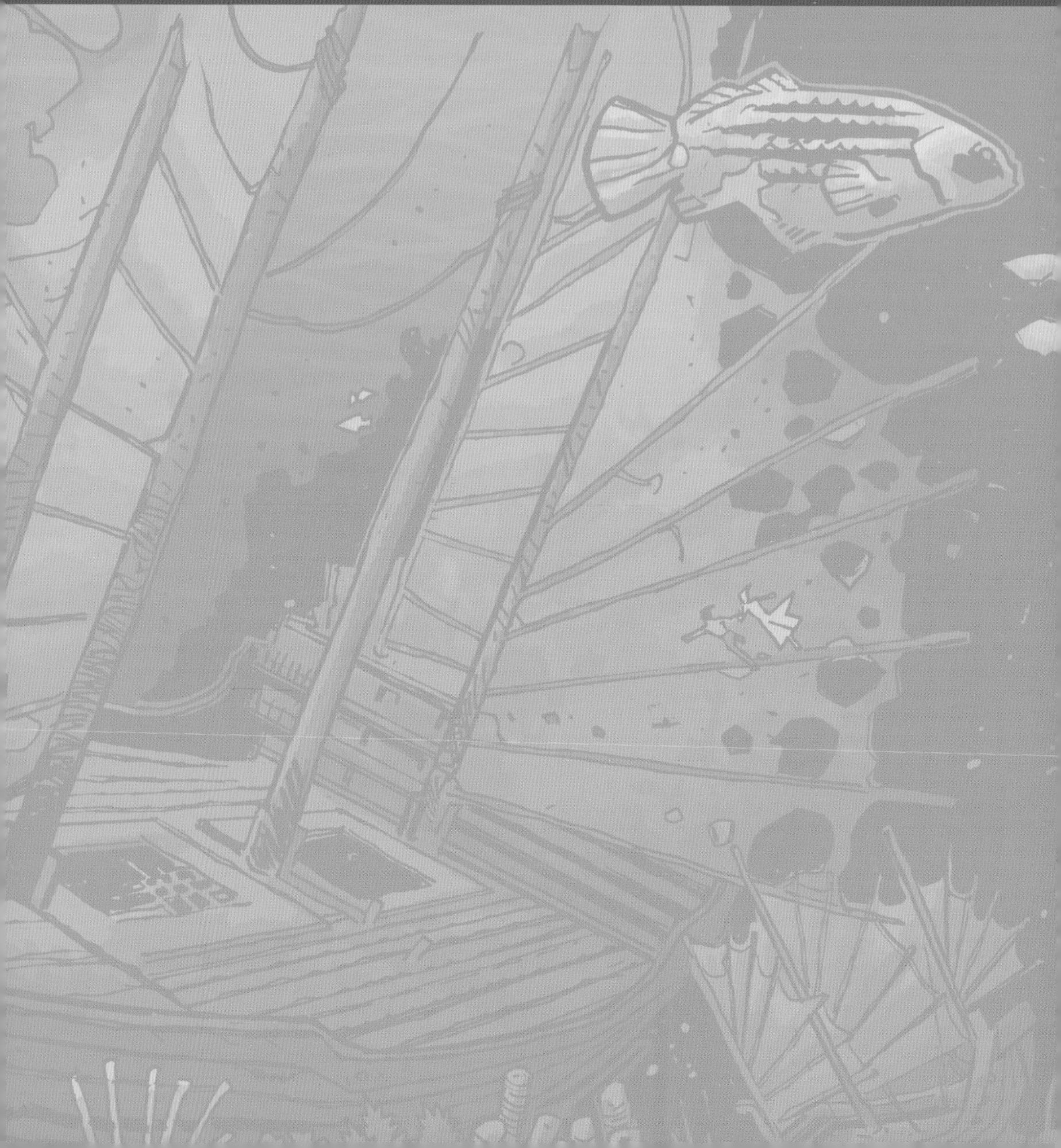

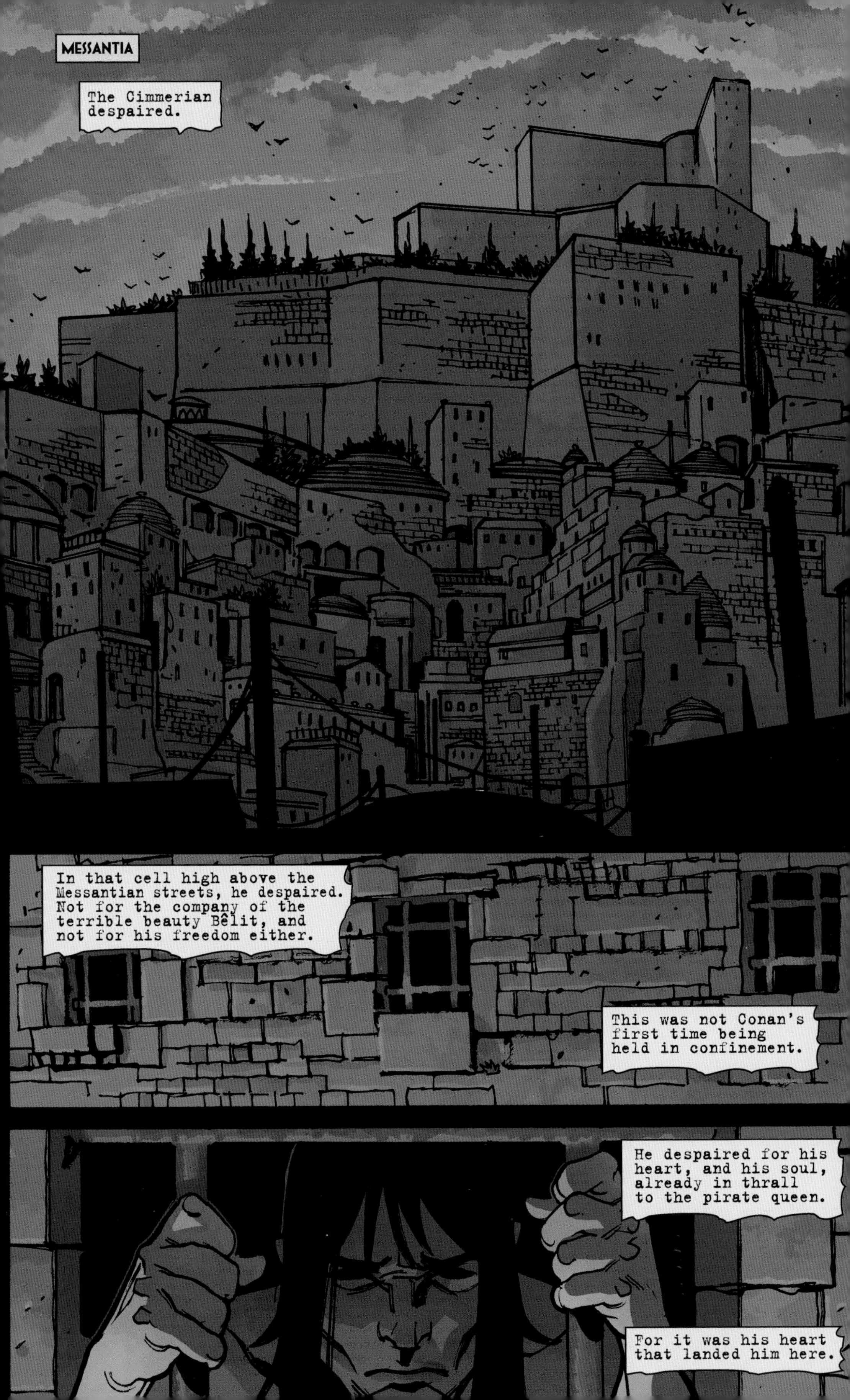
MESSANTIA
The Cimmerian despaired.
In that cell high above the Messantian streets, he despaired. Not for the company of the terrible beauty Bêlit, and not for his freedom either.
This was not Conan's first time being held in confinement.
He despaired for his heart, and his soul, already in thrall to the pirate queen.
For it was his heart that landed him here.

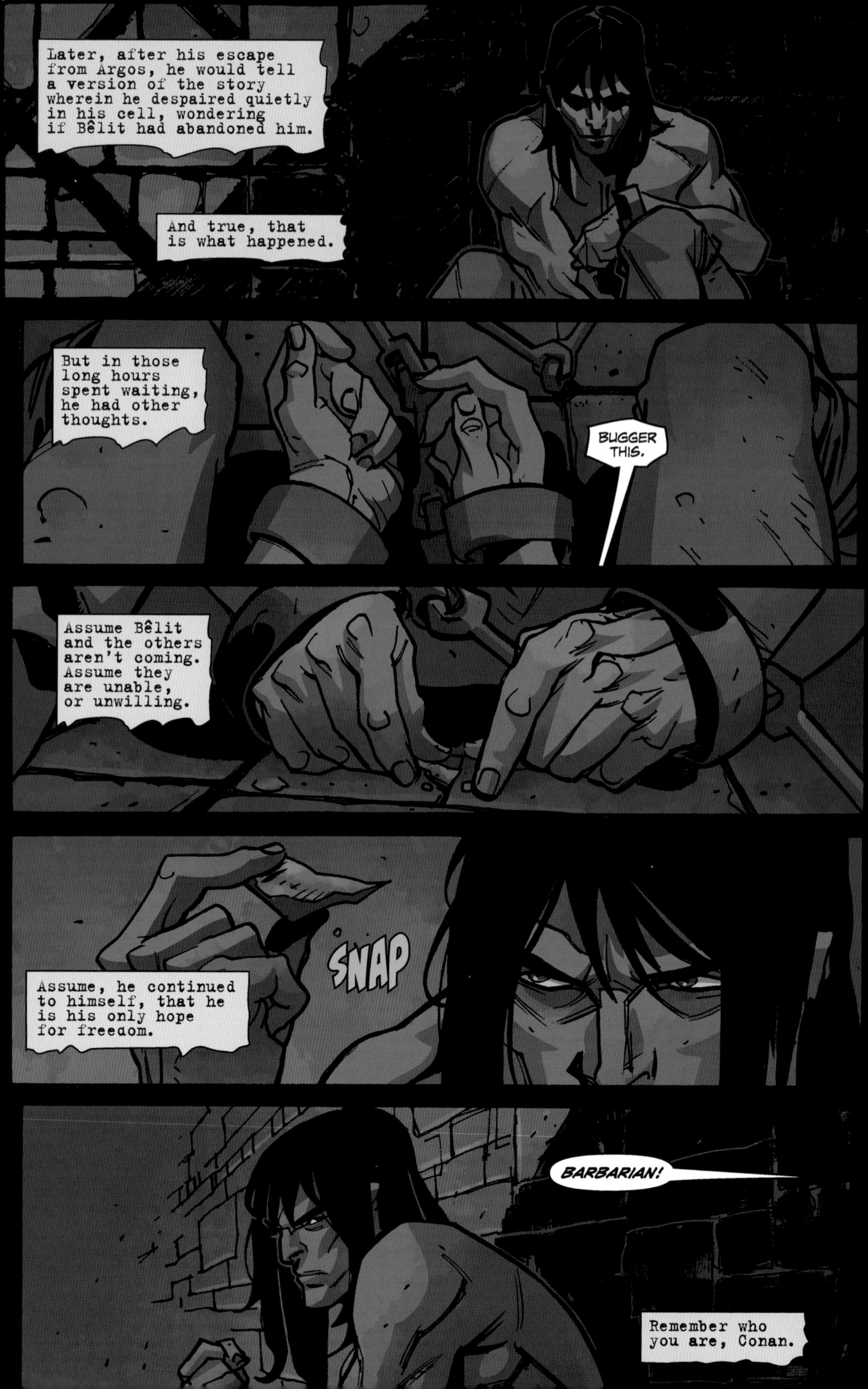

Later, after his escape from Argos, he would tell a version of the story wherein he despaired quietly in his cell, wondering if Bêlit had abandoned him.
And true, that is what happened.
But in those long hours spent waiting, he had other thoughts.
BUGGER THIS.
Assume Bêlit and the others aren't coming. Assume they are unable, or unwilling.
SNAP
Assume, he continued to himself, that he is his only hope for freedom.
BARBARIAN!
Remember who you are, Conan.

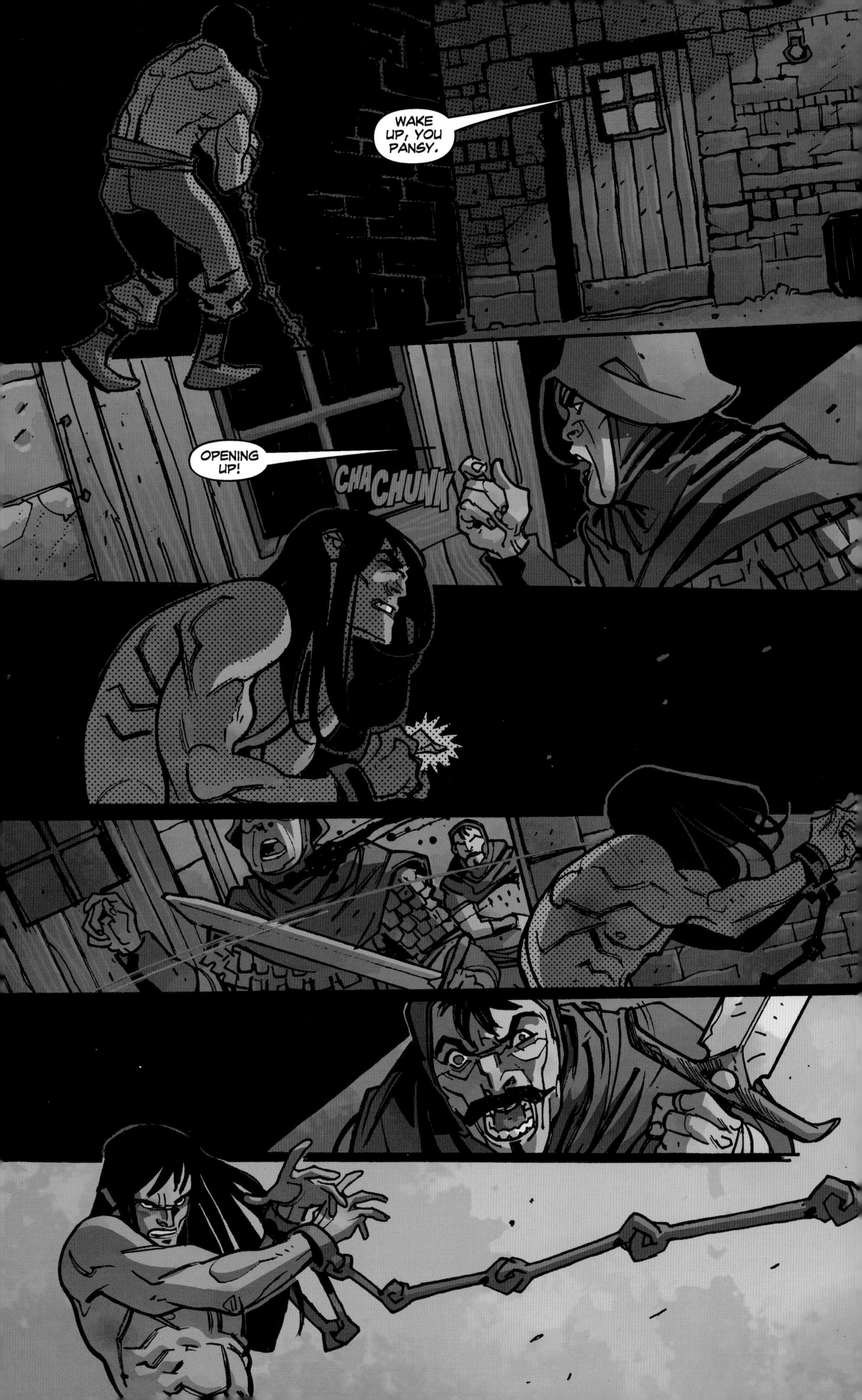
WAKE UP, YOU PANSY.
OPENING UP!
CHACHUNK

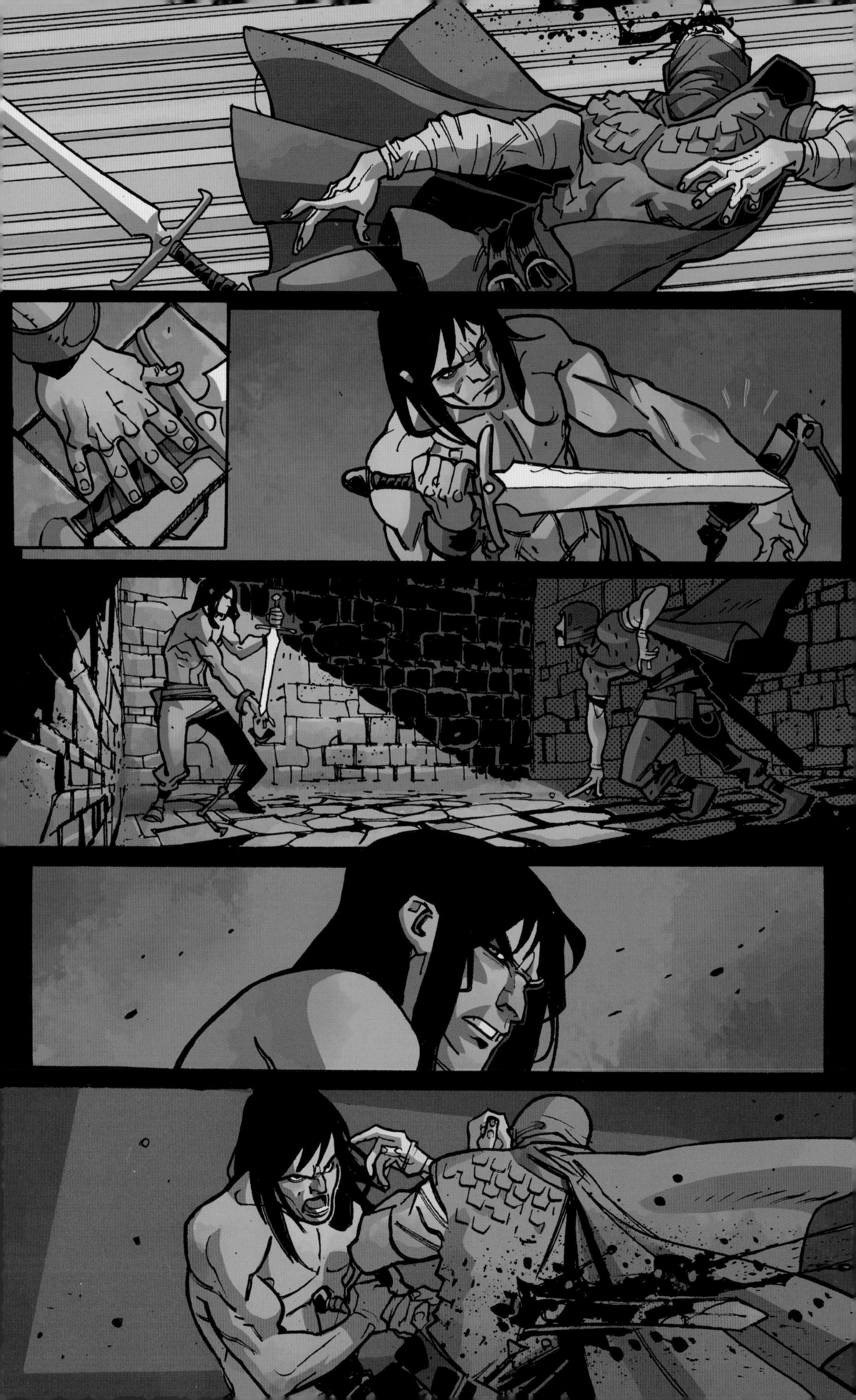

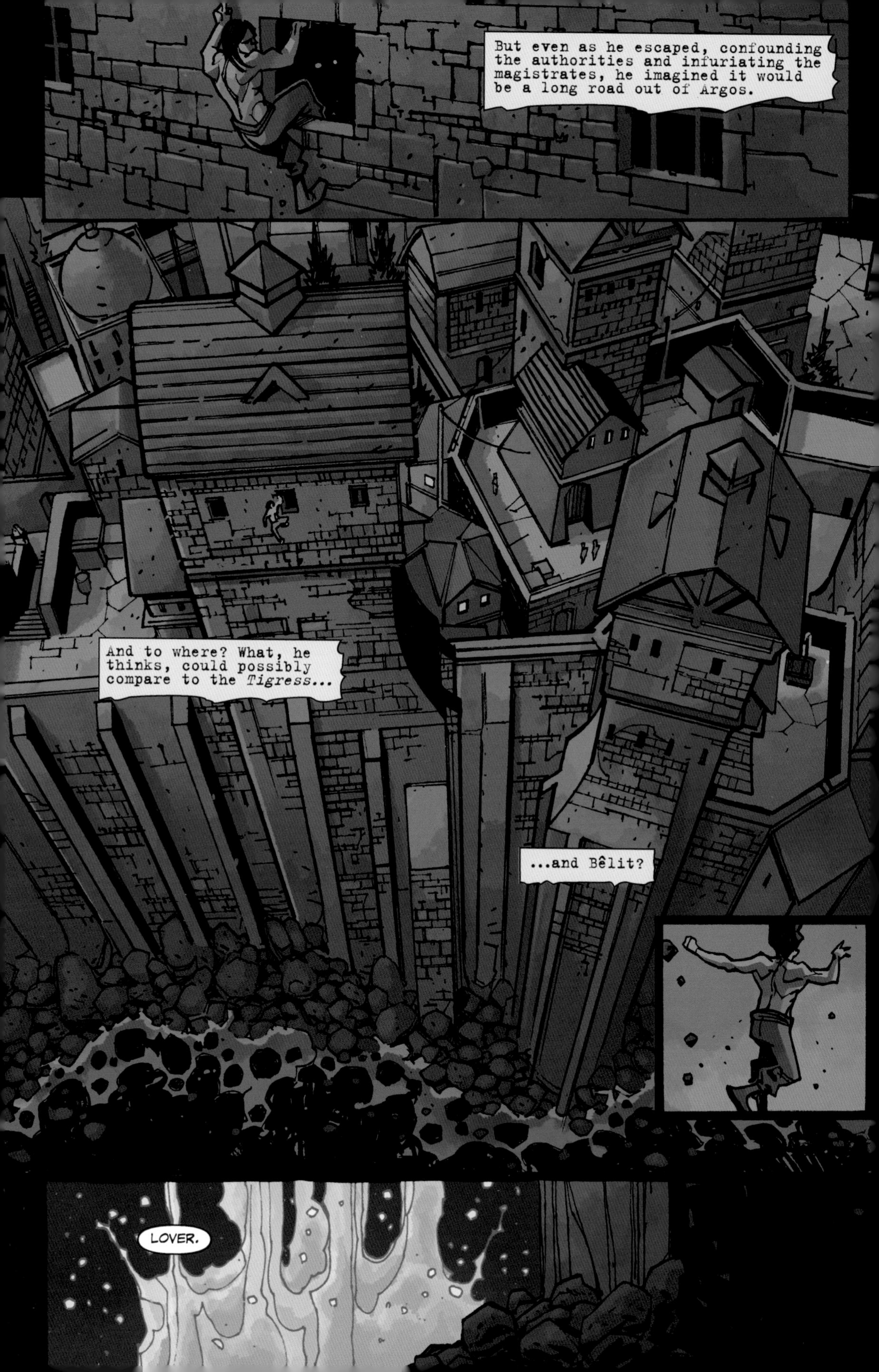
But even as he escaped, confounding the authorities and infuriating the magistrates, he imagined it would be a long road out of Argos.
And to where? What, he thinks, could possibly compare to the *Tigress*...
...and Bêlit?
LOVER.

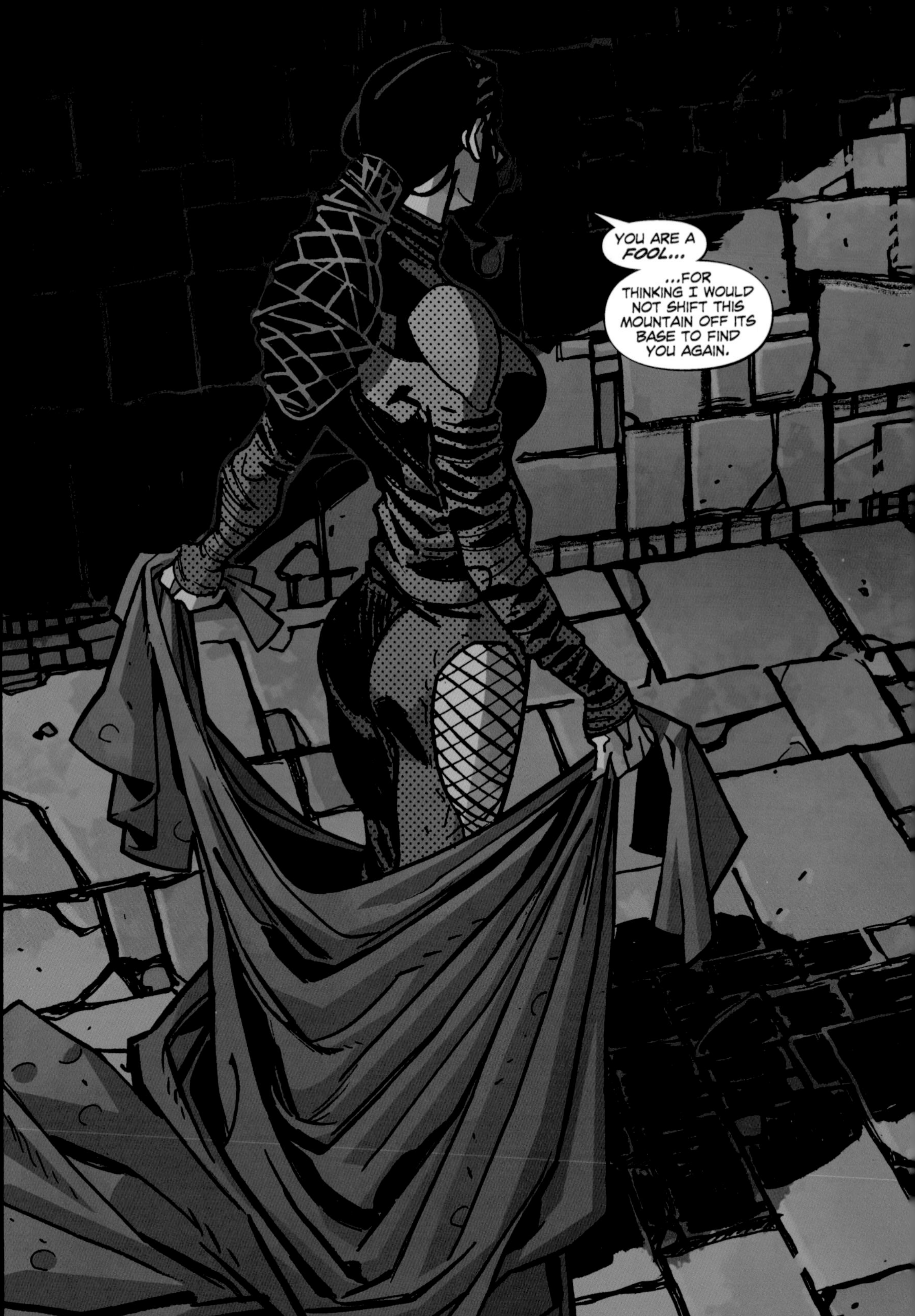
YOU ARE A FOOL...
...FOR THINKING I WOULD NOT SHIFT THIS MOUNTAIN OFF ITS BASE TO FIND YOU AGAIN.

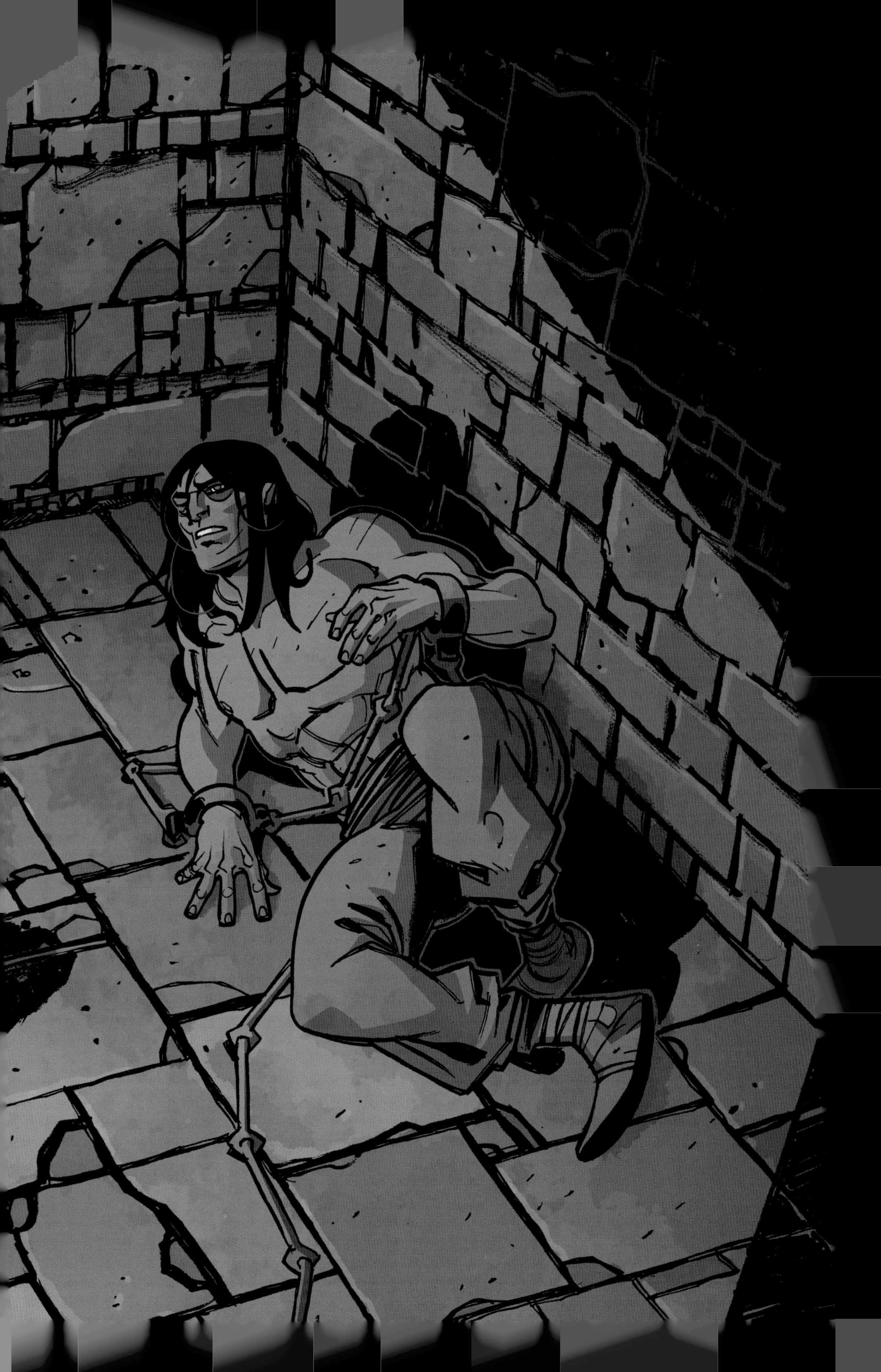

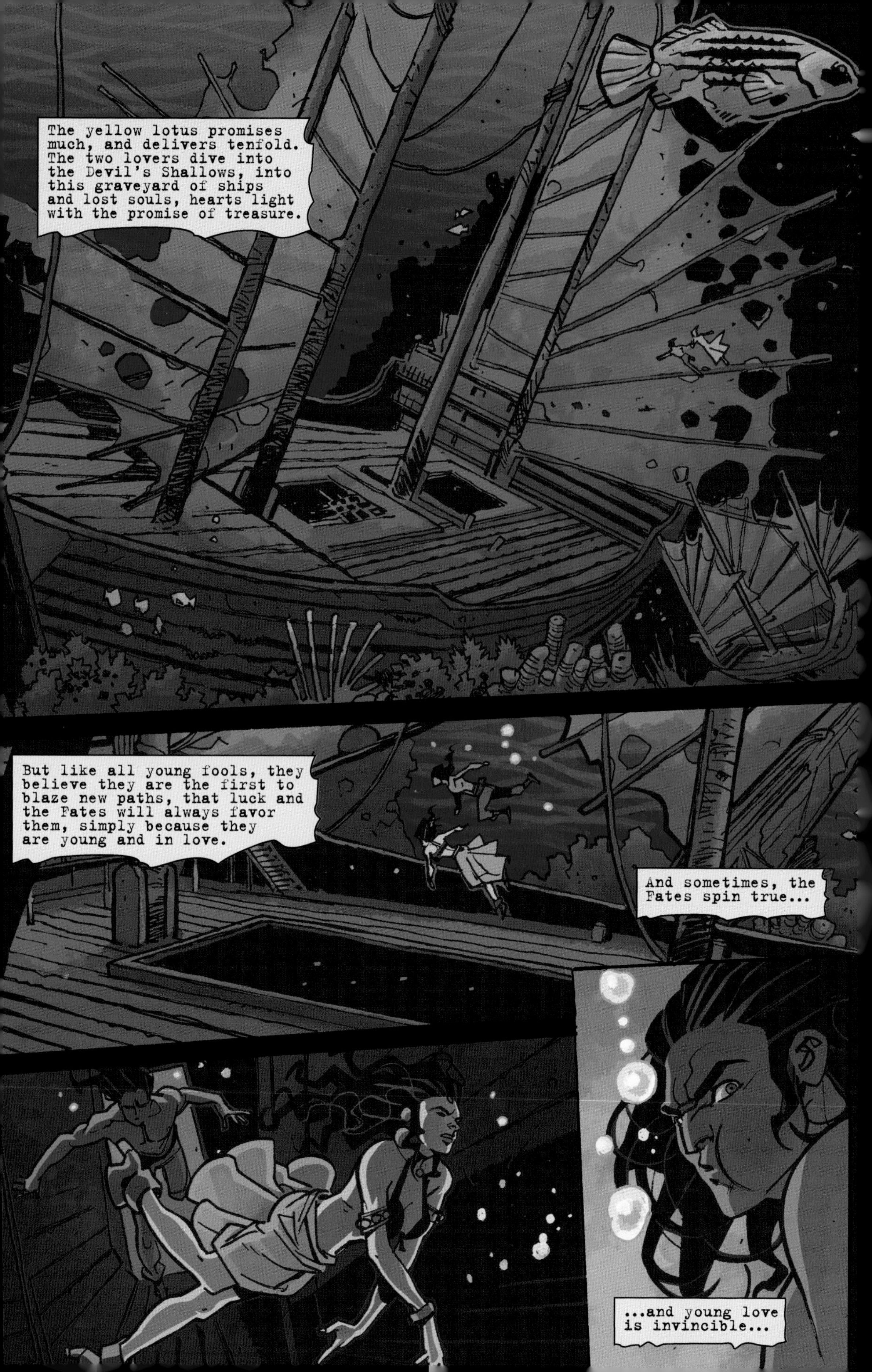
The yellow lotus promises much, and delivers tenfold. The two lovers dive into the Devil's Shallows, into this graveyard of ships and lost souls, hearts light with the promise of treasure.
But like all young fools, they believe they are the first to blaze new paths, that luck and the Fates will always favor them, simply because they are young and in love.
And sometimes, the Fates spin true...
...and young love is invincible...

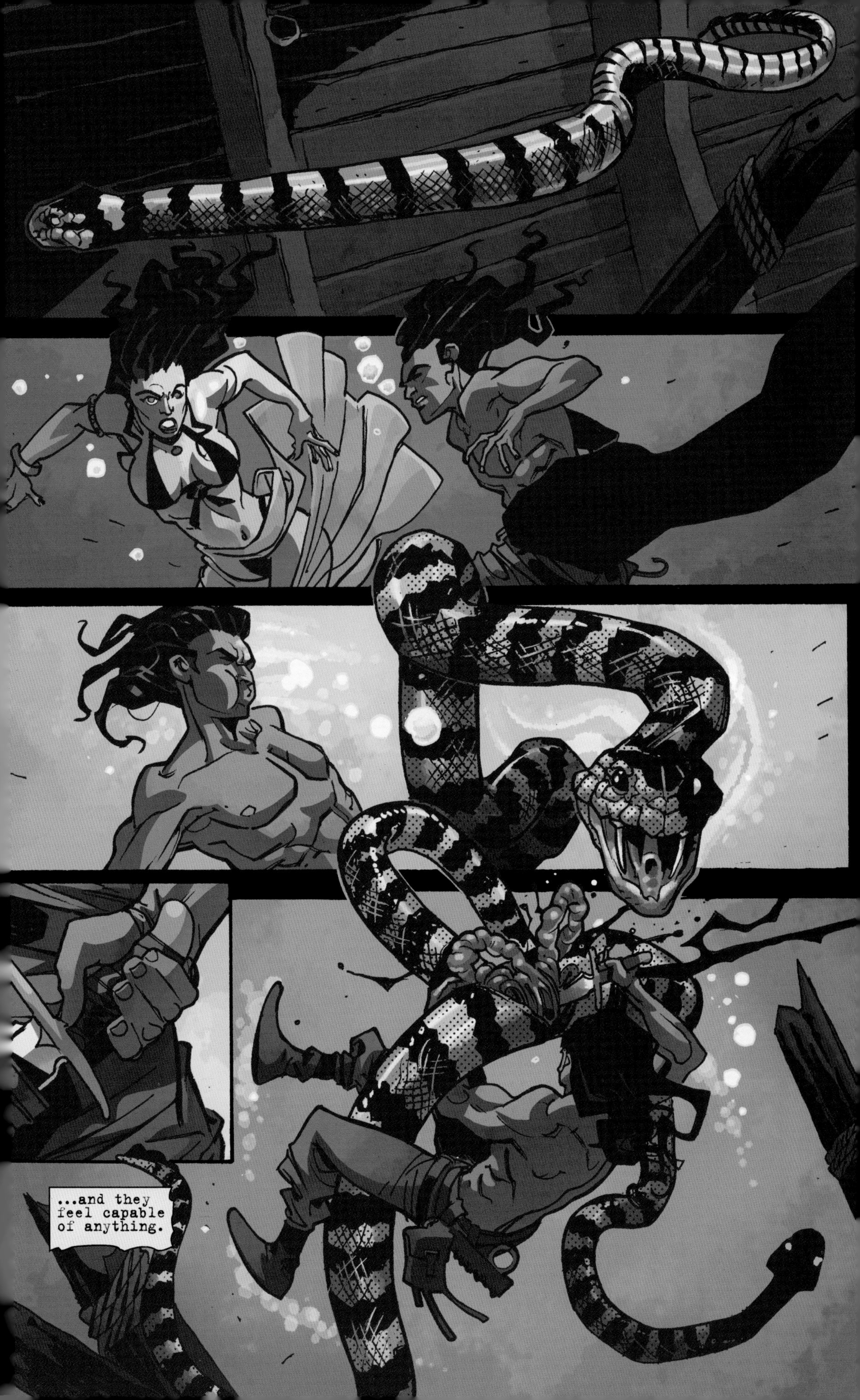
...and they feel capable of anything.

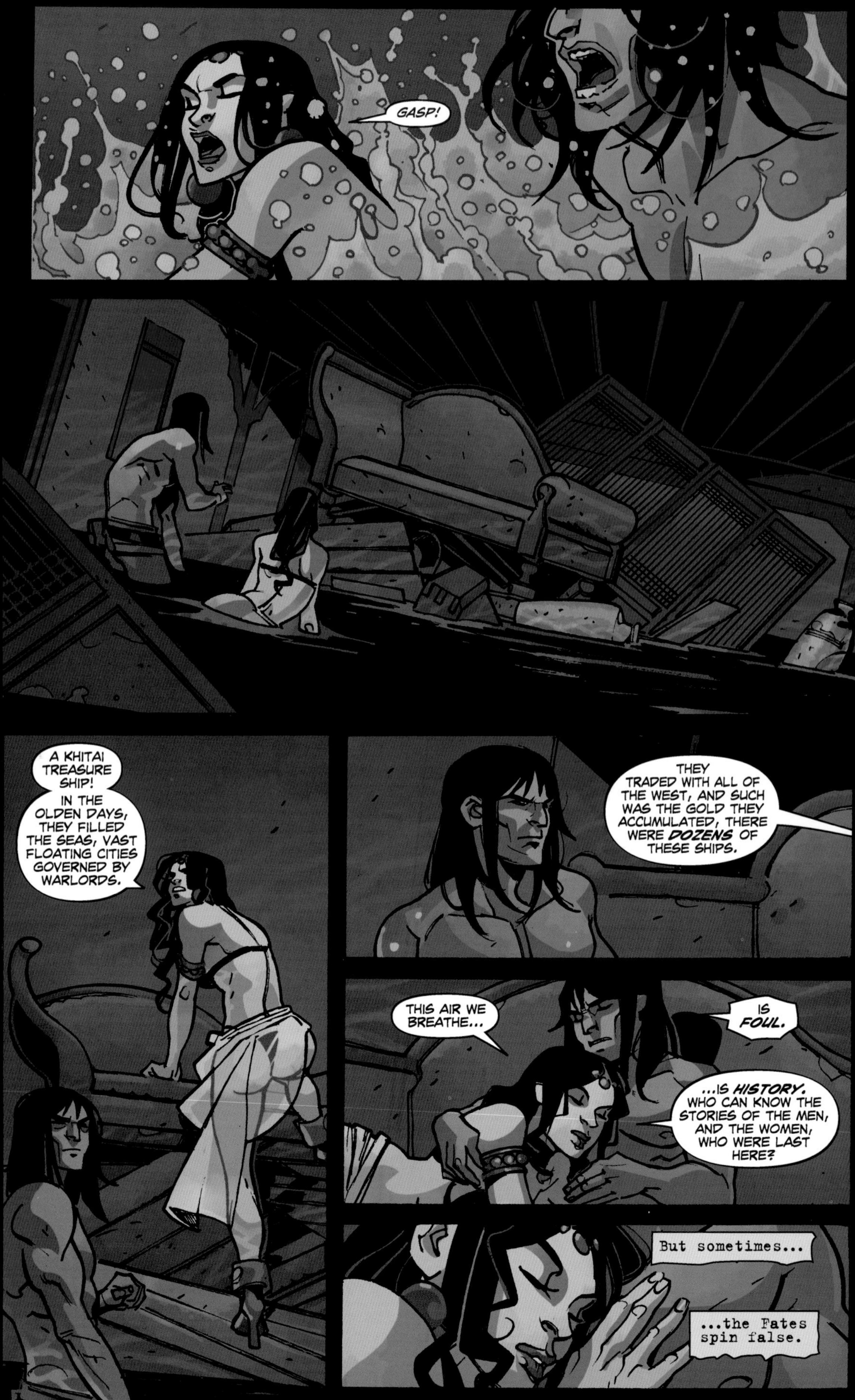
GASP!
A KHITAI TREASURE SHIP! IN THE OLDEN DAYS, THEY FILLED THE SEAS, VAST FLOATING CITIES GOVERNED BY WARLORDS.
THEY TRADED WITH ALL OF THE WEST, AND SUCH WAS THE GOLD THEY ACCUMULATED, THERE WERE DOZENS OF THESE SHIPS.
THIS AIR WE BREATHE...
IS FOUL.
...IS HISTORY. WHO CAN KNOW THE STORIES OF THE MEN, AND THE WOMEN, WHO WERE LAST HERE?
But sometimes...
...the Fates spin false.

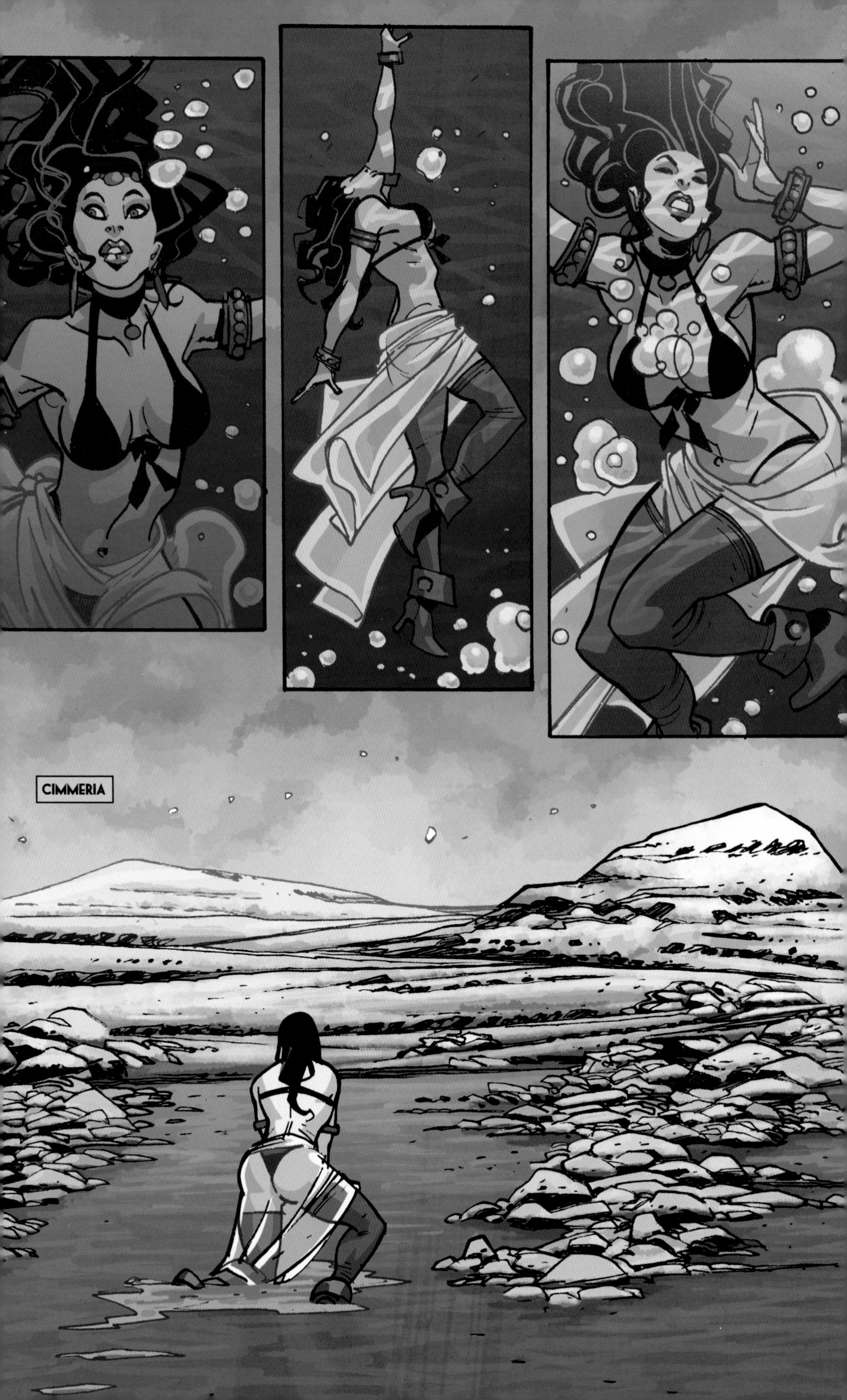
CIMMERIA

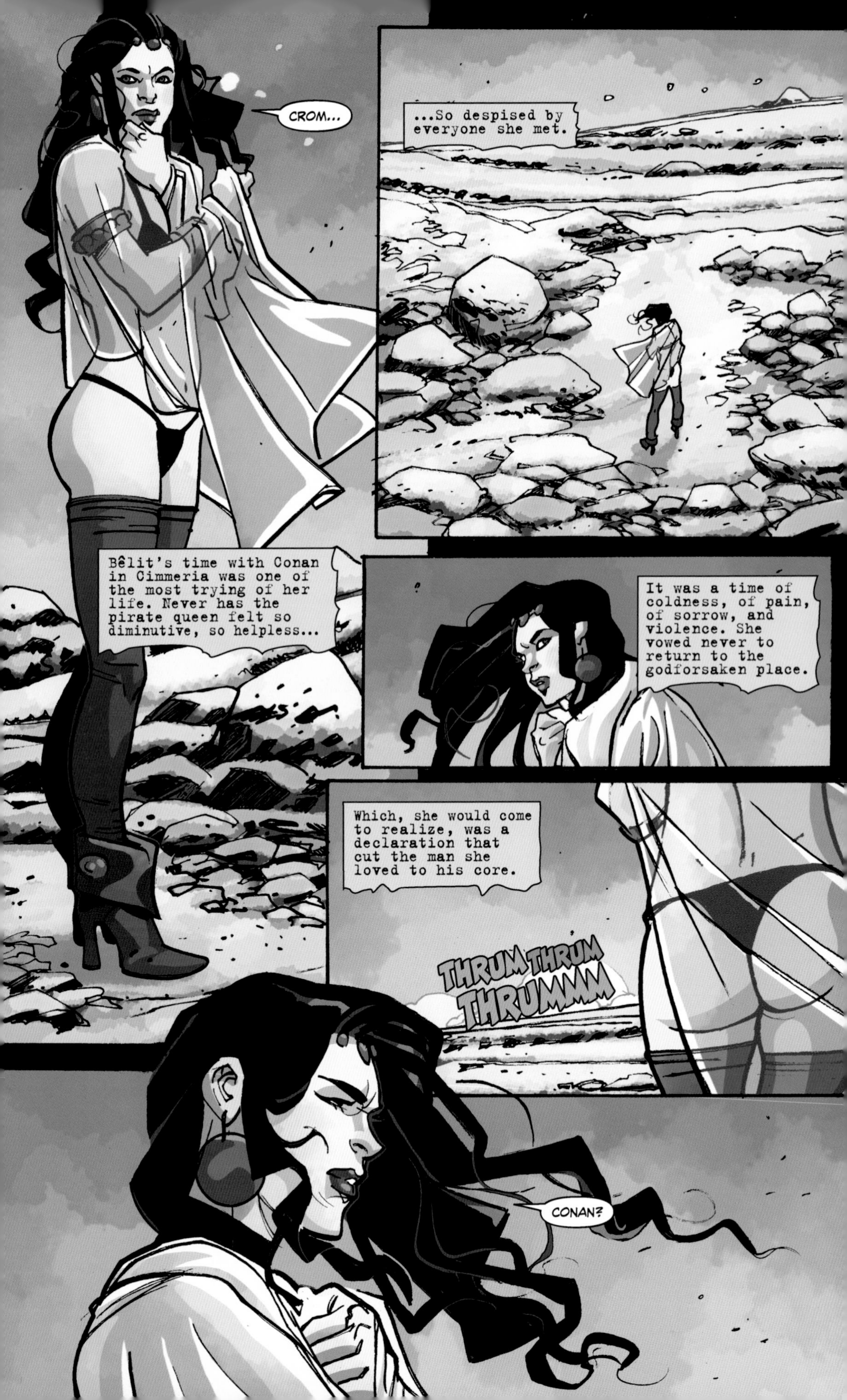
CROM...
...So despised by everyone she met.
Bêlit's time with Conan in Cimmeria was one of the most trying of her life. Never has the pirate queen felt so diminutive, so helpless...
It was a time of coldness, of pain, of sorrow, and violence. She vowed never to return to the godforsaken place.
Which, she would come to realize, was a declaration that cut the man she loved to his core.
THRUM THRUM THRUMMM
CONAN?

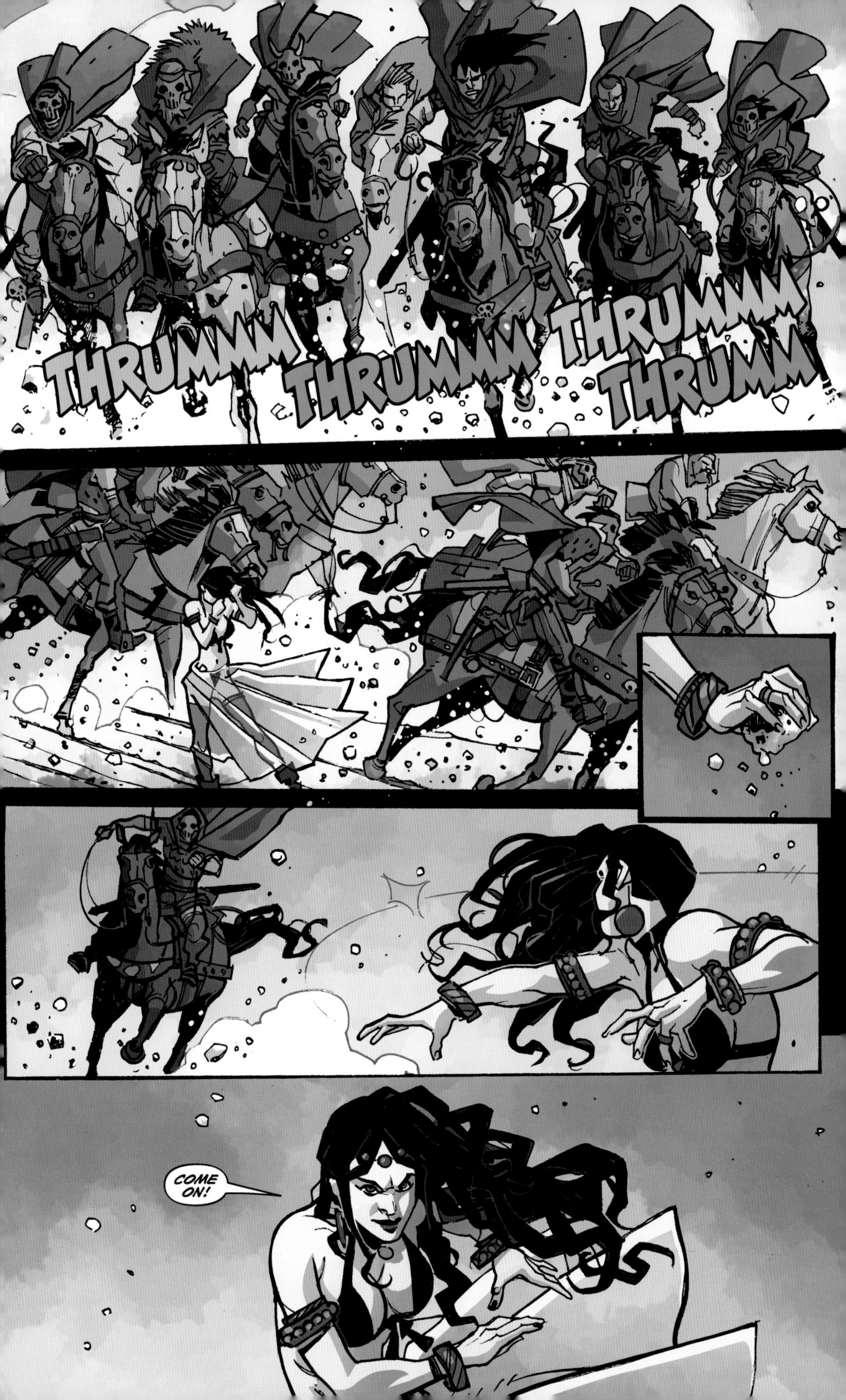
THRUMMM
THRUMMM
THRUMMM
THRUMM
COME ON!

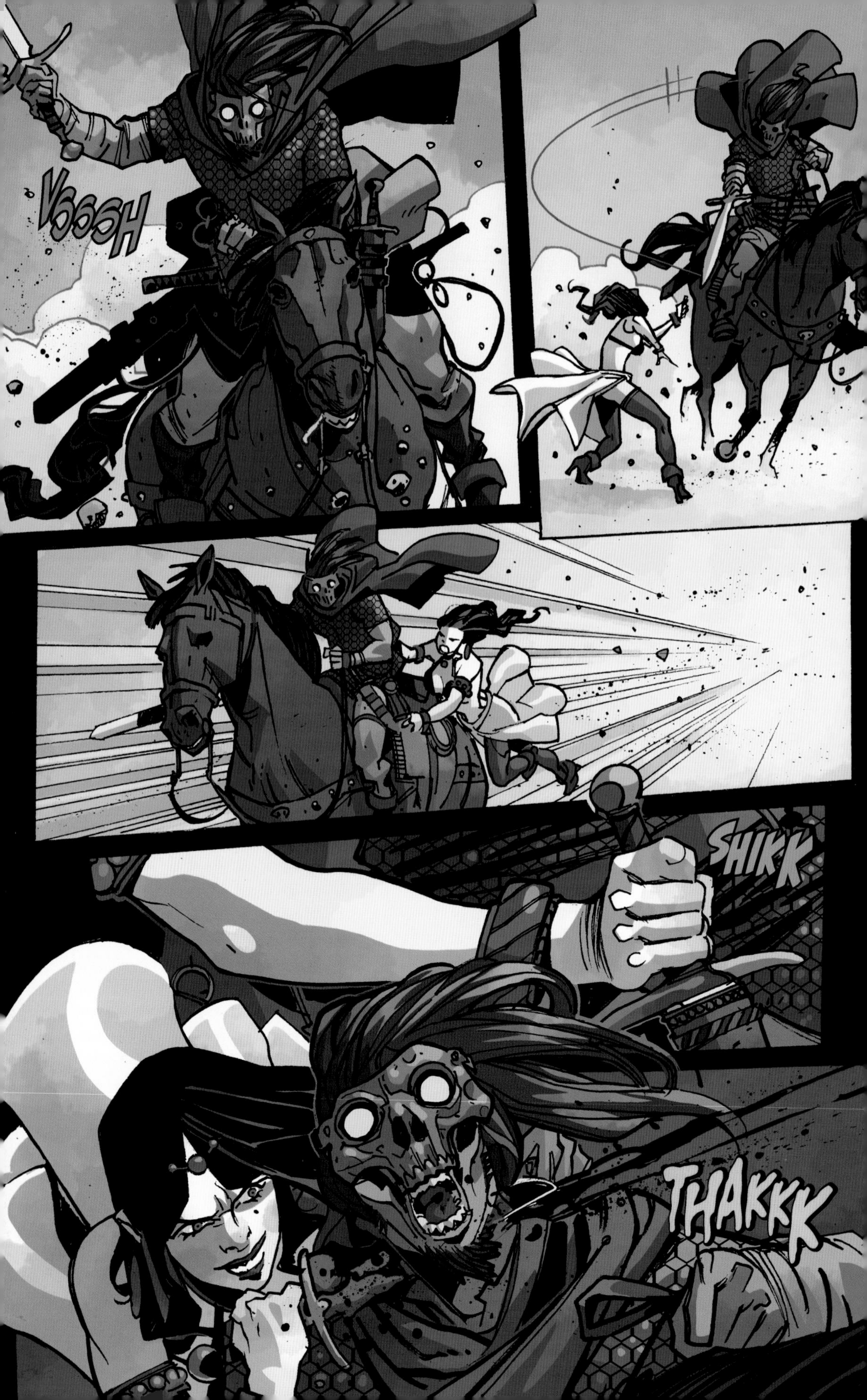
VOOSH
SHIKK
THAKKK

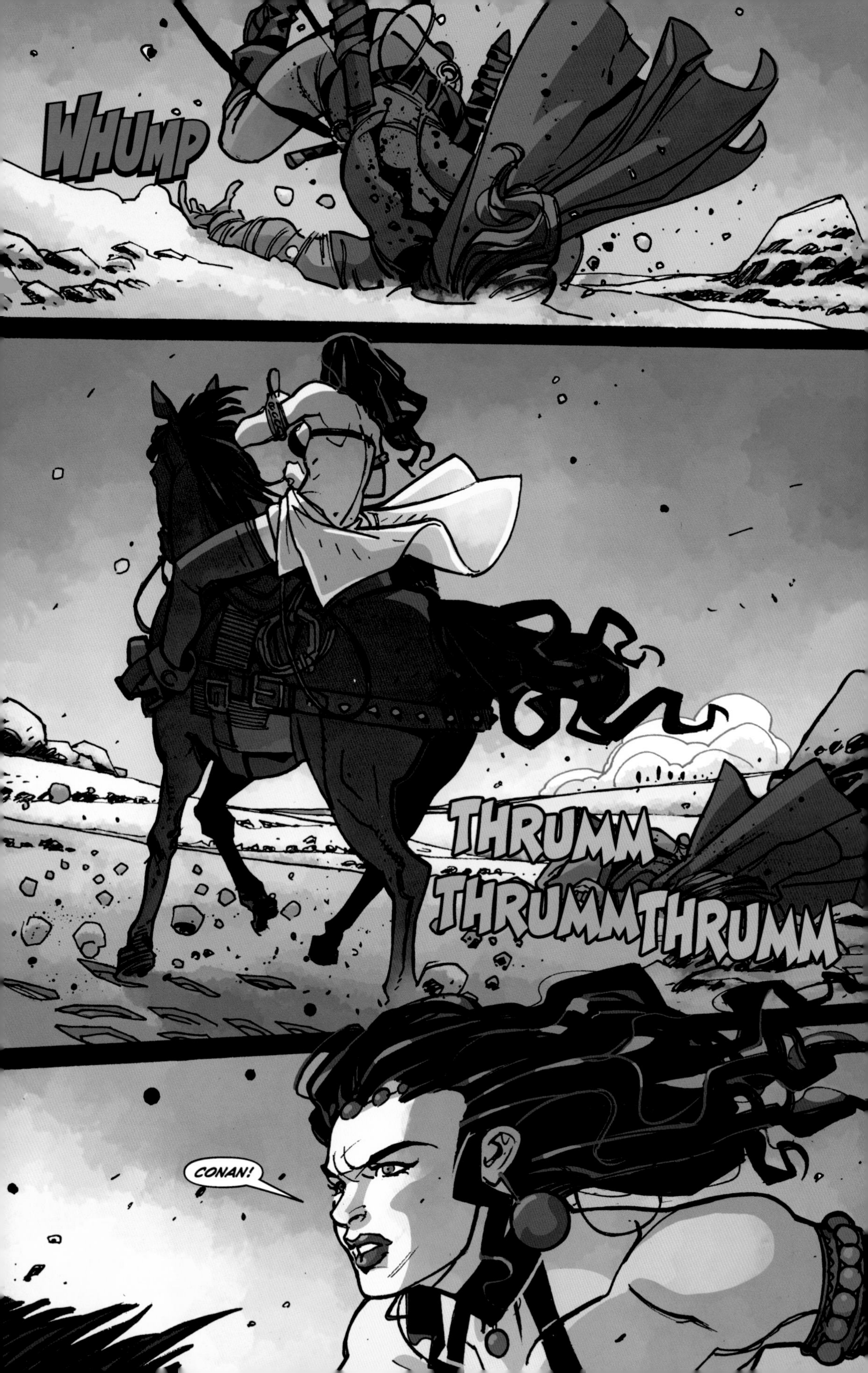
WHUMP
THRUMM
THRUMMTHRUMM
CONAN!

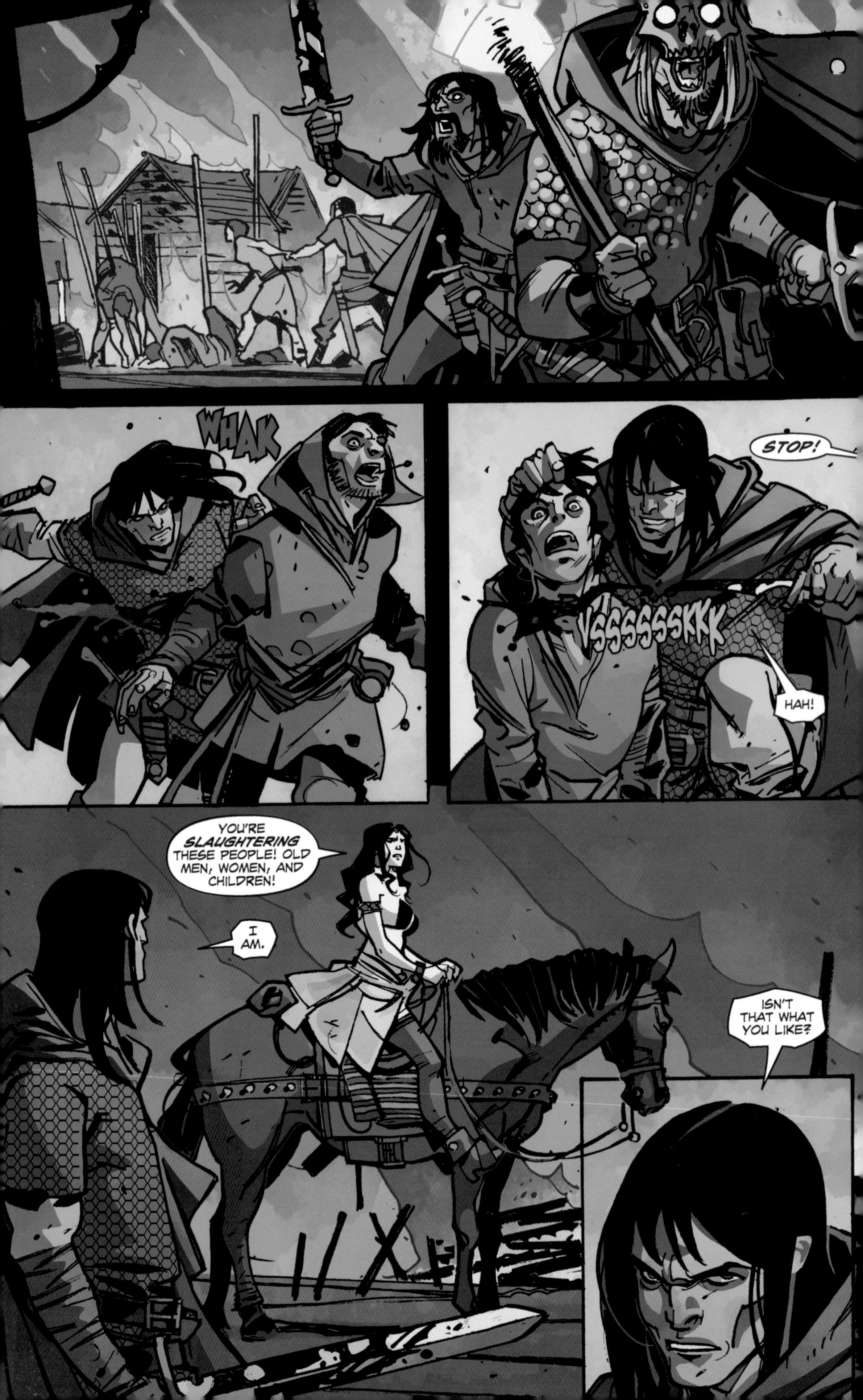
WHAK
STOP!
VSSSSSSSKKK
HAH!
YOU'RE SLAUGHTERING THESE PEOPLE! OLD MEN, WOMEN, AND CHILDREN!
I AM.
ISN'T THAT WHAT YOU LIKE?

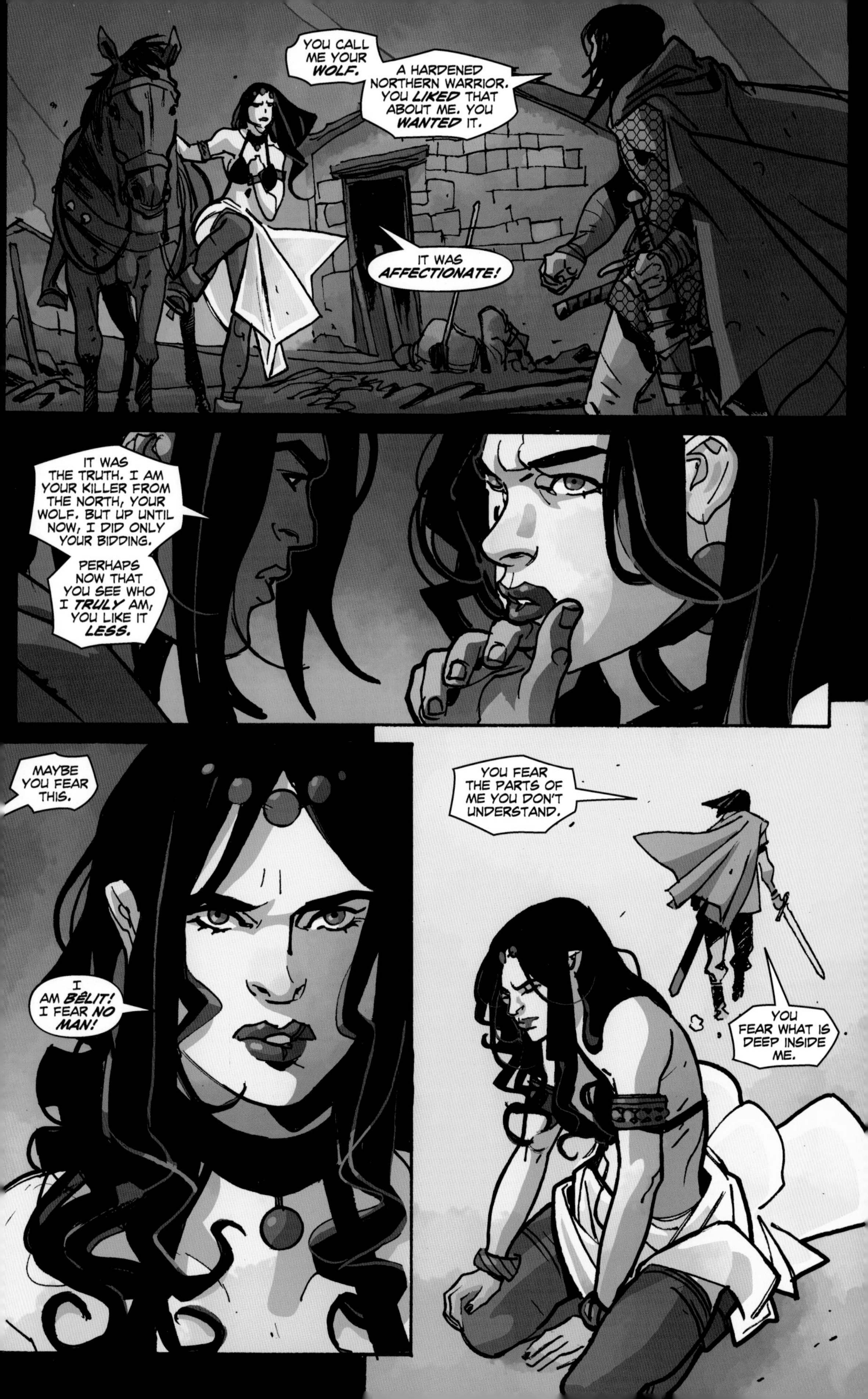
YOU CALL ME YOUR WOLF.
A HARDENED NORTHERN WARRIOR. YOU LIKED THAT ABOUT ME. YOU WANTED IT.
IT WAS AFFECTIONATE!
IT WAS THE TRUTH. I AM YOUR KILLER FROM THE NORTH, YOUR WOLF. BUT UP UNTIL NOW, I DID ONLY YOUR BIDDING.
PERHAPS NOW THAT YOU SEE WHO I TRULY AM, YOU LIKE IT LESS.
MAYBE YOU FEAR THIS.
I AM BÊLIT! I FEAR NO MAN!
YOU FEAR THE PARTS OF ME YOU DON'T UNDERSTAND.
YOU FEAR WHAT IS DEEP INSIDE ME.

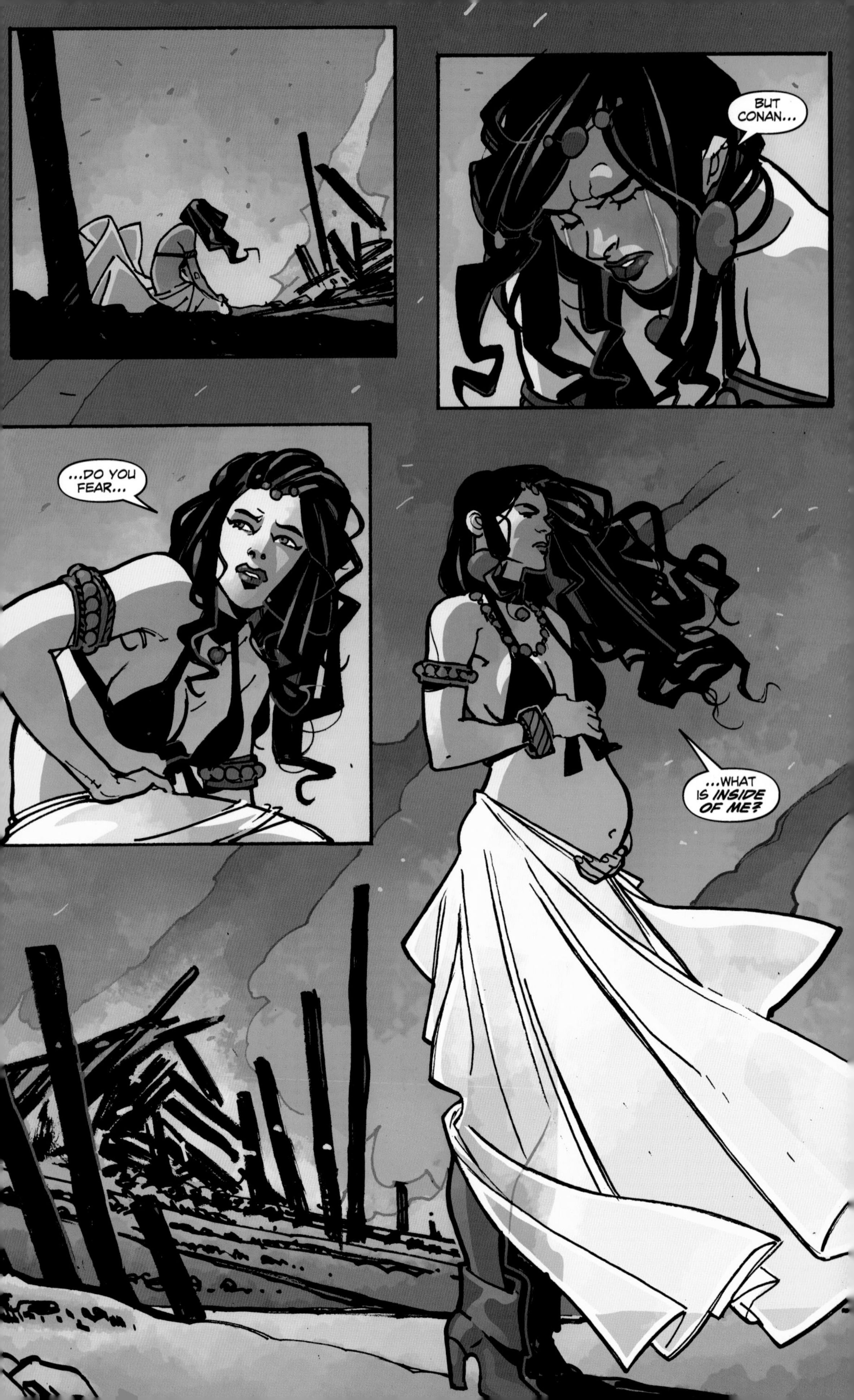
BUT CONAN...
...DO YOU FEAR...
...WHAT IS *INSIDE OF ME?*

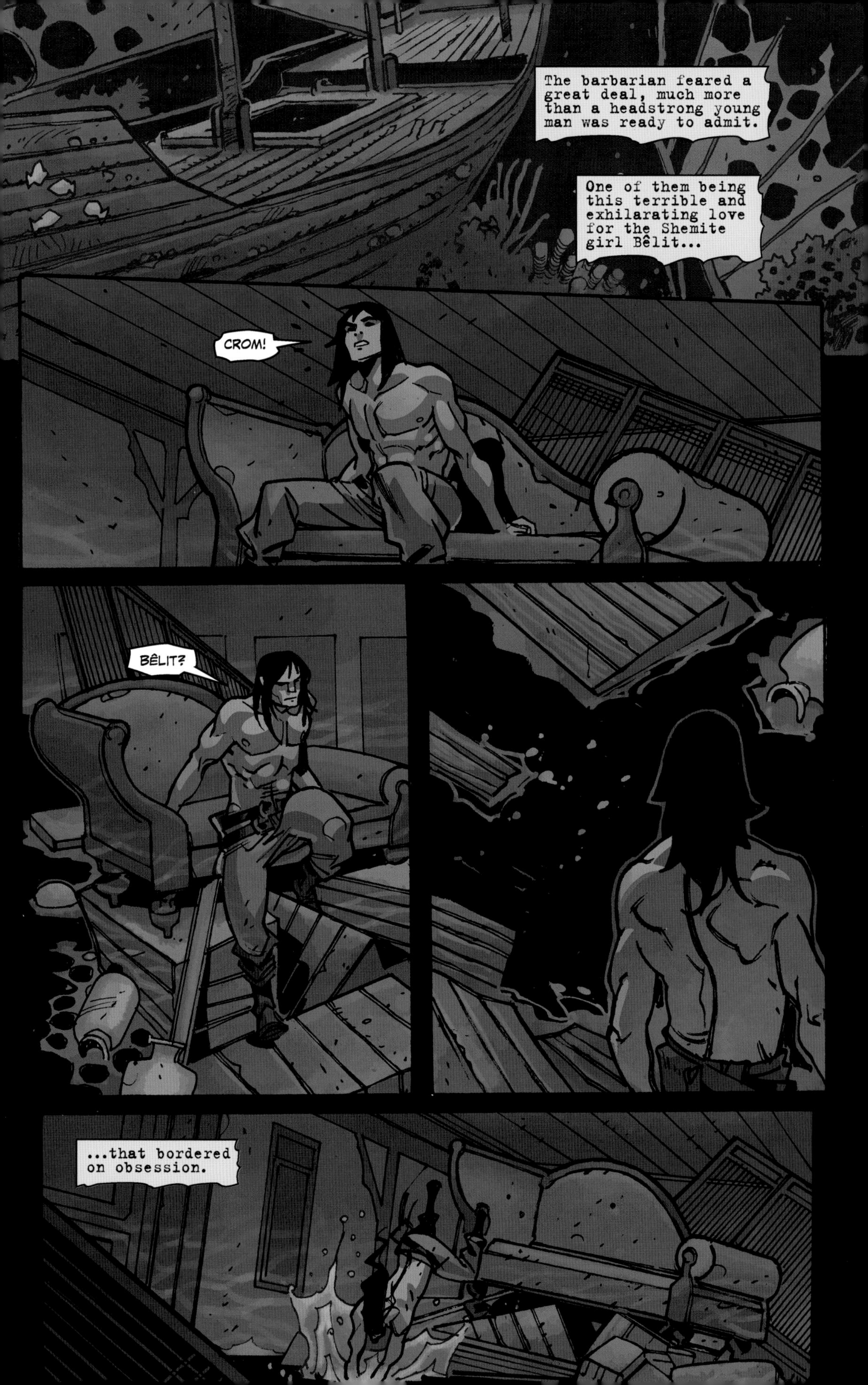
The barbarian feared a great deal, much more than a headstrong young man was ready to admit.
One of them being this terrible and exhilarating love for the Shemite girl Bêlit...
CROM!
BÊLIT?
...that bordered on obsession.

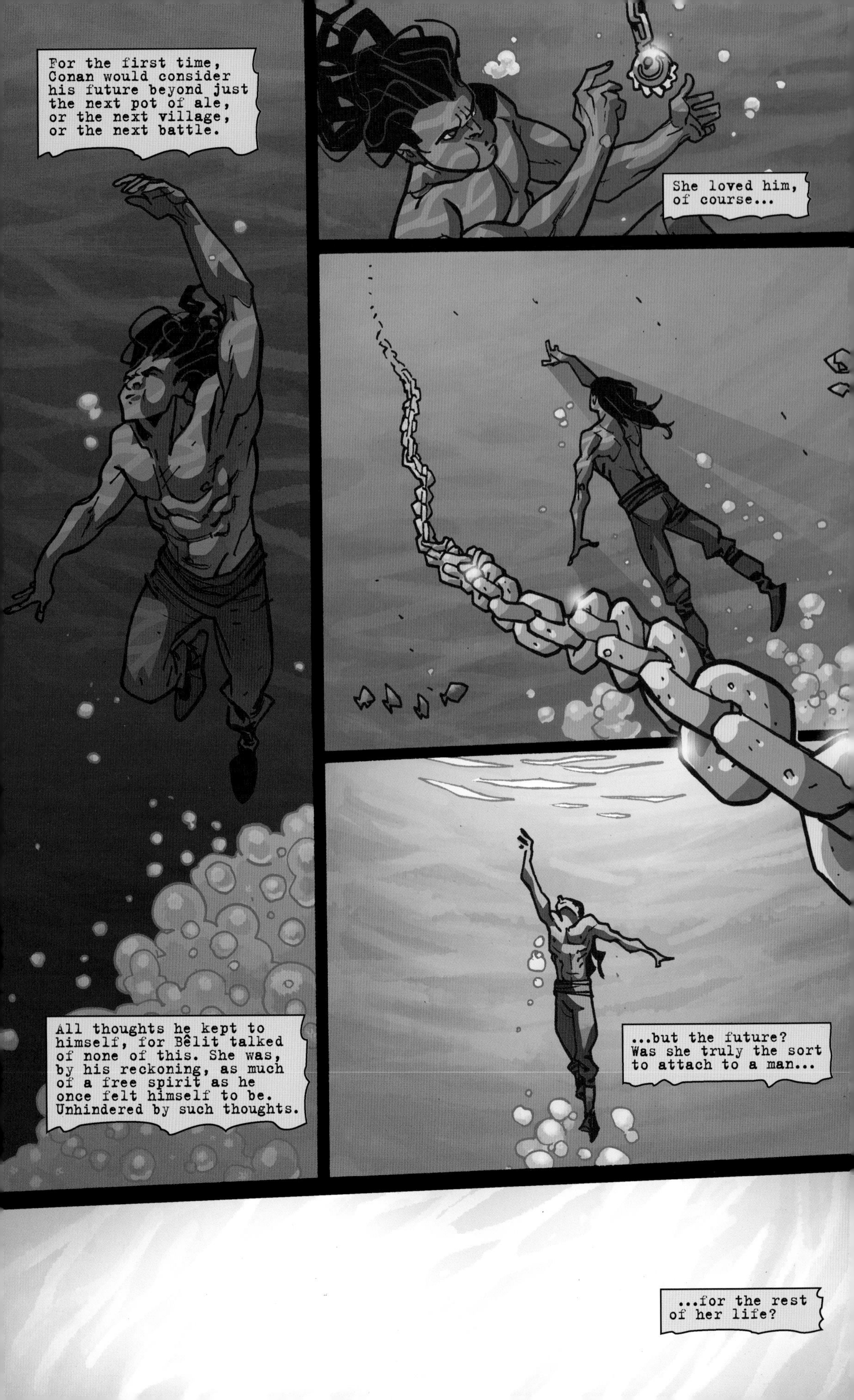
For the first time, Conan would consider his future beyond just the next pot of ale, or the next village, or the next battle.
She loved him, of course...
All thoughts he kept to himself, for Bêlit talked of none of this. She was, by his reckoning, as much of a free spirit as he once felt himself to be. Unhindered by such thoughts.
...but the future? Was she truly the sort to attach to a man...
...for the rest of her life?

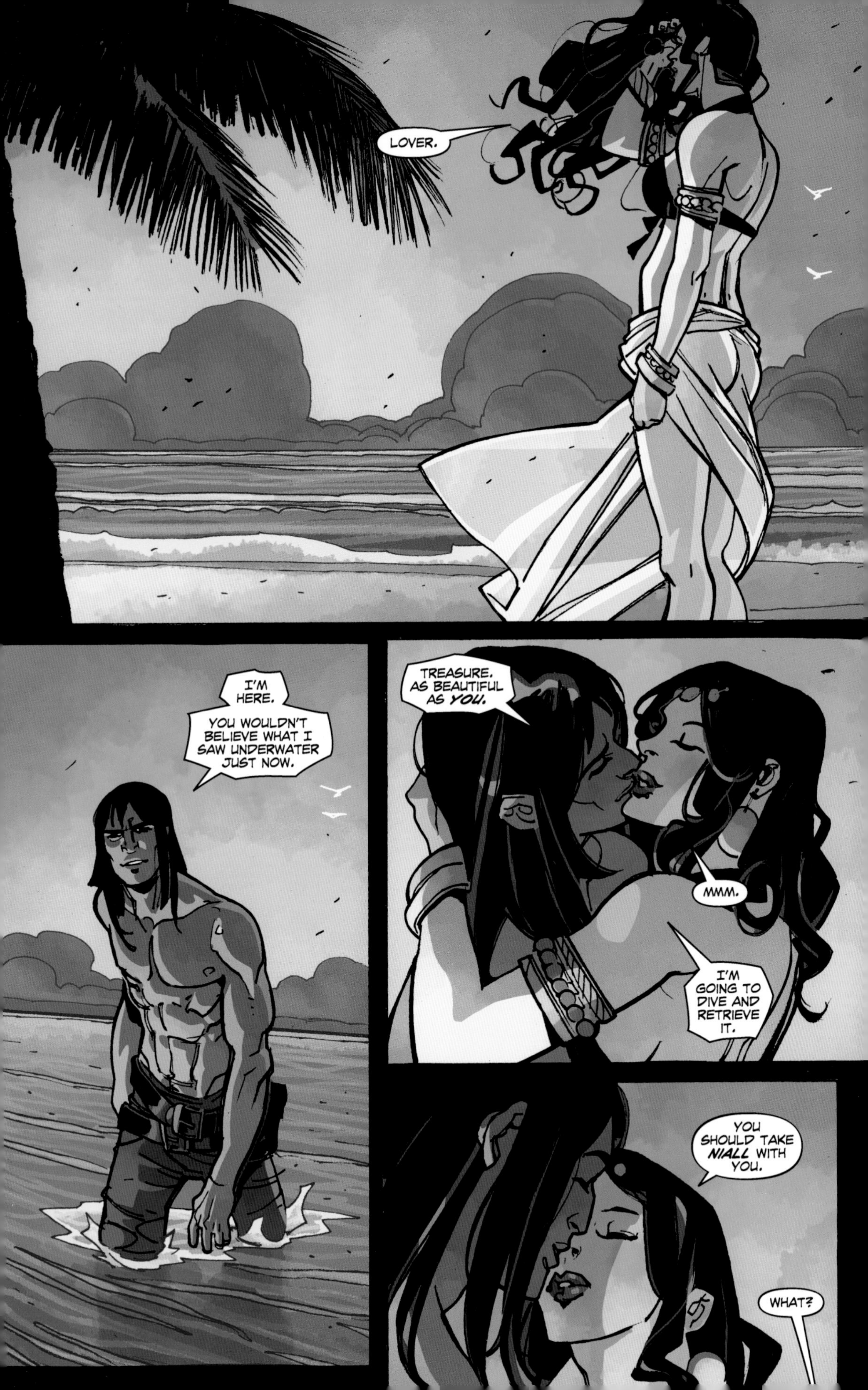
LOVER.
I'M HERE.
YOU WOULDN'T BELIEVE WHAT I SAW UNDERWATER JUST NOW.
TREASURE. AS BEAUTIFUL AS *YOU.*
MMM.
I'M GOING TO DIVE AND RETRIEVE IT.
YOU SHOULD TAKE ***NIALL*** WITH YOU.
WHAT?

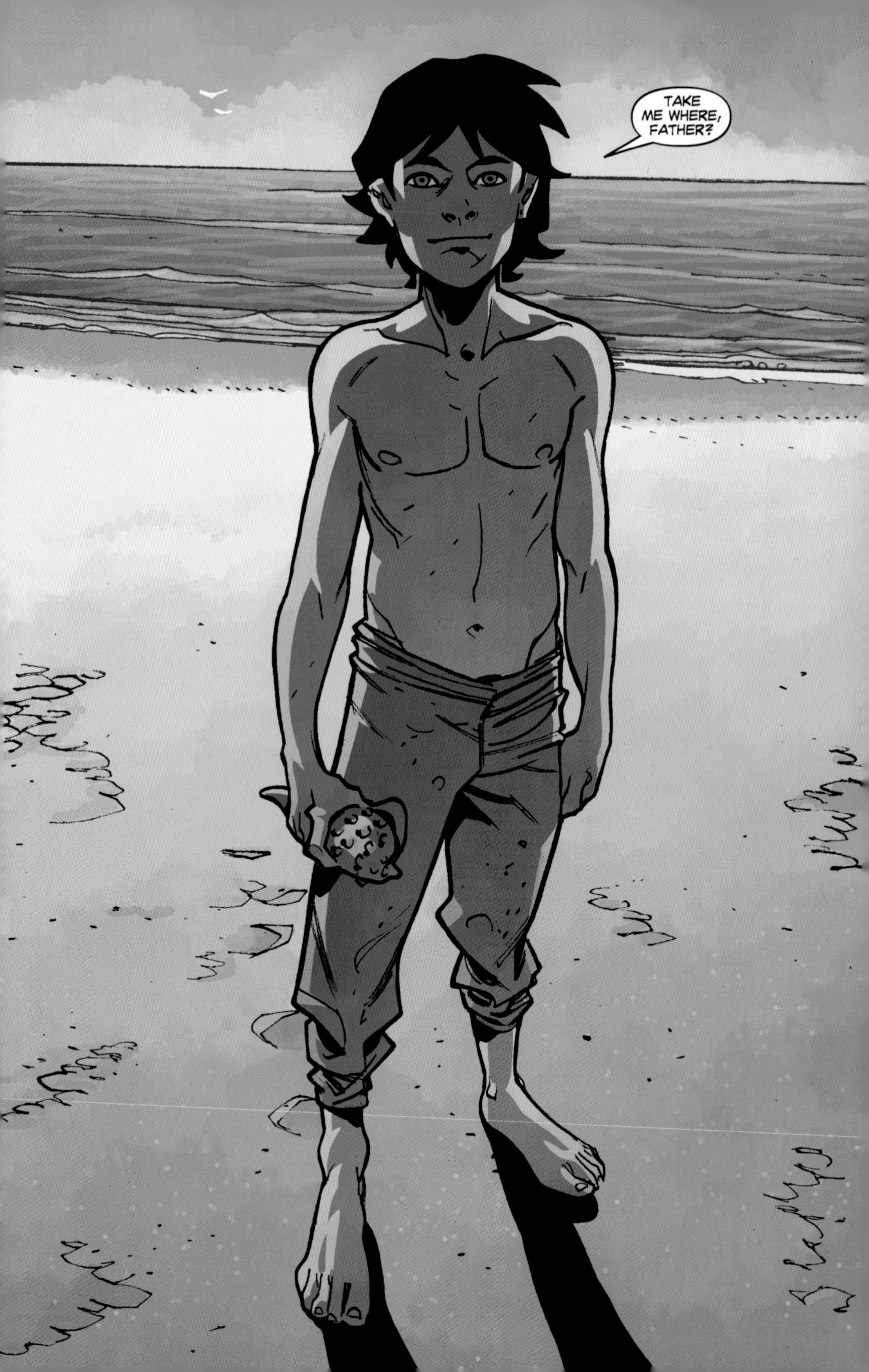
TAKE ME WHERE, FATHER?

CHAPTER SIX

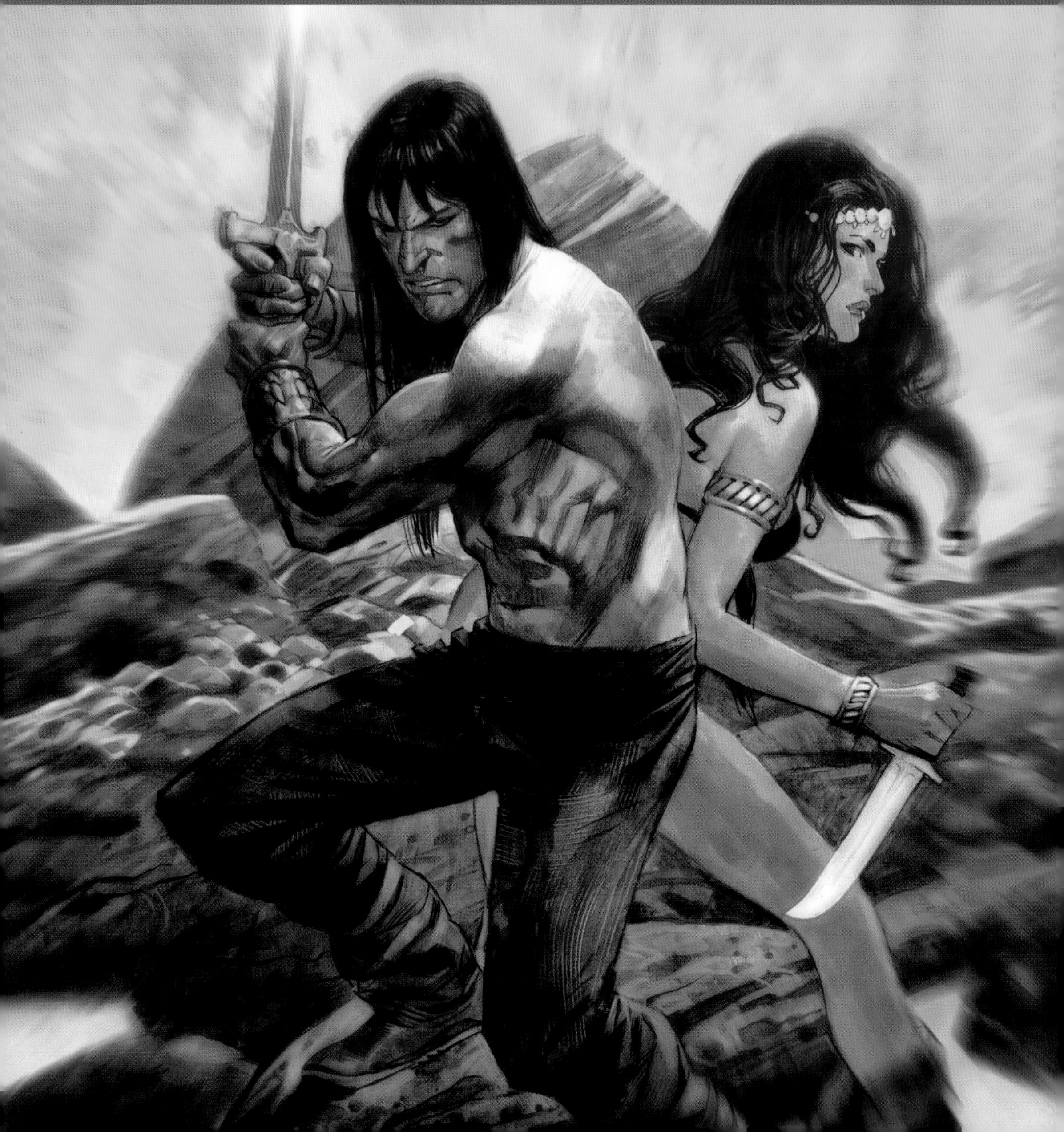

*"We should never have named it the *Tigress*."*

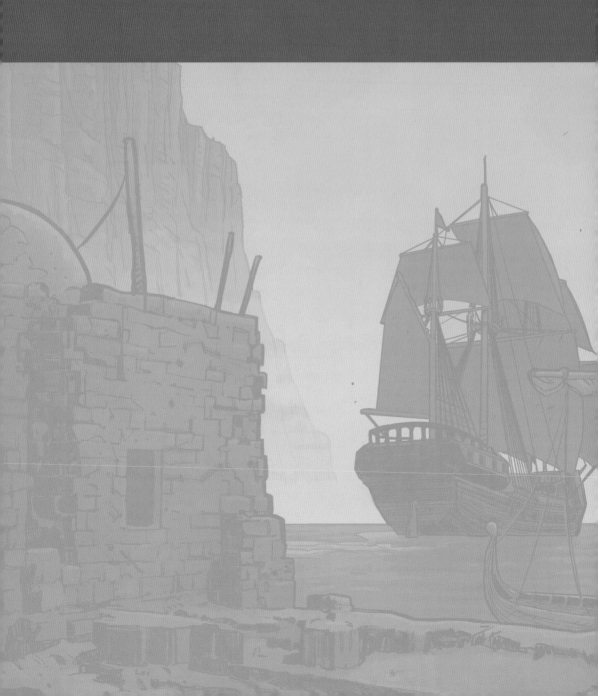

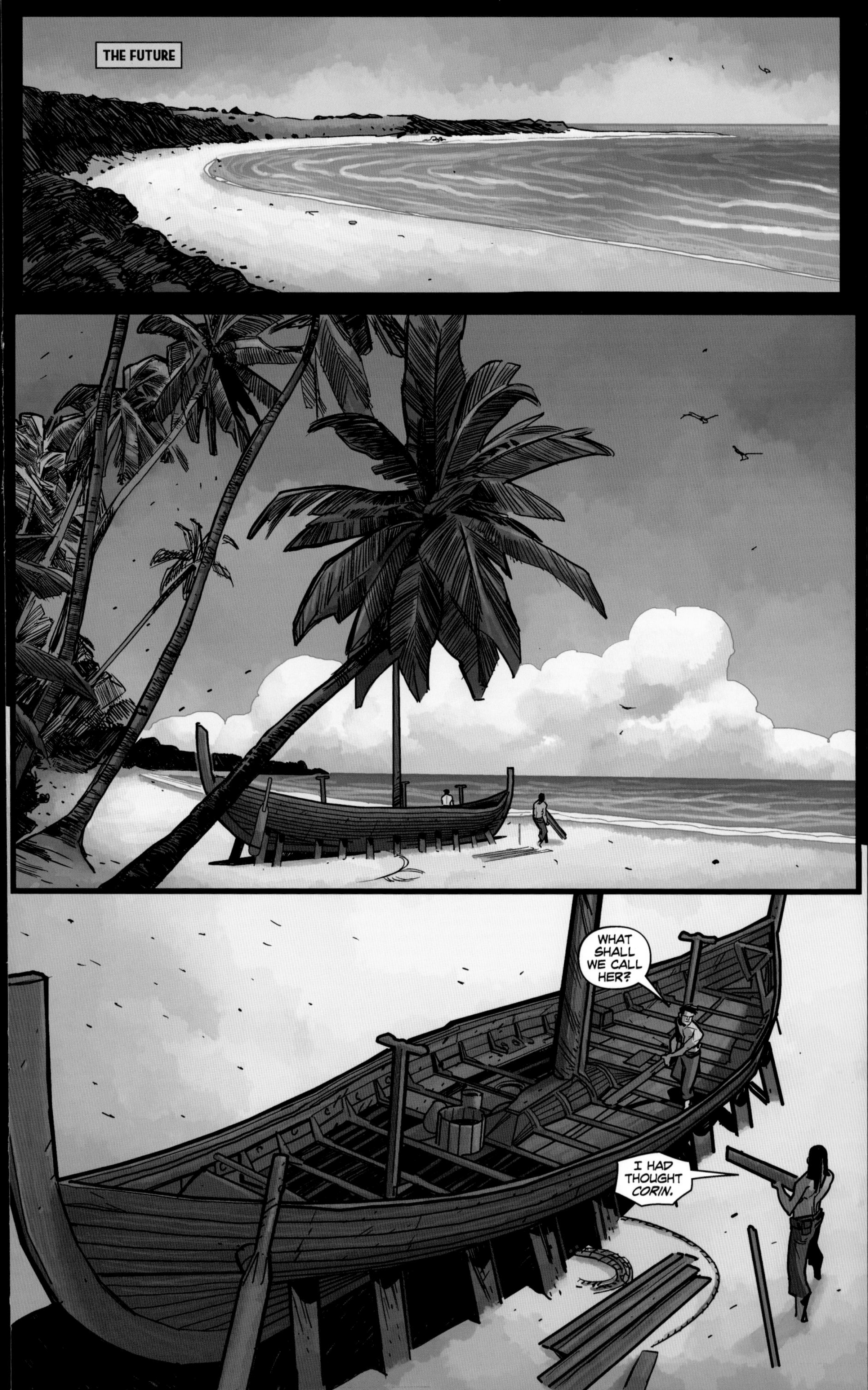
THE FUTURE
WHAT SHALL WE CALL HER?
I HAD THOUGHT CORIN.

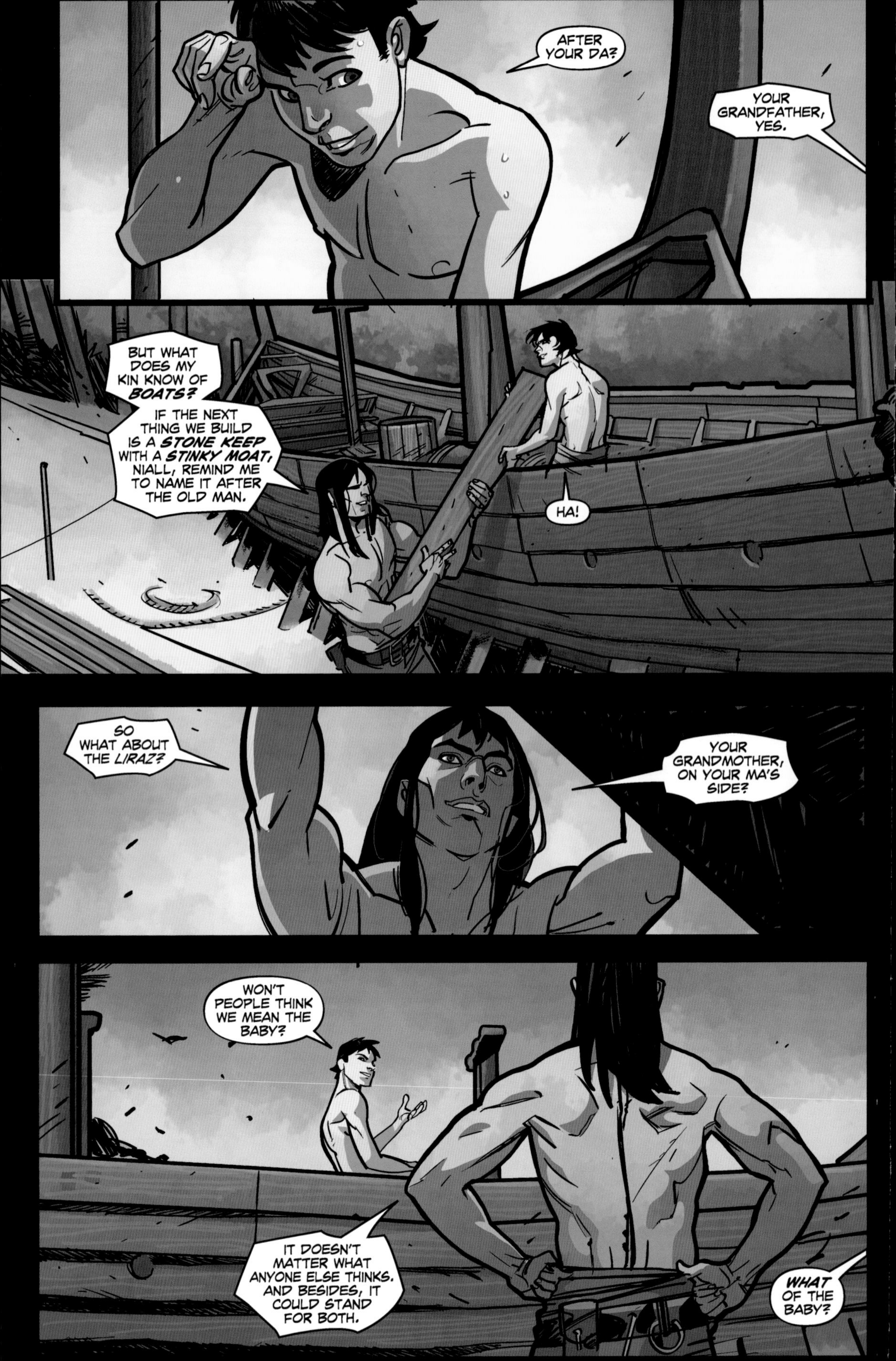
AFTER YOUR DA?
YOUR GRANDFATHER, YES.
BUT WHAT DOES MY KIN KNOW OF BOATS?
IF THE NEXT THING WE BUILD IS A STONE KEEP WITH A STINKY MOAT, NIALL, REMIND ME TO NAME IT AFTER THE OLD MAN.
HA!
SO WHAT ABOUT THE LIRAZ?
YOUR GRANDMOTHER, ON YOUR MA'S SIDE?
WON'T PEOPLE THINK WE MEAN THE BABY?
IT DOESN'T MATTER WHAT ANYONE ELSE THINKS. AND BESIDES, IT COULD STAND FOR BOTH.
WHAT OF THE BABY?

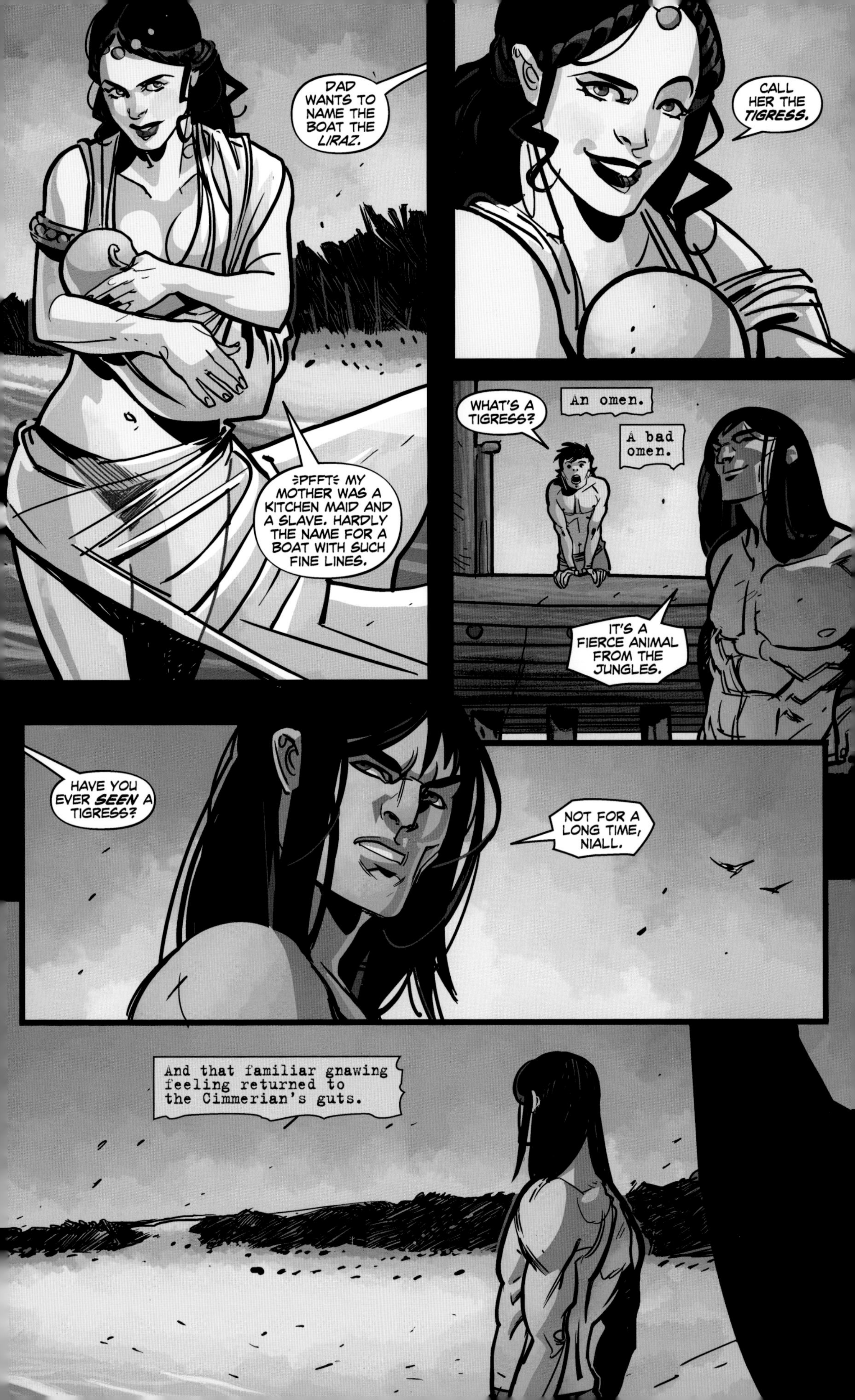
DAD WANTS TO NAME THE BOAT THE *LIRAZ*.
CALL HER THE *TIGRESS*.
PFFT! MY MOTHER WAS A KITCHEN MAID AND A SLAVE. HARDLY THE NAME FOR A BOAT WITH SUCH FINE LINES.
WHAT'S A TIGRESS?
An omen.
A bad omen.
IT'S A FIERCE ANIMAL FROM THE JUNGLES.
HAVE YOU EVER *SEEN* A TIGRESS?
NOT FOR A LONG TIME, NIALL.
And that familiar gnawing feeling returned to the Cimmerian's guts.

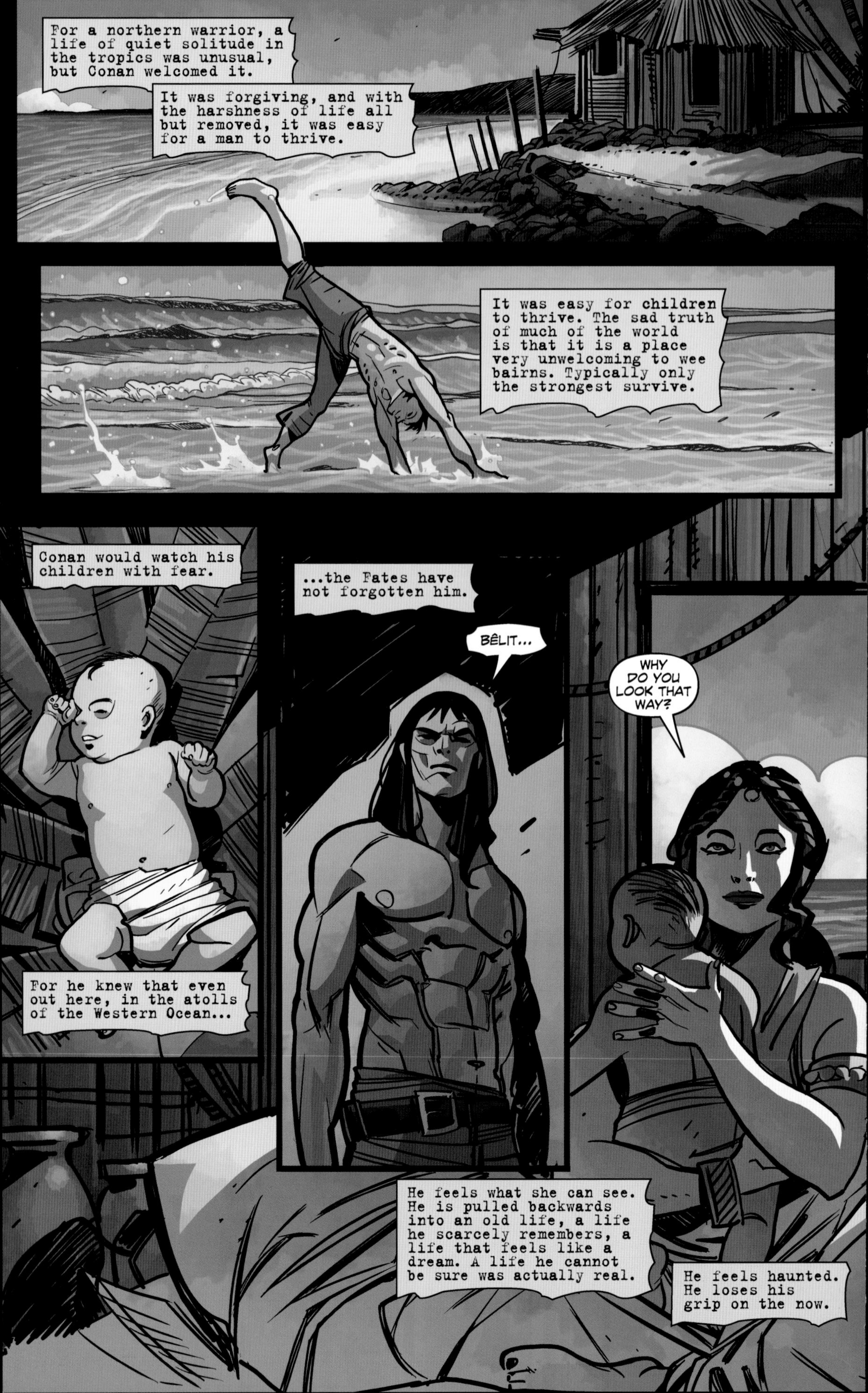
For a northern warrior, a life of quiet solitude in the tropics was unusual, but Conan welcomed it.
It was forgiving, and with the harshness of life all but removed, it was easy for a man to thrive.
It was easy for children to thrive. The sad truth of much of the world is that it is a place very unwelcoming to wee bairns. Typically only the strongest survive.
Conan would watch his children with fear.
For he knew that even out here, in the atolls of the Western Ocean...
...the Fates have not forgotten him.
BÊLIT...
WHY DO YOU LOOK THAT WAY?
He feels what she can see. He is pulled backwards into an old life, a life he scarcely remembers, a life that feels like a dream. A life he cannot be sure was actually real.
He feels haunted. He loses his grip on the now.

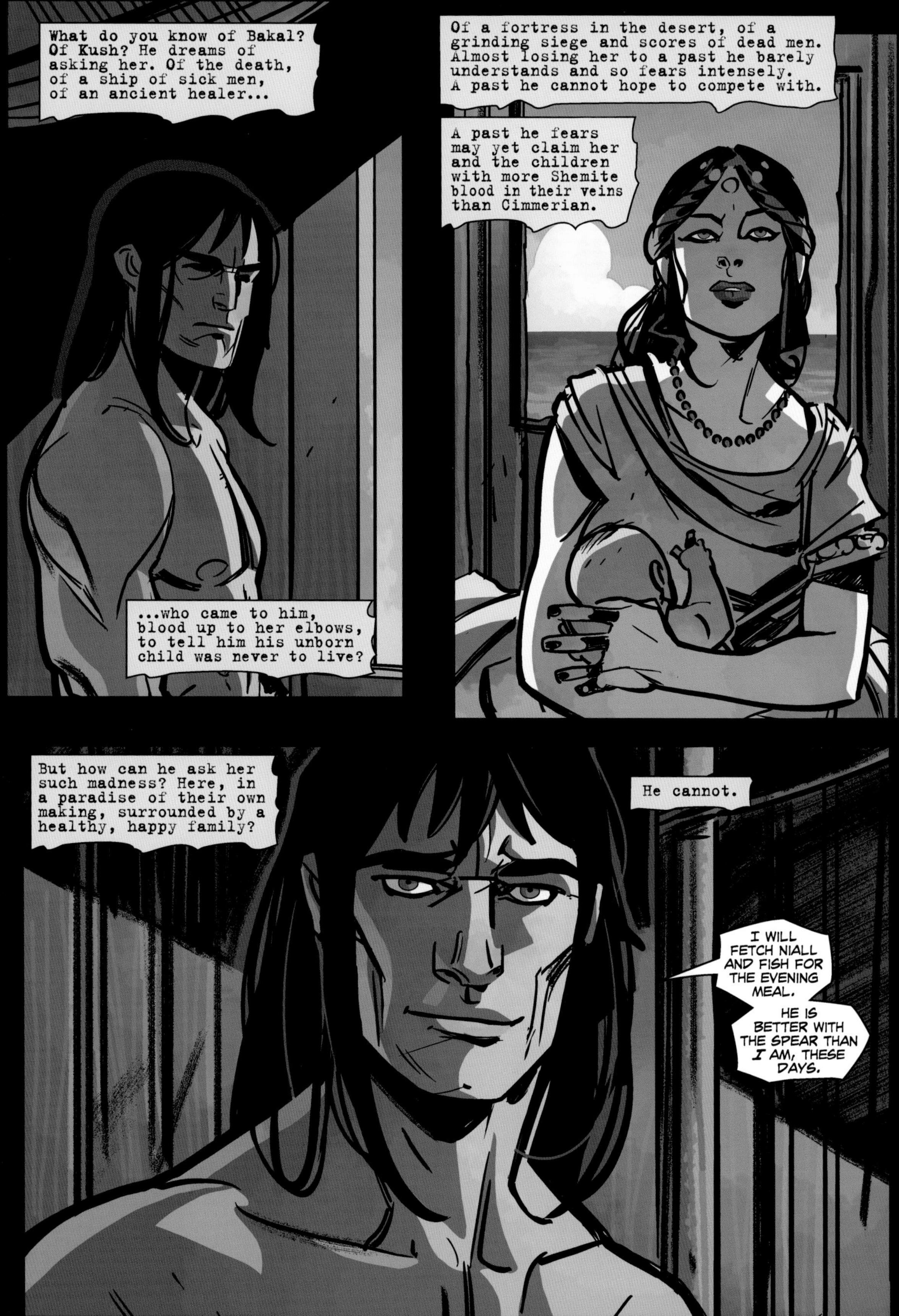
What do you know of Bakal? Of Kush? He dreams of asking her. Of the death, of a ship of sick men, of an ancient healer...
Of a fortress in the desert, of a grinding siege and scores of dead men. Almost losing her to a past he barely understands and so fears intensely. A past he cannot hope to compete with.
A past he fears may yet claim her and the children with more Shemite blood in their veins than Cimmerian.
...who came to him, blood up to her elbows, to tell him his unborn child was never to live?
But how can he ask her such madness? Here, in a paradise of their own making, surrounded by a healthy, happy family?
He cannot.
I WILL FETCH NIALL AND FISH FOR THE EVENING MEAL.
HE IS BETTER WITH THE SPEAR THAN I AM, THESE DAYS.

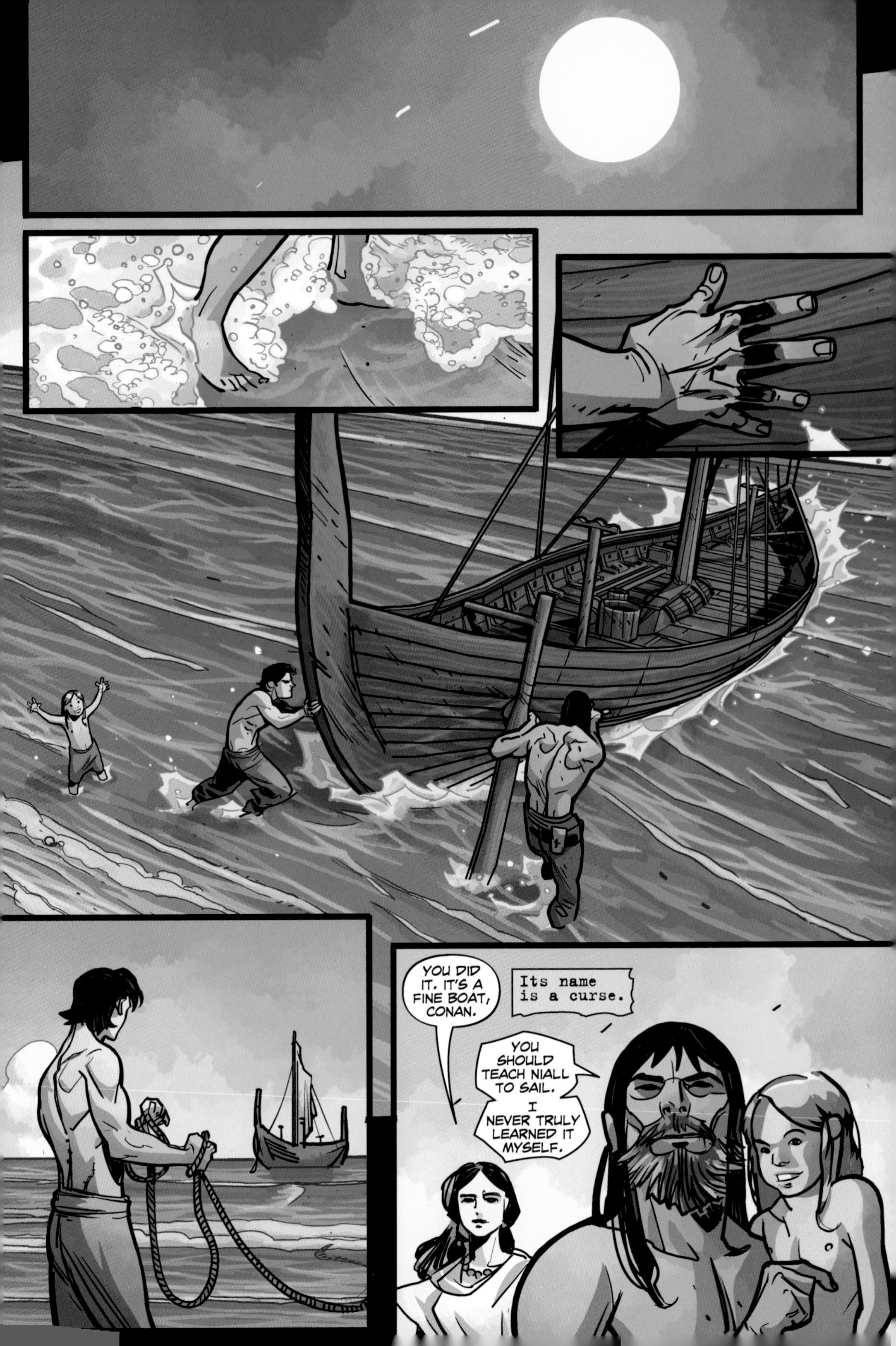
YOU DID IT. IT'S A FINE BOAT, CONAN.
Its name is a curse.
YOU SHOULD TEACH NIALL TO SAIL.
I NEVER TRULY LEARNED IT MYSELF.

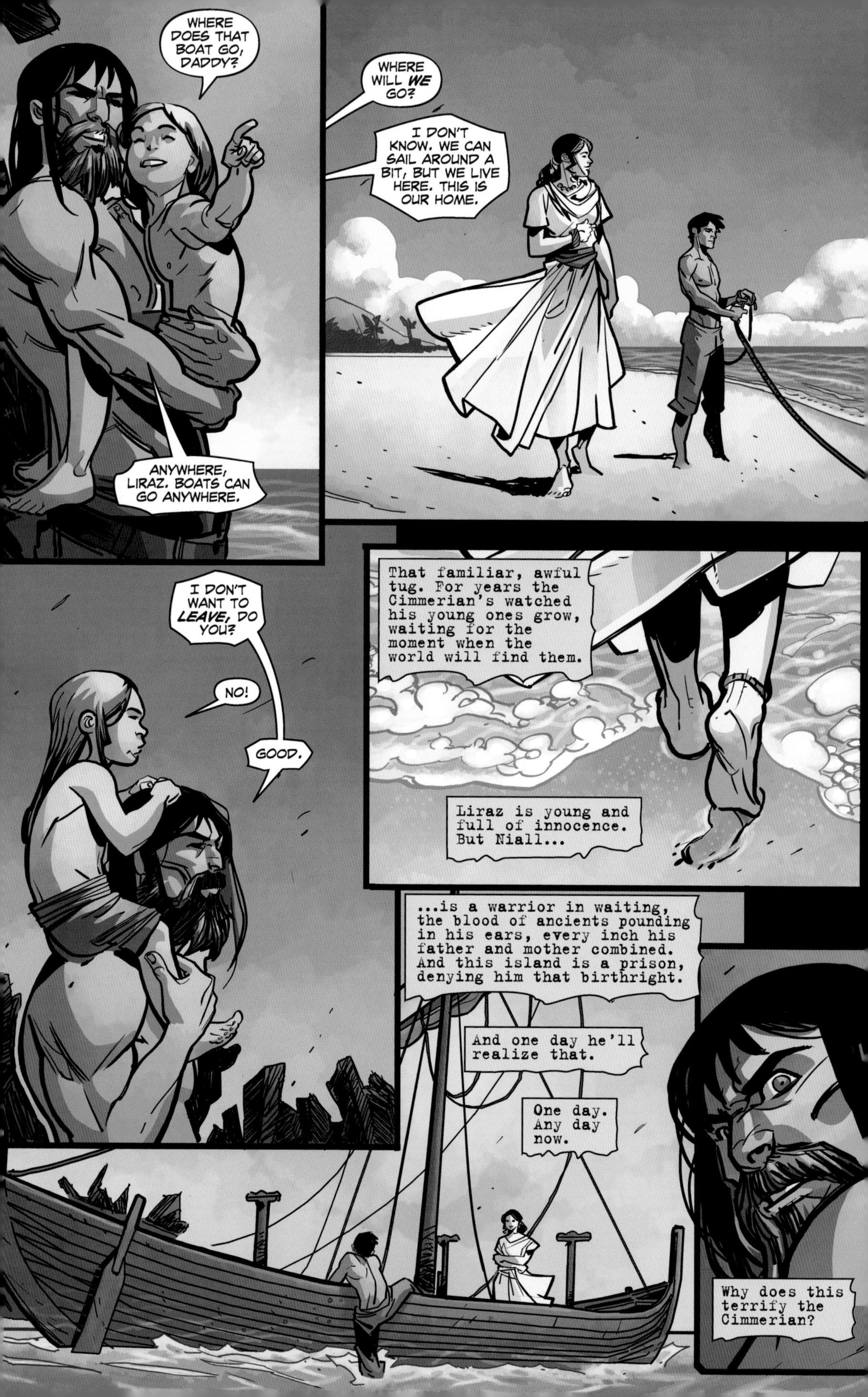
WHERE DOES THAT BOAT GO, DADDY?
ANYWHERE, LIRAZ. BOATS CAN GO ANYWHERE.
WHERE WILL *WE* GO?
I DON'T KNOW. WE CAN SAIL AROUND A BIT, BUT WE LIVE HERE. THIS IS OUR HOME.
I DON'T WANT TO *LEAVE,* DO YOU?
NO!
GOOD.
That familiar, awful tug. For years the Cimmerian's watched his young ones grow, waiting for the moment when the world will find them.
Liraz is young and full of innocence. But Niall...
...is a warrior in waiting, the blood of ancients pounding in his ears, every inch his father and mother combined. And this island is a prison, denying him that birthright.
And one day he'll realize that.
One day. Any day now.
Why does this terrify the Cimmerian?

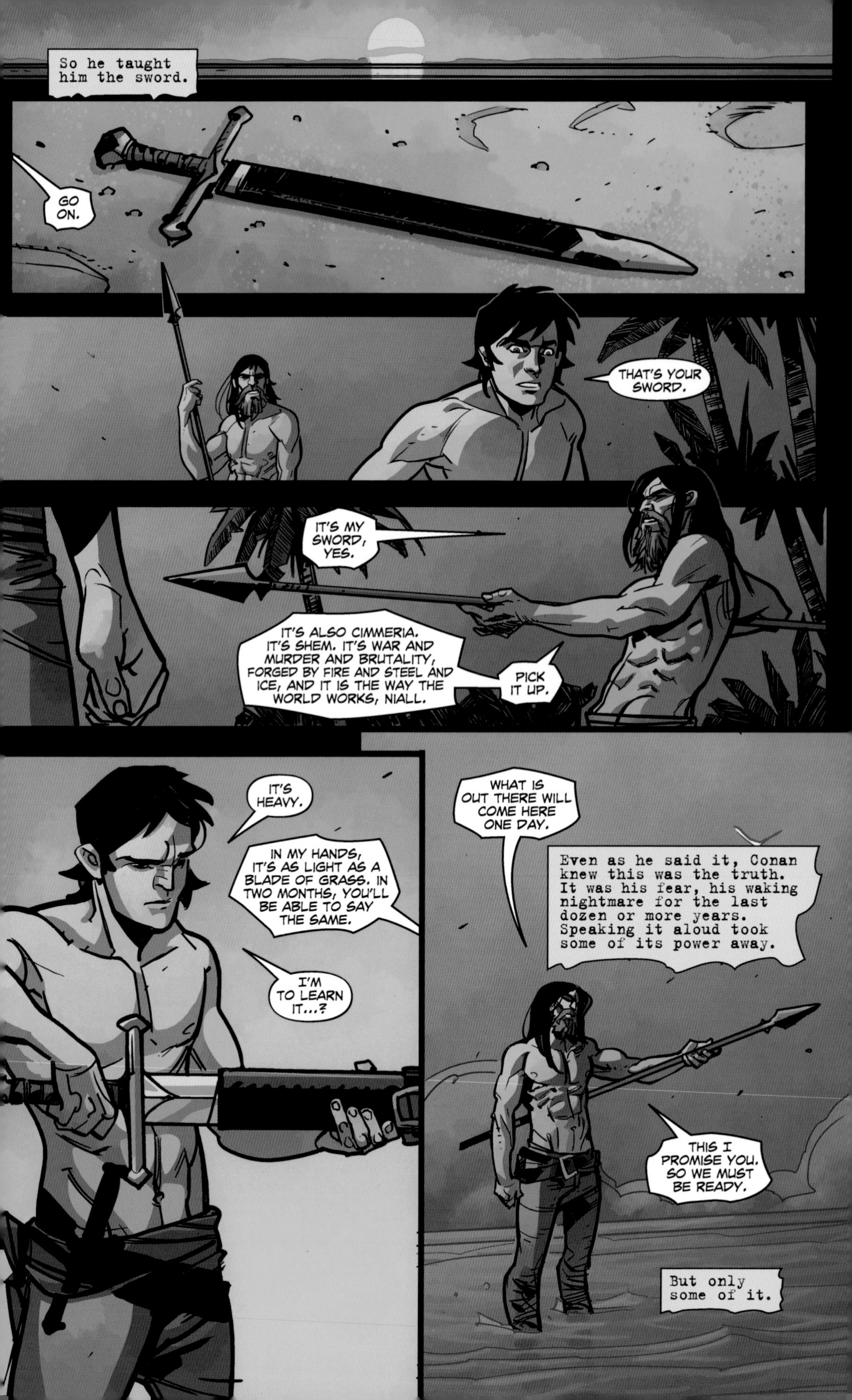

So he taught him the sword.
GO ON.
THAT'S YOUR SWORD.
IT'S MY SWORD, YES.
IT'S ALSO CIMMERIA. IT'S SHEM. IT'S WAR AND MURDER AND BRUTALITY, FORGED BY FIRE AND STEEL AND ICE, AND IT IS THE WAY THE WORLD WORKS, NIALL.
PICK IT UP.
IT'S HEAVY.
IN MY HANDS, IT'S AS LIGHT AS A BLADE OF GRASS. IN TWO MONTHS, YOU'LL BE ABLE TO SAY THE SAME.
I'M TO LEARN IT...?
WHAT IS OUT THERE WILL COME HERE ONE DAY.
Even as he said it, Conan knew this was the truth. It was his fear, his waking nightmare for the last dozen or more years. Speaking it aloud took some of its power away.
THIS I PROMISE YOU. SO WE MUST BE READY.
But only some of it.

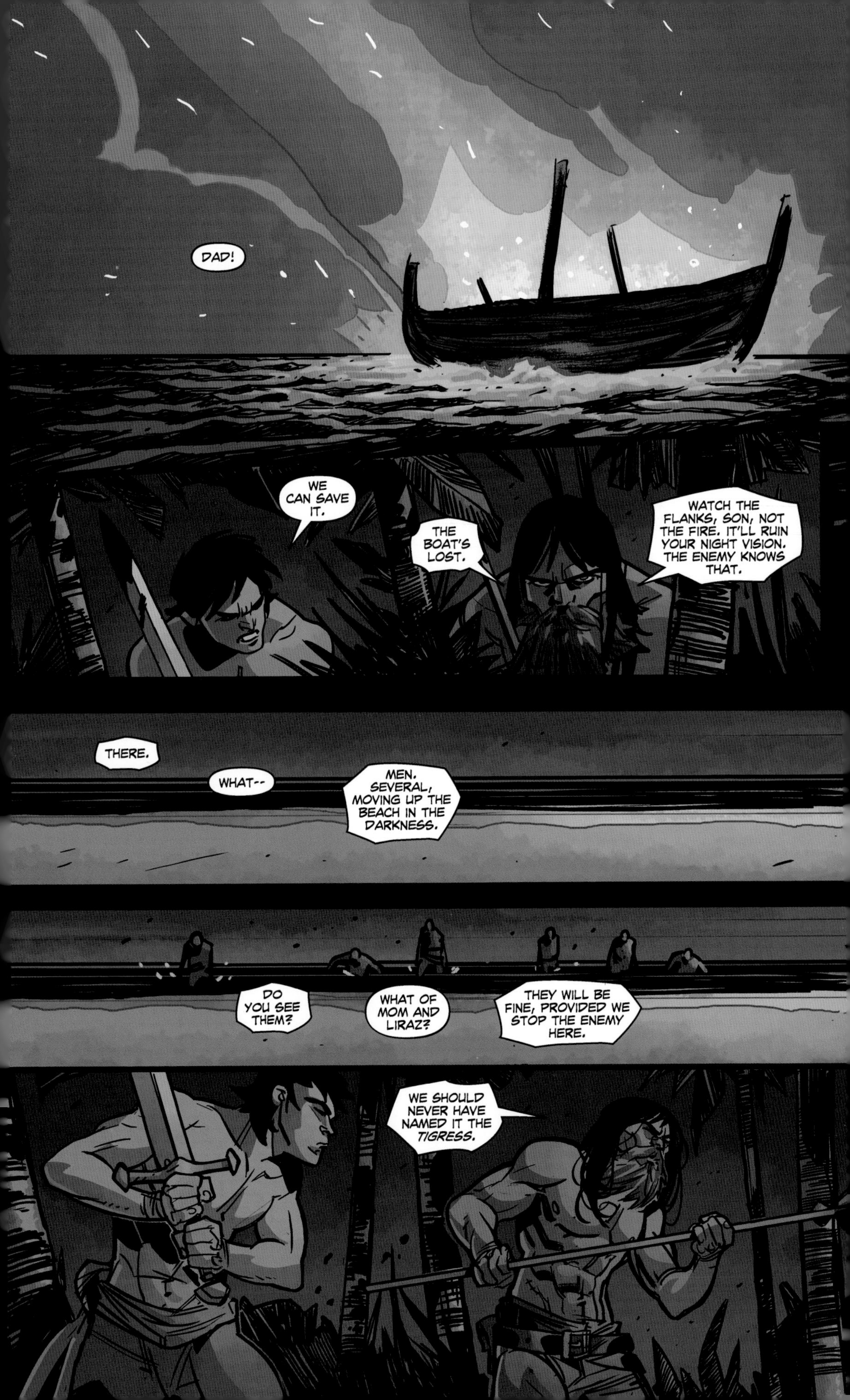
DAD!
WE CAN SAVE IT.
THE BOAT'S LOST.
WATCH THE FLANKS, SON, NOT THE FIRE. IT'LL RUIN YOUR NIGHT VISION. THE ENEMY KNOWS THAT.
THERE.
WHAT--
MEN. SEVERAL, MOVING UP THE BEACH IN THE DARKNESS.
DO YOU SEE THEM?
WHAT OF MOM AND LIRAZ?
THEY WILL BE FINE, PROVIDED WE STOP THE ENEMY HERE.
WE SHOULD NEVER HAVE NAMED IT THE *TIGRESS*.

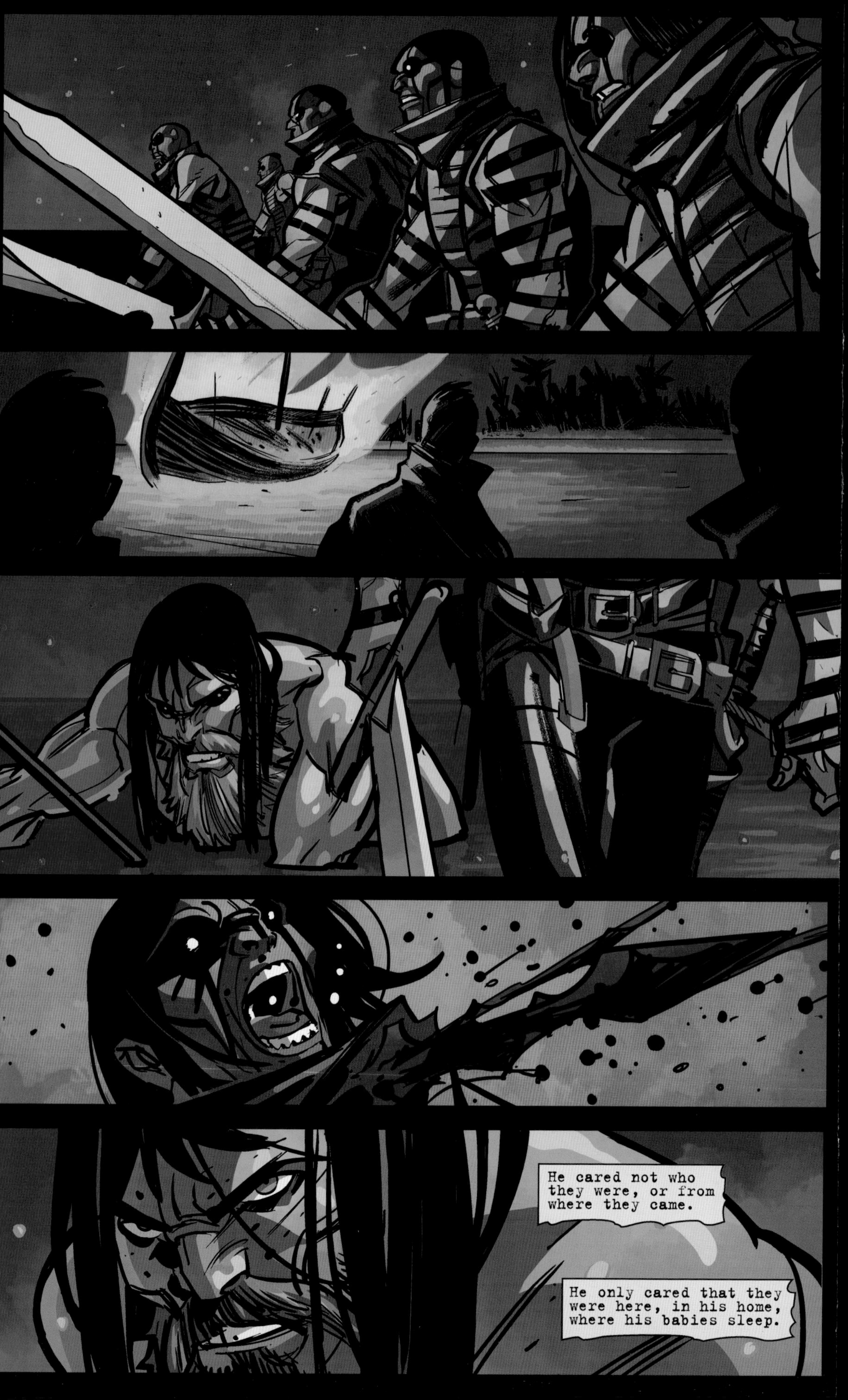
He cared not who they were, or from where they came.
He only cared that they were here, in his home, where his babies sleep.

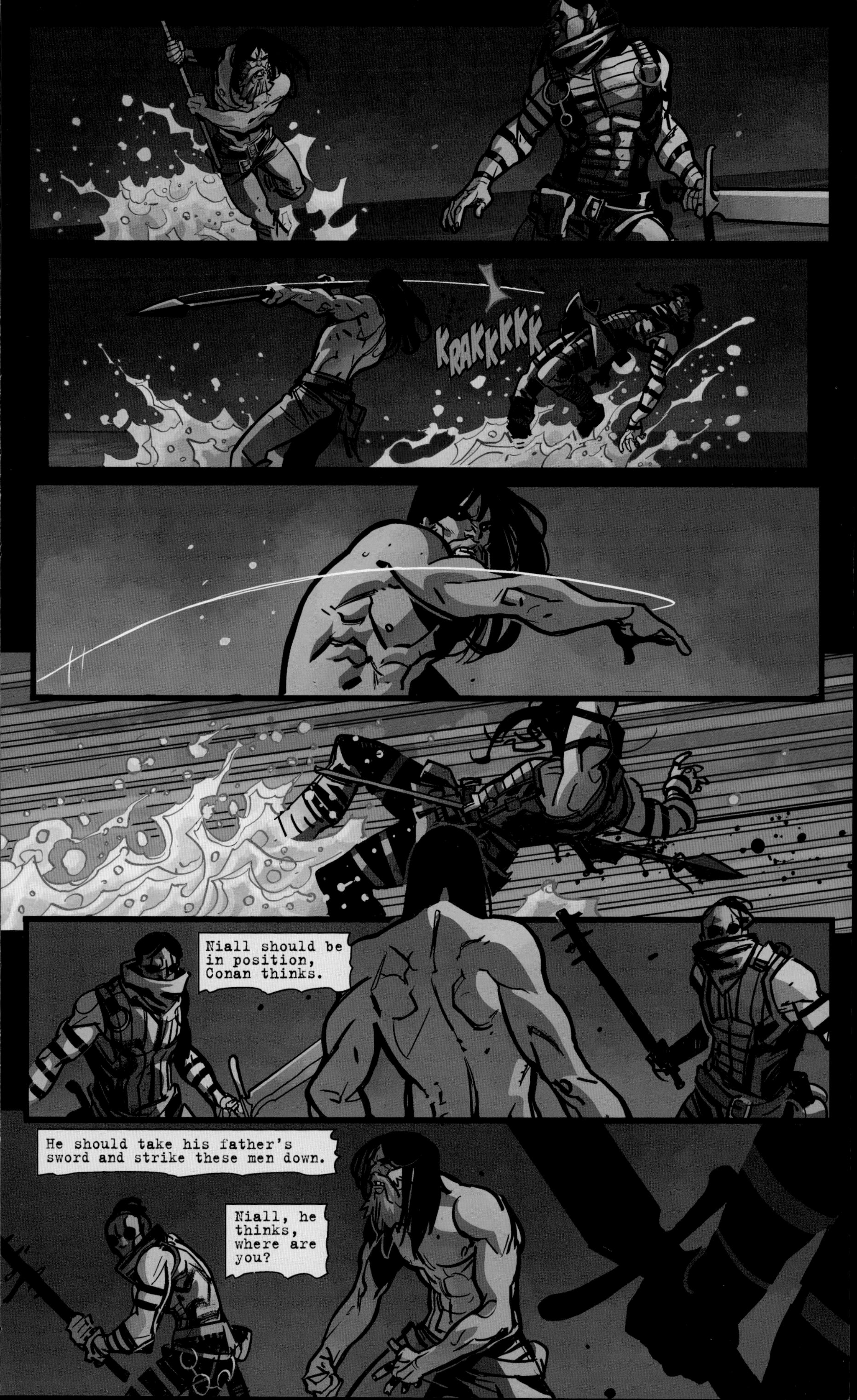
KRAKKKK
Niall should be in position, Conan thinks.
He should take his father's sword and strike these men down.
Niall, he thinks, where are you?

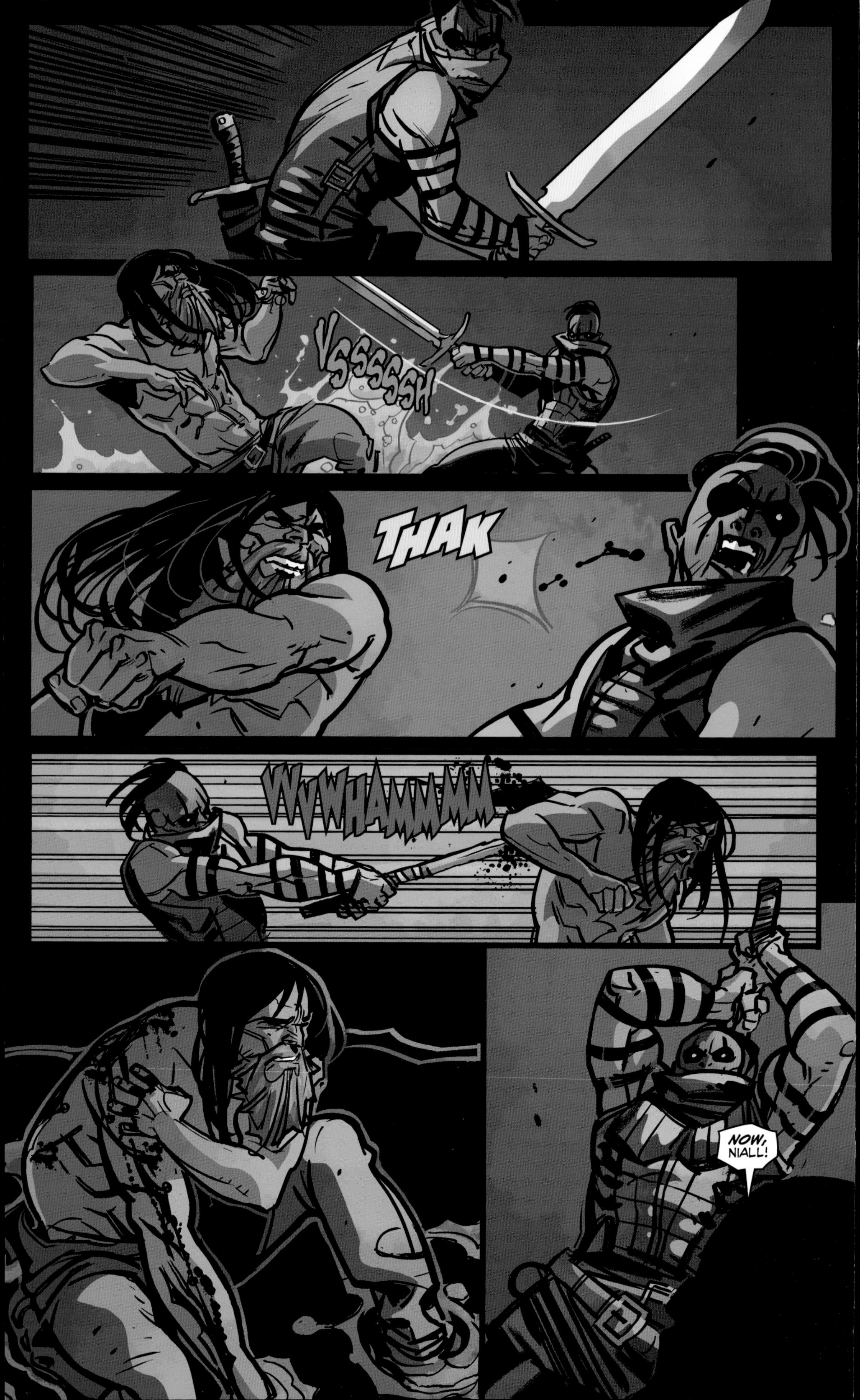
VSSSSSH
THAK
VVVWHAMMMM
NOW, NIALL!

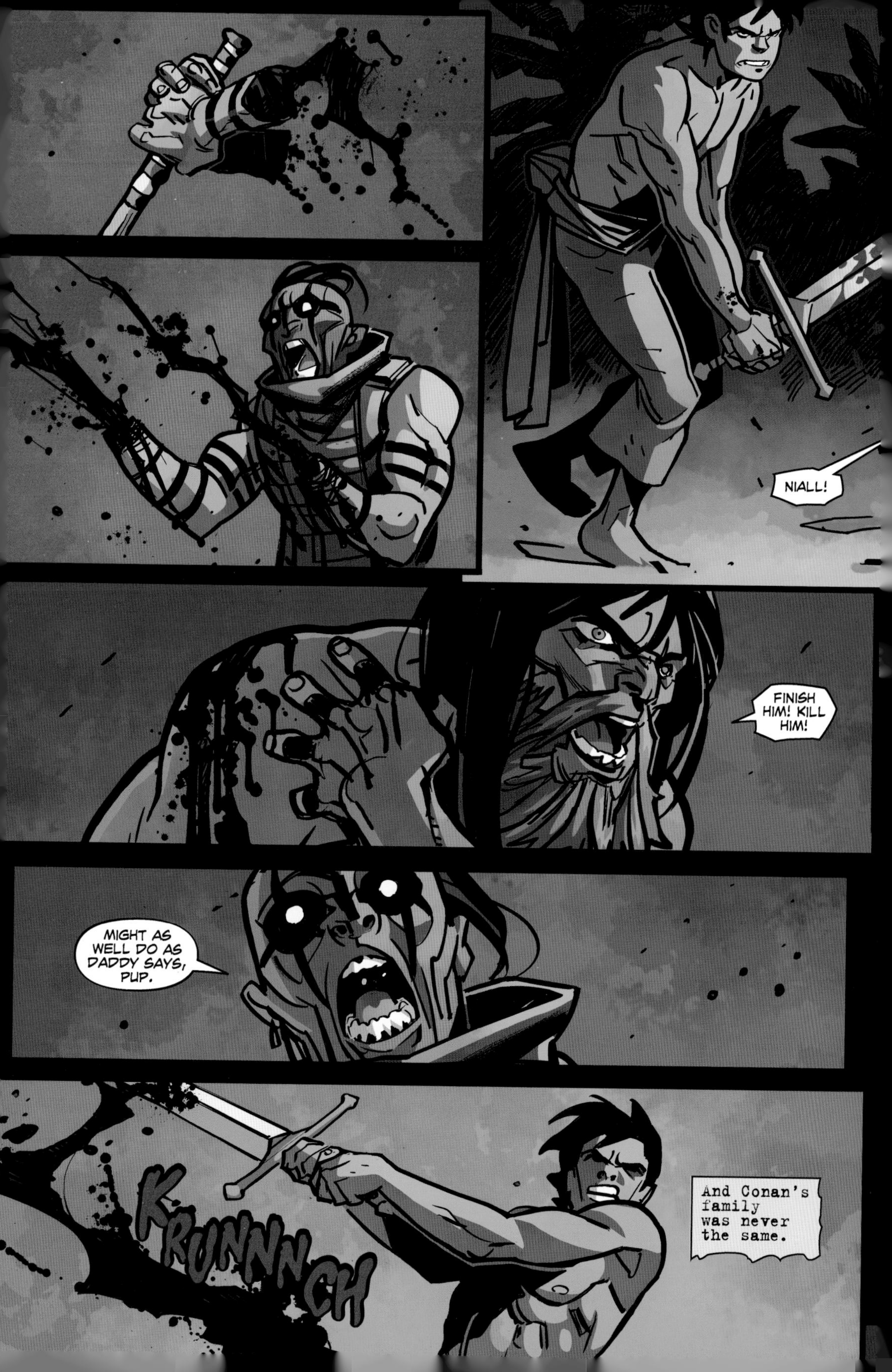
NIALL!
FINISH HIM! KILL HIM!
MIGHT AS WELL DO AS DADDY SAYS, PUP.
KRUNNNCH
And Conan's family was never the same.

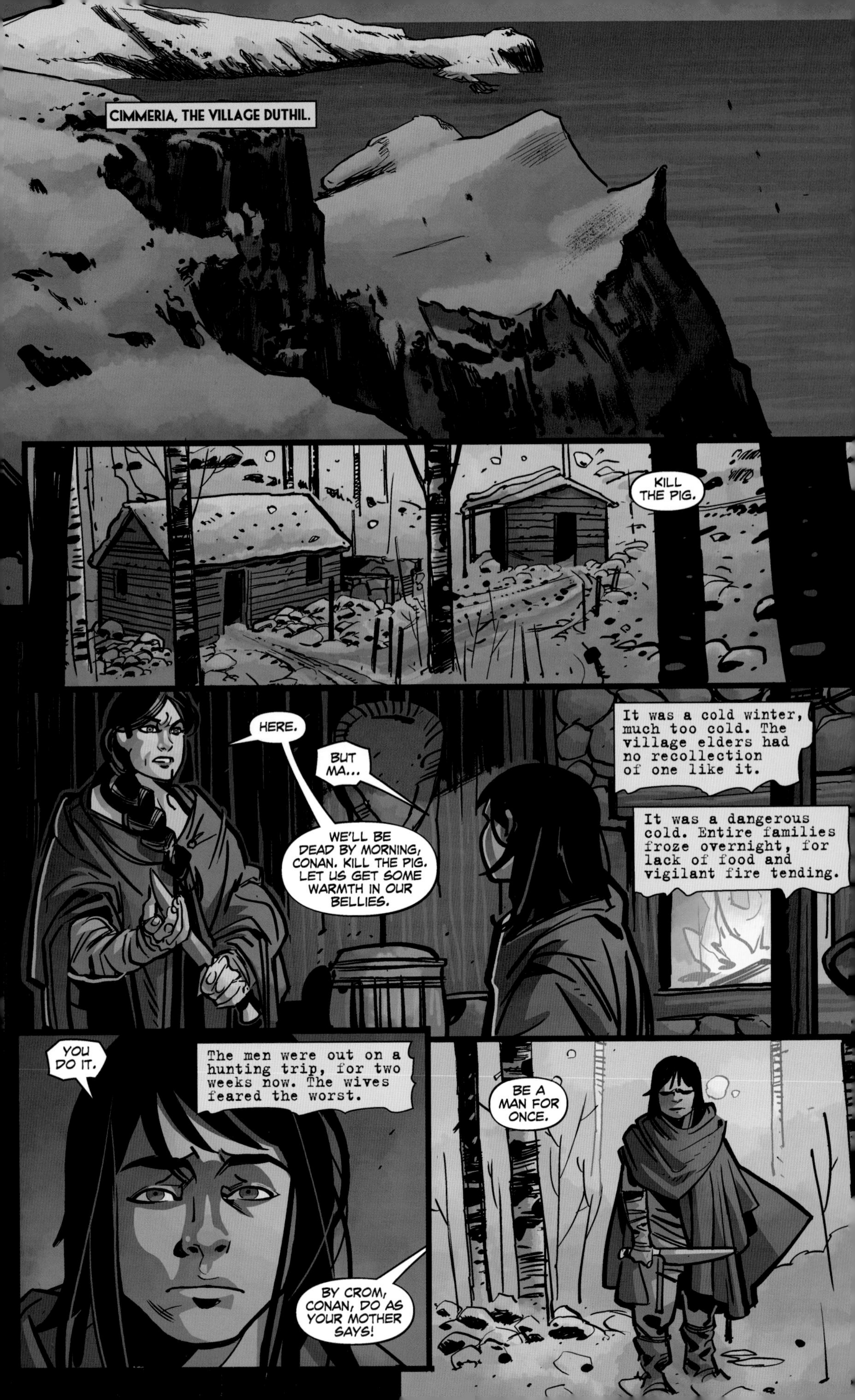
CIMMERIA, THE VILLAGE DUTHIL.
KILL THE PIG.
HERE.
BUT MA...
WE'LL BE DEAD BY MORNING, CONAN. KILL THE PIG. LET US GET SOME WARMTH IN OUR BELLIES.
It was a cold winter, much too cold. The village elders had no recollection of one like it.
It was a dangerous cold. Entire families froze overnight, for lack of food and vigilant fire tending.
YOU DO IT.
The men were out on a hunting trip, for two weeks now. The wives feared the worst.
BY CROM, CONAN, DO AS YOUR MOTHER SAYS!
BE A MAN FOR ONCE.

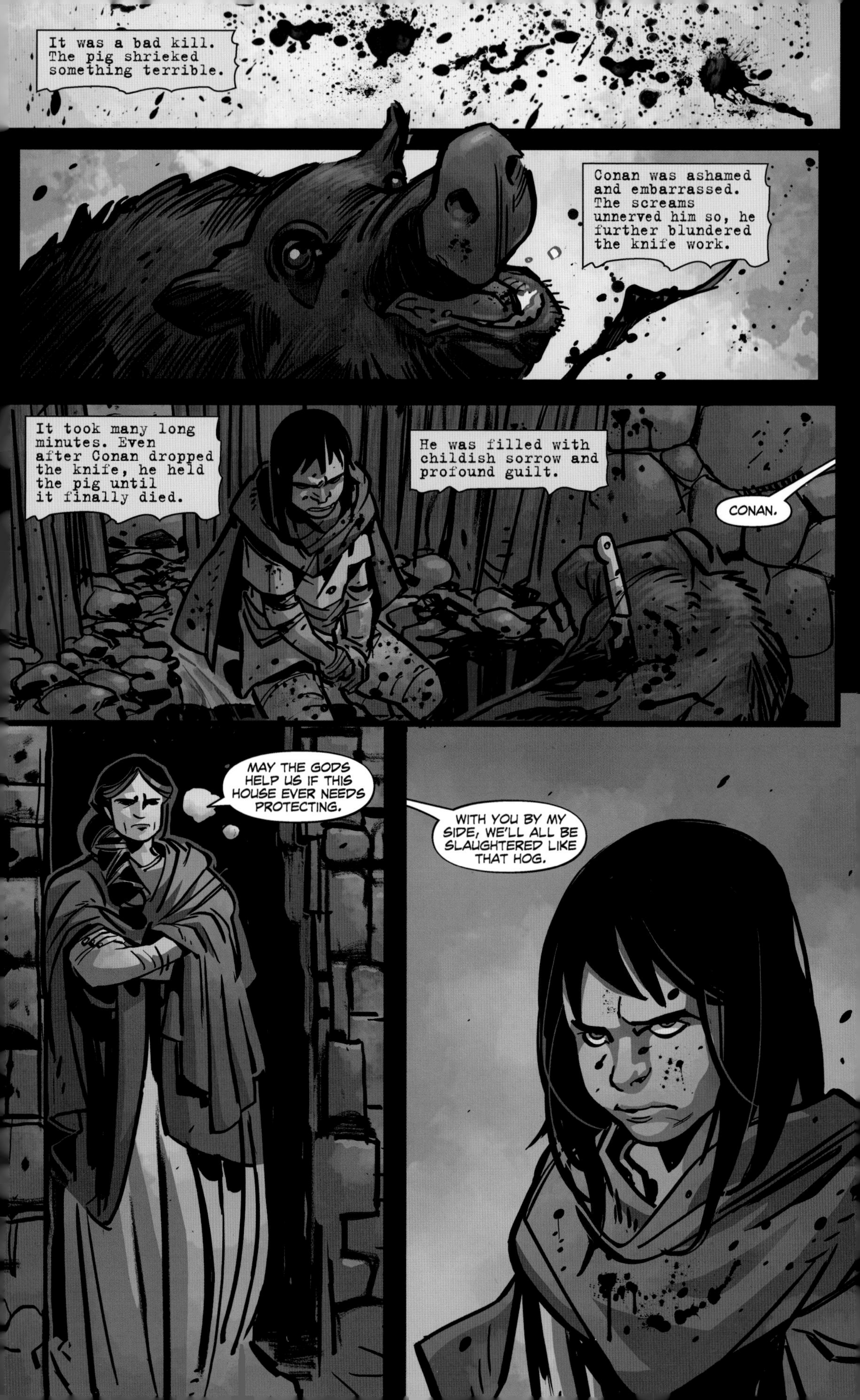
It was a bad kill. The pig shrieked something terrible.
Conan was ashamed and embarrassed. The screams unnerved him so, he further blundered the knife work.
It took many long minutes. Even after Conan dropped the knife, he held the pig until it finally died.
He was filled with childish sorrow and profound guilt.
CONAN.
MAY THE GODS HELP US IF THIS HOUSE EVER NEEDS PROTECTING.
WITH YOU BY MY SIDE, WE'LL ALL BE SLAUGHTERED LIKE THAT HOG.

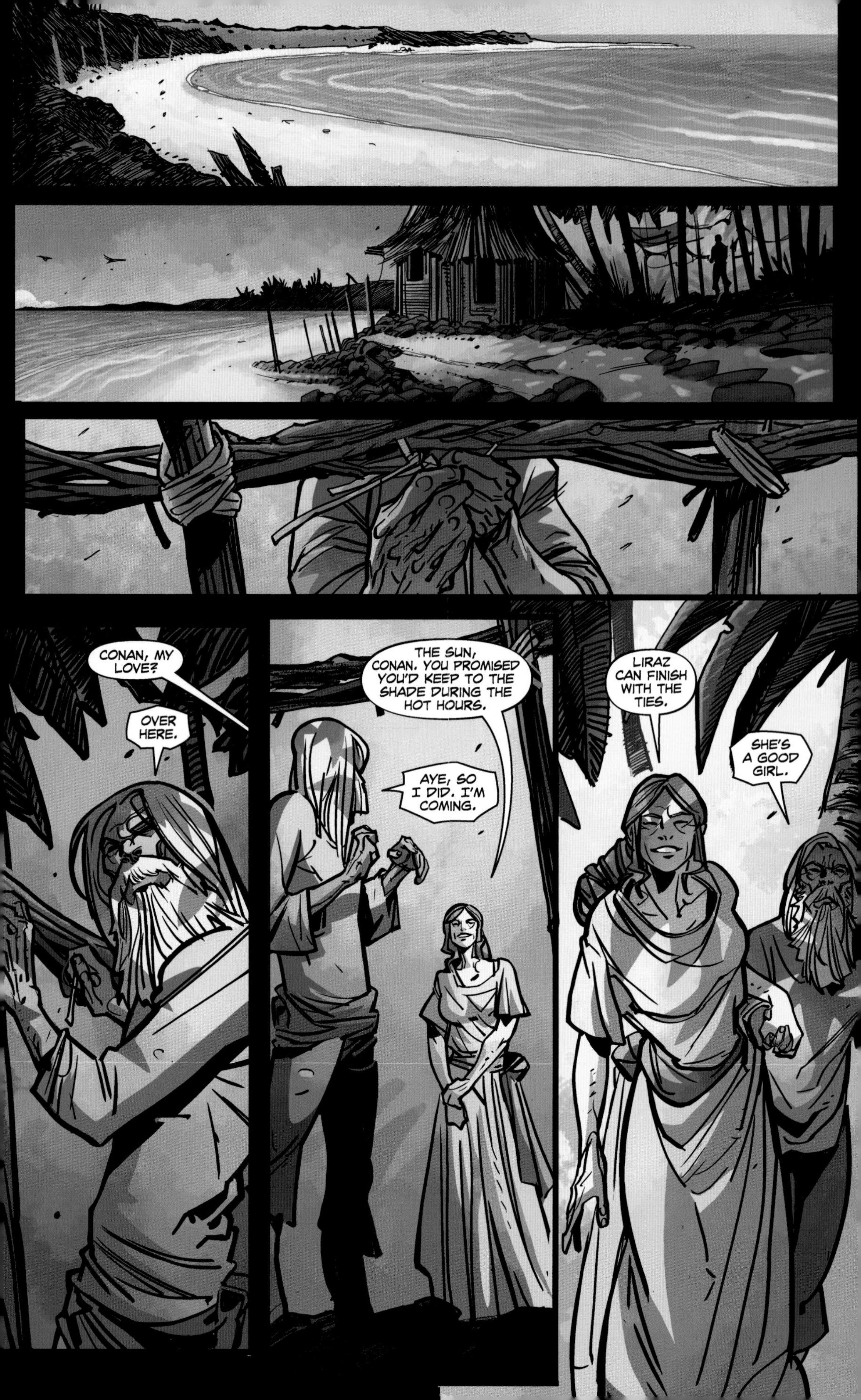
CONAN, MY LOVE?
OVER HERE.
THE SUN, CONAN. YOU PROMISED YOU'D KEEP TO THE SHADE DURING THE HOT HOURS.
AYE, SO I DID. I'M COMING.
LIRAZ CAN FINISH WITH THE TIES.
SHE'S A GOOD GIRL.

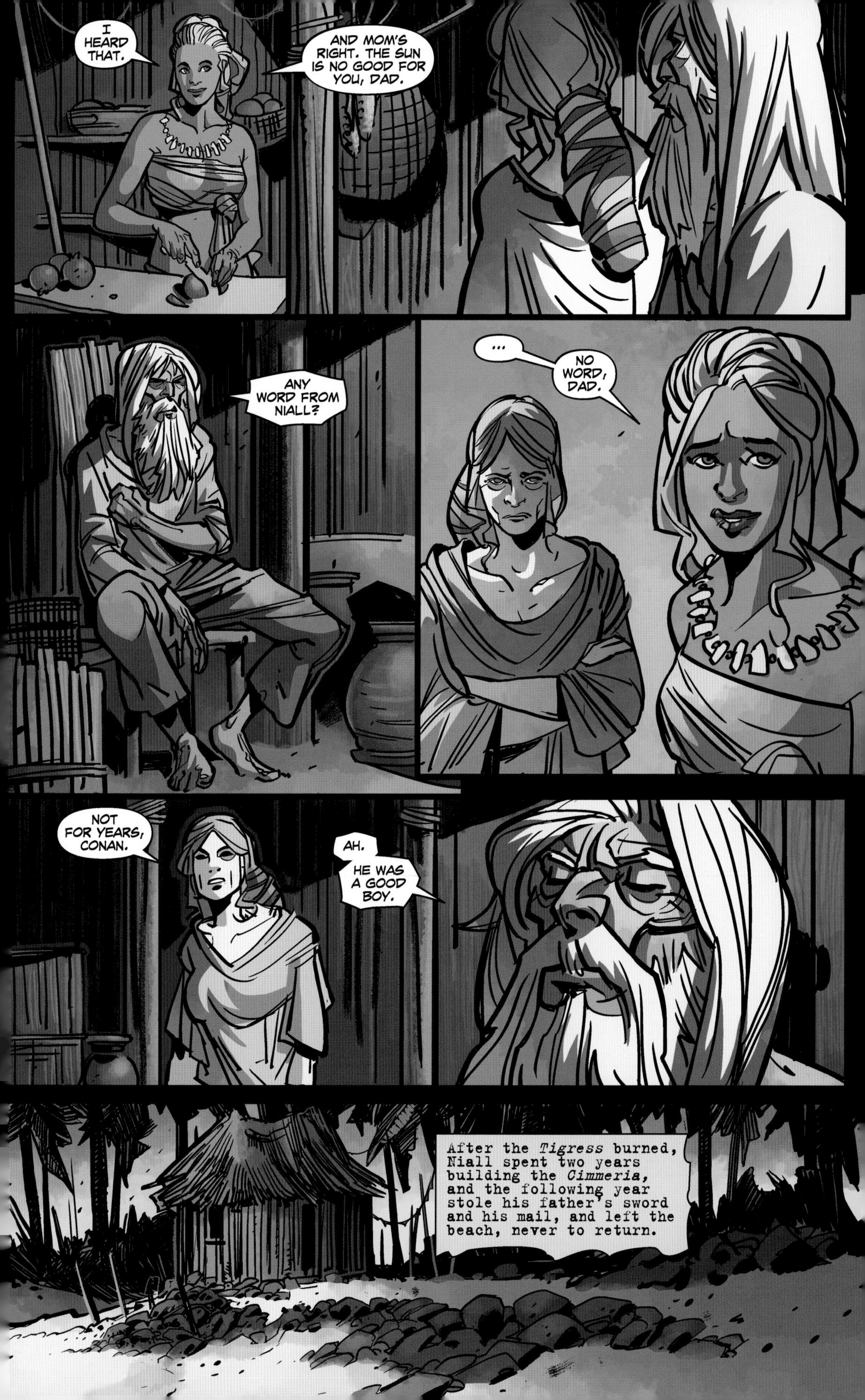
I HEARD THAT.
AND MOM'S RIGHT. THE SUN IS NO GOOD FOR YOU, DAD.
ANY WORD FROM NIALL?
...
NO WORD, DAD.
NOT FOR YEARS, CONAN.
AH.
HE WAS A GOOD BOY.
After the *Tigress* burned, Niall spent two years building the *Cimmeria*, and the following year stole his father's sword and his mail, and left the beach, never to return.

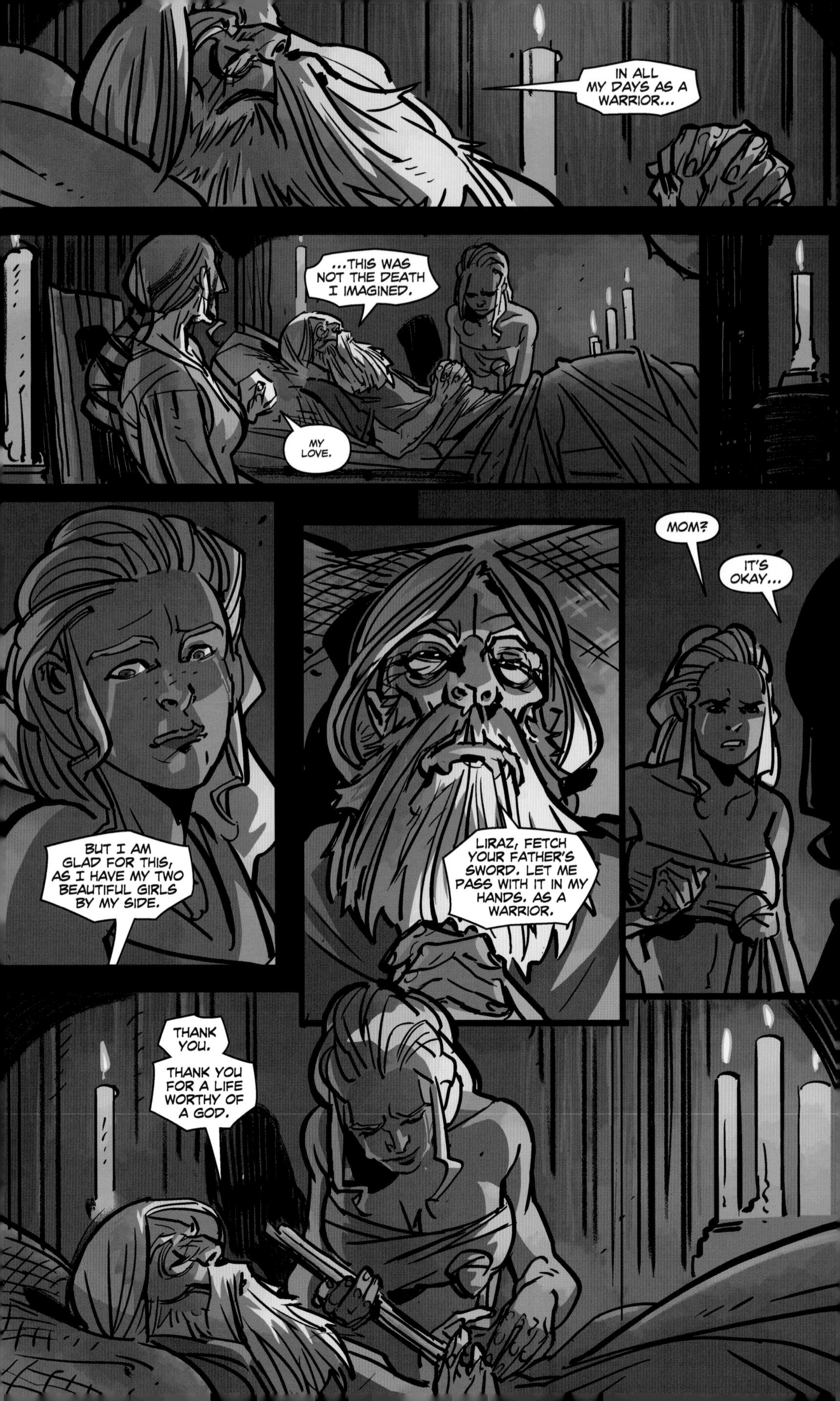
IN ALL MY DAYS AS A WARRIOR...
...THIS WAS NOT THE DEATH I IMAGINED.
MY LOVE.
BUT I AM GLAD FOR THIS, AS I HAVE MY TWO BEAUTIFUL GIRLS BY MY SIDE.
LIRAZ, FETCH YOUR FATHER'S SWORD. LET ME PASS WITH IT IN MY HANDS. AS A WARRIOR.
MOM?
IT'S OKAY...
THANK YOU.
THANK YOU FOR A LIFE WORTHY OF A GOD.

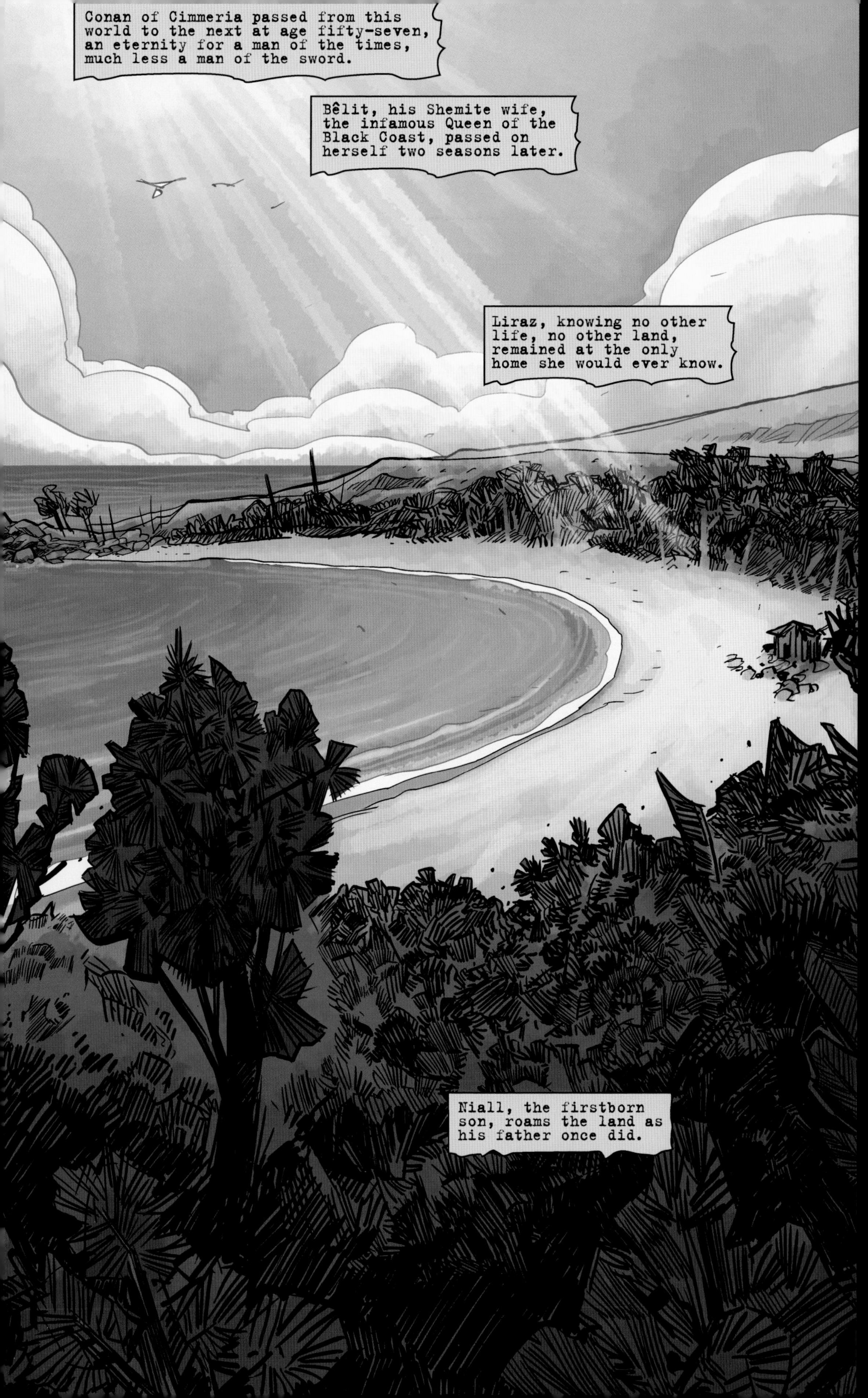
Conan of Cimmeria passed from this world to the next at age fifty-seven, an eternity for a man of the times, much less a man of the sword.
Bêlit, his Shemite wife, the infamous Queen of the Black Coast, passed on herself two seasons later.
Liraz, knowing no other life, no other land, remained at the only home she would ever know.
Niall, the firstborn son, roams the land as his father once did.

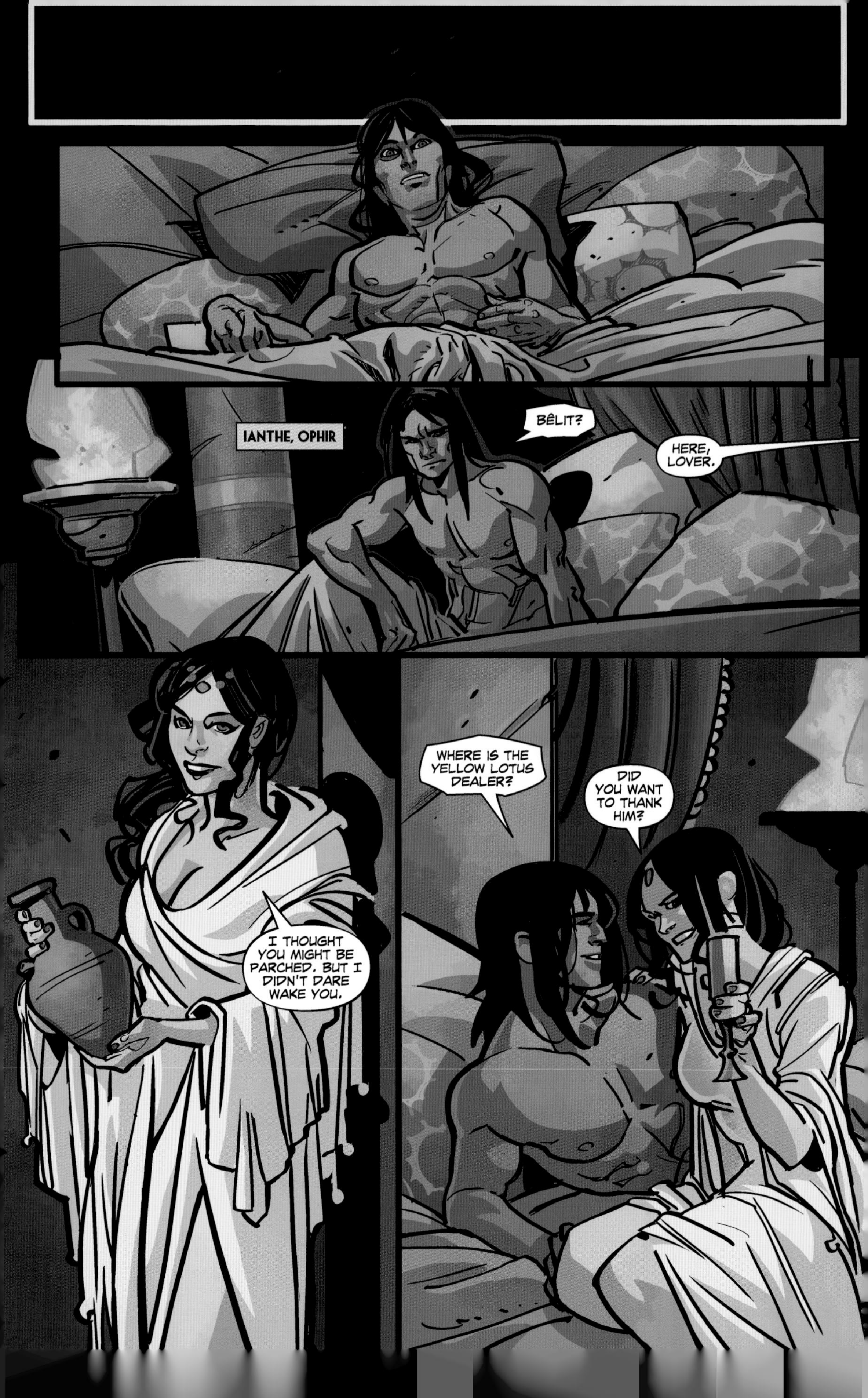
IANTHE, OPHIR
BÊLIT?
HERE, LOVER.
I THOUGHT YOU MIGHT BE PARCHED. BUT I DIDN'T DARE WAKE YOU.
WHERE IS THE YELLOW LOTUS DEALER?
DID YOU WANT TO THANK HIM?

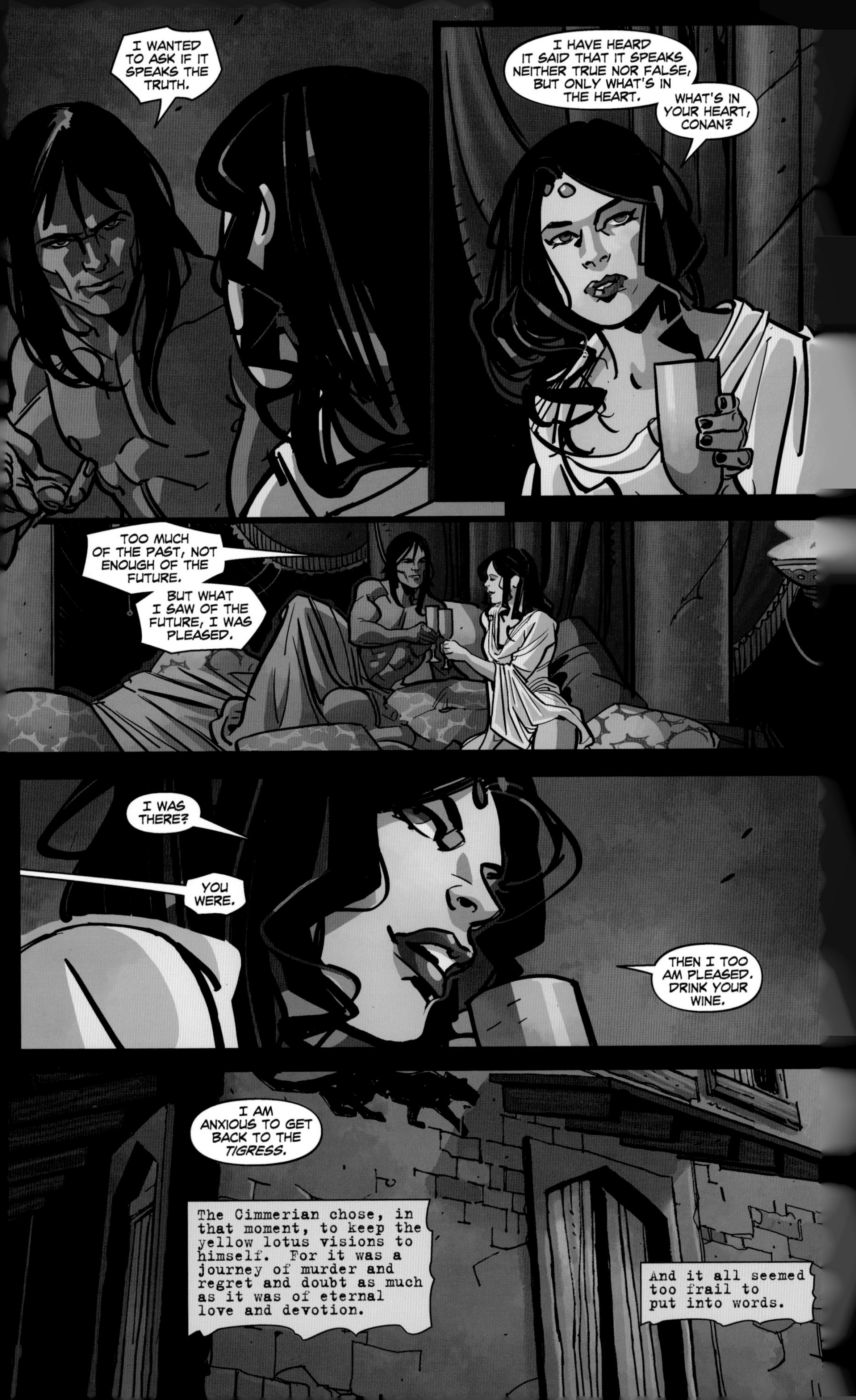
I WANTED TO ASK IF IT SPEAKS THE TRUTH.
I HAVE HEARD IT SAID THAT IT SPEAKS NEITHER TRUE NOR FALSE, BUT ONLY WHAT'S IN THE HEART.
WHAT'S IN YOUR HEART, CONAN?
TOO MUCH OF THE PAST, NOT ENOUGH OF THE FUTURE.
BUT WHAT I SAW OF THE FUTURE, I WAS PLEASED.
I WAS THERE?
YOU WERE.
THEN I TOO AM PLEASED. DRINK YOUR WINE.
I AM ANXIOUS TO GET BACK TO THE *TIGRESS.*
The Cimmerian chose, in that moment, to keep the yellow lotus visions to himself. For it was a journey of murder and regret and doubt as much as it was of eternal love and devotion.
And it all seemed too frail to put into words.

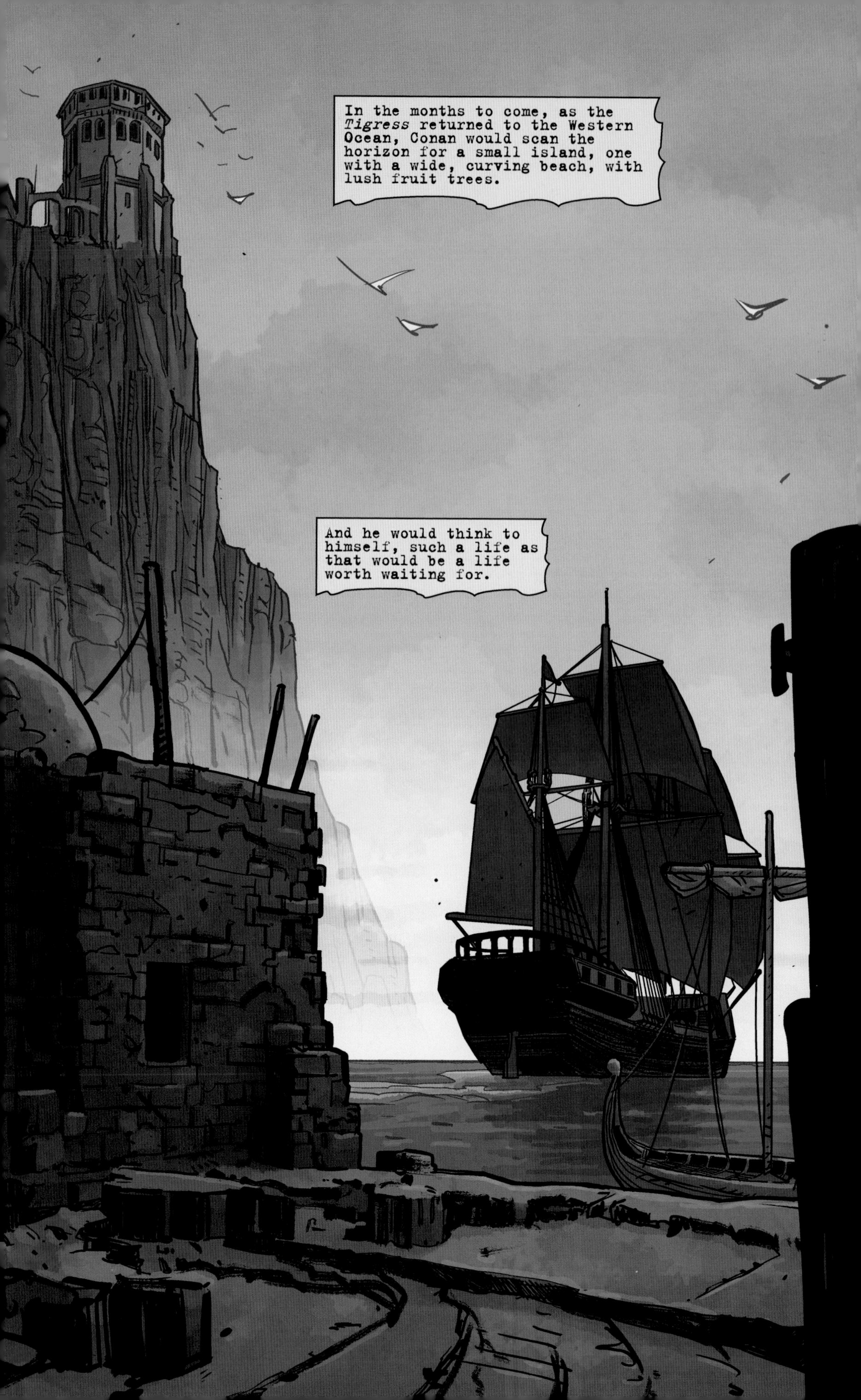
In the months to come, as the *Tigress* returned to the Western Ocean, Conan would scan the horizon for a small island, one with a wide, curving beach, with lush fruit trees.
And he would think to himself, such a life as that would be a life worth waiting for.

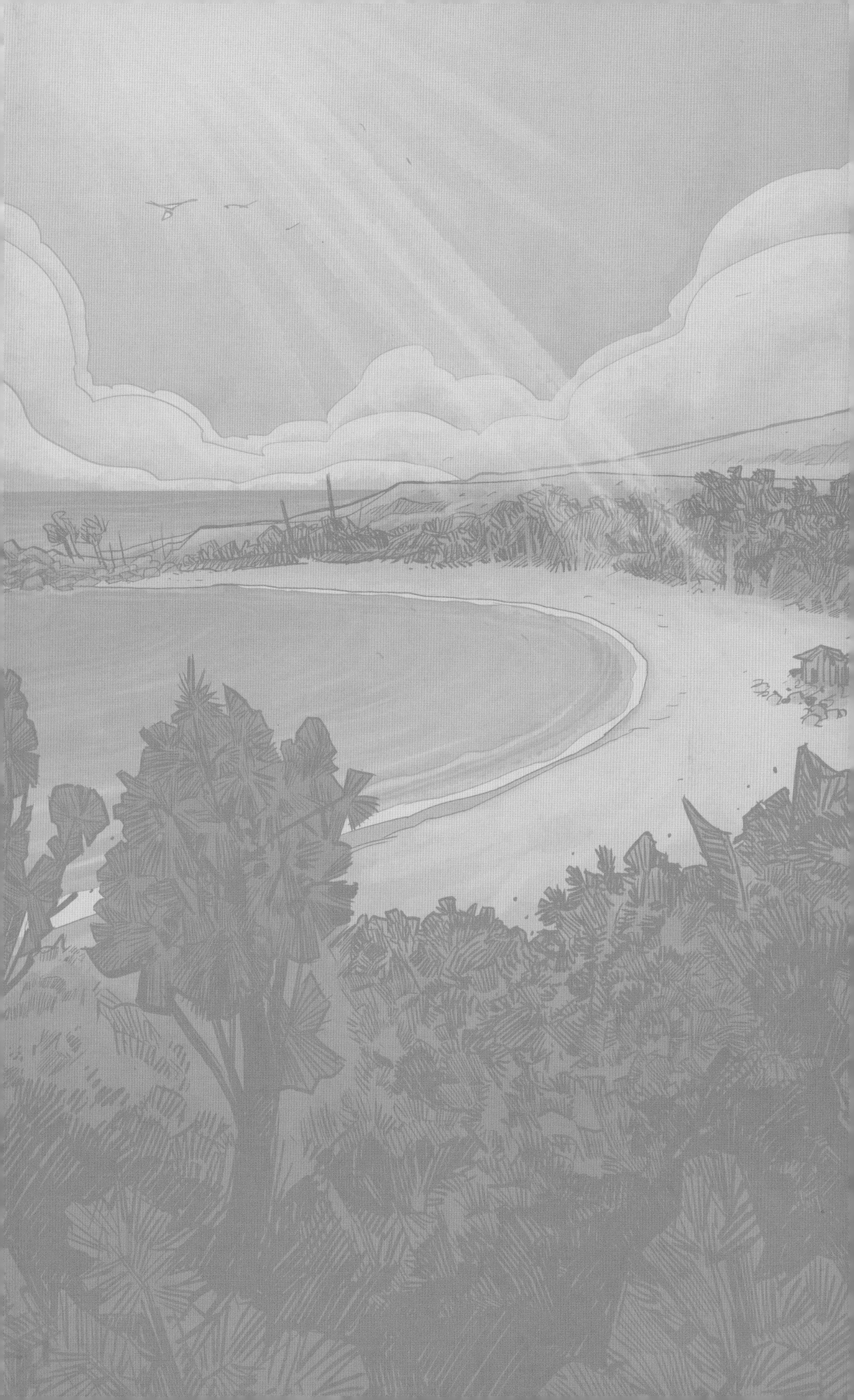

President and Publisher
MIKE RICHARDSON

Executive Vice President
NEIL HANKERSON

Chief Financial Officer
TOM WEDDLE

Vice President of Publishing
RANDY STRADLEY

Vice President of Book Trade Sales
MICHAEL MARTENS

Vice President of Business Affairs
ANITA NELSON

Editor in Chief
SCOTT ALLIE

Vice President of Marketing
MATT PARKINSON

Vice President of Product Development
DAVID SCROGGY

Vice President of Information Technology
DALE LAFOUNTAIN

Senior Director of Print, Design, and Production
DARLENE VOGEL

General Counsel
KEN LIZZI

Editorial Director
DAVEY ESTRADA

Senior Books Editor
CHRIS WARNER

Executive Editor
DIANA SCHUTZ

Director of Print and Development
CARY GRAZZINI

Art Director
LIA RIBACCHI

Director of Scheduling
CARA NIECE

Director of International Licensing
TIM WIESCH

Director of Digital Publishing
MARK BERNARDI

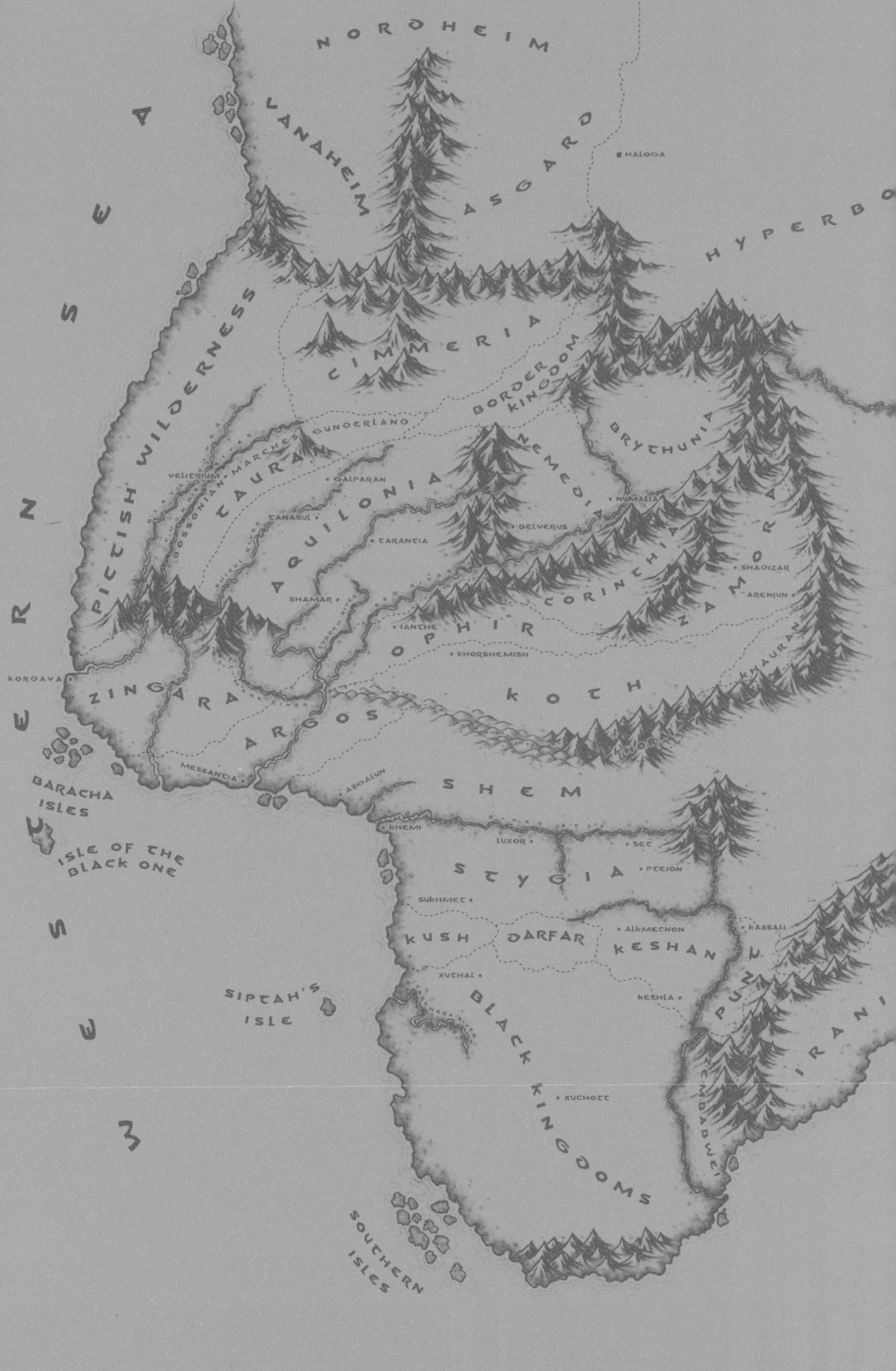
NORDHEIM
VANAHEIM
ASGARD
HALOGA
HYPERBO
WESTERN SEA
PICTISH WILDERNESS
CIMMERIA
BORDER KINGDOM
GUNDERLAND
BOSSONIAN MARCHES
TAURAN
VELITRIUM
GALPARAN
TANASUL
TARANTIA
AQUILONIA
SHIRKI RIVER
SHAMAR
NEMEDIA
BELVERUS
NUMALIA
BRYTHUNIA
CORINTHIA
ZAMORA
SHADIZAR
ARENJUN
RED RIVER
IANTHE
OPHIR
KHORSHEMISH
KOTH
KHAURAN
KORDAVA
ZINGARA
ARGOS
MESSANTIA
ASGALUN
SHEM
BARACHA ISLES
ISLE OF THE BLACK ONE
RIVER STYX
KHEMI
LUXOR
SET
STYGIA
PTEION
SUKHMET
KUSH
DARFAR
ALKMEENON
KESHAN
KASSALI
PUNT
XUTHAL
KESHIA
SIPTAH'S ISLE
BLACK KINGDOMS
XUCHOTL
IRANI
ZEMBABWEI
SOUTHERN ISLES